MALTA
CULTURE AND IDENTITY

MALTA

CULTURE AND IDENTITY

Edited by

HENRY FRENDO

OLIVER FRIGGIERI

Ministry of Youth and the Arts

1994

Published by the Ministry of Youth and the Arts

Phototypeset and printed by Grima Printing & Publishing Industries
A58 Marsa Industrial Estate, Malta.

Contents

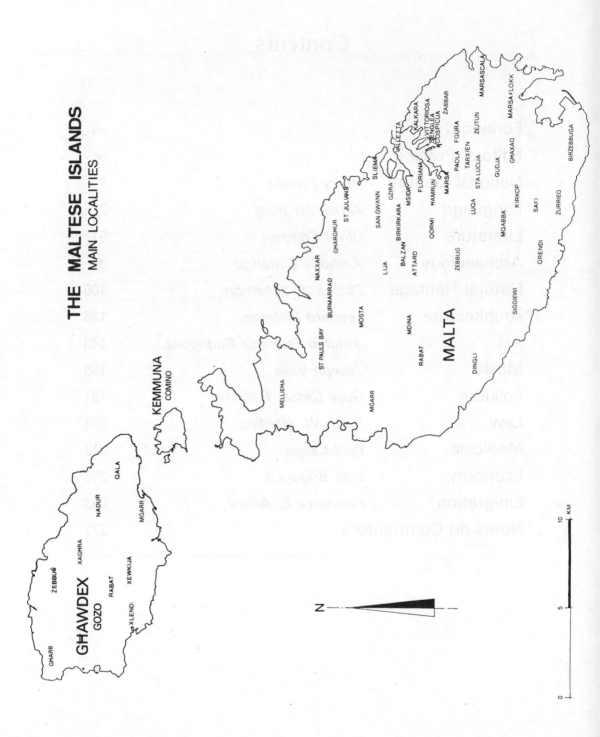

THE MALTESE ISLANDS
MAIN LOCALITIES

Foreword

I am indeed privileged and honoured to have this most welcome opportunity to join some of the foremost personalities and experts in contemporary Malta in presenting to the reader this compact but highly informative profile of Malta and the Maltese.

In a climate where sentiments flashpoint quickly and unexpectedly, commissioning contributions in a language other than Maltese was not the easiest of decisions to take. The debate called for much heart searching, spectre chasing, the playing down of emotions and above all a rational realisation that an objective had to be achieved. It was not a question of preferring one language for another – of considering to trade in the Maltese language – so signal and determining an insignia of our cultural and national diversity – but an exercise in pragmatism, designed to attract the widest possible audience.

I make no apology as we consider ourselves fortunate that the course of history was such that we now benefit from the undoubted advantage of so many generations of knowledge of written and spoken English. We have chosen the medium which affords us the best opportunity to reach out. To dress up for the occasion and tell our story.

This publication is our 'billet-doux'. It covers the dry bones of a simple cryptic means of identification with that florid southern European flesh which gives us a distinct personality and highlights our true identity. It is also a labour of love. For however clinically precise and dispassionate one tries to be there is always that strain of deep patriotic bias lurking in the subconscious which sometimes emerges spontaneously with an intense Mediterranean humanity to breathe life and soul into the body. This is us, as we know ourselves to be. Maybe as we wish to be known and want others to see and to know us. A broad brush overview, with no claim to be a complete historical and social record of a country and its people. A dozen out of a myriad aspects which shoot like stars from a vaster hazier backdrop to the prominence of centre stage.

Our culture, our identity is not just this 'mélange' of what we believe to be good, beautiful, epic and praiseworthy, a choice dictated by a burning nationalistic love of country and people. We do not portray the 'chiaroscuro' let alone contrast the darker hues which sometimes hide undeniable truths and unacceptable realities amidst the gamut of social mores and moods of a society which evolved and developed over thousands of years. For even these unpalatable and possibly shaming nuances are part and parcel of our chequered patchwork past.

Three decades of independence, a mere fraction of the aeons of a people's march since the archipelago rose Venus-like at the dawn of some far off day in a long forgotten millennium, have quickened the pace. A new spirit of adventure, primed by this new found freedom, became a motive force exploding pent up energies of thought and talent to cascade bright lights from the skies and form a colourful mosaic of Malta and the Maltese. A kaleidoscope of pluses and minuses, the conventional, the odd, the enchanting, the ugly, the profane and the sacred that is us. Whether in motley plumes or tattered rags we wear our young nationhood with justified pride.

Hon. MICHAEL REFALO
Minister of Youth and the Arts

Editors' Preface

When first asked to prepare a book of this kind by the Ministry of Youth and the Arts, our objective was to present a serious and readable kaleidoscope of Malta's culture and identity. We sought to cover the main constituent elements of this uniqueness as it was moulded and as it evolved, to indicate what was changing and where these islands and their people were heading.

It was impossible to cover every aspect of life in Malta or to go into much detail: more attention could have been given to certain periods, localities and artistic genres. To make good for this inevitable deficiency in a general work such as this, we encouraged contributors to refer in their texts to authors, patterns, trends and schools of thought that have characterised their respective areas, and we also included key bibliographical data at the end of each section to permit the reader to delve further into any particular aspect. While we sought to give some order to the entries so that these would complement and supplement one another, each section is sufficiently self-contained and may stand on its own as a valid contribution to at least an aspect, a dimension of the Malta prism. We have tried to keep to our original overall brief in the knowledge that such a book would travel far and wide and make Malta known somewhat more intimately to many.

Several of the illustrations had to be specially photographed for this production by Mr Tony Mangion, whose work speaks for itself; others were available from libraries, archives, books and private collections. We are grateful to the directors, curators, librarians and staffs of, among others, the Fine Arts Museum, the Museum of Archaeology, the Maritime Museum, the National Archives, the National Tourism Organisation, the Department of Information, the national and university libraries and other sources. We thank the geographers J.A. Schembri and N. Vella who prepared an updated map of the Maltese Islands for this book, as well as history students Simon Mercieca and Ivan Grech and secretary Yvette Attard who assisted in the collation or xeroxing of materials. Last but not least we wish to express our gratitude and appreciation to the Minister for Youth and the Arts, the Hon. Dr. Michael Refalo, and to his predecessor, the Hon. Dr. Michael Frendo, for their unwavering support in the preparation of a work for which the need had long been felt.

HENRY FRENDO
Department of History
University of Malta

OLIVER FRIGGIERI
Department of Maltese
University of Malta

National Identity

Henry Frendo

It has been said that the smaller a nation is, the more its territory has the character of 'the natal soil'. Smallness retains integrity, facilities human contact, and is more likely to have natural boundaries. In the case of the closely-connected Maltese Islands in the central Mediterranean, the feeling of 'home' (*heimat* in German) could overlap with and evolve into the feeling of 'nation' (*patria*) with relative ease.

The Upper Barracca garden in Valletta on the former Sceberras peninsula has long provided a grand-stand view not only of the magnificent harbours busy with naval, maritime and passenger activity, nor simply of the defensive and aesthetically impressive network of massive fortifications surrounding it, but also an instant sense of Malta's people: of the whereabouts of a good part of the entire population of the country. On either side of Valletta, the old Three Cities in Grand Harbour and the relatively new Sliema district across from the almost parallel Marsamxett Harbour, are clearly visible from the capital. Here, and in the 'new' (sixteenth century) capital city itself, most of the native inhabitants increasingly lived or worked. More than any other single location or artery, Valletta's deep-water, well-sheltered and strategically-located harbours have been analogous to the picture-postcard: showing, in one view, a people in the making. These harbours have been the scene of fighting and of festivity, welcoming or chasing away visitors, for thousands of years. From that one historic geographical vantage point on the hill, we can already surmise a ready means whereby size, population, territoriality, hearth and home could be 'seen' to fuse and gradually

come to life as one nation and state. The ancient Greek regard for the 'democratic' city state or *polis* was justly related to the sense of belonging and administrative manageability offered by a moderate spatial perimiter.

The land area of the Maltese Islands was (is) 122 square miles (246 square km), alongside which were several bays, creeks and inlets; hills and valleys but no mountains; few fresh water streams, no lakes or rivers; and in modern times, at least, not much vegetation or greenery. Windy but temperate, the climate was serene, the sea inviting, with rainfall mainly in winter-time, the soil sparse but intensely cultivated and protected in rubble-walled terraced fields.

The identification of people with a specific territory, with its habitat and attributes, has invariably played a dominant role in the history of nationality; even the dispersed Jews longed to go back 'home'. Malta certainly was no exception. In this long process of internalizing common traits, boundaries cease to be simply physical or visual: they become attitudinal: self-perceived and prescriptive in relation to 'others'. According to the Acts of the Apostles, when St Paul landed in Malta in the first century, the kind natives speaking their vernacular were 'barbarians' (*barbaroi*). But such incompleteness as these then inhabitants of Malta were perceived to have was merely a reflection of what the newcomers saw and defined by their own standards, just as the welcoming inhabitants themselves no doubt would have sized up and defined the strangers by theirs. Self-definition by reference and contrast to neighbours, visitors and strangers, has always been an important measure of identity: a two-sided mirror or prism for individuals and groups.

Malta was at one time remote and central, depending on what role the Mediterranean, Europe or Empire played during one epoch or another. Malteseness was chisselled out in time by the over-lap of precisely these three supra-national dimensions. Geographically the southernmost tip of the Italian peninsula from which it was separated by a stretch of sea, for southbound travellers Malta usually interrupted the route to northern Africa, just as it frequently gave haven to travellers journeying from west to east or in the opposite direction.

The earliest known inhabitants in prehistory came from Sicily. The Phoenicians knew and used Malta well before the Romans arrived in the third century B.C. and made it a *municipium*. Very few remains have been found of the subsequent Byzantine and Arab periods by archaeologists and medievalists. From the coming of the Normans in the eleventh century to Aragonese rule from Sicily in the fifteenth, Malta's feudal history largely reflected that of southern Europe, especially of Sicily. The population was small, not more than 10,000 when the Normans arrived, and less before that. A document attributed to Al Himyari would question how far Malta was permanently settled during part of the period of Arab rule (870-1091). Although Malta has nothing at all like the Islamic treasures of Sicily or Spain, the Arabic-based language apparently inherited by the Maltese from those times, and some other funerary remains until the twelfth century, would definitely suggest an Arab presence. This is also recorded elsewhere. Maltese poets of Arabic inspiration were accredited to the Norman royal court in Sicily. For this whole time span until the fifteenth century A.D., however, far the most important and spectacular remains date back to the prehistoric temple cultures which ante-date Karnak in Egypt and Mycenae in Greece.

These have been defined by leading world authorities, such as Renfrew, as the first free-standing monuments in stone: the first such temples known to man. One hypothesis is that Malta was *"l'ile sacree de la Mediterranee"*; but another would affirm the Malta prehistoric temple culture to be purely indigenous. What is beyond dispute is the importance of religion, of ritual and rite, and the artistic and architectural skills of the megalithic temple-builders themselves. A number of these extraordinary and mysterious excavated sites still stand to inspire awe and wonder.

From the Middle Ages too, by which time Malta had been fully christianized and probably (at least partly) re-christianized, it is the legacy of religion and worship that survives above all else. According to one source there were 430 Roman Catholic churches and chapels in Malta by the sixteenth century. According to another, who included privately-owned chapels, by the end of the fifteenth century there were over one thousand such places of worship. Scattered all over the Islands in villages and fields, several of these churches and chapels have survived. The most notable surviving exponent is a fifteenth century church, with its frescoes, at Hal Millieri. The overriding significance of Roman Catholic religious practices among the Maltese in medieval and early modern times emerges clearly from early descriptions of the islands and their people by Quintin in 1533, Dusina in 1575 and others.

Religion has been of the utmost importance everywhere in etching and marking out character and identity, both popular and national. Religion imparted solidarity to people: it became a symbol and a cause. A secular scholar once wrote that the spirit of Christ was 'the most powerful leaven in the development of ideals' and the church 'the greatest organizing factor in history.' Using vernaculars for communication and Latin for written record, monks were at the forefront of knowledge, of its preservation and transmission. The monotheistic faith, predicated on redemption of the individual soul, male and female alike, was also indirectly an inducement to concentrate on higher ideals and to bring about change. After the crusades and the holding operation against Islam, in the Christian European world the association of religion with nationality, and sometimes with statehood, became pronounced with the Reformation: Luther, Calvin, Henry VIII. Nestled rather cosily in the shadow of the Rome-centred Latin church, to whom state patrons from the Normans on always professed allegiance, Malta had no Reformation. The Inquisitors kept themselves occupied but were never too busy. The influence of Catholicism was all the more redoubtable in the moulding of a Maltese identity. These people, noted Quentin, kept their Semitic language, yet their Christian sentiment was so intense. Although the ruling class – officials, garrison and clergy – were often Sicilians, probably by reason of that, certain inhabitants were conscious of being Maltese. Our 'being unlike the others' may already be seen by 1500 to have been sustained and pushed forward by three seminal complexes: in culture, language-religion; in nationality, foreigner-native; and in politics, ruler-ruled.

For much of the medieval period, Malta and Gozo enjoyed a degree of internal autonomy personified in their commune or *universitas*: the old city of Mdina served as the islands' capital, with aristocrats, jurats and other notables assembling there. In the first known open manifestation of determined Maltese opposition to feudal exploitation at the hands of Don Gonsalvo Monroy in 1427-1428, it was two Mdina ecclesiastical dignitaries, don Cathaldu Cusburella and don Gregoriu di Bunellu, whom the *"università"* delegated to plead Malta's case in Palermo.

Another important development was the arrival of various religious orders, who laid the foundations for their missions, monasteries, convents, charitable institutions, schools. Augustinians and Franciscans reached Malta in the fourteenth century, Carmelites, Dominicans and Benedictines in the fifteenth. By the following century the Jesuits had established a college for higher learning which developed into Malta's university of studies. Until 1492 when they were expelled, Jews had been relatively numerous and some, like doctors, well established in Maltese society. A convent replaced their synagogue.

Neither Muslims nor Jews, neither Sicilians nor Arabs, the Arabic-speakers and fervent Roman Catholics of Hispanic-Sicilian Malta slowly took shape during the Middle Ages. With the passing of time and the curtailment of direct contact with Arabs in Malta, Maltese began to evolve into a separate language, with an often fossilized classical Arabic increasingly influenced by Romance words, expressions and concepts. An incident which deserves more attention occurred in 1481: a protest by Maltese jurats asking the bishop to dismiss a foreigner, 'who did not know Maltese', from the post of Chaplain of the Cathedral at Mdina (Città Notabile). It would seem that already by that time Maltese had assumed the character of an in-group language and was in some way a core value of nationality, or at least of marked difference: a measure by which to distinguish the native from the foreign with a certain pride of feeling. Nor was such an attachment to the vernacular limited to commoners or peasants, because the protestors were jurats. The 1481 Maltese language incident about *'il Parroco della Cattedrale che non sapeva il Maltese'* was documented by the historian Alfredo Mifsud in 1918. It happened probably some years after the first known poem in medieval Maltese was written by Pietro Caxaro, another learned resident of the Città Notabile. Again indicatively, Caxaro wrote 'Maltese' in the Roman script. In a work published in Naples in 1582, a resident of Malta's sister island Gozo, Antonio Saliba, in identifying himself described Malta as *'nostra patria'*. In 1590 a Maltese geographer, Giovanni Myriti, described Malta as *'patria mea dulcissima'*.

Modern Maltese history really begins in the

sixteenth century. To that time we can trace the origins of modern Malta. With the coming of the chivalrous European Christian order of the Knights Hospitallers in 1530, we can lay our historical anchor deep in the rocks. The state came first. The nation followed closely on its heels.

The Knights 'of Malta' progressively changed the islands and their people in eight important ways.

Politically, the Knights made Malta into a small European state. Although in 1530 the Holy Roman Emperor Charles V gave Malta and Tripoli to the Order of St John, of Jerusalem and Rhodes, in feudal tenure, *de facto* Malta came to have most of the attributes of statehood; one that never reverted to its original owner. The yearly gift of a falcon to the Emperor was largely symbolic, even if the deed of cession, in seeking to maintain a rightful balance between the nationalities, sought to regulate certain important appointments, such as the episcopacy and the admiralty. After the English Reformation, the Order in Malta was represented by seven European *Langues*, or nationalities, each of which erected its *Auberge* in the new capital, Valletta[1]. By the eighteenth century the Grand Master behaved like a European monarch, and was more or less regarded as one. A distinguished English visitor and Fellow of the Royal Society, Brydone, noted the multi-cultural Europeanity of Malta as a result of the Order's presence. 'On getting on shore, we found ourselves in a new world indeed', he wrote in 1792; 'the streets crowded with well-dressed people, who have all the appearance of health and affluence; whereas at Syracuse, there was scarce a creature to be seen; and even those few had the appearance of disease and wretchedness.' After describing the popular events of mule and donkey races held 'four times every year' by the inhabitants, he continued thus about the Knights themselves:

As Malta is an epitome of all Europe, and an assemblage of the younger brothers, who are commonly the best of its first families, it is probably one of the best academies for politeness in this part of the globe; besides, where every one is entitled by law as well as custom, to demand satisfaction for the least breach of it, people are under a necessity of being very exact and circumspect, both with regard to their words and actions. All the knights and commanders have much the appearance of gentlemen, and men of the world. We met with no character in extreme.

What most struck Brydone, however, was the composite and (it appears) rather harmonious effect of ongoing inter-personal relationships in the one government and country among the diverse nationalities living there. This effect challenged the national stereotypes in his own English mind (he also described Henry VIII as 'that capricious tyrant'):

The ridicules and prejudices of every particular nation are by degrees softened and worn off, by the familiar intercourse and collusion with each other. It is curious to observe the effect it produces upon the various people who compose this little medley. The French skip, the German strut, and the Spanish stalk, are all mingled together in such small proportions, that none of them are striking... It is still easy to distinguish the inhabitants of the north and south side of the Pyrenees, as well as those of the east and west side of the Rhine; for though the Parisian has, in a great measure, lost his assuming air, the Spaniard his taciturnity and solemnity, the German his formality and his pride; yet still you see the German, the Frenchman, and the Spaniard: it is only the caricature, that formerly made them ridiculous, that has disappeared.

Such, at their best, were the ruling class of Malta for 268 years: an aristocratic well-to-do elite, Catholic, chivalrous and celibate, committed to principles and practices so elevated and noble that it would be less than fair to expect that they all or always observed them in their daily lives. These contingents of Knights, sometimes numbering up to six hundred or so, with their retinues, their inns, houses and haunts, regarded Malta as their home, or at least as a permanent base, for ten generations. They were only expelled by Bonaparte in 1798. In the meantime, however, they had largely made Malta into

---

1. Provence; Auvergne; France; Italy; Aragon, Catalonia, Navarre; Germany; Castille, Leon, Portugal.

a modern state, with a splendid Renaissance city which Sir Walter Scott compared to a dream. They laid the infrastructure of a state. By the time they left, Malta was more organized and better catered for. New towns, suburbs and villages were established, some carrying the name of the Grand Master originally founding them, such as De Rohan (Żebbuġ) or Pinto (Qormi). Famous Italian engineers, assisted and succeeded by Maltese architects of genius such as Girolamo Cassar, planned a comprehensive system of fortifications at least as elaborate and impressive as that in Rhodes. The Conventual Church dedicated to the Order's patron saint, St John the Baptist, was constructed in the heart of Valletta, superbly adorned inside with the finest art and skill, making it one of the more magnificent churches in Europe; and so it remains in spite of the looting by Bonaparte's troops. The ceremony and pageantry which such a centre of religious and semi-religious activity permitted were necessarily unprecedented, and became intertwined with the social and cultural history of Valletta. The Grand Master's Palace, further down the Strada Reale, was another gem; as was, too, the *Sacra Infermeria*, so much larger and more imposing than the previous hospital in Rhodes. These knights were doctors as well as sailors, bureaucrats as well as *literati*; Dolomieu was a great scientist. The hospital gave rise to a Medical School, just as the concentration of edifices in Valletta, religious and secular, made the city a thriving administrative centre. It became a market city and a place for commercial and financial affairs. Malta had a mint: its own 'national' currency. Malta had a navy: its own. As Malta was never self-sufficient in wheat, elaborate grain storage facilities were built underground. Malta's dockyard, the *arsenale* (from which the Maltese word 'tarzna' is derived), became a centre-piece of the maritime-based economy. By means of an aqueduct all the way down from the high ground around Mdina to Valletta, a

more reliable water-supply system was devised, supplementing cisterns and wells. Were the Order less absolutist, Malta would also have kept her printing press, which was started in the seventeenth century but later stopped. Malta, or at any rate the Order of Malta, was diplomatically represented in some of the more important courts of European capitals. Soon enough, too, Malta had a University of Studies, a national theatre, a national library, gardens and fountains. The law courts, previously at Mdina, moved to Valletta, where town and gown mixed in a growing hustle and bustle of urban activity, with the ports nearby.

While Malta-born noblemen could not become knights, on the pretext that at law they would have been vassals, some managed to circumvent this restrictive practice by having their children born in the Kingdom of the Two Sicilies. Others however entered the service of the Order and a few managed to climb more than one rung of the ladder. Like any government, the Order could not rule without the support of the ruled: hence it was inevitable that the native inhabitants themselves get involved in almost every aspect of the Order's – and Malta's – life. Unlike their often non-resident and cynical feudal predecessors whose task was solely to collect taxes from the people, and unlike their successors, who robbed churches or measured needs on a utilitarian calculus, the Knights 'of Malta' had estates on the continent and various revenues, individual and collective, with ready access. They were also aristocrats, and Europeans, with taste, style and verve.

Psychologically, in their view of the surrounding world, the Maltese could look ahead with greater confidence, in a more outgoing way, secure on their own ground in the knowledge that for the first time they had effective protection from adversaries on land and sea. The very move from hinterland to harbour, from the old-time fortified city on the highest ground in the countryside, Mdina, to the new Renaisance peninsular city right on the water's edge, flanked by ports or open sea on three sides, was at one time real and symbolic. After the foundation stone was laid by Grand Master Jean de La Valette in 1566, building the city became priority number one, so that the Knights could move their quarters from Borgo (Vittoriosa) to the new site on higher ground on the other side of the harbour. Until the arrival of the Knights, the Borgo ('Birgu' in contemporary Maltese) had been a little fishing village which also absorbed such harbour activity as took place. The villagers would hardly have resisted any incursion from Barbary corsairs or other unwelcome visitors; in an emergency they would flee and hide as best they could. Fort Saint Angelo, which preceeded the arrival of the Knights, was the only defensive position in the harbour and not well kept or manned. The Knights did it up when they began preparing for all eventualities as soon as they arrived in Malta and set up house in the Borgo in 1530. Fort St Michael and Fort St Elmo were built and other fortifications restored, strengthened or constructed. Defence policy resumed with a vengeance after Malta's victory over the Turks in 1565, until Malta's bastions and fortifications, in Valletta and the Three Cities around the Grand Harbour, became a marvel. A deterrent in itself, Malta's defence network created an altogether novel atmosphere of stealth, a feeling of inner security which earlier generations of Maltese could not have experienced in their wildest dreams. No longer would helpless and hapless islanders go to sleep fearing plunder, rape and slavery. Mdina was to Valletta what the medieval was to the modern.

Administratively, the practices of government changed through more centralization from the urban metropolis and under the direct surveillance of the Order. This lessened or demolished the earlier communal autonomy centred in Mdina, and the role of the Maltese nobility and of the jurats, in supervising and managing internal matters. At the same time, it necessarily invited to its side and trained a novel, accommodating city-dwelling bureaucracy. Whereas earlier the emperor had been far away, only represented by frequently non-resident agents or sub-agents, now the Grand Master was on the spot, watching, with lieutenants at his beck and call, ordering people around. There was little room for dissent. The Hospitallers were after all also a military order. When an Mdina doctor, Giuseppe ('Mattew') Callus had a protest-letter to Barcelona intercepted by the Grand Master's spies, he was beheaded and his head exhibited in the main square for all to see and ruminate upon. Callus was protesting at the despotic behaviour of Grand Master La Valette, who was suppressing liberties traditionally enjoyed by the Maltese commune. The new government was also cautious with regard to traditional powers of the Catholic Church in Malta: militia captains now competed with parish priests for clients and favours. Malta became a centralized city state, ruled by foreigners from within, and rather exclusively too. In their gift, these 'kavallieri' had patronage, power, prestige, privilege and wealth. Some individual knights were erudite and philanthropic. Throughout the seventeenth century there were power struggles for status, patronage, sanctuary and jurisdiction, between the Bishop and the Grand Master and also the resident Inquisitor. In all this several took sides, but for the most part it appears that the population went on with their own prayer-and-work, family-centred lives, making ends meet and the best of an opportunity to shine, occasionally grumbling and resenting injustice or hardship as under Grand Master Ximenes. The most important Maltese attempt at a rising against the Order's degenerating rule was that led by Don Gaetano Mannarino in 1775 who briefly planted a Maltese banner on St James Cavalier at the entrance to Valletta.

Economically, the arrival of the Knights

immediately provided new work opportunities for the inhabitants, who alone had much inside knowledge of their islands as well as the *savoir faire* to service certain technical and social needs, to market and to tailor their produce and wares, and to adapt to new possibilities on offer, such as serving on the galleys or assisting in a variety of other ways in the administration of the islands. The Knights could import wealth rather than export it, distribute rather than scavange for it. Financially, they could be largely independent of local resources; they were *patrons*. They knew it, and they behaved accordingly. *Noblesse oblige*. This meant that new projects of unprecedented magnitude could be initiated, for which Maltese labour, know-how and expertise would be required; and which, in the process, provided apprenticeship and other learning experiences to those involved. This meant, too, that there was a resident consumer market for such production and manufacture as native skills and resources at one time or another could muster: olives, vegetables, cumin, sails, lace, filigree, blood oranges. A service industry became possible, indeed inevitable, meeting the daily needs and fancies of these wealthy and resident newcomers, swaggering and swashbuckling in their flowing cloaks. For many a Maltese, the Malta-based Knights provided 'a captive market'. Whether or not such reciprocities as ensued could be simply regulated by a vassal-lord philosophy, usually there was work, occasionally in abundance: in construction, using the Maltese quarries and stonemasons; on the galleys, using the Maltese sea-farers and seasoned hands; in palaces and knightly homes, the services and graces of painters and sculptors, attendants, assistants, cooks, stable-keepers and coachmen, suppliers, middle-men, protégés, servants. The Order's fortunes took a first blow with the Reformation but a second more serious one with the French Revolution: estates and revenues were soon lost, without which it became difficult to cope.

Religiously, Malta became a fief of the Lord, pressed on all sides by authorities more Catholic than the Pope. Under the Order, in fact, Malta was almost a theocracy; the frontier European Mediterranean power most opposed to the Arab advance was itself practically theocratic. Although the religious and the civil law were not one, there were the ecclesiastical and inquisitorial courts. The spiritual head of the Order, which governed the country, was the Pope; but to make doubly sure of goings-on after the Reformation the Pope also dispatched inquisitors. After their Malta posting, many of these became cardinals, two became popes. In addition, there was the Catholic bishop, in a long tradition, possibly uninterrupted since the time of St Publius, whom St Paul is held to have met and converted to Christianity in 60 A.D. Throughout the Order's period, the Bishops continued to be foreign, with possibly one exception, mostly Spaniards or Italians; these were frequently non-resident except when duty called. The hundreds of churches and chaples spread over such a relatively small space were indicative enough of the religious cults and devotions in practice at the time that the Knights arrived. New parishes came to have new, often bigger churches, as the population increased. Religious feasts and celebrations became more important and conspicuous: the country's patron saints were St Paul, St Publius and St Agatha. As in other Catholic countries, there was a great devotion to the Blessed Virgin, and saints such as St James or St Barbara. All told, not only did Malta not have wars of religion, it never had as much as a public airing of internal criticism or of denominational options or alternatives. To Maltese society under 'the Religion' – that is, the Order – Roman Catholicism was a monolith, an oath of loyalty, a state monopoly: a reinforced situation of what the islanders had inherited from their forefathers and readily accepted for their own purposes. Thus Catholicism continued to play a central and unchallenged role in Malta's life right through and for long after Reformation and Revolution on the continent, evolving into a national ethos. While religious events could be popularized and paganized, the social calendar was almost entirely a liturgical one; contact between clergy and people was close and often had a social character as much as a religious one. The place of the large domed-and-steepled church at the centre of the town or village was similar to that it occupied in the daily lives of those huddled around the square and the adjoining alleys. For a son to take up the priesthood was and long remained a dear aspiration of the average Maltese family, not unlike that which sons of the aristocracy, or their parents, had to the membership of a chivalric order.

Socially and culturally, ten generations of a manifest knightly presence in such restricted confines — of Bavarians and Frenchmen, Spaniards and Italians — necessarily rubbed off on the Maltese. Everywhere people are influenced by what they see, hear, taste and touch. To be more mobile or useful socially, it is generally the subordinates who tend to be impressed by or to seek to conform themselves to roles and models practised or put forward by superiors and men of influence. While the Maltese generally kept apart from the rulers — they had their own vernacular and value system which no doubt differed markedly from that of the average Knight — nevertheless they could not have been and were not oblivious to what went on around them, sometimes inside their very homes or towns. In battle, Maltese and knights fought on the same front, in the same galley, risking life and limb together. On another social level, we know that a section of the more literate and better endowed islanders kept contact, heads high, with the ruling class. In general, therefore, Maltese were increasingly introduced to and made use of venues for instruction, entertainment and accomplishment which the Knights brought

about or which emerged during their stay — the theatre, the library, the university, the salon, art and music, just as the lower classes engaged their skills in the navy or on construction sites, the wharves and docks, in *métiers*, crafts and services. New classes were groomed who were neither nobles nor peasants, neither wealthy nor labour hands; intermediate between the new and the old landed aristocratic hierarchies, these were clerks, artisans, supervisors, master-craftsmen, skilled labourers. Fashions and festivals, customs and manners, cuisine and leisure, education and public service were all touched, if not moulded, by the Order's long presence. Some customs, such as the pre-Lenten carnival, pre-dated the arrival of the Knights, and owe their origins to the Catholic tradition. Others started in or after the sixteenth century, or were popularised and extended. The feast of *Otto Settembre*, known to Maltese as 'il-Vitorja', celebrated the Great Siege victory of 1565. The feast of St Peter and St Paul, known as *Luminaria* (L-Imnarja), goes back as a popular festival to the period of the Knights. For example, the Knights played bowls, still a Maltese past-time today known as 'boċċi'. In the annals of history, boat and donkey races — even fireworks — similarly go back to that time, and may well precede it. Country-folk would have been less influenced than city-dwellers by the Order; here it seems that traditional dress rather continued as before, whereas in the cities there would have been more assimilation, as was to be expected. The common Maltese greetings 'bonġu' (from *'bon jour'*) and 'bonswa' (from *'bon soir'*) would date back to that time; the largest *Langue*, in number, was the French one. A word like 'missier' (Maltese for 'father') has been dated further back, to Norman times. For most practical and routine purposes of record, however, Italian, which already existed in Malta as the medium of formal education and communication, continued to be predominant throughout the Knights' stay, and thereby became a still more established 'Maltese' official language.

Ideologically, Maltese looked to Catholic Europe more steadfastly and consciously than ever before. Those who moved in government circles realised that Europe was more than just Rome, even if the Rome of popes and caesars, the closest major European mainland capital, continued to be the main focus. In the mainstream European effort to stem the Ottoman advance the Malta siege of 1565 was not as important as the Battle of Lepanto of 1571, in which Malta participated with her fleet; but for Malta the Siege was supremely important: it remained indelible in the memory and became legendary. The sociology of the Turkish siege of Malta is that it mobilized one and all, like never before, in a desperate fight to the finish between Cross and Crescent. Survival depended on the victory of the Christians against the Infidels, of the European against the Turk. Until quite recently in Malta many common people made little difference, if any, between 'Arabs' and 'Turks': those were the non-European Muslims. A chief standard-bearer of the European religion was Malta herself, raising high the eight beatitudes of 'The Religion' in the Malta Cross. As a consequence of this period, Moors were all too often slaves of the Christians; Malta sometimes had thousands of them. Several well-to-do Maltese kept slaves in their households. Christians, including Maltese and Knights, were enslaved by the Moors. The idea of Europe in Malta has its genesis as much in Roman Catholicism as in the centuries of fighting, fearing, enslaving and being enslaved by the Muslim 'Turks' or 'Moors'. These notions, sentiments and allegiances were crystallized under the Grand Masters.

Finally, the population also changed. Ideas about ethnicity and nationality are often like kith and kin. Some visiting travellers found the Maltese 'fairer in colour' than their immediate northern neighbours. Dress, hygiene, manners, attitudes, aspirations, relations and standards were influenced by military or religious rigour, by social inter-action and by the facilities offered by the Order, such as the hospital and charities. The Normans already had brought personnel to service administrative needs, and during the succession of mainly Spanish feudal lords and emissaries, other mostly Southern European individuals and families came to stay. Nor was the conduct of many individual Knights always as virgin in practice as it was *pro forma* presumed and upheld to be. The Knights brought with them from Rhodes a large entourage, mostly Rhodians, who would have mingled and mixed with the then existing population of some 20,000. By the time the Knights of Malta left in 1798, the more europeanized Maltese population had multiplied five-fold. Maltese raised large families and the conditions for a stable demographic growth were in place.

In the evolution of a Maltese nationality and identity, the 'Western' layer (the Knights of Malta) had settled on and permeated into the former 'Southern' layer (the Sicilian Normans and later feudal lords), which itself had bitten into and camouflaged the earlier 'Arabic' layer, which in turn had superseded the Graeco-Roman legacy after the Phoenician one. The 'Western' layer, carrying over in a *continuum* from the 'Southern' one – over a time span of six centuries – was the most significant, for during its tenure modern Malta came into being as a small European state.

In state-making, the Maltese nation too was being formed. No sooner had the Knights been forced out by Napoleon that the Maltese were forced to stand up for what they held to be their rights, values, interests and customs as a people. The test came upon them with an unexpected suddenness, barely three months after Grand Master Hompesch had surrendered the islands without putting up a fight. In their own insurrection against Bonapartism

Sixteenth century Maltese and Turkish ships, from a painting in the Sant Manduca collection.

Queen Victoria's statue outside the eighteenth century Bibliotecha in the "Piazza Regina".

starting in September 1798 the Maltese *patria* – not merely their *heimat* – was at stake. Against the marauding and looting French troops, grieved by broken promises and newly-imposed burdens, leaders and led rose to the challenge with courage and determination. This time, there were no knights in shining armour to hold their hands. Leadership came mainly from the professional, clerical and merchant classes: Emmanuele Vitale was a notary; Vincenzo Bugeja, a cotton merchant; Francesco Saverio Caruana an ecclesiastic. But the mass of peasants and labourers, fed up with repressive, arbitrary rule, joined in the fray in defence of religion and country. Decorously enough, the rebellion started in Mdina, where French officers were robbing the Carmelite church. To Mdina, to the pealing of church bells, the farmers hurried, armed with their tools and implements, on 2 September 1798. After taking the citadel, lieutenants and batallions were formed, cannon and shot and rations organized; the citadel at Gozo, and all the Malta villages and countryside, were soon in rebel hands. In her first siege since it was built and fortified, Valletta gave protection to the revolutionary, abusive 'infidels' from France. In Valletta and the Three Cities, besieged by the Maltese, the French garrison hid, sometimes retaliated, and slowly starved. Most Maltese city-dwellers they threw out. As was typical of the Napoleonic era throughout Europe and the Mediterranean, the announced revolutionary ideals were not very well put into practice *sur place*; as a result subject peoples thanklessly rebelled. After all, the principle of popular sovereignty had been a corner-stone of the Revolution, enshrined in the 1789 Declaration of the Rights of Man and of the Citizen. The 1798 insurrection of Malta was (and remains to this day) the first and only popular armed insurrection in the country's entire history. Thousands died during the two years that it lasted. In full alert, by general mobilisation, it brought to the fore,

combined, and sharpened the edges of the three residual or latent factors of the Maltese identity: culture, nationality and politics. The single most important cause of the insurrection – but by no means the only one – was probably religious. The course of events taken by it, incorporating Maltese from all walks of life, broadened into a bloody national resistance to a foreign despotism, with a premium set on liberty, patriotism and survival: 'us' against 'them'.

With the Neapolitan king's permission, the insurgents summoned Nelson's fleet to help them. The ensuing blockade forced the French out, but the Maltese felt badly slighted by their exclusion from the capitulation. The French left with full military honours; the Maltese licked their wounds; not a single Englishman had lost his life. But in 1800 the British had come to stay: they stayed in charge until 1964, when Malta finally gained her independence.

At the time of the Peace of Amiens in 1802 there was a prospect that Malta would revert to the Order with a Maltese *Langue* included: it would be made 'independent' and 'neutral', with guarantees from the Great Powers; but the British thought better of it and the Third Coalition against Napoleon was formed. This was a time of uncertainty, when Malta's strategic importance and the Anglo-French rivalry over it were frequently the subject of debate, of comment and caricature in the French and British press. Not wanting to return to the Order, nor willing to accept that other powers dispense of Malta's dearly-earned 'sovereignty', Maltese drew up an eloquent and up-to-date '*Dichiarazione*' of the rights of the islanders, founded on historical, juridical and philosophical argumentation. They saw allegiance to the British monarch as a compact in return for protection, but challenged his or any other power's right to dispose of the islands' destiny. A number of petitions dating to the first two decades of the nineteenth century contained a thinly-veiled presumption of

These photographs taken in Valletta in 1870 show Putirjal ("Porta Reale"), the entrance to the capital city (1); the Grand Master's Palace which became the Governor's Palace (2); the Auberge de Castille (now the Office of the Prime Minister) (3) and the Royal Opera House (4), destroyed during the Second World War.

3

4

'indipendenza'.

Such, then, was the genesis of Britain's occupation of Malta in 1800, until Malta was given to her as a possession by treaty (not with Malta) in 1815. With the exception of Gibraltar, Britain held on to Malta for longer than she did anywhere else in the Mediterranean: six generations. The 'British' layer was the last and in certain respects, the most decisively formative one in the history of Maltese culture and national identity, prior to independence. Like the Order of St John, Britain was a naval and a military power, to whom defences and docks were important. Unlike the generals whom they had replaced, the British bent backwards to keep their peace with the Catholic Church and to respect such other traditions as were irrelevant to their concerns. Unlike either, the British had an industrialized country; but, like both, they needed revenues. After 1815, they were not usually at war and cherished the *Pax Britannica*, although when war did come or was felt to be close by Malta was inevitably effected, for better or for worse. The main such 'events' after the Napoleonic era were the Crimean War (1854-1856), the Russo-Turkish War (1877-1878), the Great War (1914-1918), the Abyssinian War (1935-1936), the Second World War (1939-1945) and the war over Suez in 1956. To some extent the time and type of constitution Britain allowed Malta to have was also related to goings-on outside, in Britain and her empire, or in Europe, especially Italy. The main dates of colonial 'constitutions', up and down and up again, are themselves somewhat indicative: 1835, 1849, 1887, 1903, 1921, 1936, 1939, 1947, 1961, 1964.

The British influenced Malta considerably, especially in administration, constitutions and electoral politics, the economy, the dockyard, the forces, education. In deliberately seeking to anglicize, however, they had to contend with some five centuries of *italianità*. Viewing Malta on the field through army binoculars, measuring the people by land-size of territory, or by the naval and commercial utility of harbours, they underestimated the distinctive resilience embedded in historical and patriotic tradition and consequently the potential strength of national feeling. Anglicization was indeed largely brought about by the 1930s, by imperial *fiat*, and was more or less sealed by the joint war effort and its aftermath, in the following decade.

Throughout this fermentation, Maltese colonial nationalism emerged. In opposition to 'English, and English only', the middle class cultural nationalists raised *italianità* as their standard. Anglicization, said the British and their supporters, was to come about by means of the vernacular, Maltese (which until the 1930s had no standard orthography and not much of a literature). Until the post-war period, when Italy had discredited herself and *italianità* lost its appeal, Maltese nationalists had tended to suspect and to resist the upgrading and spreading of Maltese language education in schools, seeing this as a means for anglicization. Italian, for so long the main official language in Malta, was identified with education, public affairs, liberty, religion, and contacts in the region. English was seen as useful in some cases or for certain purposes but generally regarded as the language of domination and of despotism, an 'Anglo-Saxon tongue'. Maltese in its uncultivated state was usually dismissed as a dialect recalling the Saracen domination, too restrictive, unbecoming of a modern, secular and European society. On the other hand, by the 1880s, a growing category of people were being exposed to English or helped to realise that this could be more important to their advancement than Italian. Maltese political parties thus developed on so-called 'pro-Italian' and 'pro-English' lines, with the language battle, a clash of cultures and interests, a recurring and explosive issue in colonial politics. What this implied, of course, was an inability, in the circumstances, to reach a consensus on self-identity. Underlying the culture clash, were political and economic interests and aspirations on all sides. *Italianità* was also a buffer, a symbol, a rallying cry, frequently used interchangeably with *latinità*.

The English-Italian tussle embodied many traits which cut close to the bone of nationality, elements which are the very sinews of identity. The language question of Malta, however particular to the country, was by no means removed from concerns that continue seriously to agitate people in our own times. A Maltese historian reading the stirring *'Avenir de la Langue Française'* appeals in *Le Monde* in the 'year of Europe' 1992 may be forgiven for thinking that he was reading Fortunato Mizzi's *Malta* one century earlier. Much of the argumentation about language worth, self and nation, utility and culture, and against *'des fanatiques du tout-anglais'* is the same:

Ils oblient surtout que la langue n'est pas un vernis, une marchandise, n'est pas un matériau comme les autres: elle est ce qui porte et structure la pensée. C'est par elle qu'adviennent en nous le monde et le simple plaisir d'être soi. On n'en change pas comme on change de 'job' ou de voiture.

But in Malta's case there was also Maltese (in a French context, the *'Breton'* or *'Basque'*). Maltese gradually attracted adherents and became more creative and literary in this century, with many of those formerly using Italian starting to make use of it instead or as well. The Malta Independence Constitution of 1964 entrenched it as the national language, with English as a second language. After English, the best-known foreign languages in Malta remained Italian and French, all languages with whose countries or nationals Malta had direct contacts for long periods in the past. The multi-lingual, multi-cultural society of one time, which so impressed our English traveller as 'an epitome of all Europe', still stirred. Monolingualism certainly does not appear to be an item on Malta's national identity agenda.

In their vast majority the Maltese remain Catholics, in the same bracket with the Irish and the Poles. Freedom of conscience is not in question; with cable television and mass tourism, secularisation has been making itself felt, inviting new tensions. In the nineteenth century parishes continued to grow and develop, as did the enthusiasm of parishioners. Band clubs mushroomed from mid-century and especially from the 1870s onwards, sometimes rival ones were formed in the same town or village. Valletta had two of them before 1880. The *festa* in honour of the patron saint, or of a secondary saint, became a great village attraction: the event of the year for many villagers who took much interest in church affairs, religious and semi-religious. Fireworks became a speciality of the *festa*. The festa of the saint was also the festa of the town or village: families and friends met and made merry. *Qubbajd, pastizzi, qassatat, imqaret*, and other nougat, pastry with dates, *ricotta*, honey, typical Maltese snacks and sweets, became and remain popular. To this day, on the 15 August when seven villages simultaneously celebrated Santa Maria's feast, the night sky of Malta is ablaze with colour, resounding with petards, a quite marvellous and unique spectacle. Lay organisations and church network diehards continue to be prominent in various religious outdoor and indoor activities, such as the Good Friday ceremonies and processions.

In nineteenth century Malta the social nation came alive. More awareness of and participation in public activities, new and old, accompanied greater political organisation and mobilization especially under the umbrella of colonial nationalism, as well as the continuing growth in population. Between 1800 and 1964 Malta's population trebled from 100,000 to 300,000, in spite of mass emigration to the English-speaking world especially after 1945. Malta thus became the most densely populated country in Europe: *"una città sul mare"*, one traveller called it. *Patria* and *pajjiż* became *nazzjon* and *stat*.

An aerial view of Valletta intersecting the Grand Harbour and Marsamxett Harbour with Manoel Island and Sliema in the background.

Churchill, Roosevelt, Badoglio and Eisenhower in Malta during the Second World War.

The main political parties, Nationalist (Christian Democrat) and Labour (Democratic Socialist), in the last thirty years have at times instrumentalized the popularity of open-air *festa*-atmosphere gatherings, so that sometimes even 'mass meetings' – the appeal of which seems to be decreasing of late – came to include food-stalls, fairs, fireworks, music and song.

Until independence in 1964, Malta's national day was the *Otto Settembre* – 'il-Vitorja' – first celebrated as such by Mizzi's Nationalist Party in Valletta in 1885. This day came to recall Malta's victory in her two great sieges: 1565 and 1943; among emigrants it remained their most important feast. It was replaced by Independence Day, also in September, in 1964. In the 1970s, during Mr Mintoff's premiership, there ceased to be a consensus among the party leaderships as to the best date for Malta's national day. In 1988 it was unanimously agreed by parliament to have no less than five national 'feasts', including Independence Day (21 September 1964), Republic Day (13 December 1974), the *Sette Giugno* recalling Maltese anti-British demonstrations in 1919 when several Maltese were killed or wounded; the *Otto Settembre*; and even 31 March 1979, when 'the last British soldier left'.

Communications were facilitated first by train services (from the 1880s), then by trams, and subsequently by *char-à-bancs*, as the still throttling quaint Maltese passenger buses are known. The motor-car, a rare commodity until the 1950s, became all too popular, although it still has to share the road with trotting ponies or the horse-drawn carriage *karrozzin*. For ferrying across harbours or from ship to quay, there were always the typical Maltese multi-coloured boats, mainly the oar-driven *dgħajsa*, or occasionally one of the smaller fishing boats (*kajjik*). These had a thriving trade when Grand Harbour headquartered the British Mediterranean Fleet. More recently these have had to compete with launches, hydrofoils and helicopters

especially for the longer distances. In print journalism, Maltese newspapers started in 1838, when Britain removed the censorship: a remarkable number of newspapers, magazines and reviews were published. For the last twenty years, Malta has had three or four dailies and Sunday newspapers, in both Maltese and English. The daily Italian language newspaper *Malta* stopped being published in 1940, after a run of nearly sixty years. British-initiated locally-based radio – Rediffusion – started in the mid-1930s, after Italian wireless had begun to reach Malta. Italian TV reception and a Maltese TV station go back to the 1950s and 1960s respectively. Information-spreading, opinion-forming and public participation became features of a more modernized, more secularized lifestyle.

Introduced by the British, football became and remains the most popular national sport; but, at the Marsa Sports Club, even polo survives. Tennis too became popular, not only among younger people. Swimming has been endemic. To Maltese, the sea is in the bones. The number of professional fishermen declined over the years, as has that of farmers, but there continue to be numerous *dilettante* fishermen and farmers. Various folk events have long been associated with the sea, such as *ġostra* (the greasy pole), or the *regatta* boat-races. Horse-racing, hunting, even home pigeons have been popular for a long time, especially among the country-folk; in some areas *impromptu* guitar-accompanied folk-singing has continued to entertain select audiences, and is well patronised among some Maltese overseas communities.

In art, literature, music and theatre, a certain revival was experienced in the 1960s, especially in painting, poetry and drama. Several talented individuals have distinguished themselves, including a few stars in film or opera, composers and conductors who 'made it' overseas. Maltese creative artists and authors of all genres have tended to be somewhat handicapped

*Queen Elizabeth II and Prince Philip at the Manoel Theatre, and with parliamentarians
led by the Speaker of the House during a royal visit in 1967.
The Prime Minister, Dr Borg Olivier, is on Prince Philip's left.*

by the limited audience or market around them, or the want of adequate remuneration from official quarters for their talents: thus to go abroad, or to write or sing in a language of wider communication, was always a temptation. Recognised Maltese singers are recorded as early as the twelfth century. Musical compositions found at the Mdina Cathedral archives, which have been premiered in Malta by Maltese musicians, date back to the Middle Ages and early modern times. Others distinguished themselves in various branches of the sciences, social, natural and physical: opthalmologists, for example: Barth, Preziosi, Tabone; or a maverick like Edward de Bono. The most successful not infrequently left Malta: they went to Vienna or Paris, London or Rome, settled in Melbourne or Toronto; yet many stayed, strayed back or kept in touch.

In 1964-1965 Malta became a member of the Council of Europe, of the British Commonwealth of Nations, of the United Nations, and later of the Conference on Security and Cooperation in Europe, and of other international organisations. Until 1971, NATO's Allied Forces Mediterranean were headquartered in Malta. Before the 1987 elections parliament agreed that Malta would be neutral and not host military bases on her soil (and that the party obtaining the absolute majority of votes would govern even if the number of seats won initially did not tally).

The Maltese are and feel European. They have belonged in Europe: were its *leitmotiv* Christendom, as in 1565; or anti-Bonapartism, as in 1798; or people's democracy, as in and after 1940-1945. The contrast of shimmering light and retreating shade on the limestone that constructed the megalithic temples, the towering bastions and the anti-aircraft ranges, merges with the still clean, dazzling blue sea: but the galleys and destroyers have made way for oil tankers and cruise liners.

Since 1964 Malta has been striving to acquire the infrastructural supports required by a small state competing for markets and influence in Europe, the Mediterranean and beyond; and seeking to help uplift the quality of life, social and intellectual. The economy had to be diversified radically: for centuries this had been very largely a dependent one, with the bulk of salaried employment all too often subject to the policies, priorities and exigencies of foreign and unrepresentative governments. Public sector employment, although somewhat on the decline, remains high. Tourism (mainly from Britain, Germany and Italy), light industry (computer software, quality textiles, toys, glass), ship-repairing and some agricultural and horticultural production (including export of potatoes, tomatoes, flowers) became the mainstays of the economy. In the post-war period Maltese wines and beers started to be more professionally marketed and, after independence, also exported. The latest developments have been in offshore investment, transhipment in a free port, yacht marinas, fish-farming. Maltese tend to work hard, enjoy the family and save, and the Malta currency has been a strong one; but flair, engagement, self-confidence and openness are also precious. A respectable showing in some regional or world event by a Maltese national (as in the Eurovision Song Contest or snooker competitions), always raises a cheer. Three decades after independence, as the 'cultural cringe' slowly sheds off, we find Malta in the queue to join the European Community. The parliamentary tradition has survived in this ex-colony, past hiccups notwithstanding, and its future now appears assured. Partly due to partisan polarisation, now also on the wane, Malta's voter percentages in general elections became the highest in the world, usually over 90%. Higher education has been expanding in recent years – in 1992 the University of Malta celebrated its four hundredth anniversary. The average Maltese will be accustomed to visitors and almost invariably speak or at least understand more than one language.

Increasingly conscious of Europe, with which Malta mostly trades, Maltese are also not unaware of their own limitations, and their own characteristics. They would wish to be European without renouncing to their recognisably Maltese identity: the mould of their own ingenuity over the millenia, in an intense, varied and often difficult history. They survived as one of the world's smallest ethnic minorities, about one million in all world-wide, with their own undisputed territory and surrounding seas, with their own language too.

In Europe the closest parallel to Malta is probably Luxembourg. With a comparable resident population of somewhat less than 400,000, Luxembourg like Malta has been sandwiched between neighbouring countries and language-cultures, forging its identity at least partly by default or conscious effort. Luxembourgeois is a distinguishing German dialect, not a fully-fledged language like Maltese; it co-exists in Luxembourg with French and German. In spite of its size, Luxembourg has had a fairly eventful history, of which its continued survival as a separate nation-state in continental Europe is living proof. The Luxembourgese historian Gilbert Trausch in a 1988 study on Luxembourg's search for a national conscience concluded, by exclusion: *'Ni Français, ni Allemands, ni Belges!'* By the same token, and similarly by elimination, the Maltese position is this: *'Ni Italiens, ni Anglais, ni Arabes!'*

Bibliography

AQUILINA, Joseph, *Papers in Maltese Linguistics*, Malta Univ. Press, Valletta, 1961.
  Teach Yourself Maltese, EUP, London, 1965.
    A Comparative Dictionary of Maltese Proverbs, Malta Univ. Press, 1985.
    Maltese-English Dictionary, Midsea, Valletta, 1987-1990, 2 vols.
AUSTIN, Dennis, *Malta and the End of Empire*, Cass, London, 1971.
BEZZINA, Joseph, *Religion and Politics in a Crown Colony. The Gozo-Malta Story*
  1798-1864, Bugelli, Valletta, 1985.
BLOUET, Brian, *The Story of Malta*, rev.ed., Faber, London, 1972.
BOISGELIN, Louis de, *Ancient and Modern Malta*, Richard Phillips, London, 1805.
  2 vols. (Facsimile, Midsea, Valletta, 1988).
BOISSEVAIN, Jeremy, *Saints and Fireworks, Religion and Politics in Rural Malta*, The
  Atholone Press, London, 1965.
BOWEN-JONES, H., et (eds), *Malta: Background for Development*, Durham, 1961.
BRADFORD, Ernle, *The Great Siege: Malta 1565*, Penguin, 1964.
  The Shield and the Sword: The Knights of Malta, Fontana, 1974.
BRINCAT, Joseph M., *Malta 870-1054. Al Himyarî's Account*, Said, Valletta, 1991.
BROCKMAN, Eric, *Last Bastion, Sketches of the Maltese Islands*. Darton, Longman &
  Todd Ltd, London, 1961.
CASSAR, Paul, *A Medical History of Malta*, Wellcome Historical Medical Library,
  London, 1964.
CAVALIERO, Roderick, *The Last of the Crusaders*, London, 1960.
CREMONA, Antonio, *Vassalli and His Times*, Muscat, (May Butcher trans.,) Valletta,
  1940.
CORTIS, Toni (ed), *L-Identità ta' Malta. Kungress Nazzjonali 13-15 ta' April 1989*,
  Dipartiment ta' l-Informazzjoni, Valletta, 1989. (Contributors: G. Aquilina, A.
  Bonanno, M. Buhagiar, G. Cassar Pullicino, M. Ellul, R. Ellul Micallef, H.
  Frendo, O. Friggieri, E. Lanfranco, P. Sammut, P. Sant Cassia, P. Serracino
  Inglott, J. Vella, G. Wettinger.)
CREMONA, J.J., *The Malta Constitution of 1835 and its Historical Background*,
  Muscat, Valletta, 1959.
  An Outline of the Constitutional Development of Malta. Muscat, Valletta, 1960.
  Human Rights Documentation in Malta. Malta University Press, Malta, 1966.
CUTAJAR, Felice, *L'Occupazione Francese di Malta nel 1798*. Empire Press, Valletta,
  1933.
DENNIS, Nigel, *An Essay on Malta with Drawings by Osbert Lancaster*, Murray,
  London, 1972.
DOBIE, Edith, *Malta's Road to Independence*, Norman/University of Oklahoma Press,
  U.S.A., 1967.
ELLUL MICALLEF, R. and FIORINI, S. (eds): *Collegium Melitense Quatercentenary
  Celebrations, 1592-1992: Collected Papers*, Malta Univ., 1992. (Contributors: V.
  Axiak, J.V. Bannister, W.H. Bannister, A. Bonanno, M.G. Borg, M.P. Brincat, M.
  Buhagiar, A. Cassola, A. Cuschieri, D. De Lucca, R. Ellul Micallef, J.M. Falzon,
  A.E. Felice, S. Fiorini, M. Formosa, H. Frendo, M. Grech, J. Lauri, A. Sammut,
  P.J. Schembri, J. Tonna, A.J. Vella, K. Wain.)
FIORENTINI, Bianca, *Malta, rifugio di esuli e focolare ardente di cospirazione durante
  il Risorgimento Italiano*. Casa S. Giuseppe, Malta, 1966.
FIORINI, Stanley and Mallia-Milanes, Victor (eds.) *Malta A Case Study in International
  Cross-Currents*, Malta, 1991.

(Contributors: D.F. Allen, A. Bonanno, H. Bresc, A. Blondy, J.M. Brincat, M. Buhagiar, B. Collett, R. Ellul Micallef, D. Fenech, H. Frendo, S. Fiorini, O. Friggieri, F. Halliday, A. Luttrell, D. Mack Smith, V. Mallia-Milanes, P. Serracino Inglott, P. Vassallo, G. Wettinger.)

FRENDO, Henry, *Maltese Political Development 1798-1964. A Documentary History* (ed.), Ministry of Education and Human Resources, Malta, 1993.

"The Legacy of Colonialism: The Experience of Malta and Cyprus", *The Development Process in Small States* (eds D.G. Lockhart et), Routledge, London, 1993.

"Language and Nationhood in the Maltese Experience. Some Comparative and Theoretical Approaches", *Collegium Melitense Quatercentenary Celebrations* (*op.cit., supra*).

"Malta, Cyprus and Gibraltar: Self Identity in the British Mediterranean", *Islands and Enclaves: Nationalism and Separatist Pressures in Island and Littoral Contexts* (G. Trompf ed.), Sterling, New Delhi, 1993.

"Italy and Britain in Maltese Colonial Nationalism", *History of European Ideas*, Pergamon, Oxford, 1992, vol.14, n.4-6.

Malta's Quest for Independence: Reflections on the Course of Maltese History, Dougall, Valletta, 1989.

"Australia's Maltese Language Press", *The Ethnic Press in Australia* (A.Ata and C. Ryan eds), Academia, Melbourne, 1989.

"Storja u Għarfien: Il-Maltin min huma?", *L-Identità Kulturali ta' Malta* (*op. cit., supra*).

"Religion and Ethnic Identity in the Maltese Australian Community", *Religion and Ethnic Identity* (A.Ata ed.), Spectrum, Melbourne, 1988.

"Maltese Colonial Identity: Latin Mediterranean or British Empire?", *British Colonial Experience*, 1988 (*op.cit., infra*).

"The Condition of Malta after 1945", *The Australian People, An Encyclopedia of the Nation, its People and their Origins* (James Jupp ed.), Angus & Robertson, Canberra, 1988.

"Malta", *Lexikon zur Geschichte der Parteien in Europa* (Frank Wende ed.), Alfred Kröner Verlag, Stuttgart, 1981.

Party Politics in a Fortress Colony: The Maltese Experience, Midsea, Valletta, 1979; 2nd ed. 1991.

"Language and Nationality in an Island Colony: Malta", *Canadian Review of Studies in Nationalism*, Charlottetown, 1975, vol.3, n.1. (Catalan trans. Cesari Lleiza, *L'Avenc*, Barcelona, Sept. 1981).

Birth Pangs of a Nation: Manwel Dimech's Malta, 1860-1921, Mediterranean Publications, Valletta, 2nd ed. (in English), 1972.

FRIGGIERI, Oliver, *La Cultura Italiana a Malta. Storia e influenza letteraria e stilistica attraverso l'opera di Dun Karm*, Olschki, Firenze, 1978.

GANADO, Herbert, *Rajt Malta Tinbidel*, Klabb Kotba Maltin, Valletta, 1974-1977, 4 vols.

Jien Inħobb Nitkellem Magħkom. Maxprint Press, Malta, 1984, 2 vols.

HARDING, Hugh W., *Maltese Legal History under British Rule 1801-1836*, Royal University of Malta, 1968.

HARDMAN, William, *Malta during the French and British Occupations*, Longman, Green & Co., London, 1909.

HUGHES, Quentin, *Architecture and Military History in Malta*, Lund Humphries, London, 1969.

HULL, Geoffrey, *The Malta Language Question. A Case Study in Cultural Imperialism*, Said International, Valletta, 1993.

KOSTER, Adrianus, *Prelates and Politicians in Malta: changing power-balances between Church and State in a Mediterranean island-fortress, 1530-1976*. Vreje Universiteit te Amsterdam, 1981.

KOSTER, Adrianus, and SMITH Harrison: *Lord Strickland; Servant of the Crown*. Progress Press, Valletta 1984-1986, 2 vols.

LEE, Hilda, *Malta 1813-1914. A Study in Constitutional and Stategic Development*. Progress Press, Malta, 1972.

LUTTRELL, Anthony T. (ed), *Medieval Malta. Studies on Malta before the Knights*, British School at Rome, London, 1975.

MACMILLAN, Allister (ed.), *Malta and Gibraltar*, Collingridge, London, 1915.

MAHONEY, Leonard, *A History of Maltese Architecture*, Veritas Press, Malta, 1988.

MALLIA MILANES, Victor (ed.), *British Colonial Experience. The Impact on Maltese Society*, Mireva Publications, Malta, 1988. (Contributors: J. Bezzina, J. Boissevain, S. Busuttil, C. Cassar, A.G. Clare, D. Cutajar/E. Fiorentino, D. De Lucca, S. Howe, H. Frendo, O. Friggieri, A. Koster, V. Mallia-Milanes, P. Serracino Inglott, E.L. Zammit, G. Wettinger, A. Williams.)

(ed.), *Hospitaller Malta 1530-1798*, Mireva Publications, Malta, 1993.

(Contributors: A. Blondy, A. Bonnici, S. Bono, C. Cassar, P. Cassar, F. Ciappara, J. Gash, A.H. de Groot, A. Hoppen, Q. Hughes, S. Fiorini, M. Fontenay, A.T. Luttrell, V. Mallia-Milanes, A. Williams.)

MAZZON, Gabriella, "Politica Linguistica vs Identità Culturale: Alcuni Aspetti della Questione della lingua a Malta nel secondo '800", *Journal of Maltese Studies*, 1989-90, n.19-20.

MIFSUD, Alfredo, *Origine della Sovranità Inglese su Malta*, Malta, 1907.

MONTALTO, John, *The Nobles of Malta*, Midsea, Valletta, 1979.

PIROTTA, Joseph M., *Fortress Colony: The Final Act*. Studia Editions, Valletta, 1987-1991. 2 vols.

PORTER, Whitworth, *The Knights of St John of Jerusalem*. Simpkin Marshall & Co., London, 1884.

PSAILA, C., *Dizzjunarju Ingliż – Malti*, Aquilina, Valletta, 1947-1955, 3 Vols.

SCHERMERHORN, Elisabeth W., *Malta of the Knights*, The Windmill Press, London, 1929.

SCICLUNA, Hannibal P., *Actes et Documents relatifs à l'Histoire de l'Occupation Française de Malte, pendant les années 1798-1800 et à la fête du 14 juillet 1798 à Malte, d'après des documents pur la plupart inédits des Archives de Malte*, A.C. Aquilina, Valletta, 1979. (3rd ed.)

SERRACINO INGLOTT, Erin, *Il-Miklem Malti*, Klabb Kotba Maltin, Valletta, 9 vols., 1975-1989.

TESTA, Carmel, *The Life and Times of Grand Master Pinto, 1741-1773*, Midsea, Valletta, 1989.

Maż-Żewġ Naħat tas-Swar, Klabb Kotba Maltin, Valletta, 1979-1982. 3 vols.

VASSALLO, Mario, *From Lordship to Stewardship. Religion and Social Change in Malta*, Mouton, The Hague, 1979.

VELLA, Andrew P., *Storja ta' Malta*, Klabb Kotba Maltin, Valletta, 1971, 2 vols.

VERTOT, René Aubert de, *Histoire des Chevaliers Hospitaliers de S. Jean de Jerusalem, appellez depuis Chevaliers de Rhodes, et aujourd'hui Chevaliers de Malte*. Rollin Paris, 1726, 5 vols. (English ed. Martin & Witherspoon, Edinburgh, 1770, 5 vols.)

WETTINGER, Godfrey, and FSADNI, M., *Peter Caxaro's Cantilena. A Poem in*

Medieval Maltese, Malta, 1968.

WETTINGER, G., "Plurilingualism and Cultural Change in Medieval Malta", *Mediterranean Language Review*, Wiesbaden, 1993, n.6-7.

The Jews of Malta in the Late Middle Ages, Midsea, Valletta, 1985.

"The Militia List of 1419-20. A new starting point for the study of Malta's Population", *Melita Historica*, Valletta, 1969, vol.V, n.2.

"Early Maltese popular attitudes to the Government of the Order of St John", *Melita Historica*, 1974, vol.VI, n.3.

"Agriculture in Malta in the Late Middle Ages", *Proceedings of History Week*, Malta Historical Society, Valletta, 1981.

"The Arabs in Malta", *Malta: Studies of its Heritage and History*, Malta, 1986.

(ed.), *Acta iuratorum et Consilii Civitatis et Insulae Maltae*, Palermo, 1993.

ZAMMIT, Edward: *A Colonial Inheritance. Maltese Perceptions of Work, Power and Class Structure with reference to the Labour Movement*, Malta University Press, Msida, 1984.

Language

Alexander Borg

I

Of all the social and cultural institutions created by the inhabitants of the Maltese Islands on their long and eventful path to nationhood, their language, Maltese, is without doubt one of the most striking and original. It is, in fact, not easy for the historical linguist to account for the remarkable survival of this island vernacular in the face of the numerous socio-political upheavals that have characterized the history of this small archipelago, which 'since it was first colonised ... has never been very far from the centre of events and has often played a critical part in the making of history' (Blouet 1981: 11).

Throughout most of their medieval and modern history, these strategically located islands have been administered and culturally dominated by a succession of foreign regimes associated with linguistic power symbols of incomparably greater prestige and utility than the indigenous rural vernacular of Malta, which achieved the status of a literary medium as late as the 19th century.

What kind of language is Maltese? Briefly, the vernacular of the Maltese Islands initially developed from a medieval variety of dialectal Arabic – presumably after the Arab invasion of the archipelago in the late 9th century (870 A.D.). As noted in Thomas (1937: 117),

From the moment the Arabs had established supremacy over the Byzantines at sea, the fate of the islands of the Mediterranean was sealed, and one by one they passed into Moslem hands... They had invaded Malta at about the same time as Sicily, ruled it till 1091, and were resident for another 350 years, when they departed leaving behind them their dialect of Arabic, which is the language of the Maltese to this day.

Apart from Cypriot Arabic (§ III) – now in a terminal state – Maltese is today the only living vestige of dialectal Arabic spoken on European soil, surviving by many centuries the extinction of the medieval Arabic vernaculars of Sicily (12th century), Spain and Pantelleria (16th century).

Geographically detached from the Arabic-speaking mainland and culturally isolated from the sources of native Arabic speech, especially after the Norman invasion of the Islands in 1090 and the expulsion of the local Muslim population in the 13th century (Wettinger 1986: 98), the Arabic vernacular of the Maltese Islands evolved in line with its own internal logic and drifted away from the norms of spoken Arabic with the result that Maltese and Arabic are today not mutually comprehensible.

One important catalyst for independent linguistic development in Maltese has been the factor of language contact, first with Italian and later with English, a process that introduced into the language a considerable number of extraneous (i.e. non-Arabic) elements, mainly in the realms of phonology, syntax, and lexicon. The cumulative impact of autonomous development and language contact on Maltese has altered its structure so profoundly that though Maltese is not infrequently referred to as an 'Arabic dialect' in the linguistic and popular literature, this designation is today more appropriate as a genetic classification than as a synchronic one, since in its present form, Maltese has distanced itself structurally far too profoundly from the norms of spoken Arabic to be regarded as anything but a separate language.

27

From an erstwhile Arabic colloquial spoken by a small rural community, Maltese has gradually and spontaneously expanded as a linguistic system, winning for itself new functional domains beyond those of ordinary speech communication and popular wisdom literature (proverbs, folk-tales, etc.), e.g., those of formal and private prayer, litigation in the law courts, etc. As a literary medium it has become the repository of an interesting literary corpus (including popular novels, plays, and poetry), and of religious texts (the Bible, the Catholic liturgy). Maltese is also the language of most local journalism, and of a large body of didactic works ranging from theology to cookery.

Maltese is today, alongside English, the official language of Malta. It is, in fact, the only dialect of Arabic to have achieved this national status. It is taught at all educational levels from the primary school to university.

II

Maltese is the only national language in Europe belonging to the Semitic family, which also includes Hebrew, Arabic, Aramaic, Phoenician, Ethiopic, etc. One salient typological trait of this language family distinguishing it from other language families, e.g., Indo-European, is the root and scheme structure of most native words. Thus, the Classical Arabic word *rakiba* 'he rode' consists of:
(i) the consonantal root (*r-k-b*) associated with the notion 'riding';
(ii) a vocalic scheme (*a-i*) typical of many past tense verbs in Classical Arabic;
(iii) the final vowel (*-a*) indicating the 3rd person masculine singular.
Arabic and Maltese words displaying this specific root usually have meanings associated with the basic idea of 'riding': Arabic *rika:b* 'stirrup', *raku:ba* 'mount, female riding animal', Maltese *rikeb* 'he rode', *rikba* 'a ride', etc., (where the 'colon' symbol after a vowel indicates phonetic length).

Maltese has extended the derivational scope of this root and scheme process in an autonomous fashion and has continued to generate from native roots inherited from Arabic new words that do not occur in Classical or vernacular Arabic, e.g. Maltese *ndaħal* 'he interfered', *ndħi:l* 'interference' from *daħal* 'to enter'.

In addition to the recycling of its native elements, the expansion of the Maltese lexicon has been achieved, through massive borrowing from foreign languages, especially Italian. These borrowed elements display varying degrees of assimilation into the grammatical norms of Maltese. These different degrees of integration no doubt correlate with such factors as chronology (i.e. when the word was borrowed), and the socio-linguistic context in which the borrowing occurred.

The unusual circumstance that Maltese, a Semitic language, found itself completely isolated from the sources of Semitic speech, and in close interaction with Indo-European (principally Italian), has created a 'Semitic-Romance polarization' in the minds of many Maltese speakers as is witnessed by the movement − active in inter-war period − advocating the use of *Malti safi* 'pure Maltese'. Though no one seriously advocates the systematic elimination of all non-Arabic elements in the language, many Maltese speakers feel that the language is adopting more foreign terms that it can formally integrate. This feeling of being inundated by foreign lexicon is not new; it echoes views first expressed in the 18th century by the Maltese linguist and orientalist Mikiel Anton Vassallo (1764-1829), who earned for himself the title of 'father of the Maltese language' for his efforts at arousing a national linguistic consciousness and a responsible attitude on the part of the Maltese community of his time towards their language (cf. Cremona 1975). In recent times, the most fervent advocate for a more systematic expansion of the Semitic component of Maltese was the Maltese Hebraist and Biblical scholar Peter Paul

Saydon (1895-1971), who single-handedly translated the Old and New Testaments from their Hebrew and Greek originals into Maltese, and in the process, often resorted to innovative lexical and stylistic norms that fully exploited the generative potential of native Maltese derivational morphology as well as a certain amount of conscious borrowing from Arabic.

In practice, when two separate words – a native term and an Italian equivalent – are available in Maltese for a particular concept e.g., native *iżża ħayr* and the loan term *rringraccya* < It. *ringraziare*, both meaning 'he thanked', the selection process on the part of the individual native speaker or writer tends not to be a random one, but often reflects his cultural aspirations, educational background and, not infrequently, political affiliations. With regard to the latter point, it is generally recognized that the newspapers of the two principal political parties have developed distinct linguistic and rhetorical styles: the Labour organ inclines to the use of Semitic *Sprachgut*, while the Nationalist one is more receptive to Romance loans. The communicative functions attaching to this type of 'lexical colouring' in the context of Maltese political discourse have yet to be studied.

Throughout Malta's colonial period under British rule (1800-1964), knowledge of English was the key to social preferment. Many Maltese today are bilingual in Maltese and English; the average speaker's command of English can range from rudimentary to virtually native competence. Maltese speakers also habitually codeswitch very freely between the two languages so that a Maltese utterance is as likely as not to display embedded English lexical components – sometimes with minimal formal integration of the loaned elements to the native sound pattern. Syntactic and idiomatic calquing on English is also very common. The high status of English in Malta is evident from its diffusion to most social contexts: at home, at school and university. The tendency for young people to adopt English as a first language – usually as a strategy for enhancing their social status – would seem to present a serious threat to the transmission of unimpaired fluency in Maltese that could in the long run lead to marginalization of the language and to its ultimate demise.

Since there has traditionally been a *laissez-faire* attitude in linguistic matters within the Maltese educational system, the need for an official language policy – to *advocate* rather than to *enforce* linguistic norms in the schools and in the state bureaucracy – is keenly felt at the present time.

III

Previously we stressed the fact that, despite the patently Semitic and Arabic typology of its grammatical system, Maltese cannot in its present form be simply designated as an Arabic dialect. It is worth noting that Maltese is not a unique case in this regard since there exist a considerable number of former Arabic dialects that have survived outside the Arabic countries and are today spoken exclusively by ethnic non-Arabs, such as the Arabic vernaculars of Central Asia, Central Africa, South East Anatolia (Turkey), and Cyprus (see bibliography for sources on these dialects). The last mentioned, i.e. the Arabic dialect spoken by the Maronite Catholics of Kormakiti in the Kyrenia district of N.W. Cyprus, bears particularly close comparison to Maltese, with which it shares a number of socio-historical traits: virtually complete separation from the Arabic-speaking world, linguistic interaction across genetic boundaries (with Italian and English in the case of Maltese, with Greek in that of Cypriot Arabic), the Christian and Catholic affiliation of its speakers, as well as its Mediterranean habitat.

A linguistic analysis of Cypriot Arabic also reveals several analogous tendencies in their evolutionary profiles. It was initially these socio-historical parallels that led the present writer to undertake extensive fieldwork among the 1200-odd Arabic-speaking Maronites in Cyprus and to devote a lengthy monograph to their unusual vernacular (cf. Borg 1985). More recently, I undertook a fairly detailed comparison of Maltese and Cypriot Arabic (cf. Borg 1990), where I also indicated the significance of these marginal varieties of 'Arabic' to the historical study of mainstream Arabic.

As is often the case with linguistic relic areas, the intrinsic interest and importance of Maltese and Cypriot Arabic as objects of diachronic linguistic research surpasses by far the numerical and socio-political significance of their speaker communities. In this respect, Maltese and Cypriot Arabic invite comparison with other Mediterranean vernaculars surviving in isolation from their language families, e.g. the dialects of the Greek-speaking minorities of Calabria (Rohlfs 1933) and Corsica (Blanken 1951), the Catalan dialect of Alghero, Sardinia (Blasco Ferrer 1984), Albanian in Sicily, etc.

Three principal socio-historical factors in the evolution of Cypriot Arabic and Maltese have contributed to their estrangement from the contemporary Arabic dialect family:
a) geographical and cultural distance from the Arab countries and absence of direct contact with Classical Arabic and the mainland Arabic vernaculars, hence the complete absence of the diglossia situation typifying linguistic usage in the Arab countries (cf. Ferguson 1959, but also El-Hassan 1977) – literary Maltese does not continue Classical Arabic but is an independent local development deriving from colloquial Maltese;
b) a long history of language contact that has transformed these vernaculars, rendering them unintelligible to native Arabic speakers; in both cases there has been profound linguistic acculturation predominantly to one specific foreign language, yielding a *Sprachbund* relation-

ship with it (S. Italian in the case of M, Greek in that of Cypriot Arabic).
c) the religious factor, e.g., the Christian affiliation and European *Weltanschauung* of the Maltese and Cypriot Arabic speakers, which renders them basically unreceptive to cultural and linguistic influences from the Arabic countries. In the case of Maltese, the cultural and confessional aspects of the linguistic *Abstand* from Arabic are both reflected in the longstanding tradition of writing the language by means of the Latin alphabet (cf. the use of the Hebrew alphabet in Judeo-Arabic).

The highly analogous socio-historical and geolinguistic contexts in which these two erstwhile Arabic dialects have evolved present the historian of vernacular Arabic with what would seem to be an ideal opportunity for clarifying a number of important diachronic issues relating to the evolution of Arabic at large. Thus, since both vernaculars have traditionally been spoken by long-established Christian populations and have, as a result, side-stepped the cultural impact of Islam and the concomitant influences of Classical Arabic, they could potentially serve as useful reference points in the task of reconstructing earlier varieties of colloquial Arabic; for instance, by facilitating the identification of adstratal influences exerted by Classical Arabic on the mainstream vernaculars.

The sociolinguistic contexts of Cypriot Arabic and Maltese present a number of interesting parallels and contrasts. First of all, the size and present situation of their speaker communities should be noted. Whereas Cypriot Arabic is the native language of the 1200-odd former residents at Kormakiti village (N.W. Cyprus), Maltese is today spoken by well over 365,000 people (1984) in the Maltese Islands and by several thousand emigrants in Australia, Canada, U.S.A., Great Britain, etc. In the aftermath of the Turkish invasion and occupation of Northern Cyprus in July 1974, the majority of the Cypriot Arabic speaker community abandoned Kormakiti and have resettled in various parts of the Greek-controlled south. Previous scholars who investigated their vernacular − all of whom were able to carry out their fieldwork in Kormakiti itself − agree that this language is in its terminal stages, and that it can only be a matter of time before its speakers shift entirely to their second language, Greek, which they also speak natively − apparently without notable influence from Cypriot Arabic, though this point still needs to be looked into.

By way of contrast, contemporary Maltese − though in the long term also threatened by functional marginalization in favour of English − is today deeply rooted in the life and cultural heritage of the Maltese Islands, and shows an impressive degree of elaboration and standardization. Thus, while Cypriot Arabic has remained to this day an unwritten language, restricted mainly to the home, Maltese has been written intermittently since the 15th century, and has become − since the 19th century − the medium of a sizeable body of creative and didactic literature (cf. Friggieri 1979, *passim*). As has already been noted, it is also the usual language of religious worship, the press, broadcasting, private correspondence, etc., Maltese is today fully integrated into the school and university curricula, and despite strong competition from spoken English in most formal and informal linguistic domains − especially, but not exclusively, among the better educated − its use as a written medium seems, at least impressionistically, to be on the increase.

Finally, despite their small geographical size, the Maltese Islands constitute a fairly complex dialect area including a standard variety of Maltese, spoken in Valletta and other urban centres, and a number of rural varieties showing different degrees of phonological variation from standard speech. (For more detail on the Maltese dialect situation, see Stumme 1904, Borg 1977, and especially Puech 1994).

It is beyond the scope of the present general introduction to outline the linguistic traits, both typological and diachronic, obtaining between Maltese and the Arabic dialect of Cyprus; the interested reader can consult Borg (1990).

How different is Maltese from native vernacular Arabic? Some idea of the extent and direction of the drift from the Arabic dialect family actualized by Maltese can be obtained by examining its sound system from a historical perspective. Compared with the phonologies of the contemporary Arabic vernaculars, the sound system of Maltese represents the most salient formal factor accountable for the alienness and unintelligibility of the language to native speakers of Arabic. It is also significant in the latter respect, that whereas Maltese settlers in the West − England, Australia and the U.S. − easily shift to the majority language, e.g. English (cf. Jeger 1963 cited in Dench 1975), Maltese communities in Egypt and North Africa, retained their ethno-religious distinctiveness throughout their existence (Nachtigal 1974 [1879]: 13-14; Vadala 1906, *passim*: Price 1954: 55f) and their vernacular, and did not simply shift to the local dialect of Arabic (cf. Saada 1986 on 'Tunisian' Maltese, and Hull 1988 on 'Egyptian' Maltese). As in certain other residual varieties of dialectal Arabic spoken outside the Arab countries − e.g., in Cyprus (Borg 1985), and in Central Asia (Fischer 1961; Sirat and Knudsen 1973), no trace of phonological emphasis has been retained in the Maltese consonant system; Maltese reflexes of the OA emphatic consonants (*$ṣ$, *$ḍ$, *$ṭ$, etc.) have been systematically fused with their plain OA counterparts:

MALTESE		OLD ARABIC
sayf	'summer'	*ṣayf*
seyf	'dagger'	*sayf*
ti:n	'figs'	*ti:n*
tayn	'mud'	*ṭi:n*

though, as can be inferred from these examples, secondary reflexes have survived in the vowel system. Furthermore, all

31

Maltese dialectal varieties show far-reaching paradigmatic changes in their consonant system, e.g., reinterpretation of the Old Arabic velar and pharyngeal fricative pairs /ʻ/ and /ġ/, chiefly as vocalic length; fusion of Old Arabic /x/, /h/, and /ħ/ into Maltese /h/, loss of *hamza*, etc. Maltese has also integrated several new consonant phonemes mainly through contact with Italian, e.g., /p/, /v/, /c/, /dz/, and /c/.

The cumulative impact of these systematic departures from the phonological norms of spoken Arabic in Maltese no doubt represent an important formal correlate of the linguistic and cultural distance of its speaker community from the Arabic-speaking world, and of the *rapprochement* of Maltese to the Romance *Sprachbund*. Some idea of the estrangement of Maltese from the Arabic *Sprachraum* in the perception of native Arabic speakers can be gathered, for instance, from explicit statements by Arabic language reformers concerning the 'corrupt' state of Maltese. 'Is there an educated person who wants his language to be like that of the people of Malta?' stated the Syrian Anis Sallum (1922) – cited in Chejne (1969: 154). In a less formal vein, the Egyptian novelist Ibrāhīm al-Māzinī (in his *Ṣundūq al-dunyā*, 26-31) attempts to convey to the reader the foreignness of Maltese by 'mimicking' certain phonological traits in Maltese commonly associated with nonnative Arabic speech (e.g., confusion of Arabic, /ḫ/, /x/, and /ħ/).

The consonantal inventory is almost identical throughout the Maltese dialect area. Fairly marked differences, however, obtain between Standard Maltese (StM) and non-standard (i.e. rural) Maltese, as well as between the rural varieties themselves, specifically in the matter of vocalic inventory and morphophonemics. Dialectal diversification in the rural vernaculars of Maltese derives for the most part from differential historical treatment of the Old Arabic vowel system; note, for instance, the following differences between

StM and the dialect of Rabat in Gozo:

StM	RABAT	OA	
omm	umm	umm	mother
da:r	do:r	da:r	house
bɪ:b	be:b	ba:b	door

Thus, whereas StM has evolved a system of five vowels, all non-standard varieties of Maltese have four (Puech 1994: 17f.). In the realm of vowel morphophonemics (i.e. grammatically conditioned vowel alternation), certain non-standard varieties of Maltese display complex rules of vowel harmony (Puech 1978) and/or a set of vocalic alternations conditioned by syllabic, lexical, and pausal boundaries. Observe, for instance, the prejunctural diphthongization of OA *[i:] and *[u:] in the Rabat (Gozo) dialect:

RABAT	StM	
zarbewn	zarbu:n	shoes
zarbu:na	zarbu:na	a shoe
treyd	tri:d	you (s.) want
tri:da	tri:da	you (s.) want her

Certain conservative speakers from this dialect area also display pausally conditioned diphthongization of these Old Arabic long high vowels (Borg 1977) – a feature that is unknown in StM but well attested in certain Eastern (e.g., Lebanese) varieties of vernacular Arabic, e.g., the Šḥi:m dialect (Fleisch 1974 [1962]: 203-220), and the North Palestinian dialects spoken by the Druze (Blanc 1953: 50). The StM sound system includes the following consonant segments (special symbols are defined in the appendix):

p		t				k	
b		d				g	
	f		s	ʃ			h
	v		z	ž			
			c	č			
			dz	ǧ			
m		n					
		l					
		r					
w					y		

Some consonants are restricted to a few but well integrated loanwords, e.g. /ž/ in /televížin/ 'television', /be:ž/ 'beige', /ru:ž/ 'rouge', /dz/ in /gadzdzetta/ 'newspaper', /landzi:t/ 'bristle', /medzdza/

'kind of basket', etc.

In addition to this consonantal paradigm, the Maltese sound system has an 'abstract phoneme' corresponding only roughly in distribution to the orthographical symbol *għ* (called [a:yn] in the Maltese alphabet) and representing the reflex of the OA fricatives */'/ and */ġ/.

The schematic chart of Maltese consonants displayed above characterizes the consonantal paradigm of StM. Certain nonstandard dialects show some minor differences; as noted in Puech (1994:17), conservative speakers from the Gozitan villages of San Lawrenz, Għarb, and Żebbuġ still retain residual traces of the voiced velar fricative /ġ/ continuing the same sound in Old Arabic. Archaic consonantal traits have also been retained by speakers on the island of Malta itself, e.g., from the towns of Cospicua and Senglea, who have the uvular stop reflex [q] for old Arabic *qāf* − also noted for Valletta in the early years of the century in Stumme (1904: *passim*). The dialect of the village of Xewkija (*šewkiyya*) in Gozo, on the other hand, systematically fuses OA /q/ and /k/ into Maltese /k/: [kælb] 'dog', [kalb] 'heart'. Variant realizations also exist for Old Arabic /r/. In contrast with the apical trill [r] that is the normal S M reflex of Old Arabic *r, some nonstandard dialectal varieties of Maltese show the alveolar tap [ɾ] or the alveolar approximant [ɹ] (cf. Puech 1993: 17).

IV

What languages were spoken on the Maltese Islands before the shift to Arabic? There is every reason to believe that Arabic was not the first Semitic language to have taken root in Malta but that it was preceded by Phoenician and Punic. Blouet (1981:32) has observed that:

By the year 1000 BC the Phoenicians were trading in the western basin of the Mediterranean. It is difficult to believe that Malta was not touched at a very early age by Phoenician activity in the area, although the earliest remains of these people found so far in the

islands date only from the ninth century B.C. The Phoenicians established many colonies in the Western Mediterranean and when their homeland in the Levant was overrun, the area round Tunis...became the new heartland of their activities. The Carthaginians colonized the Maltese Islands in the eighth and seventh centuries BC and built several important temples on the islands including the one that has recently been excavated at Tas-Silġ near Marsaxlokk... Malta was strongly controlled by Carthage and Punic culture appears to have put down deep roots.

That Phoenician and Punic were spoken in ancient Malta need not be seriously doubted; what is not clear at this stage is how late Punic survived there. The Romans wrested Malta from the Carthaginians in 218 BC during the Second Punic war (Livy XXI, 50, i) but the Romanization of the local population appears to have proceeded very slowly since Diodorus Siculus (v, 12), writing about 150 years after the Roman invasion, could still refer to the Islands as Phoenician colonies. Equally striking is the fact noted in Bonanno (1992: 15) that

The earliest Latin inscription, one of a public nature, is dated to the beginning of the imperial period, a good two centuries after the Roman conquest.

Mayr (1909: 110-112), which is, as far as I know, the only scholarly attempt at reconstructing the linguistic situation in Malta in the early centuries of our era, i.e. between 60 AD, the date of the Paul's shipwreck, and the beginning of the 4th century AD − when written sources relating to Malta come to a halt − suggested that during this period Punic probably held its ground among the common people, with Greek and Latin being spoken alongside it by the upper class:

During this period the population of Malta lost to a large extent its Phoenician character, which ultimately had to yield to the superiority of the Graeco-Roman culture. It would appear from the admittedly vague indications to hand that the Punic language held its ground for a rather long time. Quite apart from the Neo-Punic inscription mentioned above, which, if it really belongs to Malta, could very easily have been produced during this period, one can conclude from a place in the Acts of the Apostles [Ch.XXVIII, 1-11; A.B.], that when Paul suffered shipwreck in Malta

(60 AD), the peasants of Malta were largely Punic-speaking. There the inhabitants of the coast of Malta, who hosted Paul in a friendly manner, are called βαρβαροι, an expression which would hardly have been applied to a Greek- or Latin-speaking population. In support of this view one could cite an inscription in Greek — engraved on an amphora discovered in the ruins of a warehouse-like building... in the Grand Harbour area — the Phoenician name *ḥlm* attested elsewhere too. The lettering and discovery site relate the amphora to the latter imperial or Byzantine period.

The Greek language which in the preceding period emerged very prominently alongside Phoenician held its ground in the face of competition from Latin. Whether the inscription of L. Castricius Prudens, dating from Tiberius' reign, was put up by himself, his relatives, or the community, it serves to show that Greek still fulfilled an important function in Malta... Particularly noteworthy is the fact that Roman names sometimes occur in Greek script, which also shows that during the imperial age, Greek was widely used in Malta.

During this time Latin was the official language; which naturally became more and more extensively used by the common people. Its position invites comparison with the way English today is spreading on the island. [My translation from German, A.B.]

It is most unlikely that Punic was still spoken in Malta when the Arabs arrived in the 9th century. Bonanno (1989: 11) noted the increasing impact of Greek cultural influences that 'had started to filter in the whole Punic world in the third century B.C.' and that in Malta

"grew stronger as a result of the more intensive intercourse between Sicily and the Maltese Islands". This situation appears to have endured with little change till the beginning of the sixth century A.D. when Malta was absorbed, together with Sicily and its islands within the Eastern Empire (cf. also Bonanno 1981).

Given the fact that the islands eventually passed under the hegemony of Byzantium after the break-up of the Roman Empire in 395 AD, it is more likely that after approximately 370 years under Hellenic rule, the inhabitants of the Maltese islands shifted to Greek, particularly since the 'Byzantine Renaissance had revived Greek as an important language in both Southern Italy and Sicily during the sixth and seventh centuries' (Di Pietro and Selim 1967: 19).

Greek lexical elements in Maltese may never have been quantitatively significant, and what has survived today is difficult to date and to assign to its proper diffusional path, particularly since Malta has since the 16th century had a small Greek community that may have been the immediate source of the Greek loans in Maltese.

The oldest Greek lexical stratum probably harks back to the time of the Byzantine/Arabic cultural cross-fertilization in the 7th and 8th centuries. Note, for instance, the presence in Maltese of Arabized Greek terms in the toponymic domain, e.g. the name *Xlendi* (in Gozo) (šlendi) < χελανδιον (with fronting of palatalized Gk. *x* > š), which also appears as a Greek loan in Middle Arabic: *šalanda:* (Fück 1955: XX). Ahrweiler (1966: 91) lists the *chélandia* among the *bateaux légers* of the Byzantine navy, which kept an important base at Malta:

Un archonte et drongaire de Malte (Mélitè) est connu par son sceau, daté du VIIe-VIIIe siècle. Le haut titre de drongaire que porte le commandant de cette île témoigne de l'importance de l'escadre chargée de la garde de ce poste frontalier. A notre connaissance, il n'est question nulle part ailleurs du commandement maritime de Malte. (Ahrweiler 1966: 87)

Other Maltese placenames of likely Greek origin include Mistra, and Birgu, presumably < πυργος, (showing the expected shift from Greek [p] to Ar. [b]), and Luqa, the last-named probably continuing Ar. *lu:q* 'poplar' ultimately < Gr. λευκη . Outside the toponymic realm, Colin (1970) identified the Maltese Grecisms *šabsa:la* (Soldanis 175v, 18th century) 'beehive' < κυφελη , and *cunnariyya* 'carrot'. The last mentioned term has been integrated into several other Mediterranean languages. Saydon (1954) drew attention to a few Maltese religious terms of Greek origin which he interprets as relics of the Byzantine rite in the church of Malta.

VI

What kind of Arabic did Maltese evolve

from? In other words, which variety of colloquial Arabic was spoken in Malta during the early Middle Ages? Since written documents reflecting the linguistic situation in Malta start much later, i.e., towards the end of the 15th century, e.g. *Peter Caxaro's Cantilena* (Wettinger and Fsadni 1983) — the earliest continuous text in Maltese — it is not possible to determine with accuracy what kind of Arabic was used during the early centuries that witnessed the genesis of the Maltese language. In the absence of early documentary attestations of the vernacular of the Maltese Islands, comparison of the present-day language with the contemporary Arabic dialects can be helpful in reconstructing the past history of Maltese, making due allowance for the obvious fact that the Arabic dialects themselves have no doubt undergone considerable change in the course of the centuries.

Maltese is customarily grouped with the North African Arabic dialect area (Nöldeke 1904) on the basis of a number of grammatical traits shared with vernaculars spoken in the old sedentary centres of North Africa, e.g. Tripoli, Tunis, and Algiers. One highly diagnostic morphological feature — among others — that bears out this areal classification occurs in the morphology of the verb; it is the so-called *nekteb-nektebu* imperfect:

MALTESE	JERUSALEM	TUNIS
n-ikteb	*a-ktub*	*n-ekteb*
n-iktb-u	*n-uktub*	*n-ektb-u*

OA	
a-ktub	I write
n-aktub	we write

where the Maltese prefix [n-] represents the first person marker in the singular quintessentially typical of the Maghrebine dialects (cf. Blanc 1974). There are, however, other formal traits that link Maltese with the Arabic dialects of North Africa, most of which were noted by the linguist and orientalist Nöldeke in his aforementioned 1904 review of Hans

Stumme's *Maltesische Studien* (Leipzig, 1904); the most important include the following: the long stem vowel in the third person (f. and pl.) of finally weak verbs:

MALTESE	JERUSALEM	TUNIS
hallı:-t	*xalla-t*	*xalla:-t*
bke:-w	*biky-u*	*bka:-w*

OA	
xalla-t	she left
baka-w	they wept

the verbal pattern *Qtā:l* for verbs relating to physical states and defects (*twa:l* 'he grew tall', *sfa:r* 'he became pale'), the use of *bı:š* 'in order to' and *alı:š* 'why', and of the conjunction *illi*, etc. (for further details, see Borg 1978: 345). Numerous items of lexicon are also of North African (occasionally Berber) provenance: *hallas* 'he paid', *fellu:s* 'chick', *gendu:s* 'ox', *farta:s* 'bald', etc.

Alongside these indisputably North African Arabic features Maltese also displays a set of linguistic traits (comprising chiefly phonological and lexical traits) that are unknown in the Maghreb but well attested in the Levant. Thus like the dialects of Cairo, Jerusalem, Beirut, and Damascus, etc., Maltese retains the accent on the first syllable of words harking back to the Old Arabic word pattern CVCVC:

MALTESE	JERUSALEM	OLD ARABIC
bá'ar	*bá'ar*	*baqar* cows
ríkeb	*ríkib*	*rakib* he rode

In the numerals 'three' through 'ten' Maltese retains, like many Eastern dialects, reflexes of *tā' marbūṭa* (a [-t-]) that acts as *liaison* between the numeral and the following noun); thus, the numerical expression 'five thousand' (*xamsatu a:la:fin* in Classical Arabic) is realized as *hames-t-elef* in Maltese, *xams-t-ala:f* in Jerusalem, but *xems a:la:f* in Tunis. In the realm of lexicon, several commonly used terms in Maltese lack cognates with similar meanings in the North African dialects but are well attested in the Levant:

MALTESE	MEANING	LEV.AR.
čamfar	to reprimand	šafar (Cairo)
zarbu:n	shoes	zarbu:l (Aleppo)
zokra	navel	zukra (Galilee)
kaħħal	he plastered (wall)	kaħħal (Aleppo)

A more systematic documentation of Eastern features in Maltese can be found in Borg (forthcoming).

How is one to interpret the multiple areal affiliations of Maltese with the contemporary dialects? Rossi (1936: 213) – echoing Stumme (1904: 83) – noted simply the following, without attempting any historical explanation:

The conclusion must be accepted that Maltese is an Arabic dialect which in some ways shows resemblances to the Eastern Arabic dialects, in many others recalls the Arabic dialects of the Maghrib... A study of the Maltese lexicon, to show how affinities with Arabic dialects, Eastern and Western, may be explained, and how word-fossils have been preserved in Maltese, is still to be undertaken.

One could hypothesize that the Eastern elements in Maltese hark back to former settlement of Eastern (possibly Christian) Arabs in the Maltese Islands; this is an attractive theory but lacks supporting historical evidence. Another possible explanation is that the combination of so-called 'Eastern' and 'Western' features in Maltese was at one time more widespread in mainland Arabic and that Maltese has retained this combination on account of its speaker-community's isolation from mainstream Arabic (for further detail, see Borg, forth.).

Rossi mentions the matter of word fossils in Maltese. These do in fact occur. One finds, for instance, a few lexical Aramaisms that seem to be either unattested or rare in contemporary vernacular Arabic at large:

MALTESE	MEANING	ARAMAIC
šandar, išandar	he broadcast	šaddar he sent

Since Maltese did not come into direct contact with Aramaic, these admittedly rare pre-Arabic Semitic features in Maltese were most likely inherited from some variety of Arabic – presumably Eastern – displaying an Aramaic substratum!

Given the isolation of its speakers from the sources of native Arabic, the vernacular of the Maltese Islands no doubt began to deviate from the mainland varieties well before it became exposed to the external impact of foreign languages. As Renfrew (1987: 122) has noted in a different linguistic context:

It is certainly the case that when groups speaking the same language separate and are no longer in contact, marked differences in vocabulary and in forms of expression gradually emerge. A good example is Polynesia, where, since the islands are very remote from each other, and interactions are few, the consequences of divergence are particularly plain.

Separation from the realia of mainland Arab culture has primarily meant, for Maltese, a notable degree of lexical loss for concepts relating to material culture; the loss has been made good in part by massive borrowing from the geographically closest language area: the Italian-speaking mainland, particularly in the realm of non-basic lexicon: fyu:ra 'flower', annima:l 'animal', payyi:z 'country', li:ǧi 'law', vapu:r 'ship', etc. The effects of linguistic isolation on Maltese are perhaps most clearly discernible in the way the language has recycled and restructured native Arabic Sprachgut to expand the lexicon. A highly noteworthy example of this particular strategy of relexification occurs in the realm of function words, adverbs, etc., many of which have been locally generated via lexical fusion of discrete Arabic elements, and, in this form, appear to be unique to Maltese:

MALTESE (ORTH.)	LITERAL TRANSLATION	MEANING
madankollu	with all of this	nevertheless
għalfejn	whereto	why
minħabba	out of love of	because
kemmixejn	how much + nothing	a little
għadilli	yet + that (conj.)	although

The originality of Maltese in recycling Arabic lexicon also comes into play in the form of semantic shifts:

MALTESE		ARABIC	
ħafna	much	ħafna	handful
wisq	too much	wasq	cargo (Cairo)

The geographically peripheral position of Maltese vis-à-vis the Arabic *Sprachraum*, has yielded another evolutionary characteristic associated with marginal or isolated areas: a tendency towards linguistic conservatism. Thus despite its extraneousness to the Arabic-speaking world, Maltese interestingly retains certain Old Arabic words attested in Classical Arabic but completely lost in the contemporary Arabic dialects:

MALTESE	MEANING	OA
mindu	since	*munδu/muδ*
qatt	never	*qaṭṭu*
seta, yista	to be able	*isṭa:ʿ, yusṭi:ʿ*

The first example is particularly interesting in that Maltese *mindu* harks back directly to proto-Arabic **min* + *δū*: in other words, Maltese has retained /i/ in the first syllable and not harmonized it with /u/, as has happened in Classical Arabic. This feature and the actual retention of final /u/ — only optional in Classical Arabic — renders the Maltese forms of this word older even than its Classical counterpart!

At the time of the Norman conquest of Sicily (1061-1091) the dominant language in Sicily was Arabic (Varvaro 1988:1). This author describes the linguistic situation in Norman Sicily in the following terms:

Non c'è dubbio che la lingua prevalente nell'isola fosse l'arabo, ma da un lato bisogna distinguere tra dominanza sociolinguistica (indiscutibile) e diffusione reale (che non è detto fosse generale) e d'altro canto sarebbe indispensabile conoscere quanto ed in che modo l'arabo parlato si differenziasse già da quello scritto e sopratutto letterario, che ci è abbastanza ben noto, grazie alla circostanza che esisteva e ci è in parte giunta una ricca produzione poetica e scientifica.

The issue of the likely nature and extent of the *Abstand* between colloquial and written in Arabic in Sicily at this time is not as open-ended as Varvaro here suggests when seen in the wider context of the socio-linguistic evolution of Arabic as a whole. Thus S. Hopkins' *Studies in the grammar of early Arabic* (Oxford, 1984), which is based on Muslim Arabic papyri datable to between the 7th and early 10th centuries A.D., corroborated the general impression

emerging from previous research carried out on Middle Arabic (i.e. the literary or semi-literary Arabic written by Christians, Jews, and occasionally Muslims) that the dichotomy between vernacular and literary Arabic probably dates back to the earliest historical stages of sedentary Arabic. Hopkins sums up his important findings as follows:

From the data collected in the present work the most important result is undoubtedly the recognition that in almost every case in which the language of the Arabic papyri deviates from Classical Arabic, it deviates unmistakably in the direction of Middle Arabic, typologically akin to most of the modern colloquials. ...A large proportion of the features attested here in mediaeval Jewish, Christian and, to a lesser extent, Muslim Middle Arabic, many of which are familiar today from modern dialects, occur here for the first time. This fact speaks for a very impressive continuity in colloquial Arabic usage, and the roots of the modern vernaculars seem to lie very deep. (Hopkins 1984: xlvi)

It is therefore probably idle to suppose that the colloquial Arabic norms of the Arabs in Sicily were more 'classical' than elsewhere in mainstream spoken Arabic. B. Isserlin's comparative study of phonetic aspects of Sicilian Arabic and Maltese (1977) strongly suggests that the medieval Arabic vernaculars of Sicily, Malta, and, presumably, Pantelleria were very similar. Like contemporary Maltese, Sicilian Arabic has been classified with the North African Arabic vernaculars (Blau 1968) responding to Di Pietro and Selim 1967).

VII

With the re-romanization of urban Sicily initiated under the Normans (Bonfante 1986: 47), Romance linguistic influences from Sicily began to infiltrate the speech of the Maltese islanders. Varvaro (1988: 3-4) is probably right in suggesting that the greater part of the Romance elements in Maltese were acquired during the period 1091-1530, preceding the administration of the Order of Knights Hospitallers of St John of Jerusalem (1530-1798). The administration of the Knights (1530-1798) ushered in a new era of intense consolidation and expansion especially of urban life in the Maltese Islands, particularly based on Malta's maritime potential. By this time, the vernacular of the Maltese Islands was generally referred to as 'Maltese' rather than 'Arabic'. (Wettinger 1993: 154)

It has generally been recognized that the period of the Knights witnessed the exposure of Maltese to literary forms of Italian. I suggest that the intense maritime activity of the Maltese during this period also provided the context for systematic exposure to the Mediterranean Lingua Franca (see §IX). Until the second half of the nineteenth century, when popular education became available to an increasing number of Maltese, there can be no doubt that knowledge of Italian was a prerogative of the clergy and the upper classes. Camillo Spreti, a Knight from Ravenna, who compiled a description of Malta in 1764 noted that the islanders 'understand little Italian and speak less' (cited in Luke 1960 [1949]: 133).

One area where Maltese has brought to bear a great deal of creativity is that of accommodating foreign (mostly Italian) linguistic elements. Though most Arabic vernaculars spoken along the Mediter-ranean littoral have come under the impact of Italian (and/or other Romance languages) as the languages of trade or higher culture, it is probably true to say that Maltese has surpassed all the Arabic dialects described so far in its receptivity to Italian *Sprachgut*.

In this connection, it would be valuable to have comparative data from other Arabic vernaculars spoken by non-Arabs e.g., the Jews of Tripoli, who are known to have undergone extensive acculturation in Italian. Though supporting documenta-tion from various historical periods is lacking, it is obvious that Italian components in Maltese have been assimilated at different periods and via different diffusional channels.

From the annexation of the Maltese Islands by the Normans (1090) until the arrival of the Knights of St John (1530), the vernacular of Malta no doubt came under the influence of S. Italian (Sicilian, Calabrian, etc.). The contact with Sicilian occurred with two linguistic registers, i.e. both ordinary vernacular Sicilian and chancery Sicilian as used by notaries, Church functionaries, etc. Contemporary Maltese has retained many everyday terms of both vernacular and learned character:

MALTESE	MEANING	SICILIAN
flišku:n	bottle	flascuni
buti:r	butter	butiri
bečču:n	pigeon	picciuni
canga	beef	chianca
pastart	cauliflower	bastardu
kabočča	cabbage	cappucciu
inkwi:na	anvil	incunia
gverta	blanket	cuverta
pitacc	exercise book	pitazzu
gri:zma	Confirmation	crisima
li:ği	law	liggi
so:ru	nun	soru

As is the case in its Arabic component, the Romance component in Maltese tends to display a conservative character. Observe, for instance, how Maltese retains Old Sicilian [mb] and [nd] clusters which in contemporary Sicilian have undergone levelling to [mm] and [nn] respectively:

MALTESE	MEANING	SICILIAN
lukanda	inn	lucanna
gamblu	shrimp	gammaru

In fact, as was recognized in Wagner (1932), the comparative investigation of Maltese and Southern Italian dialects could benefit not only the historical study Maltese, but also that of Sicilian itself which has, for instance, retained numerous reflexes of Arabic terms (cf. Pellegrini 1972); cognates of these still occur in contemporary Maltese, e.g. the element *racal-* in placenames deriving from *raḥal*, which in Maltese still means 'village'.

Fifteenth-century documentary material in this literary medium is now becoming available (e.g. Wettinger 1993a); the linguistic description of literary Sicilian as used in medieval Malta will furnish the historian of the Maltese language with important insights into the sources and chronology of learned Romance lexicon in medieval Maltese.

Under the administration of the Knights of St John, the use of Sicilian in the courts and among the legal profession was replaced by that of literary Italian. The following is an excerpt from a *Transcript of legal proceedings against the Englishmen of the Barks Roe and Rainaldson and the merchant John Lucas*, published in A.P. Vella (1972: 79-160) from the archives of the Inquisition in Malta. In this work, the author attempts to reconstruct the circumstances of an alleged Elizabethan-Ottoman conspiracy in the late 16th century. The document reproduces the Inquisitor's question in Latin and the answer in Italian:

Interrogatus: Quas artes exercuit in Anglia et de quibus sustinuit dictam eius uxorem?

Respondit. In Inghilterra io facevo arte di marinaro et di questo vivea et non avevo intrata nessuna: et moglie mia è ben piovera et sa cucir, et vive di quello. (Vella 1972: 107)

(What was your profession in England and how did you support your aforementioned wife?

In England I worked as a sailor and made my living from this; I had no other income. My wife is quite poor but can sew and supports herself this way.)

The established character of Italian as the language of culture in Malta is reflected in the fact that Maltese writers during the nineteenth century and later invariably established their reputations as writers of Italian before turning to the use of their native vernacular (cf. Grech 1961: 13). One such writer was the national poet of Malta, Dun Karm, who started writing in Maltese in 1912, having spent the preceding thirteen years experimenting with Italian models (Friggieri 1979: 112). By the turn of the present century the use of Italian was so well established among educated Maltese that Nöldeke (1904) expressed the view that it was only a matter of time before it would replace Maltese. Nöldeke could not have foreseen the events that were to lead up to WWII when Malta, as a British military base, became the target of the Axis forces. Whereas the cult of Italian among the Maltese had been retained throughout the British colonial administration, often at the cost of much friction with the colonial regime (cf. Frendo 1991 [1979] *passim*), the outcome of WWII had the effect of undermining the former position of Italian and preparing the way for its replacement by English.

IX

One source of Romance lexicon in the evolution of Maltese that has not received systematic attention in the existing literature is the Mediterranean Lingua Franca (in the sense of Kahane and Tietze 1958). The term *lingua franca* is most commonly used to refer to a language of wider communication employed across a fairly extensive geographical area, its function being that of a contact language used between speakers of mutually unintelligible languages. Aramaic, Koiné Greek, and Latin, have all, at different times, fulfilled this role. One such language today is Swahili, a Bantu language originally spoken in Zanzibar and the adjacent coast, the use of which has spread at a commercial language across East Africa and the Congo. Trade languages of this kind are sometimes barely more than pidgins suitable for communication at a fairly rudimentary level, e.g. Melanesian Pidgin English.

The Mediterranean Lingua Franca (henceforth MLF) was another pidgin or highly degrammaticalized contact vernacular (Kahane 1983: 8) which is generally believed to have originated in the Eastern Mediterranean during the Crusades, and was apparently still used in the 19th century along the North African coast, especially in Algiers, where it was called *sabir*. Hall (1966: 6) notes that 'in some parts of North Africa, *sabir* or *petit-nègre* still survives; the most recent information indicates, however, that it is on its way out'.

The first important study on the MLF

was Hugo Schuchardt's classic 'Die Lingua Franca' (1909), a concise work whose insight and originality placed it at the focus of the discussion relating to pidgins and language genesis. In the second paragraph to this work, the author cites an intriguing statement from a work on human geography by F.P.W. von Richthofen (1908:102f.) to the effect that the MLF was 'a kind of Italian originating from Malta and thoroughly intermingled with Arabic elements' (Schuchardt 1909: fn.2). the cryptic nature and informal character of this remark renders its precise bearing vis-à-vis the language situation in Malta – as perceived by von Richthofen – somewhat difficult to determine. It is most unlikely that this scholar was thinking of Maltese itself since the professional linguistic literature in German dealing with the vernacular of the Maltese Islands had already established the origin and character of this language (cf. Gesenius 1811; Sandreczki 1876, 1879; Stumme 1904, etc.). Another difficulty here is the precise meaning to be attached to 'Lingua Franca'. I would here like to suggest that by reason of several historical factors relating specifically to the pre-occupation of the Maltese with the sea, the use of the MLF must have been fairly normal in Malta throughout the administration of the Knights of St John. In their voluminous lexical study, *Lingua Franca in the Levant* (1958), the authors, H. and Renée Kahane and Andreas Tietze, study the MLF impact on Turkish and restrict the term MLF to 'vocabulary alone, and within vocabulary to nautical terms...borrowed by Turkish from the West during the period beginning with Turkish navigation in the Mediterranean in the 13th-15th centuries and continuing through the 18th century, when the Mediterranean nautical terminology was as yet unaffected by the international terminology of modern techniques that permeates it in the 19th century' (p.VIII). Their comparative material from Mediterranean languages other than Turkish embraces several dialects of Arabic and Maltese.

The impact of nautical vocabulary on general lexical usage, though quite considerable, has not been recognized in diachronic work on Maltese. Italian nautical terms in Maltese are common in metaphorical or idiomatic usage *nna:vika, yinna:vika* 'to do housework, to tinker' (Aquilina 1990: 893) < It. *navigare* 'to sail'; *sassla* 'cloth scoop for collection (in Church)' < It. *sassola*, (< Sic. *sassula*) glossed in Petrocchi (1900) as 'specie di pala o cucchiaia per votar l'acqua delle lance'; *sorǧa, ysorǧi* 'to sit down' < It. *sorgere* 'to moor'. Some of these, especially when they entail Romance loans of North Italian provenance are almost certain to have been filtered through the MLF: Maltese *perżu:t* 'ham', *tornavi:t, pitra:vi* 'beetroots' (all from Venetian). MLF: Maltese *perzu:t* 'ham', *tornavi:t*, items of general (i.e. non-nautical) vocabulary, e.g., Maltese *sptar* 'hospital' (cf. Ar. *sbita:r*).

The immediate social contexts of such loans are not difficult to visualize. As noted in Mallia-Milanes (1992: 15):

By the time the Hospitaller Order of St John had settled in Malta (in 1530 A.B.), its corsairing activity had already had a chequered history of its own.

Under the Knights (1530-1798) 'privateering...would eventually develop into an important industry, an increasingly vital source of wealth for the island's economy' (*op.cit.* 17-18). Earle (1971: 121) states that in the 1660s, 30 active corsairs operated from Malta; the personnel involved in this activity (comprising crews, soldiers, and slaves) were in the region of 4000, so that 'one-fifth of the adult male population was engaged in the *corso*'. As Mallia-Milanes attempts to show, the privateering exploits of the Maltese corsairs were far from being restricted to the central Mediterranean but frequently ventured into Levantine waters against Muslim shipping. Military engagements against the Barbary states were the order of the day, and the capture, presence and disposal of large numbers of slaves in

Malta must have created ample opportunities for contact with MLF. In his *Corsairs of Malta and Barbary* Peter Earle notes, for instance, that

Malta as a centre of privateering compares very favourably with its much better-known rival, Algiers, from the second half of the seventeenth century onwards. Estimates for the sixteenth century put the Algerian fleet at about 50 or 60 units, and Father Dan estimated the fleet to consist of 80 ships in 1634, of which 70 were sailing-ships. But by the period 1674-6 the Algerian fleet was only between 26 and 35 ships, including those owned by the state, i.e. virtually identical in size to the Maltese fleet plus the Maltese navy. (1970: 122)

Later, when the *corso* lost its *raison d'être*, the Maltese appear to have been among the first Europeans to settle in North Africa. Thus Ettore Rossi (1968: 271-272) speaks of 'la presenza di numerosi Maltesi a Tripoli, come a Tunisi e ad Alger. Già nel 1804 in una lista delle persone che stanno sotto la protezione del console britannico a Tripoli, in tutto un centinaio figurano quasi unicamente cognomi maltesi'. On his visit to Tripoli in 1862, the German traveller and orientalist Gustav Nachtigal (1974 [1879]: 13) noted:

Beside the Hara [i.e. the Jewish Quarter, A.B.] lies that part of the Muslim town where the Maltese have made their home, and impressed their characteristic stamp upon the neighbourhood. This element is abundantly represented in all the coastal towns of Tripolitania, Tunisia and Algeria; it has the most intimate connections with the Muslim population, displays indefatigable activity, admirable business acumen and exceptional thrift, and by its vigour and adaptibility has been of the greatest importance for the development of the whole life of these regions.

Price (1954: 60) notes that by 1842 the emigration movement from the Maltese Islands 'had been in existence long enough to produce well-defined Maltese settlements all along the southern and eastern shores of the Mediterranean'. By 1885 there were 15,000 in Algiers and Constantine, 11,000 in Tunis; and 3000 in Tripoli (*op.cit.*: 230). The substantial presence of the Maltese community in Algiers is noteworthy from the linguistic viewpoint, since this city had been the most important centre for the diffusion of *sabir*. The famous

Dictionnaire de la Langue Francque ou petit mauresque, composed specifically for the French forces stationed in N. Africa appeared (in Marseilles) in 1830. The work's anonymous author notes in his preface:

La langue francque ou petit mauresque, très-répandue dans les états Barbaresques, lorsque les corsaires de Tunis et d'Alger rapportaient de leurs courses un grand nombre d'esclaves Chrétiens, est encòre employée par les habitans des villes maritimes, dans leurs rapports avec les Européens. (p.5 cited from Cifoletti 1989).

Notwithstanding its Arabic origins, Maltese itself as spoken by *colons* from Malta, not only retained its formal distance from native Arabic but also achieved to some extent the role of an intercommunal linguistic medium between various European groups (Italians, Greeks, Arabs, etc.) reserved for certain sociological situations, and Maltese *Sprachgut* became common coin among Europeans and Arabs alike. The *Trésor de la langue française (dictionnaire de la langue du XIXe et du XXᵉ siècle)* notes that in the Algerian French argot, the term 'maltais' meant '*cabaretier*', apparently '*par allusion à de nombreux Maltais qui avaient la profession de cabaretier en Algérie*'. The port of Algiers appears also to have employed many Maltese since a special 'language' was developed there which *Arts et litteratures* (1936: 38-40) refers to as '*le jargon franco-hispano-maltais du port d'Alger*'. We possess a very fine description of the Jewish Arabic dialect of Algiers: Marcel Cohen's classic work, *Le parler arabe des Juifs d'Alger*, published in 1912. It is difficult not to be struck by some of its similarities to Maltese, particularly in the lexical domain:

ALG.AR. (COHEN 1912)		MALTESE	
[ˈ]aːrɒnǧ	orange amère	[ˈ]arinǧ	oranges
ċɒrċɒr	murmurer (ruisseau)	cercer	shed (liquid)
bɒttia	tonneau	bettiyya	barrel
pɒrtmone	portemonnaie	portmóni	purse
nanna. nannaːti	ma grand'mère	nannti	my grandmother

Highly striking is one particular idiosyncratic semantic treatment of the Italian

KTŶB YL KLŶM MÂLTI

MFYSSER BYL-LATIN U BYT-TALJÁN

SIVE

LIBER DICTIONUM MELITENSIUM

HOC EST

MICHAELIS ANTONII VASSALLI

LEXICON

MELITENSE-LATINO-ITALUM

CUI POST AUCTARIUM ACCEDUNT

APPENDIX ETYMOLOGICA ET COMPARATIVA
ET DUO INDICES VOCUM LATINARUM AC ITALICARUM

MELITENSIBUS NUMERO RESPONDENTIUM.

VOCABOLARIO MALTESE

RECATO NELLE LINGUE LATINA E ITALIANA

*Al quale viene premesso un ragionato Discorso, e dopo il Supplemento
si aggiungono un' Appendice etimologica e comparativa,
e due Indici Latino l' uno e l' altro Italiano*

QUALI PER VIA DI NUMERAZIONE CORRISPONDONO ALLE VOCI MALTESI.

ROMAE APUD ANTONIUM FULGONIUM

MDCCXCVI.

SVPERIORVM PERMISSV.

Vassalli's dictionary of the Maltese language published in Rome in 1796

MICHAELIS ANTONII

VASSALLI

MYLSEN

PHOENICO-PUNICUM

SIVE

GRAMMATICA

MELITENSIS

ROMAE MDCCXCI.

SUMPTIBUS AUCTORIS

APUD ANTONIUM FULGONI

Praesidum Facultate

Vassalli's grammar of the Maltese language published in Rome in 1791

A. CREMONA

TAGĦLIM

FUQ IL-KITBA MALTIJA

L-EWWEL KTIEB

MALTA

THE EMPIRE PRESS

1935

Cremona's grammar book published in 1935

loanword *capace* to mean 'perhaps':
Maltese *kapa:ẽi yiği* 'he may well come',
Alg. Ar. *kapa:š iği* 'peut-être bien qu'il va
venir' (très proche de l'idée: "il viendra
probablement").

It should also not be forgotten that the
port of Valletta (*Il-Port il-Kbir*) was itself
highly cosmopolitan, e.g., during the 19th
century. In 1809, on his way to Nubia, the
Swiss traveller and orientalist John Lewis
Burckhardt visited Malta and wrote:

The port of Valletta has lately been declared a free
port, and this will render it for a long time to come
the centre of trade from Gibraltar as far as Odessa.
The numerous Greek traders find themselves better
protected here than in their own lands... You may
well conceive I avoided all intercourse with these
persons from Barbary. I often met parties of them in
the streets... The trade between Malta and Barbary,
especially that with Tripoli and Tunis, acquires daily
more vigour and vitality. (Burckhardt 1822: X)

On a visit to Valletta in 1844, the novelist
W.M. Thackeray recorded having heard
the 'chatter of all nations' (*From Cornhill
to Cairo*, September 5th).

X

In view of the present lack of a modern
systematic description of Maltese in
languages other than Maltese itself, it may
be useful to conclude this introduction to
the language with some general indications
as to how the letters of the Maltese
alphabet correlate with the sound system of
the spoken language, if only to enable the
interested linguist or general reader to avail
himself of printed texts in Maltese for the
purpose of personal study.

The present Maltese orthography,
standardized in 1934, is the product of a
long but intermittent literary tradition
harking back to the late Middle Ages. It is,
however, only from the 18th century
onwards that Maltese has been written with
any degree of continuity, though descriptive
accounts of the language, necessarily
entailing attempts at orthographic
representation, were compiled before then:
for instance, the recently discovered *Regole
per la lingua maltese*, which is thought to
date back to the late 17th century (cf.
Cassola 1988: 63).

The Maltese orthography presents a
number of pitfalls for those unfamiliar
with the spoken language. Thus except for
the digraph *ie*, which is generally (though
not always) realised long, Maltese does not
ordinarily mark vocalic length. The
circumflex is sometimes used to avoid
ambiguity: *qartas* 'to wrap in paper' as
distinct from *qartâs* 'a paper cornet for
wrapping groceries' (Aquilina 1990: 1134).

The Maltese alphabet

a, A – a low central vowel, long or short: *qam* 'he rose' ['a:m]; *wasal* 'he arrived'
[wásal];

b, B – a voiced bilabial stop: *bir* 'well' [bi:r]; *aħbar* 'piece of news' [aħba:r]; *bieb* 'door'
[bı:p];

ċ, Ċ – a voiceless alveolar affricate: *ċar* 'clear' [tša:r]; *keċċa* 'he expelled' [kéttša];

d, D – a voiced dental stop: *dar* 'house' [da:r]; *beda* 'he began' [béda];

e, E – a mid front vowel, long or short: *erbgħa* 'four' [é:rba]; *deheb* 'gold' [de:p]; *dell*
'shadow' [del];

f, F – a voiceless labiodental fricative: *fiehem* 'he explained' [fíyem]; *siefer* 'he travelled'
[sı:fer]; *ħlief* 'except' [ħlı:f];

ġ, Ġ – a voiced alveopalatal affricate: *ġar* 'neighbour' [ǧa:r]; *riġel* 'foot' [ríǧel];

g, G – a voiced velar stop: *gżira* 'island' [gzi:ra]; *niggeż* 'he pricked' [nígges];

h, H – a letter that continues etymologically the OA laryngeal fricative /h/, but is
phonetically identical with ‹ħ.›

44

ħ, H – a voiceless fricative with a widely variable point of articulation including velar, pharyngeal, and laryngeal realizations: *ħafer* 'he forgave' [ḥáfer]; *baħar* 'sea' [báħar]; *riħ* 'wind' [rı:ḥ];

i, I – a high front vowel, long or short: *iben* 'son' [íben]; *irid* 'he wants' [iri:t];

j, J – a palatal glide: *jiena* 'I' [yı:na]; *sejjer* 'going' (m.) [séyyer];

k, K – a voiceless velar stop: *kelb* 'dog' [kelp]; *beka* 'he wept' [béka];

l, L – an alveolar lateral resonant: *lagħab* 'he played' [la:p]; *mielaħ* 'salty' [mí:laḥ];

m, M – a bilabial nasal resonant: *mera* 'mirror' [méra]; *komma* 'sleeve' [kómma];

n, N – an alveolar nasal resonant: *neħħa* 'he took away' [néħḥa]; *bnin* 'beneficial' [bni:n];

għ, Għ – a digraph usually continuing Old Arabic ['] and [ġ] yielding mostly vocalic length in stressed positions: *għamel* 'he made' [a:mel], and [ḥ] when closing word-final stressed syllables: *qiegħ* 'bottom' ['ı:h];

o, O – a mid back rounded vowel, long or short: *omm* 'mother' [ómm]; *għoli* 'high' [ó:li];

p, P – a voiceless bilabial stop: *pastas* 'rude' [pastá:s]; *kappar* 'capers' [kappá:r];

q, Q – a voiceless glottal stop: *qal* 'he said' ['a:l]; *qorti* 'lawcourt' ['órti];

r, R – an apical trill: *raba'* 'fields' [rába]; *morr* 'bitter' [mor];

s, S – a voiceless alveolar fricative: *seraq* 'he stole' [séra']; *biss* 'only' [bis];

t, T – a voiceless dental stop: *tar* 'he flew' [ta:r]; *kattar* 'he increased' [káttar];

u, U – a rounded high back vowel, long or short: *usa'* 'wider' [ú:sa]; *iżur* 'he visits' [izú:r]; *ġurat* 'grasshopper' [ǧurá:t];

x, X – a voiced or voiceless alveopalatal fricative: *xorob* 'he drank' [šórop]; *televixin* 'television' [tèlevǐžin];

ż, Ż – a voiced alveolar fricative: *żar* 'he visited' [za:r]; *beża'* 'he feared' [béza];

z, Z – a voiced or voiceless alveolar affricative: *gazzetta* 'newspaper' [gadʣétta]; *zekzek* 'he tutted' [cékcek]; *gezzez* 'he bundled together' [géttsets].

Appendix

Phonetic symbols and abbreviations

[ ]	:	enclose phonetic transcriptions
[:]	:	vocalic length, e.g. [a:] long *a*, as opposed to [a], short *a*
[æ]	:	a front low vowel, like *a* in Eng. *pan*
[ɑ]	:	a more backed *a* like the vowel in Eng. *tar*
[ı:]	:	the Maltese vowel usually written *ie*, approximating Eng. [ı:] in *lid*
[i:]	:	the Maltese vowel usually written *i*, approximating *ea* in Eng. *lead*
[θ]	:	voiceless interdental fricative, like *th* in Eng. *thick*
[ð]	:	voiced interdental fricative, like *th* in Eng. *this*
[ṣ]	:	voiceless emphatic sibilant
[ḍ]	:	voiced emphatic dental stop
[ṭ]	:	voiceless emphatic dental stop
[ḍ̵]	:	voiced interdental emphatic fricative
[š]	:	voiceless alveopalatal fricative, like *sh* in Eng. *ship*
[ž]	:	voiced alveopalatal fricative, like *g* in Eng. *beige*
[c]	:	voiceless alveolar affricate, like *ts* in Eng. *cats*
[ʣ]	:	voiced alveolar affricate, like *ds* in Eng. *lads*
[ɾ]	:	alveolar tap
[ɹ]	:	alveolar approximant

45

[č]	:	voiceless alveopalatal affricate, like *ch* in Eng. *church*
[ǧ]	:	voiced alveopalatal affricate, like *j* in Eng. *jeep*
[x]	:	voiceless velar fricative, like *ch* in German *Buch*
[ġ]	:	voiced uvular fricative: like *r grasseyé* in French
[q]	:	voiceless uvular stop
[']	:	voiceless glottal stop, like *t* in Cockney *bottle*
[h]	:	a voiceless glottal fricative, like *h* in Eng. *hat*
(f.)	:	feminine
(m.)	:	masculine
M	:	Maltese
MLF	:	Mediterranean Lingua Franca
(n.)	:	noun
(pl.)	:	plural
StM	:	Standard Maltese
⇐	:	derives synchronically from
⇒	:	yields synchronically
<	:	derives historically from
>	:	yields historically
~	:	cognate with

Bibliography

AHRWEILER, Hélène, *Byzance et la mer: La marine de guerre, la politique et les institutions maritimes de Byzance aux VIIe-XVe siècles*, Paris, 1966.

AL-MAZINI, Ibrahim, *Sunduq al-Dunya*, Cairo (n.d.).

AQUILINA, Joseph, *Maltese-English Dictionary*, 2 vols, Malta, 1987-1990.

ARBERRY, A.J., *Dun Karm, poet of Malta*, Cambridge, 1961.

BERQUE, Jacques, *Le Maghrib entre deux Guerres*, Paris, 1962.

BERTRAM, Thomas, *The Arabs*, London, 1937.

BLANC, Haim, *Żtudies in North Palestinian Arabic*, Jerusalem, 1953.
> The nekteb-nektebu Imperfect in a variety of Cairene Arabic. *Israel Oriental Studies* IV, Tel Aviv, 1974.

BLANKEN, G., *Les greces de Cargèse (Corse). Recherches sur leur langage et sur leur histoire*, Tome IV, partie linguistique, Leiden, 1951.

BLASCO FERRER, E., *Grammatica storica del catalano e dei suoi dialetti con speciale riguardo all'Algherese*, Tübingen, 1984.

BLAU, Joshua, To which dialect group did Sicilian Arabic belong? *Journal of the American Oriental Society* 88: 522-523, 1968

BLOUET, B., *The story of Malta*, Malta, 1981 [1967].

BONANNO, A., Malta in the third century, *The Roman West in the Third Century* (A. King and M. Henig, eds), Oxford, 1981.
> Malta's changing role in Mediterranean cross-currents from prehistory to Roman times. Malta: *A case-study in international cross-currents. Proceedings of the First International Colloquium on the history of the Central Mediterranean held at the University of Malta, 13-17 December 1989* (S. Fiorini and V. Mallia-Milanes, eds), Malta, 1989.
> *Roman Malta*, Malta, 1992.

BONFANTE, Giuliano, La continuità del latino in Sicilia, *Mediterranean Language Review* 2: 47-49, 1986.

BORG, Alexander, Reflexes of pausal forms in Maltese rural dialects? *Israel Oriental Studies*, No.7:211-25, 1977.
> *A historical and comparative phonology and morphology of Maltese*, Ph.D. diss., Hebrew University, Jerusalem, 1978.
> *Cypriot Arabic*, Stuttgart, 1985.
> Observations on some evolutionary parallels and divergences in Cypriot Arabic and Maltese. To appear in the proceedings of the *Congreso internacional: Interferencias lingüisticas arabo-romances y paralelos estra-ibericos, Madrid 10/14 de diciembre de 1990*.
> Lexical influences from the Mediterranean Lingua Franca in contemporary Maltese. To appear in *Romania Arabica*, 1994.
> The non-Maghrebine elements in Maltese. To appear in *A collection of articles in honour of the sixtieth birthday of Professor Heikki Palva*, Helsinki.

BURCKHARDT, J.L., *Travels in Nubia* (2nd ed.), London, 1822.

CASSOLA, A., *Regole per la lingua maltese*, Malta, 1988.

CHEJNE, Anwar, *The Arabic language*, Minneapolis, 1969.

CIFOLETTI, Guido, *La lingua franca mediterranea*, Padova, 1989.

CINI, Antonio, *La reconciliazione nella questione della lingua: ossia un disegno di riforma degli studi ginnasiali*, Malta, 1903.

COHEN, Marcel, *Le parler arabe des juifs d'Alger*, Paris, 1912.

COLIN, G.S., Emprunts grecs et turcs dans le dialecte arabe de Malte. *Mélanges Marcel Cohen*: 229-231, 1970.

"Supplément au dictionnaire maltais" (see Vanhove 1991), 1991.

CREMONA, A., *Mikiel Anton Vassalli u żminijietu*, Malta, 1975.

DENCH, G., *Maltese in London*, London, 1975.

DI PIETRO, Robert J. and George D. SELIM, The language situation in Arab Sicily, *Linguistic Studies in memory of Richard Slade Harrell*, Washington D.C., 19-35, 1967.

EARLE, Peter, *Corsairs of Malta and Barbary*, London, 1970.

EL-HASSAN, S.A., Educated spoken Arabic in Egypt and the Levant: a critical review of diglossia and related concepts. *Archivum Linguisticum* IX (new series) 1: 32-57, 1977

FERGUSON, C.A., Diglossia. *Word* 15: 325-340, 1959.

FISCHER, Wolfdietrich, "Die Sprache der arabischen Sprachinsel in Uzbekistan". *Der Islam* 36:385-399, 1961.

FLEISCH, Henri, *Études d'arabe dialectal*, Beirut, 1974.

FRENDO, Henry, *Party politics in a fortress colony: The Maltese experience*, Malta, 1991 [1979].

FRIGGIERI, Oliver, *Storja tal-letteratura Maltija*, vol.I, Malta, 1979.

FÜCK, Johann, *Arabiya*, Berlin, 1950.

GESENIUS, W., *Versuch über die maltesische Sprache zur Beurtheilung der neulich wiederholten Behauptung, dass sie ein Ueberrest der altpunischen sey, und als Beytrag zur arabischen Dialektologie*, Leipzig, 1811.

GRECH, P., Introduction to Arberry 1961: 1-53, 1961.

HALL, Robert A., *Pidgin and Creole Languages*. Ithaca & London, 1966.

HOPKINS, Simon, *Studies in the grammar of early Arabic*, Oxford, 1984.

HULL, Geoffrey, Vicende e caratteristiche del maltese parlato in Egitto. *Incontri Siculo-maltesi. Atti del convegno su Malta-Sicilia, contiguità linguistica e culturale (Malta, 4-6 aprile 1986)*, Malta, 1988.

ISSERLIN, B., Sicilian Arabic and Maltese. Some remarks on their phonetic inter-relations. *Journal of Maltese Studies* 11: 19-25, 1977.

JEGER, L., "London Maltese", *Guardian* (Feb. 14, 1936).

KAHANE, Henry and Rénee, Introductory essay: Aspects of Mediterranean Linguistics. *Mediterranean Language Review* Vol.I: 7-9, 1983.

KAHANE, Henry and Rénee & TIETZE, Andeas, *Lingua Franca in the Levant*, Urbana, 1958.

LUKE, Sir Harry, *Malta: An account and appreciation*, London, 1960 [1949].

MALLIA-MILANES, Victor, *Venice and hospitaller Malta 1530-1798*, Malta, 1992.

MAYR, Albert, *Die Insel Malta im Altertum*, München, 1909.

MICALLEF, G., *Memorandum on the Maltese language put before the Royal Commission. Its nature and paternity, its shortcomings and the possibility of its use in the Courts of Law*, Malta, 1931.

NACHTIGAL, Gustav, *Sahara and Sudan*, Vol.I, London, 1974 [1879].

NÖLDEKE, Theodor, Review of Stumme 1904. *Zeitschrift der deutschen morgenländischen Gesellschaft*, LVIII: 903-920.

PELLEGRINI, G.B., *Gli arabismi nelle lingue neolatine*, vols. I and II. Brescia, 1972.

PETROCCHI, P., *Novo dizionario universale della lingua italiana*, Milano, 1900.

PRICE, C.A., *Malta and the Maltese: A study in nineteenth century migration*, Melbourne, 1954.

PUECH, Gilbert, A cross-dialectal study of vowel harmony in Maltese. *Chicago Linguistic Society* 14: 377-389, 1978.
Ethnotextes maltais, Wiesbaden, 1994.

RENFREW, Colin, *Archaeology and language*, London, 1987.

RICHTHOFEN, F.P.W., VON, *Vorlesungen üben allgemeine Siedlungs- und Verkehrsgeographie*, (ed. Otto Schlüter), Berlin, 1908.

ROHLFS, Gerhard, *Scavi linguistici nella Magna Grecia*, Halle-Rom, 1933.

ROSSI, Ettore, "Malta". *Encyclopaedia of Islam*, Vol.III: 213-214, 1936.
Storia di Tripoli e della Tripolitania dalla conquista araba al 1911. (Edizione postuma a cura di Maria Nallino), Rome, 1968.

SAADA, Lucienne, Maltais en Tunisie. *Gli interscambi culturali e socio-economici fra l'Africa settentrionale e l'Europa mediterranea. Atti del congresso internazionale di Amalfi, 5-8 dicembre 1983*, Napoli, 1986.

SANDRECZKI, C., Die maltesische Mundart. *Zeitschrift der deutschen morgenländischen Gesellschaft* 30: 723-737, 1876.
Die maltesische Mundart (II). *Zeitschrift der deutschen morgenländischen Gesellschaft* 33: 225-247, 1879.

SAYDON, P.P., Traces of the Byzantine rite in the church of Malta. *Melita Theologica* VII, no. 1-48, 1954.

SCHUCHARDT, Hugo, Die Lingua Franca. *Zeitschrift für romanische Philologie*, XXXIII. Band: 441-461, 1909.

SIRAT, A.S., and KNUDSEN, E.E., Notes on the Arabic dialect spoken in the Balkh region of Afghanistan. *Acta Orientalia* XXXV: 99-101, 1973.

STUMME, Hans, *Maltesische Studien*, Leipzig, 1904.

SOLDANIS, G.F., AGIUS DE, *Damma tal-Kliem Kartaginis mscerred fel fom tal Maltin u Ghaucin*, 4 vols. (MS preserved at the Malta National Library), 1750.

THOMAS, Bertram, *The Arabs*, London, 1937.

VADALA, G., *Malte et ses dépendances*, Malta, 1906.

VANHOVE, Martine, Un manuscrit inédit de Georges S. Colin: le "Supplément au dictionnaire maltais;" edition partielle et commentaires. *Matériaux arabes et sudarabiques*, MAS-GELLAS, Nouvelle Serie No 3: 137-225, 1991.

VARVARO, Alberto, La lingua in Sicilia e a Malta nel medioevo. *Incontri Siculo-Maltesi. Atti del II convegno su Malta-Sicilia; contiguità e continuità linguistica e culturale (Malta, 4-6 aprile 1986)*, Malta, 1988.

VELLA, A.P., *An Elizabethan-Ottoman Conspiracy*, Malta, 1972.

WAGNER, Max Leopold, Zu einigen arabischen Wörtern des Sizilianischen und Süditalienischen. *Zeitschrift für romanische Philologie* LII: 641-670, 1932.

WETTINGER, G., and FSADNI, M., *L-Għanja ta' Pietru Caxaru*, Malta, 1983.

WETTINGER, G., The Arabs in Malta. *Malta: Studies of its heritage and history*, Malta, 1986.
Plurilingualism and cultural change in medieval Malta. *Mediterranean Language Review* 6-7: 144-160, 1993.
1993a.

Some General Works on Maltese

AQUILINA, Joseph, *The structure of Maltese*, Malta, 1959.
Papers in Maltese Linguistics, Malta, 1961.
BORG, Alexander, *A historical and comparative phonology and morphology of Maltese*.
(Ph.D. diss., Hebrew University), Jerusalem, 1978.
COHEN, David, Le système phonologique du maltais. *Études de linguistique sémitique et arabe*. The Hague, 1966.
SCHABERT, Peter, *Laut- und Formenlehre des Maltesischen anhand zweier Mundarten*, Erlangen, 1976.
SUTCLIFFE, E.F., *A grammar of the Maltese language*, Oxford, 1936.

Literature

Oliver Friggieri

The Maltese literary background

A history of Maltese culture may be said to reflect in various ways the history of the whole community. Since, much more than in the case of larger countries, Malta could never do without foreign contacts, necessarily causative of a complex process of influences, adaptations and reactions (and consequently only through a study of a set of assimilations can the scholar arrive at a true definition of a Maltese identity), such a history, be it political, social or cultural, is bound to assume a comparative character. This may be all the more so owing to the fact that what one may euphemistically call foreign contacts were nothing less than foreign occupations. The conditions which characterize and modify the process of, say, a political history of subordination may boil down to be the inalienable causes of analogous conditions in the cultural field.

The basic distinction is linguistic and not necessarily cultural or psychological. Considering the two major languages which assumed, contemporarily or subsequently, the role of primary media for the elaborate expression of a community's feelings, experiences and ambitions, one has to start by distinguishing between Italian and Maltese. (The presence of English is relatively too recent to be defined as another proper channel through which Maltese literature could seek new bearings. English-Maltese literary interaction can be traced back directly to the modern poets and novelists who effected a radical transformation in the sixties of this century). The dialectical relationship between Italian and Maltese has been looked at, up to a few years ago, as controversial, or worse still, as the unhappy and not easily reconciliable intercourse between a Latin culture, the presence of which in the island goes back many centuries, and a Semitic one, characterized mainly by the basic Arabic structure of the popular language which, owing to the island's uninterrupted contacts with the outer world, adopted a Romance superstructure. One has to define the nature of the apparently contradictory dialectic Italian-Maltese from a purely linguistic point of view. The language question, forming a central part of the island's romantic experience, owes its origin to the active presence of Italian exiled rebels in Malta during the Risorgimento, on the one hand, and to the constant British efforts to introduce English and eradicate the traditional cultural language, on the other. After getting a clear perspective of the language question, which constituted one of the major political preoccupations between 1880 and 1939, one may proceed to deal exclusively with the literary question, since languages which find themselves in interaction within the borders of the same community are also bound to develop cultural and particularly literary cross-currents.

The Arabs conquered Malta in 870 A.D. and thus laid the foundations for the language we now call Maltese. With the Norman conquest in 1090 A.D. the language of the island started to find itself open to extra-Arabic influences, a process which has widened its vocabulary and syntactic patterns, and practically exposed it to a completely different way of life.

Considering the traditional presence of both languages in Malta, the first conclusion is that Maltese is prior to Italian as a spoken language, whilst there is hardly any proof that Italian was ever adopted as the habitual speech medium by any local section of the population. When Maltese started to be written in the 17th century and then on a much wider scale in the 18th and 19th centuries, Italian had already established itself as the only and unquestionable cultural language of the island and had a respectable literary tradition of its own. One of the earliest documents in Italian, for instance, dates back to 1409. Among the earlier literary works it is worth mentioning *La Historia di Malta nuovamente composta in ottava rima, per Antonio Pugliese, l'anno 1565 delli 10 di maggio*, published in Venice in 1585 and preserved at the National Library of Malta. The list of later works written and published in Malta by Italian writers includes *San Paolo a Malta*, an epic which Vincenzo Belloni (1839-1878) issued in 1875 after having spent five years in the island. Since the appearance of the first book printed locally, *I Natali delle Religiose Militiae de' Cavalieri* (1643) by Geronimo Marulli, Malta has seen the constant development of Italian publications, mainly historical and literary. This tradition was interrupted only a few decades ago, that is, more than a century after the real birth of a national literary tradition in the vernacular.

This considerable deposit of literary output throughout the centuries, a large section of which is still in manuscript form at the National Library of Malta, is the work of both Maltese and foreign writers (who happened to live or spend a period of their life on the island) alike. Thus, whilst Maltese has the historical priority on the level of the spoken language, Italian has the priority of being the almost exclusive written medium, for official and socio-cultural affairs, for the longest period. The native language had only to wait for the arrival of a new mentality which could integrate an unwritten, popular tradition with a written, academically respectable one.

On the other hand, if one seeks to identify the literary spirit of the Maltese throughout the centuries, one should only find it obvious to include, and give causative prominence to, the said Italian-oriented Maltese production, thus rendering it the first, or preliminary, phase of the whole spectrum. This approach would seek to establish the extraliterary motives which debarred Maltese from all cultural manifestations, and why it was socially dishonourable to use it. Alongside this dichotomy, resulting in the co-presence of two distinct social stratifications, one should also seek to define the proper character of the Italian tradition, something which can be done through a comparative analysis of the peninsular literature and of its forms of assimilative participation in the island during a series of cultural epochs, such as Renaissance, Baroque, Illuminism and then the first inklings towards Romanticism.

Romanticism, both Latin and German, revalued the Illuminist concept of cultural diffusion and while questioning and negating the true significance and practicability of cosmopolitism, fostered the cult of national languages. This epoch, fundamentally based on the discovery of the sense of personal and national individuality, coincides with the first serious efforts towards the rediscovery of Maltese as one of the most ancient patrimonies of the new emerging nation, as Mikiel Anton Vassalli (1764-1829) calls it in his famous *Discorso preliminare*, the introduction to his *Vocabolario maltese* published in Rome in 1796. The antiquity of a popular language featured very significantly in the concept of nationalism which European romanticism sought to form and preach. One of the more important results of Vassalli's political and scholarly contributions is the embryonic development of a nationalistic way of thinking which centred around two basic aspects of the 19th century philosophy and aesthetics: (i) the affirmation of the singular and collective identity (an experience emanating from the absolute devotion the romantics had for sentiment and passion, as opposed to the old and undisputed right enjoyed by the "goddess reason" which underlay, as evinced in almost all poetics since Aristotle, all previous works of art modelled with architectural precision and in a state of psychological equilibrium); and (ii) the cultivation and diffusion of the national speech medium as the most sacred component in the definition of the *patria* and as the most effective justification both for a dominated community's claiming to be a nation and for the subsequent struggle against foreign rulers.

This new national religion promulgated by romantic Italy pervaded Malta during the period of the Risorgimento when writers, journalists and political rebels sought refuge in the island, and alongside their activity in favour of a united and independent homeland engaged themselves in an analogous mission: that of inviting the Maltese themselves to fight for their own political and cultural rights against the British colonial domination. This started to give rise to an ever wider utilisation of the native language and to the gradual growth of an indigenous literature fully aware of the political, social and cultural rights of the community.

The two genres which characterize the fullest development of Maltese literature are the poetic and the narrative. Theatre as a definitely aesthetic experience in the modern sense is only a recent achievement. Consequently, in giving a panoramic picture, any basic assessment is bound to be conducted in terms of the work of the poets and the novelists, with the particular contribution of the dramatists dovetailing into this mainstream.

Prose

History as a national mythology

The historical novel, based on a subjective compromise between objective data and a personal disposition to recreate them according to one's political commitment, flourished most during the Italian Risorgimento. In recalling the heroic achievements of past generations, the novelist sought to revitalize forgotten myths and give dignity to the contemporary national cause. The idealized depiction of remote historical experiences is emotionally transformed into a vision where past and present are projected towards an immediate future. The objective representation of facts, characters and environments is simply a pretext for rendering history an epic in which the martyrdom of the individual and the national family is the only valid contribution.

In his search for an identification of the *patria* the novelist is only concerned with translating the glories of the past into a spectacular scenery which is bound to be repeated at the moment in question. Structurally, his work tends to assume the form of an alternation between the depiction of creatively sublimated historical events and the passionate exhortation of his fellow citizens towards national unity and redemption. The logical progression of facts which constitute a plot is coupled with the formation of a patriotic philosophy based on a local mythology full of well-known heroes and an anonymous multitude of faithful, and equally valorous, forefathers. The Mazzinian dialectic right-duty is translated into a pragmatic religion: God has given to every citizen the right to a homeland, but it is the citizen's own duty to build it up.

This set of thematic components synthesizes the main character both of the Italian historical novel of the Risorgimento period and of the Maltese one, written in Italian and then in Maltese, of the late decades of the 19th century and of the first half of the 20th. The reasons for this harmonious assimilation, already hinted at in broader terms, are essentially two: (i) local writers had an exclusively Italian education and consequently they either wrote in the island's (incidentally Italian) cultural language according to the prevalent "foreign" criteria or sought to translate them into their early Maltese experiments; as a matter of fact the more important writers, such as Ġan Anton Vassallo (1817-1868), Ġużè Muscat Azzopardi (1853-1972), Anton Manwel Caruana (1838-1907) and later Anastasju Cuschieri (1876-1962), Dun Karm (1871-1961) and Ninu Cremona (1880-1972) started their literary experience in Italian; and (ii) the island's political situation easily presented itself as analogous to, if not even as the direct side-effect of, the peninsula's unification movement. This was enhanced all the more by the active presence of such prominent exiles as Gabriele Rossetti, Francesco Orioli, Luigi Settembrini, Francesco Crispi, Rosalino Pilo, Tommaso Zauli, Sajani, Francesco De Sanctis and many others.

Various rebels were very active as journalists and literary writers, and their participation in the cultural life of the island contributed a lot towards the diffusion of the concept of literature fully committed with the national cause. On the other hand, numerous non-Italian writers visited Malta from time to time and recalled such experience in their memoirs. The list includes the names of George Sandy (1611), Patrick Bryden (1770), Samuel Taylor Coleridge (1804), Lord Byron (1809, 1811), Sir Walter Scott (1831), Hans Christian Andersen (1841), William Makepeace Thackeray (1844), D.H. Lawrence (1920) and Rupert Brooke (1915).

The Maltese historical novelists writing in Italian, such as Ġan Anton Vassallo (*Alessandro Inguanez*, 1861, and *Wignacourt*, 1862), Ferdinando Giglio (*La Bella Maltea ossia Caterina Desguanez*, 1872), Ramiro Barbaro di San Giorgio (*Un Martire*, 1878) and Gaetano Gauci (*Il Condannato al Supplizio del Rogo*, 1905, *L'Ultimo Assalto del Forte San Michele*, 1907, *Maria Valdes*, 1909, and *Notte di Dolore*, 1915) were creating a socio-literary

atmosphere which, in the long run, had to make them realize that the national cause could be expressed effectively only through the language of the people, adequately handled according to the people's own aptitudes. The new dimension which Maltese, as the traditionally neglected idiom of the masses, profoundly needed was now provided by the modern aesthetics which conceived the popular speech medium as the best one for expressing the heightened emotion of a whole nation and as the only one which could suit the new content of art: the construction of a national identity in terms of its differentiating factors, the first of which was the language itself.

The process of local political emancipation and the history of the earlier stages of literature in the vernacular amply testify to the fact that this modern conception owes its dynamic presence in Malta, and particularly within the literary circles, to the island's complex participation in the Italian Risorgimento. This immediately suggested an inherent contradiction with regard to Maltese nationalistic literature written in Italian. It was now up to open-minded writers to employ the uncultivated dialect in order to express congruently this vision which concerned literature, politics and society in an equal manner. On the other hand, the Maltese novelist, like any other colleague, was faced with an added challenge, since he was simultaneously expected not only to interpret a national experience in Maltese but also to make the dialect assume a respectable literary character.

This double programme was decidedly pursued by Anton Manwel Caruana whose *Inez Farruġ* (1889), considered to be the first literary novel in Maltese, succeeded in fusing stylistic ambition with patriotic involvement, thus initiating a movement of language-cum-literature revival which lasted up to about two decades ago, when a new crop of writers reacted against traditional obsolete patterns in order to come to terms with a thoroughly different reading public.

The structure of the Italian historical novel assumed a twofold nature: the author could either derive his central plot from known history and set it within a fictitious surrounding, or peripheral plot (e.g. Massimo D'Azeglio's *Niccolò de' Lapi*), or create a central plot himself and insert it harmoniously within the limits of a historically authentic, although partially transformed, background. This second structure, popularized mainly by Manzoni's *I Promessi Sposi*, was chosen by Caruana whose primary aim was to establish a constant parallelism between a (fictitious) family problem and a (historical) national crisis. A structural analysis of the plot scheme would show that the parallelism is so meticulously built up that it ultimately reduces the private affair (or central story) to an allegory of the population's unfortunate condition under foreign rule (the outer plot). A synthesis of the two narrative models was attempted by Ġużè Muscat Azzopardi, whose *Toni Bajada*, 1878, *Viku Mason*, 1881, *Susanna*, 1883, *Ċejlu Tonna*, 1886, *Ċensu Barbara*, 1893, and *Nazju Ellul*, 1909, revolve around the figure of an artistically modified 'historical' protagonist who comes to life against a similarly reconstructed historical setting. This compromise reached further stages of development through Ġużè Aquilina's *Taħt Tliet Saltniet* (Under Three Reigns), 1938, and Ġużè Galea's *Żmien l-Ispanjoli* (The Time of the Spaniards), 1938, *San Ġwann* (Saint John), 1939, and others. Other novels of minor creative value which fall within the general outlines of this category are Ġ. Vassallo's *Mannarino*, 1888, C.A. Micallef's *Sander Inguanez*, 1892, S. Frendo De Mannarino's *Il-Barunissa Maltija* (The Maltese Baroness), 1893, and L. Vella's *Bernard Dupuó*, 1898, *Isolda*, 1902, *Bint il-Ħâkem* (The Ħâkem's Daughter), 1907, and *Nikol Ghabdul*, 1907-1908.

These novelists' constant preference for protagonists chosen from within the zone of well-known national patriots is another major step in the romantic direction. The almost religious cult of heroes (the more important being Mikiel Anton Vassalli and Dun Mikiel Xerri) was enormously fostered through their aesthetic reincarnation and furnished the hitherto submissive community with another unifying emblem and with a fundamental justification for the claim of ethnic distinction and ancestral dignity.

The main line of progression, however, seems to be the way in which later novelists have gradually moved away from Caruana's elegaic *leitmotif* and arrived at a vision of victory. This passage from the negative to the positive, from the elegy to the epic, not only implies a radical shift of emphasis (the future instead of the past) but also proves that the narrator was abandoning his former role of dignified chronicler and assuming that of a prophet or leader. This transformation is explainable through reference to the political situation which in the first decades of the twentieth century reach higher levels of development.

Together with the formative discovery of a hitherto neglected epos, this narrative tradition recognized the fundamental poetic and creative value of popular heritage. Following the footsteps of Herder, the brothers Schlegel, Tommaseo, Berchet and other famous theorists of cultural democracy, romanticism had long declared its deep respect for folklore, oral and written traditions of the lower classes, and the more primitive, or less urbanized, aspects of the people. The instinctive national family, as opposed to the tempered academic artificer, became the truest poet. (This aesthetic dialectic assumed locally the nature of a parallelism with the socio-cultural distinction between Italian, the vehicle of the restricted elite, and Maltese, the spontaneous means of expression of the less educated masses). Within this context this school of writers' insistent sublimation of the local patrimony – the language, the popular traditions, the physical beauty of the average young countryman and countrywoman, the landscape – acquires an aesthetic, as well as political, justification.

Alongside this group of democratically oriented literary novelists, another movement of popular writers, more directly appealing to the less educated category of society, was contributing in an analogous manner towards the fusion of the narrative pattern, socio-political involvement and the newly-born awareness of the intrinsically creative value of folk traditions. Although further to the extraliterary implications of the said Italian-Maltese dialectic, the distinction between the literary historical novel and the popular historical one implies another class stratification within the restricted spectrum of readers of Maltese (as opposed to those of Italian), the basis for their being distinct, or different, is, apart from literary intentions, rather a question of varying emphasis on related aspects of the people theme: the literary type stresses the collective political and patriotic involvement, whereas the popular type dwells extensively on the socio-familiar condition, thus giving ample room for the consideration of non-political private and public events, mainly unfortunate and tragic. Whilst the literary type subdues a central plot for the sake of an ideal content, the popular one treats its own one on a purely narrative level which is exclusively concerned with arousing pathos as a personal experience and not with conducing the reader to conceive his acquired emotion as something he is sharing in common with other fellow citizens and which he should dutifully translate into action.

This segment of the historical novel, although not strictly literary, has an indirectly aesthetic touch inasmuch as its thematic content is immediately derived from the romantic vision of life, whereas the formal aspect is openly geared to the less sophisticated tastes of the majority.

Horror and social inquiry

Horror, violence, the nocturnal and the spectral depiction of life were looked at by many romantics as excellent vehicles for the formation of a tragic image of human existence. The romantic experience had a profound aptitude for terror, and consequently many novels, while maintaining throughout a light sprinkling of historical veracity, preferred the socialization, rather than the previous idealistic nationalization, of an event. Such an event normally centred around a sensational murder or an unhappy love affair which ended up dramatically. Spectres, ruthless villains, haunted houses, ruined castles, deserted palaces, secluded passages, superstitions, popular experiences of the supernatural, gloomy settings and corpses are coordinated into one suggestive whole which motivates awe and suspense. The more important novelists of the Gothic type, Arturo Mercieca [*Carlo de Von Hove, jew il-kefrija tal-bojja Goldo* (Carlo de Von Hove, or the cruelty of the hangman Goldo), 1899, *Inez jew bint l-imgħallaq, ġrajja ta' Malta, kurjuża u tal-biża'* (Inez or the hanged man's daughter, a tale of Malta, curious and macabre), 1901, *Ix-Xebba ta' Wied Żnuber* (the maid of Żnuber Valley), 1912, *L-għerien tal-katavri jew it-tallâb Kalabriż* (The cave of the corpses or the beggar from Calabria), 1924], A.E. Borg [*Luċija jew il-vittma tat-tradiment* (Lucia or the victim of betrayal), 1907, *Marija jew vendetta ta' baruni* (Maria or the baron's vengeance), 1908, *Amalja mart l-assassin* (Amalia the murderer's wife), 1910], G. Cumbo [*Katavru spjun – qalb ta' Venezjan* (The spying corpse – heart of a Venetian), 1935, *L-id tal-mejjet jew l-iben ta' Monte Cristo* (The dead man's hand or the son of Monte Cristo), 1937] and numerous others had an enormous success and contributed very much to the diffusion of both the Maltese novel as such and the horror taste.

Analogously to this narrative production, the *tijatrin*, or popular theatre, sought to be melodramatic either through comedy or through tragedy. Far-fetched and highly complicated plots had to develop easily into an uninterrupted series of exaggerated features. Put together, and normally divided into three acts, these were intended to motivate either laughter or horror. Substantially it is only the same technique — melodramatic reconstruction — which explains both the basic nature and the popular success of the two apparently distinct, or even opposite, genres.

Apart from focusing attention, however crudely, on socio-moral and environmental characteristics, the horror story paved the way for future writers and started to invite them to abandon the long worn-out national conception and to substitute it by a deeply felt preoccupation with the immediate social hardships of a certain section of the population. Gradually the emphasis began to be shifted from the outer to the inner world, although no novelist could ignore their reciprocal cause-effect relationship, thus admitting their inalienable coexistence and then depicting it in terms of a set of socially aware individuals who sum up in their personalities the condition of a commonly poor community silently heading for a class war.

The earliest dialectic found in the Maltese novel's characterization, the foreigner and the native, developed itself into a purely democratic one, the privileged and the deprived, although doubtlessly there is no clear-cut distinction in this direction between the historical and the social novel. For instance, Caruana's *Inez Farrug* had already pointed out basic social differences between the rulers and the ruled, whilst Aquilina's *Taħt Tliet Saltniet* (Under Three Reigns) had also suggested a reform of social structures alongside, or better, as a prominent side-effect of, the political emancipation.

The reformist novelists, such as Ġużè Ellul Mercer (*Leli ta' Ħaż-Żgħir*, Leli of Ħaż-Żgħir, 1938), Ġwann Mamo (*Ulied in-Nanna Venut*, The Children of Grandma Venut, 1930), Ġużè Bonnici (*Il-Qawwa ta' l-Imħabba*), The Force of Love, 1938, *Ħelsien*, Freedom, 1939), Wistin Born (*Is-Salib tal-Fidda*, The Silver Cross, 1939), Ġużè Orlando (*L-Ibleh*, The Simpleton, 1948), Ġużè Chetcuti (*Id-Dawl tal-Ħajja*, The Lamp of Life, 1958, *Imħabba u Mewt*, Love and Death, 1961, *L-Isqaq*, The Alley, 1962, *It-Tnalja*, The Plier, 1964, *Nirien ta' Mħabba*, Fires of Love, 1967) and Ġorġ Zammit (*Ix-Xhud li ma deherx*, The Witness who did not turn up, 1964) assumed the role of critical observers of characters, of typical situations and environments, and applied their objective investigation towards creating a literature meant to instigate social consciousness and inquiry into the problems of the lower classes. Such a critique had to be conveyed through a faithful analysis of spoken linguistic schemes. This is also what realist playwrights, such as Ġino Muscat Azzopardi (b. 1899), Ġużè Diacono (b. 1912) and Ġużè Chetcuti (b. 1914), sought to do in order to put on stage a totally faithful reproduction of what actually happened in daily life. The more important aspects of familiar and social ethics, such as love and hatred, sincerity and hypocrisy, offered the widest range for their typical thematic field, whereas characters, environments, dictions and customs aimed at rendering in an almost documented manner the objective appearance of sensory phenomena. The empirical world of these writers, therefore, was necessarily deprived of their own subjective consciousness and its depiction had to reject any sort of sublime idealization.

This socio-literary disposition provided a new opportunity for Maltese to widen considerably its lexical registers and syntactic patterns through a bare-faced confrontation with a sector of society the literary transcription of which had hitherto been seriously forbidden. The extension of both the thematic field and the stylistic stock stressed all the more the principle that literature, and particularly the narrative genre, had to exist, flourish and justify its development only insofar as it depicted society in the light of its real problems. Man was no longer examined and valued in virtue of his being a citizen, but in respect of his belonging to a particular province, a city or a village. Instead of embracing the whole nation and bringing forth all its space and time dimensions, the new plot structure evolved within the restricted domains of a particular milieu. The present substituted the past and the former epic motive transformed itself into a social inquiry based on class distinction, a new category within the earlier unspecified grouping of all citizens forming one ethnic family.

The self and the outer region in conflict

The young revolutionary writers of the sixties, united under the banner of the *Moviment Qawmien Letterarju*, the Movement for the Promotion of Literature, founded in 1967, and progressing apace with the new wave of revival which invaded universities and social structures alike in Europe and in America, proposed for themselves a radical cross-examination of all the previous literature which may be summed up in a twofold manifesto: (i) the critical revaluation of traditional works, aimed at discarding all the thematic and formal components which led to sterile alienation and to decadent imitation, and (ii) the introduction of fresh contemporary motives and of a set of stylistic devices which could enable their adequate expression. All human experiences became aesthetically valid in themselves, and languages started to be looked at simply as a mental abstraction, potentially subject to all possible creative deviations (lexical, syntactic, semantic, etc.) and not as an already codified set of objective rules demanding full adherance and unquestionable reproduction.

New novelists like J.J. Camilleri (*Aħna Sinjuri*, We are rich, 1965, *Il-Għar tax-*

Xitan, The Cave of the Devil, 1973, *Is-Sejħa ta' l-Art*, The Call of the Earth, 1974), Lino Spiteri (*Tad-Demm u l-Laħam*, Of Flesh and Blood, 1968, *Ħala taż-Żgħożija*, Wasted Youth, 1970), Frans Sammut (*Labirint u Stejjer Oħra*, Labyrinth and Other Stories, 1968, *Il-Gaġġa*, The Cage, 1971, *Samuraj*, Samurai, 1975) and Oliver Friggieri (*Il-Gidba*, The Lie, 1977, *L-Istramb*, The Misfit, 1980) suggested a thorough examination of society, conceived of as an irrevocably sorrowful confrontation between the individual and the collective complex. At times the former reduces itself to a microcosmic manifestation of the latter and occasionally the two become the extreme poles of an irreconciliable dialectic. For the first time in Malta local novelists, as well as the poets, dared speak out in unequivocal terms, pinpoint the most serious maladies of their community and indirectly suggest a diversification founded on integrity, the immediate consequence of the elimination of sanctified hypocrisy which they believed to detect in religion, society and family life.

Although scrupulously faithful to the literary rendering of factual truth (whence the gradual formation of a modern style), Lino Spiteri seeks the implied significance, the enigma which may underlie empirical experience and which may follow from a sensible re-examination of the data in order to rediscover them according to the logic of purified emotion, the writer's spiritual condition, as opposed to the logic of reason, the functioning of which constitutes the preliminary stage of this double process. Heightening crude reality (the result of a peaceful fusion of Christian education and Socialist orientation) and redimensioning it in terms of his own sensibility, Spiteri transforms the factual into the possible, the stale and commonly unnoticeable event into a uniquely unrepeatable experience. Through the subjective elaboration of observed objectives, biography and reportage attain universality, and the particular, be it personal or social, becomes predicable of all humans. This is why Lino Spiteri's short story, like J.J. Camilleri's novel, is often simultaneously explainable both through a Maltese and through an anonymously human reiteration. It is not only the said new (or better reactionary, if put in its true historical perspective) awareness of society which accounts for such a choice, but also the rejection of nationalism as an irrelevant myth (a major theme and a psychological state already exhausted in the previous decades) and the preoccupation with the idea of man the mind as opposed to man the citizen.

Spiteri's and other authors', such as J.J. Camilleri's, could not possibly take an exclusively literary, or formalistic, slant, but had to be deeply rooted in, or motivated by, a sense of dissatisfaction with the human, and then incidentally Maltese, condition. On the other hand, Spiteri's literary language, whilst striving to activate hidden potentialities, rules out all the unwanted remnants of *decorum*, simplifies commonly used structures and coins new ones, thus creating a fresh, fluent diction. Remaining faithful to his original background, Spiteri even employs dialectisms, but his constant intention is to alternate concisely detached descriptions and lyrical passages, and consequently to produce a series of closely related vignettes which proclaim the disguised poetic character of an otherwise uninspiring concrete situation. From the point of view of a history of literary technique, Spiteri may be said to be contributing to the now prevalent fusion of two different genres, the poetic and the narrative, and to be giving evidence that their traditionally acclaimed distinction is here purely phenomenological. An analysis of the two devices (description and lyricism), taken separately and also as components of one complete texture, is perhaps the best approach towards a definition of his style.

Frans Sammut, still enamoured of a literary speech which suggests the conscious choice of a convinced purist, similarly presents an experiment in new structures and lexical adventures. His sentences, at times ironically rhetorical and at others sharp and provocative, are the eloquent recollection of a disturbed ego persecuted by a strange world which is at the same time hauntingly real and vaguely symbolic, internal and objective. The lack of a definite distinction between the two frontiers as well as their continuous interaction transform description into experience, the empirical into the psychological, a process which is both stylistic and thematic. For instance, logical congruity is frequently ignored when grammar passes from the dialogue to the monologue and vice-versa. Secondly, Sammut's characters are normally the humanized version of an environment or the ill-placed end-product of its antithesis, and therefore their external activity is always necessarily related to the internal one, an aspect which is by far the most insistent throughout his narratives.

This interpretation may explain the central role of splendid unsociability bestowed on anti-heroes whose sole problem is communicability but whose fundamental redeeming feature is their own failure to come to terms with the outer world. Whilst all this is again directly traceable back to its immediate origins (the Maltese social context), one is hardly justified in not seeing it as just a pretext for the exemplification of the human situation itself. Sammut's individual, remotely resembling a combination of the Dostoyevskyan sublime idiot and Camus' sceptical social hermit, always betrays traits of Maltesism used as prime matter for the ultimate formation of a human type. In other words, he universalizes according to the dictates of a localized version of man as such.

The substantial confrontation between the epic of the traditional historical novelist and the elegy of the modern one is only too evident. Whereas the former strove to formulate a positive definition of an idealized *patria*, the latter disclaims it and renders it a sterile, or at least an unfortunate, anonymous territory where people are necessarily humans and only incidentally citizens. It is, however, the same *patria* in disguise and employed as the object of a critique which is the result of a love-hate relationship very typical of all modern Maltese literature. Oliver Friggieri's *Fil-Parlament ma jikbrux Fjuri* (In Parliament no Flowers grow), 1986 and *Fil-gżira Taparsi jikbru l-Fjuri* (In the island of Taparsi flowers grow), 1991, further emphasized and illustrated the sharp dualism.

Within this framework of a closely related genre one can appreciate better the historical significance of the central role played for the first time by drama. The real birth of a modern literary theatre in Maltese goes back to the first appearance of Francis Ebejer (1925-1993) in 1950. A bilingual writer, Ebejer strove hard and faced controversy and prejudice to introduce in local drama the modern idiom of a highly evocative technique which ably related crude reality to a wide texture of symbolism and suggestive relevance. The influence of European and American theatre is immediately detected, and it is all absorbed and assimilated in terms of his own personality in search of the contemporary international spirit. Since his first Maltese radioplay, *Ċpar fix-Xemx* (Fog in the Sun), 1950, he started to create a nervous awareness of what stage reality actually was. Insistently obsessed with the conception of human experience as a turbolent sequence of contrasts and meaningful absurdities, he gradually went on to identify the inherently metaphorical, or better allegorical, nature of theatre as such. The nationwide success of his prize-winning plays, such as *Vaganzi tas-Sajf* (Summer Holidays), 1962, *Boulevard*, 1964, *Menz*, 1966, immediately brought about an authentically literary approach to drama. People, especially those who usually refrained from attending a stage representation in Maltese, flocked to the island's national theatre every time Ebejer

came out with a new work. Consequently, Ebejer finally achieved in drama what Anton Manwel Caruana had done with the novel in 1889 and what Dun Karm, the national poet, started to do from 1912, when he dedicated himself to poetry in Maltese.

The implied discontent with previous popular and pseudo-literary dramatic efforts underlies Ebejer's radical transformation and, on the other hand, explains and amply justifies the categorical negation proposed by Oreste Calleja (b.1946), a playwright of significant inventiveness, in 1972: "The deficiences of Maltese theatre are innumerable. The Maltese theatre does not exist."

Partly indebted to Ebejer's own versatility in dramatic conception and linguistic flexibility according to a variety of conditions, environments, characters and thematic contents (all elements manifesting the direct, almost obvious, influence on him of Beckett, Ionesco, Pinter and others) Calleja is similarly engaged in depicting a highly allegorical, dramatically entertaining vision of a definite set of human dilemmas. Some of his situations are the most original in the whole of modern drama. His *dramatis personae*, like those of the modern novelists and the young poets themselves, are helplessly in search of a thorough personal fulfilment of which they are fatally destined to remain deprived owing to certain socio-psychological phenomena which are always exerting their influence on them. The problem of identification (already present in some of the more important prose and poetry works of the thirties) is at the core of this version of being human and of being Maltese alike. It is actually difficult to distinguish between the localized and the universally minded critique since the two borders normally overlap. The characters of both Ebejer and Calleja are ultimately a subtle fusion of environmental and cosmopolitan features.

Ebejer's second phase, which may be said to have started with his *Il-Ħadd fuq il-Bejt* (Sunday on the Roof), 1971, is fundamentally Maltese, in the sense that it transforms a series of typically localized versions of human experience into a quasi-ludicrous national self-portrait. Its basic structure is perhaps derived from the island's popular theatrical tradition, mostly typified in the form of the *farsa*. The inevitable love-hate complex which modern Maltese writers manifest in treating environmental conceptions is present to the extent that it gives room to a plot, drastically reduced in terms of its traditional component parts, which is superficially comic or satirical and basically elegaic, deeply rooted in a hidden stratum of personal delusion. Essentially, it is a feeling shared by all writers of this period.

Alfred Sant (b.1948) is significant for his novel *L-Ewwel Weraq tal-Bajtar* (The first Palms of the Prickly Pears), 1968, and for his plays, particularly *Fid-Dell tal-Kattidral* (In the Shadow of the Cathedral), 1977. Deeply conscious of the function of every word in his text, Sant manipulates language in a manner which reveals both a tense psychology and an uncodified approach to grammatical equilibrium. Departing from a substantially negative appraisal of life, he portrays a delicately ironical image of either Maltese ways of life or of unqualified human conditions. At times his narrative tends to resolve itself into a series of vignettes which may betray his strange love for familiar and social structures he actually wants to discredit. At times, however, poetry is allowed to feature prominently, and somehow paradoxically, even in objectively uninspiring situations. This tendency to transform drama into poetry is also the most typical feature of the plays of Doreen Micallef (b. 1949).

Poetry

A cultural dualism

The aesthetic myth of the people as the truest poet, a basic principle which determined the real character of romantic art, is the primary motive of the revival of Maltese as a means of literary, and especially versified, expression. The European movement, largely inspired and determined by the democratic spirit of great liberal thinkers, may be said to have revolved around Herder's fundamental distinction between *Kunstpoesie* (poetry of art) and *Naturpoesie* (poetry of nature). Latin romanticism subsequently started to adopt this dialectic as its creed and to see in the first component the poetry of the traditional and outdated past, and in the second one the authentically inspired expression of a new emerging generation endowed with the right to translate its own genuinely primitive feelings into poetry which was necessarily uncultivated, spontaneous and instinctive in form and content.

This dualistic conception of poetry, and of art in general, amounted to the distinction between classicism, now looked at as an elitist and socially barren culture, and romanticism, a movement fully aware of contemporary political and social features and problems which the modern artist had to interpret according to the dictates of a whole native milieu. Whereas in the major European literatures (such as the Italian, in which the heredity of the Renaissance was still alive) this new conception sought to assume an anti-classical identity, in the case of a small island like Malta, where the traditional Italian literature of the Maltese proved to be the concern of a numerically restricted and socially privileged class, it did not only imply a radical reaction against a worn-out aesthetic vision but also a hitherto unprecedented formation of a national awareness which inevitably had to be both political and linguistic.

Ġan Anton Vassallo's triple contribution

Ġan Anton Vassallo (1817-1868) is the

first important poetic personality to effect the earliest traces of development in the said direction. Being fully equipped with an Italian academic education, he soon started to participate in the new aesthetic vision and to form a poetics totally oriented towards democratic experience. The people were to inspire the poet and to suggest to him the lexical, structural and thematic components.

Vassallo's contribution has a triple character. He introduced into Maltese the pathetic or sentimental attitude which represents man as an emotional creature in search of self-attainment through love. The dialogue with nature which surrounds human sensibility is transformed into the intimate document of man's psychological journey. Alongside this subject-object relationship the poet presents a fresh awareness of the troubled soul as the central unit within the texture of all human experiences. The second component of Vassallo's poetry is satirical. Man is not only conceived of as a victim of superior forces which are continuously exerting their influence on his sensibility – thus motivating a type of poetry which is thematically negative and pessimistic and stylistically delicate, melodious and rhetorically direct – but also as an active protagonist of a social environment. His romantic fables seek to caricature a set of public aspects and to render stale folkloristic material a spectacular panorama of what actually underlies the truest identity of a humble class-ridden society. Animal psychology, class conscience, personified sensitive, animate and inanimate entities, dramatized traditions, dictions and situations of particular sectors of society are fused into one whole in order to create a colourfully critical interpretation of contemporary life.

Vassallo was actually trying to do in Malta what Fiacchi, Perego, Gozzi, Casti, Passeroni, Batacchi, Pignotti and many others were doing in Italy. Thematically and structurally, his fables are an integral part of the movement. This pedagogical

aspect of romanticism flourished enormously in the island and may be said to be one of the major means by which the native idiom acquired a nationwide justification for its popular-literary cultivation.

But the poet's focal conception of man is essentially nationalistic. It is man the citizen, as opposed to man the disillusioned lover or man the social animal, that determines to the greatest extent the character of his poetic vision. The heroic past is brought back to life through a dramatic re-elaboration which puts people, events and environments on an equal footing and which looks at history as an uninterruptedly evolving present, thus suggesting that the idealized *patria* of the romantics is potentially on the verge of being actualized in definite political terms. Through such an elimination of any mental barrier between past and future, the new image of the nation is put to life in a manner analogous to that of the all-seeing prophet.

This three-fold character of Vassallo's contribution to Maltese poetry marks the initial phase of a relatively long period conducted on the same lines by the future poets. Minor authors like Ludovico Mifsud Tommasi (1795-1879), Richard Taylor (1818-1868), Ġużè Muscat Azzopardi (1853-1927), Anton Muscat Fenech (1854-1910), Dwardu Cachia (1858-1907), Manwel Dimech (1860-1921) and others continued to develop further the democratic orientation of poetry and to widen their sources of inspiration through a better understanding of social structures and a more flexible manipulation of popular diction according to a set of literary criteria. The romantic axiom that poetry is a depository of national truth explains what actually happened on the poetic level. On the other hand, the school of Maltese poets writing in Italian sought to drive home this vision of man and the country. But since now it was only popular sensibility which could inspire works of art – a basic truth insistently proclaimed and

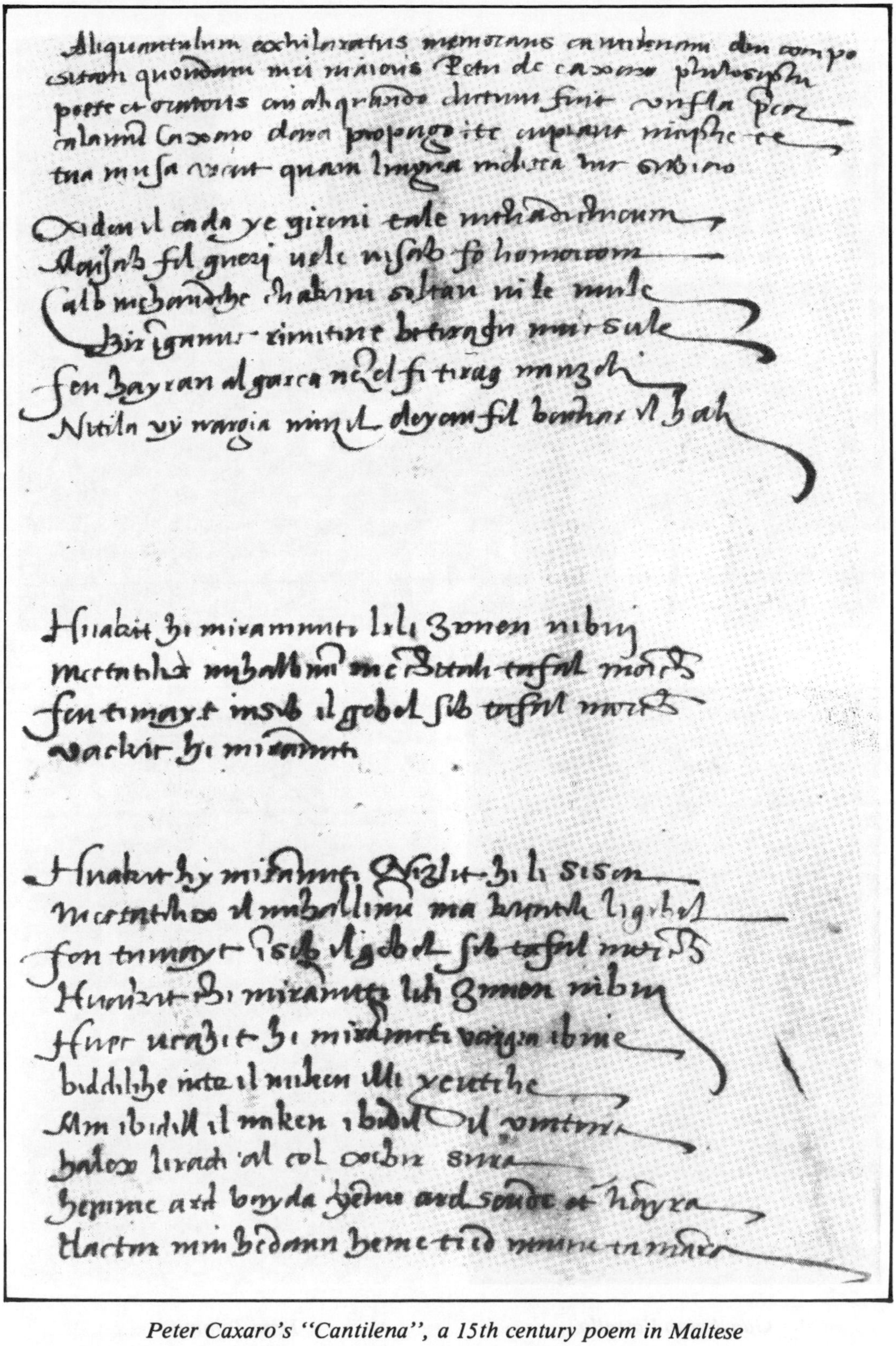

Peter Caxaro's "Cantilena", a 15th century poem in Maltese

Dun Karm

Ġan Anton Vassallo

Temi Zammit

Ġwann Mamo

Rużar Briffa

Karmenu Vassallo

Francis Ebejer

65

diffused in Malta through the island's participation in Italy's romantic experience, and particularly through the vast local activity of the Italian exiled rebels (1804-c.1860) – and since Maltese was rapidly assuming a central role which was ultimately destined to substitute, at least partly, the traditional cultural role of Italian, this group of writers found themselves faced with a decisive dilemma. They had either to come to grips with the new situation (that is, through resorting to the handling of Maltese as their artistic medium and through reaching a compromise with the immediate aspirations and the real educational standards of the majority), or to isolate themselves considerably from the mainstream and to reduce themselves to a consciously isolated socio-literary cast.

Maltese became an official language in 1934. Although the language question emphasized the basic distinction between Italian (as a living evidence of a rich Latin patrimony) and Maltese (as a then so-called unworthy Semitic dialect which served as a mere vehicle of popular communication), for the literary historian it is still more important insofar as it motivated a further distinction within the Maltese language literary movement itself. Some writers sought to purify the written idiom from all non-Semitic derivatives (an attitude analogous in various ways to the Italian purist movement, led by Antonio Cesari and others, which during the Napoleonic era tried to restore the modern language according to the Italian of the "*aureo Trecento*"). Others, however, believed that an effective democratization of literature in Maltese could not be adequately carried out without using lexical and structural patterns which, although carefully and intelligently selected, were also totally faithful to the actual choices of the contemporary population. The purist movement – represented mainly by A.M. Caruana (1838-1907), who sought to eliminate as much as possible non-Semitic loan words from his novel *Inez Farrug*,

1889, and from his *Vocabolario della Lingua Maltese*, 1903, and by Annibale Preca (1830-1901), who strove to give an all-embracing Semitic origin to common words of Romance derivation, particularly to place-names and surnames, in his *Malta Cananea*, 1904 – was later on succeeded by a group of liberal thinkers who faithfully reiterated the linguistic democratism of the Italian romantics. Napuljun Tagliaferro, Ninu Cremona, Dun Karm and Ġ. Aquilina were openly in favour of a natural fusion of Semitic and Romance words which ultimately reflected both the truest image of popular spirit and a synchronized version of the spoken language.

Consequently, many of the romantically oriented poets of the early twentieth century (like Ġ. Muscat Azzopardi, A. Cuschieri, N. Cremona, Dun Karm) soon found that the new challenge, being both political and aesthetic, could not be adequately faced if not through their translating (and partly modifying) their own 'Italian' romantic conscience into Maltese. Others, however, failed to accept the intrinsic value of the popular idiom and continued to write romantic poetry which, paradoxically enough, could not reach any more its basic aim, that is, popular communication. The implied aesthetic contradiction is indirectly present in certain Maltese poems which proclaim the myth of a national language.

The contemporaneity of the two schools, though linguistically much different and socially opposed, may appear, at first sight, to be analogous to the thematic and formal distinction between the old literature still written according to the Latin tradition and the new literature written according to some Semitic philosophy and technical apparatus. Maltese was looked at, up to a few decades ago, as a mere corrupt Arabic dialect, the 'poverty' of which was further proved by its lexical assimilations from Sicilian and Italian. Since the Maltese community had, and still has, a Catholic orientation, and since the local writers who either abandoned Italian to start experimenting with Maltese or initiated their creative activity through Maltese were not in any way alien to the Italian tradition, they were repeatedly reminded of their being '*educati italianamente*'. One can only speak, therefore, of a harmonious fusion of the older and the new tradition, a historically organic continuation of one complete process. The modern usage of the native language instead of the more respectable one and the consequent democratization of literature are only new bearings within the same linear development.

In spite of the well known fact that Latin romanticism amply exploited various extra-European sources of inspiration, and notwithstanding the basic Semitic character of Maltese, Vassallo insisted that local writers were duty bound to interpret and sublimate the real identity of the country. In practical terms this meant that, as it subsequently proved to be, they were only expected to insert themselves within the wider current of the Latin tradition and to find the adequate channels through which they could adopt a linguistic medium of Semitic origin according to a set of non-Semitic formal and thematic components which were part and parcel of the island's cultural orientation. When one bears in mind that Vassallo was fully aware of the need of diffusing the popular language and of creating a poetic corpus which faithfully reflected the community's innermost experiences, one can only conclude that in this way he was advocating the organic fusion of a Semitic language and a Latin spirituality which henceforth was destined to prevail in all future literary works:

"*Sacrificheremo pure vanità filologiche e interessi maggiori, a più alto fine; facciam ogni sforzo per ispingerci verso l'occidente nonostante l'orientalismo della nostra lingua. All'Oriente, bellissimo nelle pagine di Chateaubriand e Lamartine, diamo soltanto un saluto poetico; sien essi però i nostri sguardi, i nostri sospiri, per l'occidente*".

Dun Karm: nationalism and solitude

Maltese only needed then to assume this respectability and to be identified with culture, apart from folklore, popular comedy and religious ritual. This was the challenge which expected and needed a master of both languages, gifted also with a sublime poetic character, since the poetic genre was actually the most popular and ideally the most suitable to involve the majority in this socio-cultural encounter. Such a poet could not possibly be one who was outside the *only* group of dedicated Maltese authors, that is, those who cultivated the Italian tradition and sought to develop it locally. The situation is commonly labelled as linguistic but in reality was deeply rooted in social and ideological substrata. It only lacked the presence of a unifying spirit who also happened to be a resourceful author who had already let European, and especially the Italian risorgimental, romanticism exert far-reaching influences on his identity to make him take the irrevocable decision of giving both Italian and Maltese their respective due in terms of time-space conditions which are always changing. In fact Dun Karm (1871-1961) was endowed with a deep sense of historicism and could easily accept the challenge in its entirety, but only 'failed' to see any incompatibility between the two linguistic media on the creative level.

Since he wrote exclusively in Italian up to 1912 (his first poem goes back to 1889), when he started to write in Maltese he did not undergo a substantial or radical change, but retaining the formal and ideological features he had already developed in his first literary phase, he passed on to assert the same dignity in regard of the native language. The fact that this event of major importance in the literary evolution of Maltese did not take the form of a total re-examination but just of a healthy fusion of past and present is further evinced by the other equally significant fact that Dun Karm went on to write occasionally in Italian even after the year of his linguistic 'conversion' (1912).

Dun Karm succeeds in sublimating for

the first time the vision of a glorious nation and transforms its long history into a lyrical epic full of heroes and spectacular events. Through the dramatic reincarnation of such patriots like Dun Mikiel Xerri, Vassalli and La Valette, and through the depiction of a varied series of folkloristic vignettes, he unifies in one complete whole the always relevant glories of the past and the verifiable merits of contemporary life. A group of national figures, romantically conceived of as the fathers of the country (a direct participation in a central motive of Italian nineteenth century inspiration, particularly elaborated and diffused by Foscolo, with whom Dun Karm takes part in an ideal but intimately passionate dialogue, and whose *I Sepolcri* he translated into superb Maltese), and an anonymous multitude of faithful citizens form one ethnic entity distinctly characterized by its religious chorality in deeds and intentions. The Mazzinian emblem of 'God and the People' as well as the thinker's doctrine of one's right to have a homeland and consequently one's duty to construct it assume an essential importance in the poetry of Dun Karm (and then of his numerous followers). Metaphors, similies, rhetorical devices, poetic forms, emotional adjectivizations and other lexical choices easily define this poetic corpus as significantly risorgimental according to the Italian models which are here revisited and experienced by a mature spirit and reorganized according to the needs and suggestions of an immediate historical situation.

The subject-object dilemma of the romantic conscience is also actively present in Dun Karm. In complete contrast with the nationalistic, outward-looking component of his poetic personality, there is the equally important aspect of his solitude, a main motive which is insistently expressed in poems which evoke the fatally remote figure of his mother and which depict a loving nostalgia for the countryside where the poet's sensibility revives the past and seeks to indulge in an ego-id relationship which is both physical and spiritual. The landscape, previously transformed into a figurative version of the island's differentiating factors which form and justify its national definition, is now spiritualized according to one's own internal universe and reduced to an objectivized projection of a disturbed human psychology. Even if christianized and ethically restrained, the *Sehnsucht* motive, the urge for the nostalgically exotic, is typical of Dun Karm's real individuality.

Poetry as a lyric

The thematic field of subsequent romantic poets was destined to evolve within analogous limits. This was partly due to Dun Karm's literary influence on his contemporaries as well as to a sort of a collective participation in one general experience, aesthetically romantic and historically Maltese, which was bound to make itself evident in terms of a common trend, a *courant commun*, to use Van Tieghem's comparative language. Although substantially and stylistically very distinct from one another, Rużar Briffa (1906-1963), Ġorġ Zammit (1908-1990), Anton Buttigieg (1912-1983) and Karmenu Vassallo (1913-1987) gradually eliminate the remnants of patriotic inspiration and adopt a thoroughly subjective, inward-looking attitude. Instead of socio-political preoccupations, their lyricism at its best presents a second stage of the main romantic evolution, an intensified investigation of man as a passionate victim of his sensations as well as of the supreme forces of nature with which (or better, with whom, since the world of empirical data is always personified and frequently transformed into an ethereal, omnipresent feminine figure) they can develop a psychological relationship. Since this is their particular way of passing from monologue to dialogue, from isolation to extrapersonal commitment, the focal character of their poetry is self-confessional, at times overtly diaristic.

Ružar Briffa imposes upon his own sensibility a set of time-space limits which transcend their original sensory data insofar as they convey the imaginative sublimation of a suffering soul. Ġorġ Zammit seeks the mysteriously religious significance of creatures and objects with which he is hauntingly surrounded and sees in empirical data a mystic manifestation of infinity which is both external and spiritual. Anton Buttigieg omits the ideal-real dichotomy by depicting reality (which is largely vegetative and sensitive) according to an ideally antropomorphicized conception. His seemingly descriptive poetry, richly suggestive and allusive, is only a sublimated projection of his own internal universe.

Karmenu Vassallo, whose first poetic phase (1932-1944) is basically determined by Leopardi's poetics of socio-psychological exclusion on the one hand, and poetry of negation, as evinced by his central lexical choices and syntactic patterns, on the other, has a contrasting identity: he is perhaps the only Maltese poet ever to reveal a subtle affinity with the *Sturm und Drang* state of soul (a directly Italian, and indirectly German, assimilation), but he also ends up by denying humanity in general, and poets in particular, the possibility of ever creating illusions. This anti-Kantian negation is evidently traceable back to both philosophical and literary spirits of modern Europe.

The modern movement: controversy, reconstruction and detachment

The uninterrupted repetition of these and other romantic motives, as well as the imitative reproduction of a definite set of related formal components, by a group of minor poets whose literary activity coincides chronologically with that of the said major ones (a span of time ranging approximately from the thirties up to the sixties of this century) is the immediate cause which necessitated the recent anti-romantic controversy conducted by a new crop of young poets, like Charles Coleiro (b. 1935), Victor Fenech (b. 1935), Achille Mizzi (b. 1936), Daniel Massa (b. 1937), Mario Azzopardi (b. 1944), Philip Sciberras (b. 1945), Oliver Friggieri (b. 1947), Albert Marshall (b. 1947) and others. Alongside the mainstream of the young generation, however, Anton Buttigieg contributed and is still contributing to a sort of formal compromise between the older and the modern type.

The modern period is characterized by the radical contestation of the thematic content (predominantly patriotic, traditionally religious and ecclesiastical, nocturnal, introvert and emotional) of the previous literary school which, as happens to all movements which prolong their existence too much, started to bear evidence of decadence and extinction in the uninspiring work of numerous minor poets. The new version of the cerebralists, regarding both literature (and particularly the verse form) and Maltese society (which had long started to modify its identity and to experience different modes of thinking and behaving), goes back to the sixties of this century when the new national awareness naturally ought to have given rise to more complex attitudes in the creative field.

In 1949 Ġužé Aquilina had already pointed out the need of a thorough regeneration of Maltese poetry. He suggested that poets had to give due importance to technical, especially metrical, experimentation and to the exploration of a new self, much more creatively subjective according to the trends of modern knowledge and experience. He also implied that such a renewal was necessarily destined to introduce new syntactic structures in the language which the traditionalists had only handled in an almost anonymously uniform manner and in accordance with the old norms of grammatical equilibrium and academic decorum. However, it was only an article published by the present writer in 1966 which finally put forward the quest for a radical modernization of literature, and particularly of poetry. Discussion soon started to gain momentum, mainly owing to the participation of other budding poets and prose writers, like Mario Azzopardi, Albert Marshall, Raymond Mahoney, Philip Sciberras, Achille Mizzi, Joe A. Grima, Charles Casha, Alfred Degabriele. The other points of reference were various major modern writers, such as Thomas Mann, Ernest Hemingway, Evelyn Waugh and Graham Greene about whom Peter Serracino Inglott, himself a poet and a critic as well as philosopher, wrote a series of articles on *Il-Ħaddiem* during the period 1966-1967. Modern foreign poets, like Vladimir Mayakovsky, Yevgeny Yevtushenko, Salvatore Quasimodo, Petr Bezruc, Dylan Thomas and Pedro Salinas started to be translated into Maltese by the local poets themselves.

The critical appraisals of the members of this reformist group repeatedly referred to what the major international exponents of modern poetry — like Pound, Eliot, Apollinaire, Mallarmé, E.E. Cummings, Ungaretti, Claudel, Valery, Alain Robbe-Grillet — had already declared and adhere to.

In 1946 Aquilina's second edition of his anthology *Il-Muża Maltija* (The Maltese Muse) featured Wallace Gulia (b. 1926), Marjanu Vella (1927-1988) and Charles Coleiro, all of whom gave evidence of being preoccupied with a set of modern themes and of being fully conscious of the need of experimenting with new poetic forms and syntactic structures, as well as of giving a cerebral flavour to their metaphors.

During the period 1966-1972 a number of shared anthologies of modern verse were widely covered and discussed in the leading newspapers and gradually motivated a public debate which ultimately assumed a social, political and religious character, beside its basic literary one. *Kwartett* (Quartet), 1965, by J.J. Camilleri, V.

Fenech, D. Massa, C. Vella; *Dħaħen fl-Imħuħ* (Smoke in the Minds), 1967, by Ġ. Borg, O. Friggieri, A. Marshall; *L-Għar ta' l-Enimmi* (The Cave of Enigmas), 1967, by A. Mizzi; *Priżmi* (Prisms), 1968, by L. Cachia and Ph. Sciberras; *Antenni* (Antennae), 1968, by M. Azzopardi, J.J. Camilleri, V. Fenech, R. Mahoney; *Analiżi '70* (Analysis '70), 1970, by M. Azzopardi, V. Fenech, O. Friggieri, D. Massa; *Mas-Sejħa tat-Tnabar* (The Call of the Drums), 1971, by M. Azzopardi, O. Friggieri, A. Mizzi; and *Dwal fil-Persjani* (Light in the Blinds), 1972, by M. Azzopardi, J. Friggieri, O. Friggieri, R. Mahoney, Ph. Sciberras are the main documents of a radically new approach both to literary values and to human behaviour alike.

The idea of publishing shared anthologies is to the credit of Victor Fenech, who edited *Kwartett* (Quartet) in 1965. Three Maltese poets, Joseph Abela, Manwel Cassar and John Sciberras, had already produced *Tlitt Iqlub* (Three Hearts) in 1953, but it remained an isolated case. Fenech got the idea in 1965 on seeing some Northern House poetry pamphlets, published in sets of four authors, and he thought the scheme could be adopted locally with some modifications. In 1962 Penguin Books had already launched their "Penguin Modern Poets" series, featuring some thirty poems by each of three modern poets in a single volume. The idea gathered momentum in the literary life of the island and a whole spate of shared anthologies soon appeared in the market. Running parallel to these were the more traditionally Maltese 'collective anthologies', involving single works by a large number of writers. In recent years the trend has slowed down considerably.

The titles of these shared anthologies are in themselves a clear indication of a substantially untraditional way of creating metaphors. Whilst former book titles had an exclusively sentimental touch (e.g. *Weraq mar-Riħ*, Leaves in the wind, 1932, by N. Cremona; *Dell ta' l-Imgħoddi*, Shadow of the past, 1936, by T. Vassallo;

Fanali bil-Lejl, Nocturnal Lamps, 1949, by A. Buttigieg; *Il-Waltz tad-Dellijiet*, The Waltz of the Shadows, 1949, by Ġ. Pisani; *Fuq Ġwienaħ il-Għana*, On the Wings of Song, 1964, by Ġ. Zammit), the modern ones prefer to select their imagery from the immediate world of urban, industrialized experience (e.g. *Antenni*, Antennae), or to reveal the detached frustration of a distressed psyche (e.g. *Dħaħen fl-Imħuħ*, Smoke in the Minds; *L-Għar ta' l-Enimmi*, The Cave of Enigmas). Such a deliberate substitution of emotional metaphors by a set of others which are rather cerebral, mathematically precise, logically coherent but apparently too densely inter-related to be easily comprehensible, is one of the most consistent features of the new poems themselves. This proves further that the modern poetic experience is necessarily transferred from the warm abode of the heart, as the so-called seat of passions, to the labyrinth of the mind, now considered as a paradoxically delicate, fragile machine which cannot actually insert itself adequately within the predetermined confines of an objective, impersonal complex.

The romantics had repeatedly sought to sublimate the conception of poetry as the intimate revelation of the heart and had equated their own work with an aesthetic reconstruction of autobiographical data. The following book titles are just a few typical examples of this fundamental orientation: *Kwiekeb ta' Qalbi* (Stars of my Heart), 1944, by K. Vassallo; *Moħba tal-Qalb* (The Heart's Secret Path), 1945, by F. Camilleri; *Mill-Milja ta' Qalbi* (From the abundance of my Heart), 1956, by V. Ungaro; *Tlitt Iqlub* (Three Hearts), 1953, by J. Abela, M. Cassar and J. Sciberras; *Meta toħlom il-Qalb* (When the Heart dreams), 1962, by G. Delia. On the other hand, although Charles Coleiro is one of the first protagonists of the modern movement, the title of his book, *Mirja ta' Qalbi* (Mirrors of my Heart), 1964, indicates his reluctance to part irrevocably with tradition.

Notwithstanding the impression of optimism which these poets suggest, an intelligent examination of their innermost self shows a deep dissatisfaction with themselves and with the outer region which surrounds them. At times the subject-object rapport betrays the presence of an existentialist attitude (Sartre, Camus, Ionesco and Brecht as well feature in their manifestos) and consequently the inherent frustration ends up with transforming the apparently indomitable protagonist into a sceptically hostile victim of superior forces. The best instances of this psychic dialectic are provided by Victor Fenech, Philip Sciberras, Mario Azzopardi, Carmel Attard and Doreen Micallef. From the point of view of poetic technique, this incapability of coming to terms with the world of sensory experience results in metaphorical density. Symbols seem to breed and over-populate the poem without leaving any marginal space for literal or rhetorical intervals. Pure poetry proved to be difficult for the average reader and for some of the traditionalists as well.

As social animals these poets only develop a love-hate relationship with their environment. This dualism is also characteristic of some modern Maltese novels and short story collections such as Alfred Sant's *L-Ewwel Weraq tal-Bajtar* (The first Palms of the Prickly Pears), 1968, Frans Sammut's *Il-Gaġġa* (The Cage), 1971, and *Samuraj* (Samurai), 1975, and Oliver Friggieri's *Il-Gidba* (The Lie), 1977, *Fil-Parlament ma jikbrux Fjuri* (In Parliament no Flowers grow), 1986, and *Fil-gżira Taparsi jikbru l-fjuri* (In the island Taparsi flowers grow), 1991.

Protest, the elimination of traditional taboos and the negation of rigid socio-religious rituals, the search for a different identification of a true individual and national self, and other unfamiliar motives were conveyed through a range of poetic forms which amply reflected the extralit-erary involvement of the group and the fresh cultural orientation of the younger generation. Polyphonic prose, projective verse, the *recit*, cut-out and concrete poetry and other unconventional techniques, generally of an English or an American modern origin, aimed at provoking a critical confrontation between the authors and the widest possible range of readers and at providing poetry with an authentic justification for its existence and then for its diffusion among people from all walks of life.

Thematically, this attitude implied that all human experiences are inherently adequate to be considered as prime matter for poetic transformation and sublimation, whilst from a purely formalistic point of view it evidently proclaimed the belief that all aprioristic literary codes had to be done away with. Consequently, the definition of a poem in terms of its genre became only an *a posteriori* conclusion. Practically this amounted to the conscious elimination of generic distinctions and of the traditionally supreme recognition granted to the adherance to a prescribed set of stylistic precepts.

The *Moviment Qawmien Letterarju*, informally set up in November 1966 and officially founded in January 1967, was meant to organize this whole process of literary revival and to fuse all innovations in one concerted effort. Writing was intended to be translated into experience which had to go far beyond the restricted boundaries of normal literary routine. The title of the movement's magazine itself, *Il-Polz* (The Pulse), launched in July 1967, immediately indicated that these poets and writers were detecting an intimate relationship among rhythm, pulse, beat and jazz music. (It is impossible to isolate this mentality from that of the Beat Generation poets of the fifties and the sixties, such as Jack Kerouac, Allen Ginsberg and Gregory Corso). As a matter of fact, their radio literary programme was called *Beat and Literature*, whilst they soon embarked on a series of public recitals of poetry and pop music. Night clubs, hotels, streets and squares were the new venue for experiencing literature conceived of as a happening rather than as just a written work. The poet was not to be any more, to quote Dylan Thomas, "a person of words" but "a person of words in action," and the poem was gradually becoming "an event, a happening, an action perhaps, not a still-life or an experience put down, placed, regulated." Such activities were obviously intended to substitute the previous ghetto-like gatherings of traditional literary societies.

Whereas the sixties form a short, turbulent period of experimentation, public debate and controversy, the seventies and the eighties are actually the period when literary equilibrium was finally reached. The best examples of modern Maltese verse illustrate the general conclusion that the modern trends, modified and adapted to the conditions of the Maltese temperament, had to be channeled through a path where the inquisitive self and the environment of an ancient, solitary island form one unique whole. A brief account of the contributions of the more important contemporary poets may suffice to justify these assertions.

Mario Azzopardi, perhaps the angriest among the poets who made their presence felt in the late sixties, is himself a prominent exponent of the new current. His fine lyrical vein is an indication, albeit paradoxical, of inner tranquillity, since the real world is now the one within the self. The rebel has adopted the behaviour of a mystic constantly in search of ultimate truths. The objective world is now interiorized and symbols, equally original and disturbing, form the suggestive language of an inward-looking pilgrim talking only to himself. On the other hand, Achille Mizzi is highly sensuous and evocative, densely allusive and at times really obscure. He only knows the mood of a grave thinker perceiving the essence of existence through subtle images. His metaphors are frequently passionate but are intelligently formed as an effort to reconcile what is empirical with what is psychological. His poems at times suggest a sort of relationship between human life and scientific technique. Eternity and history constitute a world of sharp confrontation. The self is at times lost but individuality is a sense animating all his works.

Doreen Micallef's main concern is the transformation of verse into a monologue conducted along different levels of awareness. This psychological condition is largely reflected in the syntactic patterns and the lexical choices she adopts in all her poems. Daniel Massa has contributed considerably to the renewal of Maltese verse especially in the field of symbolization, the choice of vocabulary, the formation of new rhythms, and the widening of the thematic content. His poetry is highly allusive and gives significance even to the minutest detail. Carmel Attard is essentially a lyric poet revisiting the past with the specific intention of renewing schemes and metaphors and of eliminating the rather abrupt distinction between tradition and modernism. Nostalgia and subtle irony are fully made use of in order to create an environment that is equally intimate and indifferent.

Philip Sciberras is deceptively descriptive and constantly philosophical. His deep sense of futility, at times utterly pessimistic, is combined with a profound faith in the innermost intuitions experienced by man when subjected to a thorough psychospiritual divestment. Social relevance is only of secondary importance to him, although some of his better works are effective owing to their dependence on known events. Oliver Friggieri transforms his own experience into a paradigm of universal suffering and insists on the relationship between love and death, God and history. Man's inability to communicate and to come to terms with existential and social dilemmas is eventually explained as the real essence of the human condition. Emotional content and philosophical principles constitute the major sources of his inspiration.

Other poets like Albert Marshall, Joe Friggieri and Ġorġ Borg still maintain a highly lyrical note, choose their vocabulary from the registers of sentiment and intimacy, and dwell on the potentiality of poetry as a means towards self-identification. Their world is universal, rarely national, even if social relevance creeps in at intervals.

From an exclusively literary point of view, the reaction of the young poets was systematically directed against the typical components of some of the previous models: stereotyped phraseology, the purely emotional metaphorical nucleus, strict metrical formality, syntactic patterns which appeared to be obstinately distinct from traditionally unknown syntagmatic, paradigmatic, graphological, grammatical and lexical deviations. Consequently, openly declaring the absolute need of a radical renewal of forms and contents, these poets started to give great attention to English and American poetry. Among other things, the traditional sharp distinction between prose and poetry began to be considered as simply mental and phenomenological, and in no way substantial. Following Olson's dictum that the artist should escape towards, and not from, reality, and anxious to formulate a different poetic register, much more flexible and immediate, Victor Fenech and some others gradually eliminated the dichotomy. They did this mainly through the adoption of an utterly unpredictable anti-poetic diction, in which Wallace Stevens had already recognized "that truth, that reality to which all of us are forever fleeing," but, needless to say, the process is much more complex and aims at a fusion of both genres.

This attitude, which is both literary (since it concerns a taste and a choice regarding the written medium) and psychological (since it involves a new conception of what is humanly poetic or immediately translatable into poetry) has recently resulted in a harmonious fusion in Fenech's prose poems. In virtue of his latest creations Fenech has not only found the ultimate equilibrium towards which his poetry has been constantly heading since

73

the earliest published experiments in the sixties, but has also inserted Maltese poetry within the mainstream of international prose poetry production. Since the publication of Oscar Wilde's *Poems in prose* in the *Forthnightly Review* of July 1894, experimentation in this direction led to a highly creative synthesis of the narrative structure and the distinctive features of metaphorical composition. The works of Solzhenitsyn, who almost identified this genre with a recreated version of the traditional allegorical fables, and those of an impressive number of French poets, such as René de Obaldia, Pierre Bettencourt, Henri Pichette, Marcel Béalu, André Hardellet and Julien Gracq, have provided the Maltese writer with a reliable point of reference which admits a wide range of minor variations within the spectrum of its own basic definition. As a matter of fact Ġorġ Borg's *Stejjer minn tarf ir-Raħal* (Tales from the Village outskirt), 1977, claim to be poems in prose and are intimately related to Wilde's poetic fables in terms of narration and allegory, but are also different owing to the inclusion or exclusion of other aspects. (On the other hand, the prose of the major romantic poets, such as Dun Karm, Anton Buttigieg, Ġorġ Zammit and Karmenu Vassallo has always maintained a poetic spirit throughout, even if these writers were not aware of any literary fusion of the two genres which up to a few years ago were considered as mutually exclusive).

Being almost nervously conscious of their foreign contemporary colleagues − the most important ones being T.S. Eliot, Ezra Pound, G.M. Hopkins, the Liverpool poets, the English social poets of the thirties and others − the protagonists of this group could at last claim that they were moving apace with the most recent revivals. The initial historical disadvantage of Maltese literary evolution was finally surpassed.

The problem of identity

Contemporary Maltese writers are almost unanimously engaged in portraying man in his eternal, absolute dimension. The romantics had succeeded in discovering the national self, and their basic intuition regarded man as a citizen, an inhabitant of a historically rich island. Alongside this conception the earlier writers themselves insisted on individuality as the prerogative of man as a human being and not simply of man as a mere member of a tiny community. Identity, both collective and personal, human and national, was seen in itself as the real essence of existence; national pride and personal distinctiveness are basically the complex offshoots of the same historical achievement. As this consciousness reached maturity and was fully developed on the creative level, it seemed that the time was ripe for a profounder revision of such an attainment. The exploration of the most diverse literary forms emanates from a deep urge to use all given means to attain self-fulfillment.

On the political plane Malta moved consistently ahead and made considerable strides in its efforts to be inserted in the contemporary outside world. Social and economic advancements brought about a different view of life and a set of new demands. The intercourse with foreign countries increased and international criteria had to be kept in mind as a constant point of reference. In trying to come to grips with this intriguing challenge writers know they have to face it both as keen observers of their immediate milieu and as intellectual interpreters of existence itself. The national and the universal levels at times overlap and are definitely engaged in a continuous relationship. The principle of individuation, sought after, discovered and sublimated by the previous writers, has since the seventies assumed subtle shades of meaning. Self-knowledge has gradually become a sort of collective conscience uniting writers together in search of something unknown. Although it initially had a decidedly Maltese point of reference, Maltese literature has since travelled much in diverse directions and is constantly heading towards a condition where man, the sea, the ancient land, the sun, the landscape and all the obvious characteristics of an island, traditionally identified with the real nature of a country, assume a cosmic, ambiguous significance.

The basic problem to be faced by the Maltese writer will long be how to strike a middle course between the two extremes of being faithful to the place of origin and belonging to the outer world. Citizenship will go on assuming the double role of national identification and universal significance. The archetypal pattern of man the traveller is still the one most insistently adopted to portray the image of the self in search of justification in terms of history and relevance in terms of new demands and conditions.

Insularity has always been transformed into paradigm, a state of being which is both local and cosmic in implication. The island which the romantics have discovered and idealised to assert their own identity has eventually been transformed into a symbol of the human condition itself. Man himself is now an islander reaching out for the wide world where an alternative way of being can be explored. French Existentialism has exerted great influence on most modern writers and it has paradoxically provided them with the necessary intellectual content whereby to justify their own predicament of members of a small island community.

As writers make great efforts to attain a higher degree of social relevance, their spiritual condition seems to be more identifiable with that of the inward looking mystic. Traditional religiosity has been largely substituted by a deeper sense of the mystery encompassing existence itself. They have more questions to put than answers to provide. The island itself is perhaps going through such a process of self-reappraisal. Traditions and myths which poets and novelists since the sixties have been divesting of any merit and dignity are now being similarly treated by the younger generation itself. Perhaps the impact these writers had on the population has been much greater than they themselves ever imagined. It all leads to the conclusion that even in such a tiny state writers can really play a decisive role in the process of modernisation.

Bibliography

Publications by Oliver Friggieri

I. Books

La cultura italiana a Malta — Storia e influenza letteraria e stilistica attraverso l'opera di Dun Karm, Leo S. Olschki, Firenze, 1978, pp.168.

Movimenti letterari e coscienza romantica maltese, Guido Miano, Milano, 1980, pp.56.

Cross Winds — An Anthology of Post-War Maltese Poetry, Wilfion Books, Renfrewshire, xxxiv + pp.106.

L'esperienza leopardiana di un poeta maltese; Karmenu Vassallo, Edizioni Spes, Milazzo, 1983, pp.120.

Storia della letteratura maltese, I, Edizioni Spes, Milazzo, 1986, pp.400.

Saggi sulla letteratura maltese, Università di Malta, 1989, pp.168.

II. Critical Studies

"Il poeta nazionale di Malta — osservazioni linguistiche", *Le lingue del mondo*, Firenze, XLII, 5, 1977, pp.421-422.

"La cultura italiana a Malta nell'Ottocento e nel primo Novecento, *Il Veltro*, Roma, 16, 1977, pp.36.

"A History of Maltese Literature: its Nature and Extension", *Le lingue del mondo*, Firenze, XLIII, 6, 1978, pp.502-505.

"A Brief Survey of the History of the Maltese Novel" (in Arabic), *Al Fusul*, Tripoli, 1979, pp.238-249.

"New Bearings in Modern Maltese Poetry", *Trends*, Renfrewshire, Vol. 2, 4, 1979, pp.45-54.

"L'incontro ideale tra il Leopardi e un poeta maltese: Karmenu Vassallo", *Critica letteraria*, Università di Napoli, VIII, 28, 1980, pp.526-558.

"Trends in Modern Maltese Poetry" (in Arabic), *Almujtam'a*, Damascus, 1980, pp.44-45.

"Relazioni storico-culturali tra romanticismo italiano e romanticismo maltese", *Silarus*, Salerno, XVII, 98, 1981, pp.1-7.

"Gian Antonio Vassallo — l'introduzione dell'eredità romantica italiana nella poesia maltese", *Critica letteraria*, Università di Napoli, IX, 33, 1981, pp.717-744.

"Mario Azzopardi: Malta's New Experience Through Poetry", *The Journal of Commonwealth Literature*, Oxford, XVI, 1, 1981.

"Modern Trends in Maltese Literature", *Portland Review*, Oregon University, Vol. 27, 2, 1981, pp. 32-33.

"Il contributo dei poeti alla trasformazione socio-politica di Malta", *Atti-Convegno Internazionale*, Cagliari, 1981, pp.69-82.

"Aspects of Maltese Literature" (in Greek), *Kanali 14*, Athens, 80, 1981, pp.69-82.

"A History of Maltese Literature: its Nature and Extension", *Revue*, Paris, 20, 1981, pp. 28-30.

"Una introduzione alla storia della poesia maltese", *Il delfino*, Torino, XII, 63, 1982, pp. 17-18.

"Il romanticismo italiano e l'inizio della poesia maltese", *Otto Novecento*, Varese, VI, 1982, pp.5-40.

"Cenni sulla fortuna di Dante nella letteratura maltese", *Studi danteschi*, Firenze, LIV, 1982, pp.175-190.

"Il romanticismo italiano e la nascita della letteratura maltese", *Il delfino*, Torino, XII, 65, 1982, pp.6-8

"Influssi manzoniani sul poeta nazionale di Malta, Dun Karm", *Silarus*, Salerno, XVIII, 101-102, 1982, pp.4-12.

"Una pagina della storia risorgimentale italo-maltese – il caso Zauli Sajani", *Il delfino*, Torino, XII, 67, 1982, pp.14-19.

"Letteratura e lingua nell'isola di Malta", *La grotta della vipera*, Cagliari, 22-23, 1982, pp.26-31.

"An Introduction to the History of Maltese Literature" (in Macedonian), *Kulturen Zivot*, Skopje, 6, 1982, pp.31-33.

"La critica e la letteratura delle minoranze: aspetti dell'esperienza maltese", *Atti – Convegno internazionale*, Cagliari, 1982, pp.95-105.

"Elementi leopardiani nella riflessione estetica di un poeta maltese: Karmenu Vassallo", *Silarus*, Salerno, XIX, 105, 1983, pp.21-27.

"Dun Karm, il poeta nazionale di Malta – la scoperta dell'ispirazione popolare", *Il delfino*, Torino, XIII, 69, 1983, pp.6-9.

"Literature and language in the island of Malta" (in Greek), *Delfika Tetradia*, Athens, I, 1983, pp.41-45.

"L'esperienza foscoliana di Dun Karm, il poeta nazionale di Malta", *Il delfino*, Torino, XIII, 71, 1983, pp.9-20.

"Gian Antonio Vassallo 1817-1868", *Il delfino*, Torino, XIII, 73, 1983, pp.7-12.

"La letteratura maltese: l'esperienza di un piccolo popolo mediterraneo", *Impegno 80*, Mazara del Vallo, V, 13-15, 1983, pp.8-11.

"Dal secondo Ottocento al primo Novecento: nuove aperture romantiche in alcuni poeti minori maltesi", *Critica letteraria*, Università di Napoli, XI, 39, 1983, pp.335-348.

"The Evolution of Poetry in Malta" (in Norwegian), *Vinduet*, Oslo, 38, 1984, pp.66-70.

"Malta and the Poetics of National Awareness: A Brief Account of Modern Poetry", *Scripta Mediterranea*, Toronto University, V, 1984, pp.39-54.

"La lingua leopardiana del dolore in un poeta maltese: Karmenu Vassallo", *Il delfino*, Torino, XIV, 80, 1984, pp.18-21.

"The Evolution of Poetry in Malta", *The Journal of Commonwealth Literature*, Oxford, XIX, 1, 1984, pp.22-26.

"An Account of Contemporary Maltese Poetry", *Revue*, Paris, 24, 1984, pp.36-38.

"Malta cristiana e il suo poeta", *Litterae Communionis*, Milano, 10, 1984, pp.42-49.

"Malta come una minoranza nazionale – problemi di identità e di partecipazione", *Prometeo*, Messina, IV, 15, 1984, pp.53-62.

"Riflessi pirandelliani nella letteratura maltese", *Studi pirandelliani a Malta*, ed. S. Milioto, Palumbo, Palermo, 1985, pp.51-62.

"Gian Antonio Vassallo – la lirica della patria in un poeta maltese dell'Ottocento", *Cenobio*, Lugano, XXXIV, 2, 1985, pp.146-153.

"Influssi manzoniani sul poeta nazionale di Malta, Dun Karm", *Il delfino*, Torino, XV, 84, 1985, pp.10-16.

"In Search of a National Identity: A Survey of Maltese Literature", *Durham University Journal*, Durham, LXXVIII, 1, Dec. 1985, pp.121-136.

"Il poeta nazionale di Malta: aspetti dell'identità culturale", *Prometeo*, Messina, V, 19, 1985, pp.25-36.

"Dun Karm, the National Poet of Malta", *Revue*, Paris, 28, 1985, pp.30-32.

"Influssi manzoniani sul poeta nazionale di Malta", *Arcadia*, Berlin – New York, 21, 3,

1986, pp.276-284.

"Il poeta nazionale di Malta, Dun Karm – la fede tradotta in lirica", *La vallisa*, Università di Bari, 14, 1986, pp.5-24.

"Rużar Briffa: un poeta lirico maltese", *Prometeo*, Messina, VI, 23, 1986, pp.9-17.

"An Account of Maltese Poetry" (in Serbo-Croat), *Istra*, Pula, 1-2, 1986, pp.101-108.

"Ġwann Mamo and Maltese Literature" (in Russian), *Inostrannaya Literatura*, Moscow, 3, 1986, pp.245-246.

"Malta and the Poetics of National Awareness", *Revue de Littérature Comparée*, Tours, 2, 1986, pp.207-218.

"The Language Question in Malta: A Search for National Identity" (in Serbo-Croat), *Zivot*, Zagreb, 5-6, 1986, pp.492-495.

"La evolucion de la poesia en Malta" (Spanish-English parallel text), *Equivalencias*, Madrid, 10, 1986, pp.128-141.

"Malta and the Poetics of National Awareness", *Nouvelle Europe*, Luxembourg, 50, 1986, pp.21-29.

"Malská literatura – výras malého stredomorskeho národa", *Svetova Literatura*, Prague, 4, 1986, pp.234-236.

"Appunti per una indagine sui rapporti letterari tra Malta e la Sicilia", *L'editore e l'isola*, ed. C. Ruta, Pozzallo, 1986, pp.58-74.

"Dun Karm, Malteski Narodni Pjesnik", *Kalnik s Titom u Nama*, Karlovac, 1.1.1987, p.5.

"Poetul National al Maltei", *Romania Literara*, Bucarest, 26, 25.6.1987, p.21.

"Evolutia poeziei in Malta", *Steaua*, Bucarest, XXXVII, 6, 1987, pp.50-51.

"Ġwann Mamo – Maltsky autor spchecenskoreformnich romanu", *Svetova Literatura*, Prague, XXXIII, 5, 1987, pp.244-246.

"Dun Karm – the National Poet of Malta: a Lyrical Interpretation of Life and Citizenship", *Outrider*, Queensland University, 2, 1987, pp.17-24.

"Dun Karm, the National Poet of Malta", *Atenea*, Universidad de Puerto Rico, VI, 1-2, 1986, pp.117-123.

"Reprezentanti ai romanuliu maltez", *Romania Literara*, Bucarest, 34, 20.7.1987, pp.20-21.

"Dun Karm Dichter Maltas", *Merian*, Hamburg, I, Jan. 1989, pp.88-90.

"Dun Karm, the National Poet of Malta", *Nouvelle Europe*, Luxembourg, 58-59, XVII, 1988, pp.24-27.

"Dun Karm, the National Poet of Malta – A Lyrical Interpretation of Life and Citizenship", *Poetry*, Orissa, India, XIII, 1-2, 1988, pp.1-12.

"Rapporti letterari tra Malta e la Sicilia: prospettive veriste nella narrativa maltese", *Critica letteraria*, Università di Napoli, XVI, 58, 1988, pp.125-140.

"La visione della patria in Dun Karm, il poeta nazionale di Malta", *Civiltà mediterranea*, Palermo, Ott. 1988, XI, 13, pp.19-22.

"Dun Karm, Bard Naiseanta Mhalta", *Gairm*, Glasgow, 141, 1988, pp.145-150.

"Il romanticismo italiano e la nascita della letteratura maltese", *In oltre*, Brindisi, 3, giugno 1989, pp.121-124.

"Dun Karm, le poete national de Malte", *Sources*, Poesie des Regions d'Europe, cahier n. 2, Belgium, 1989, pp.3-11.

"Dun Karm, the national poet of Malta", *Boletim*, University of Parana, Brasil, 17, July-Dec. 1989, pp.27-40.

"La visita di Luigi Capuana a Malta", *Spiragli*, Marsala, 11, 4, 1990, pp.24-29.

"Maltese Literature and National Consciousness during British Colonial Rule 1800-1964", *Canadian Review of Studies in Nationalism*, Prince Edward Island, XVII, 1-2,

1990, pp.205-217.

"Dun Karm − problematica foscoliana e superamento cristiano", *Letture*, Milano, 46, no.474, 1991, pp.107-116.

"Rużar Briffa, un poeta lirico maltese", *Spiragli*, Marsala, 111, 2, 1991, pp.24-31.

"Prospettive veriste nella narrativa maltese", in *Malta e Sicilia*, ed. R. Sardo − G. Soravia, Edizioni CULC, Catania, 1988, pp.147-162.

"Dante, Foscolo, Leopardi nella letteratura maltese", *Sudpuglia*, Lecce, XVII, 4, dic. 1991, pp.131-139.

"Ġużè Muscat Azzopardi", *Poetcrit*, Maranda, India, V, Jan. 1992, pp.17-19.

"Dun Karm, the national poet of Malta: a lyrical Interpretation of Life and Citizenship", *World Literature Today*, Oklahoma, Winter 1992, pp.47-50.

"Influenza della letteratura italiana fuori d'Italia: la fortuna di Vincenzo Monti presso il poeta maltese Dun Karm, *Quaderni*, San Paolo, Brasil, nuova serie, 2, marzo 1992, pp.81-95.

"La fortuna di Vincenzo Monti in Dun Karm, il poeta nazionale di Malta", *Arcadia*, Berlin − New York, 26, 3, 1991, pp.290-302.

"La storia della poesia romantica, maltese: considerazioni metodologiche", *Arenaria*, Palermo, VIII, 22, 1992, pp.17-23.

"Dante Foscolo Leopardi nella letteratura maltese − e il dialetto diventò lingua", *Sudpuglia*, Lecce, 4, dic. 1991, pp.131-139.

"Linguistic and Thematic Cross-currents in Early Maltese Literature", *Unimar*, Maringa, Brasil, 14, no.1, 1992, pp.133-141.

"Critical Notes on Five Maltese Authors", *Outrider*, Queensland, Vol. 9, 1-2, June 1992, pp.249-263.

"Points of Contact between Italian Romanticism and Maltese Literature", *Forum Italicum*, New York, Vol.26, no.2, Fall 1992, pp.364-379.

"Cenni sulla fortuna di Dante, Foscolo e Leopardi nella poesia maltese", *Studi d'Italianistica nell'Africa Australe*, University of South Africa, Vol.5, 1, 1992, pp.103-116.

"Dun Karm, the National Poet of Malta" (in Serbo-Croat), *Stvaranje*, Montenegro, XLVII, May 1992, pp.468-472.

"Rapporti tra letteratura maltese e letteratura italiana − intervista a Oliver Friggieri", *Profili Letterari*, Lugano, II, aprile 1992, pp.72-78.

"Linguistic and Thematic Cross-currents in Early Maltese Literature", *Atenea*, Universidad de Puerto Rico, XII, 1-2, 1992, pp.39-48.

"Dun Karm e Vincenzo Monti a confronto − Nostalgie del perduto amore", *Sudpuglia*, Lecce, 4, dic. 1992, pp.115-123.

"La cultura maltese e l'Italia − l'isolamento come sfida e tema letterario", *Sudpuglia*, Lecce, 1, marzo 1993, pp.115-121.

"Leopardi e la letteratura maltese − quattro passi nella solitudine", *Sudpuglia*, Lecce, 2, giugno 1993, pp.117-121.

"Maltese Literature under the Knights of St John", *Durham University Journal*, Durham, LXXXVI, 1, January 1994, pp.51-58.

Archaeology

Anthony Bonanno

Until future archaeological discoveries prove otherwise, only the last 7000 years of the 50,000 years of man's existence in his present form of both physical and cultural evolution — that of *Homo Sapiens Sapiens* — can be documented archaeologically on the Maltese islands. His first presence on the islands is not testified before 5000 B.C., that is, not before he learnt to grow his own food and to construct sea-craft that was reliable enough to enable him to brave long distances of open sea. Although there were long periods of time, each of thousands of years, namely during the Ice Ages, when the Maltese archipelago was physically connected by land to Sicily and the European continent as a result of drastic falls in sea levels, no traces of human activity have been recorded pertaining to those times. The human molars once reputed to be characteristic of Neanderthal man and to have been found in a Pleistocene context at Għar Dalam are no longer held to constitute reliable evidence.

In spite of this, two eminent Italian scholars, Professor Emmanuel Anati, of the Centro Camuno di Studi Preistorici, and Professor Francesco Fedele, of the Istituto di Antropologia of the University of Naples, have in recent years postulated, admittedly as yet on the theoretical level, a human presence before the Neolithic age. Indeed, recent developments in prehistoric studies in other parts of the Mediterranean, in particular the Franchthi Cave in the gulf of Argos in Greece, have revealed that man had started to brave the seas as early as the Mesolithic (around 10,000 to 8,000 years ago), rather than, as it used to be believed, in the Neolithic (from 6000 B.C. onwards).

So, in these scholars' view, he could equally well have reached the Maltese islands in the earlier period. On the more tangible level, Emmanuel Anati and his wife, Ariele Fradkin Anati, have in their possession photographic documentation of "paintings" from one of the most popular and frequented caves of Malta which have been proposed as evidence for such an early human presence. The extremely draughty galleries of Għar Ħasan are far from ideal for the preservation of such paintings and this "evidence" has not yet received confirmation by further checks and scientific controls *in situ*.

Throughout the Palaeolithic (or Old Stone Age) man remained in almost total subjection to his environment for his survival. But even after he made the first, and most decisive, steps to harness nature by means of agriculture and stock-raising, man remained — and will always remain, to varying degrees — under the influence of the environment. The greatest influence exerted by man's immediate environment on his cultural development can be seen in his tools and in his architectural as well as other artistic manifestations. Where, for example, wood was abundant architecture was expressed predominantly in that material; where it was lacking and stone was available the latter made possible the creation of enduring feats of architecture and wonderful sculptural monuments.

No visitor to the Maltese islands can help being struck by the predominance of stone in their landscape. Since the beginning stone must have exerted — as it still does — a very strong impact on human life on them: it provided the main

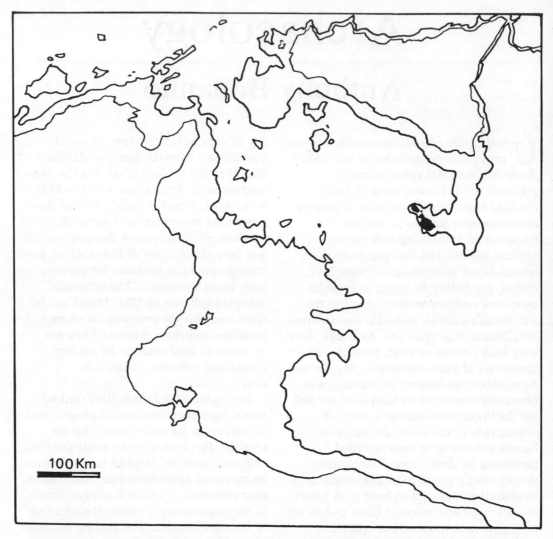

Map showing the extended shoreline of Sicily and North Africa during the maximum Würm glaciation around 18,000 years ago (after Shackleton, van Andel and Runnels). (Anati p.70)

MALTA'S GEOLOGICAL FORMATIONS	COLOUR CODE	MAXIMUM THICKNESS
Upper Coralline Limestone	Green	175m.
Greensand	Green	16m.
Clays	Blue	75m.
Globigerina Limestone	Yellow	227m.
Lower Coralline Limestone underlain by Clays and dolomitised limestone	Pink	120m. (visible) 2999m. (Naxxar borehole)

resource for buildings, both domestic and religious, as well as for some rudimentary tools. Consequently, a brief review of the geological formation and general landscape of the islands is probably helpful at this stage in order to understand better the cultural developments described in the following pages.

The Natural Setting

The Maltese archipelago consists of three major islands, of decreasing size (Malta, Gozo and Comino) and some islets. It lies right in the centre of the Mediterranean about 100 kilometres south of Sicily. The whole surface area does not exceed 320 square kilometres. There is virtually no difference in the geological formation between the islands except that Comino appears much more barren than the other two larger islands, and that Gozo has preserved proportionally much more of its clay layer and appears, therefore, much greener and more fertile. The islands' exposed rocks are all sedimentary, having been deposited on the bed of a warm sea, known as the Sea of Tethys, in the Tertiary era (around 30 to 7 million years ago).

At some point in the Pliocene the Maltese group of islands was forced up by tectonic movements. At various times during the following geological period, the Pleistocene, as a result of the accumulation of water as ice around the poles, the sea level was much lower than it is at present, so low in fact that the Maltese islands were merely the highest points on an irregular tongue of land extending southward from nearby southeast Sicily. This land bridge was submerged each time the sea level rose with the partial melting down of the ice caps during the interglacials and, finally, after the last (*Würm*) ice age, thus leaving those same high grounds exposed, as islands, almost precisely at the centre of the Mediterranean sea.

Starting from the topmost layer and working one's way down in the geological stratigraphy one meets first a fragmented crust of relatively hard, semi-crystalline limestone known as Upper Coralline which often breaks up naturally into blocks of varying sizes that the temple builders of the late Neolithic found ready for use in their impressive religious constructions. Even the Romans seem to have preferred this stone for their buildings wherever it was readily available, in particular in the areas around Rabat.

Beneath the Upper Coralline is a thin and very uneven layer of Green Sand, of hardly any significance to the cultural development of the islands. On the contrary, it is the underlying layer of Blue Clay which has made early life possible on the islands as it arrested the downward percolation of rain water into the upper layers and forced it to flow sideways and sprout out in life-giving springs. It seems to have been the only source of water exploited by Neolithic man, just as it was provided by nature, without any effort on his part to store it or to extract it. In the Bronze Age several bottle-shaped pits were hewn in the rock surface inside the village settlements for storage of either grain or, more probably, water. Later on, in historical times artesian wells were sunk through the Upper Coralline layer to reach the upper water table trapped above the Blue Clay one. This clay also played an important role in the life of primitive man as it provided the earliest building material for the wattle-and-daub and mud-brick used in domestic architecture. Clear and consistent traces of mud-brick were discovered in the 1960s among remains of hut constructions of both the Neolithic (at Skorba) and the Bronze Age (at Borġ in-Nadur). Even better preserved were those uncovered in 1987 in the construction of Temple Period semi-interred huts at Għajnsielem, Gozo. Although we have no hard evidence to confirm it the roofing system of the temples themselves is likely to have made use of clay to render it impermeable. Finally, the Blue Clay layer provided also the raw material for the local

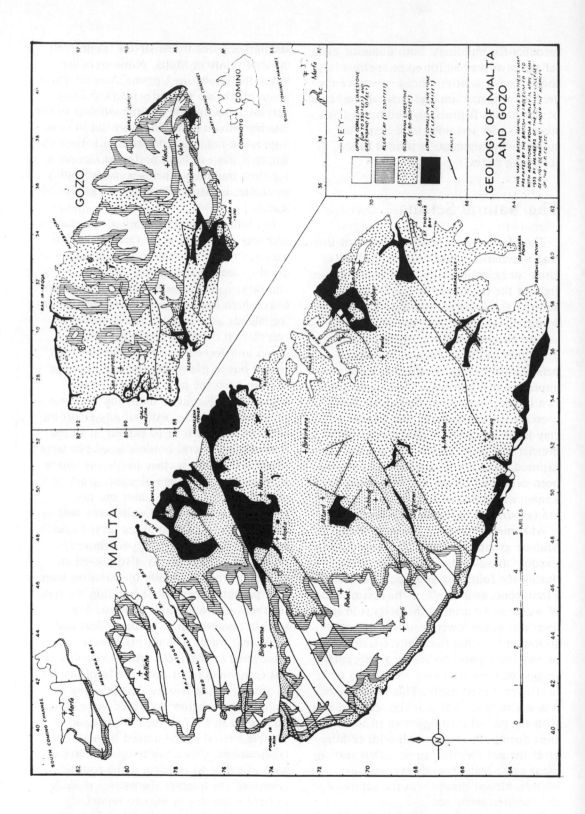

Geological map of the Maltese Islands (after Pedley, Zammit Maempel or Alexander).

production of pottery vessels and of some of the prehistoric anthropomorphic figurines, such as the well-known 'Venus of Malta' and 'Sleeping Lady'. From ancient historic times onwards, then, fired clay was recycled when it was used in *cocciopesto* floors or in cement linings of cisterns after being pounded into tiny fragments.

The layer of Globigerina Limestone below the Blue Clay has been, since the Temple Period, the source of an ideal building stone with its soft, easily worked and weather resisting texture. We find it used for temple construction in the eastern part of Malta, as well as at Ħaġar Qim, whereas it was employed only for some internal structures and decorated blocks inside the other temples that were built on Coralline outcrops, such as the Mnajdra and Ġgantija temples. It was also the preferred medium for sculptural decoration both in prehistoric and in historic times. The few known sculptures of the Roman period which seem to be of local production were carved in this material, although the large gravestone of the comic actor and lyre player Hermolaos, now kept in the Museum of Roman Antiquities in Rabat, and a sarcophagus preserved in a private house in Mdina, both carrying sculptural decoration in relief, are in the harder Coralline limestone.

Lower Coralline has more or less the same consistency and structure as Upper Coralline. Stone from this layer is also sometimes used for temple construction in prehistoric times whenever it provides the setting for them. The best example is the Mnajdra complex.

Before the end of the Pleistocene era the landscape of the Maltese Islands must have had a greatly different appearance from the present one. Large quantities of bones of Pleistocene exotic fauna, like dwarf elephants and hippopotami, that one encounters also in other islands of the Mediterranean were discovered in several caves (like that of Għar Dalam) and fissures (like the one near Mnajdra), as well as in open deposits (such as at Mrieħel) only in Malta. None have yet been discovered in Gozo or Comino. From these and other related remains it would not be too hazardous to suggest that these islands must have had a much thicker tree cover, a much richer vegetation between a quarter-of-a-million years ago and man's first interference with the natural habitat of the islands some 7000 years ago. A systematic field survey and other studies being undertaken on a regular basis by the Maltese competent authorities and Malta University teachers in co-operation with a team of foreign specialists are expected to throw revealing light on the evolution of the environment of the islands and of their habitat.

The Earliest Colonisers

When the earliest inhabitants arrived on the islands, around 7000 years ago, almost certainly from the nearest land, the larger island of Sicily, they found a very different landscape from the denuded, rocky and arid one we experience around us at present. Although it is likely that the process of soil erosion had already started through natural agents, such as the wind and the alternation of increasingly differentiated dry and wet seasons, the natural environment of the islands was yet untouched by man. Unfortunately, in the past no records were taken from excavations of relevant layers for proper analysis in order to throw light on the ecosystem prevalent on the archipelago at the time when man started to interfere with it. Consequently, we are not in a position to tell what kind of trees and plants thrived on it. It would be correct to presume, nevertheless, that the islands were much more wooded than they have been since, although this assumption still requires confirmation from future applications of palaeobotanical and palaeozoological analyses to soil samples representing this period. Nor is it possible to tell exactly

The Pleistocene fauna of the Maltese islands (after Adams 1870). (Anati p.66)

what kind of animals roamed that virgin landscape except, perhaps, that they were the same as those in existence just before the final retreat of the glaciers and the consequent, definitive rise of the sea level at the end of the last ice age, some 10,000 years ago, which left the Maltese archipelago detached from the continent ever since. Some species, such as the bear, seem to have gone extinct by the time of man's arrival, while others, like the wild boar and deer, survived for much longer since their bones turned up occasionally in Temple Period contexts. There were definitely no domestic animals and the first specimens of goats, sheep, cattle and pigs had to be shipped over the relatively long stretch of sea that separated the new home of the colonisers from Sicily, together with the first range of domesticated seeds for cultivation.

The foremost preoccupation of these early farmers after setting up home on the islands was the reclamation of agricultural land for farming. If we are right in presuming that at that point in time the islands had a much more extensive tree cover, then this reclamation could only be done at the expense of the woods. It is well known, however, that land thus reclaimed loses its naturally acquired fertility after only a few years, and it would seem that these prehistoric farmers found it necessary to leave the land fallow for a number of years to allow it to regain its fertility before it could be sown again. Meanwhile, new land had to be procured and thus, the heavier demands made on the limited available land accelerated the process of denudation which in time led to soil erosion and the loss of precious rain water into the sea.

These problems do not seem to have become acute before the end of the following period of Maltese prehistory, more than 2500 years later. During this early Neolithic period there were no phenomenal rises in population. Nor were there any astounding cultural achievements as there were in the following age. Malta's

earliest inhabitants lived in natural caves, such as that of Għar Dalam, which abound in the Maltese limestone geology, and in small, scattered villages. Only one of these has been properly explored, at Skorba, near Żebbiegħ. Their primitive abodes consisted of small oval huts built of sun-dried mud-brick or wattle-and-daub over low stone foundations. The same type of construction technique was extended to religious architecture an example of which was discovered in the same prehistoric village of Skora. Inside the so-called 'Skorba Shrine' fragments of the earliest representations of the human form were found – small, unmistakably female figurines which have been connected with the worship of a Mother Goddess, a goddess of fertility representing Mother Earth, that is commonly believed to have been the object of worship among most Neolithic farming communities.

The Temple Builders

Things start to become more complex and sophisticated in the second period of Malta's prehistory which is characterized by those astounding buildings, shaped of huge stones, that are known as megalithic temples. A new migratory wave, originating from the same source as that of the first inhabitants, that is southeast Sicily, seems to have replaced or completely subdued, at least culturally, the previous early Neolithic population. This new population brought with it some new ideas, a different cultural background. Its first recorded manifestations are collective underground tombs, examples of which were first discovered at Żebbuġ, Malta, and more recently at Xagħra, Gozo. This type of collective tombs was to develop in time into huge underground cemeterial complexes like the unique Hypogeum of Ħal Saflieni. From the Żebbuġ tombs comes a mysterious piece of sculpture, a stylized, very abstract human head with the facial features suggested by incised

Stylized clay figurine, possibly a representation of a Mother Goddess, from the Brochtorff Circle in Gozo.

lines and holes. A similar one, smaller and perhaps less refined, came forth from the Xagħra tombs. What is stranger still in these heads is the fact that they have nothing in common with the later characteristic anthropomorphic sculpture of the temple culture which developed gradually from this new population.

What is obvious about this cultural development is that while contacts with the outside world, namely with Sicily, Lipari and Pantelleria, as well as Italy and beyond were maintained, these were limited to the continued importation of raw materials for tools — such as flint and obsidian — as well as some ritual objects (like the green stone axe pendants). In brief, traffic in either direction was restricted to the material culture. For the rest, starting from the third phase of this period, the *Ġgantija* phase, this people of farmers initiated a cultural development of great consequence, but in total isolation, without inspiration from outside and without any apparent influence directed towards the outside. This cultural phenomenon, made possible by an efficient, surplus producing, agricultural economy, an equally efficient, even if primitive, social organization and a deeply-rooted, literally stone-moving belief in a great religious idea, brought about the conceptualization and the realization of such feats of architectural ingenuity as the Ġgantija temples and those of Ħaġar Qim and Mnajdra.

In their efforts to understand the processes of the cultural evolution of mankind several scholars found it, and still find it difficult to accept that such a grand culture as the one that produced the impressive Maltese temples could possibly develop independently of the great cultural movements that brought to bear on virtually all the lands bordering on the Mediterranean at the time. It is within this mental framework that we ought to try to understand the diffusionist theories that prevailed in the first half of our century, from Montelius and Elliot Smith to Gordon Childe's view of 'the irradiation of European barbarism by Oriental civilization'.

That prevalent view of the diffusion of ideas and civilization from east to west did not exclude the formulation of at least one theory which held that the cradle of Mediterranean civilization was not to be sought any longer in the east, as it had always been thought, but at the centre of the same sea, namely Malta. Luigi Maria Ugolini, writing in the 1930s favoured the view of an irradiation of civilization from the centre (*ex medio lux*) rather than from the east (*ex oriente lux*). Of course this idea has never taken root in the scholarly world but the very fact that it occurred to a serious archaeologist like Ugolini as a possible explanation of the Maltese megalithic phenomenon, is a reflection of the impact produced by this surprisingly advanced prehistoric culture on the modern mind. Indeed, in the wake of the 'radiocarbon revolution' and of the consequent upheaval in the traditional diffusionist framework, especially the establishment of the chronological priority of the Maltese temples to other megalithic phenomena both to the east and to the west of them, there were others who expressed the possibility of the idea of megalithism and its associated art having its origin in Malta from where it reached the rest of the Mediterranean.

As early as 1959 John Evans suggested that the inner shape of the Maltese temples was in the first place inspired by that of the underground collective tombs, such as those of Xemxija. Others have proposed the simple, round or oval domestic hut as the model for the most primitive form of temple. From that point onwards a logical evolution can be traced from the simple trefoil plan to the final one consisting of six apses and a shallow niche arranged symmetrically along a central axis which departed from a monumental trilithic entrance placed in the middle of a slightly concave facade. Even the building material evolved from the relatively small, sometimes shapeless, blocks of stone to carefully dressed, gigantic, ashlar blocks. The phenomenon of the temples would thus appear to have taken place locally in isolation, without any intervention from outside the islands.

Whatever our conclusions on the origins of the ideas inspiring the building of the Maltese prehistoric temples and the social and religious forces that made them possible, there is no doubt that between 5600 and 4500 years ago the Maltese islands were inhabited by an extraordinary people, extraordinary not because they were stronger or better built than us, but because they were highly intelligent and resourceful. They were certainly both technologically and artistically well endowed. Evidence of their advanced technology lies in the sheer size of the stone blocks used and, in many cases (such as at Ħaġar Qim, Tarxien and Mnajdra), in the perfect interlocking between them to provide a solid structure according to a preconceived architectural design. It will suffice to observe the high quality of the sculpture that used to adorn certain parts of the temples, both the statuary and the carvings in relief, as well as the perfection of design of the hand-moulded ceramic product, to convince oneself of the artistic genius of this people.

A ranked social organization based on chiefdoms has been suggested for the temple people, one that made possible great feats of public – or, rather, religious – building by means of a co-ordinated communal effort. Evidence of class ranking can also be gleaned in certain structural features that suggest the restriction of access to the inner parts of the temples to the chosen few.

The breakdown of this delicate social structure might well have been one of the causes of the apparently sudden collapse of this extraordinary culture. Other causes could have been a natural calamity, pestilence or the total depletion of the islands' natural resources through overexploitation. I would incline towards

the latter explanation. The appearance of certain close similarities in architecture, in pottery design and decoration, in some other parts of the Mediterranean roughly at the same time as the disappearance of the temple culture from Malta tends to suggest the abandonment of the islands by its population as a result of a compounded series of adverse natural and anthropogenic disasters.

The Bronze Age Warriors

The temple culture met with a mysterious, somewhat abrupt, end towards the middle of the third millennium B.C. Although some scholars claim to glean signs of cultural decline before the final collapse, the only possible evidence for a situation that might have led to it is a tendency towards an increasing re-trenchment of the dominating class vis-a-vis the rest of the population. Some attempts at explaining the final collapse appear more plausible than others but all remain based on varying degrees of conjecture. What is certain is that the temple people were, soon after 2500 B.C., replaced by a succession of three migratory waves originating from different sources on the European littoral of the Mediterranean, either from the north or from the northeast.

All three successive cultures show clear signs of the insecurity of the times (in sharp contrast with the peaceful tranquillity that reigned in the previous period): copper weapons, naturally defensible settlements on high ridges or flat hilltops, at times even fortified villages. So far scholarly research has mostly focused its attention on the more spectacular feats of art and architecture of the previous period, but it may well be that the Bronze Age reserves for us some unexpected surprises with regards to the denouement of the Maltese scenario at the dawn of European history when Crete was fast becoming the seat of the earliest European civilization, that splendid civilization named after the mythical king Minos, followed immediately and absorbed by the Mycenaean one which dominated the whole of the Aegean area in the second half of the second millennium. There are signs of close contacts between the Bronze Age inhabitants of the Maltese islands and these two civilizations, such as the dark stone bead with symbols in gold inlay that look identical to some characters of the Minoan script, and a fragment of a Mycenaean cup.

The *Tarxien Cemetery* people cremated their dead and deposited their charred remains in urns inside the ruins of the Tarxien temples. As yet we have not discovered any of their settlements as we have for their successors, the *Borġ in-Nadur* people, who lived on flat-topped hills and ridges which were sometimes fortified with 'Cyclopean' walls on the more vulnerable sides. We also find allusions in later Classical writers, such as Lycophron, Callimachus and Ovid, which can be interpreted as distant recollections of these contacts between the Aegean world and the contemporary inhabitants of these islands.

Lycophron relates how a group of Greek warriors settled in Malta in their wanderings around the Mediterranean as they were prevented by the gods from reaching their homelands after the long siege and destruction of Troy. Callimachus identifies Gozo, the second largest island of the Maltese archipelago, with the Homeric Ogygia, the island of Calypso, on which Odysseus was shipwrecked and spent seven of his ten-year-long *nostos*. Ovid connects the legendary reign of a king of Malta, Battus by name, with Anna, the refugee sister of Dido, queen of Carthage who, according to another legend, gave hospitality to another Homeric hero, Aeneas the founder of Rome.

The Cart Tracks

After the megalithic temples the most mysterious phenomenon of Maltese archaeology is that of the cart tracks. Traditionally they have been assigned to the Bronze Age. They do not seem to have any relation to the temples and no serious attempt has been made to connect the tracks with the megalithic constructions. I do not claim to have the final word for explaining these markings on the Maltese rock surface but my frequent encounters with them both in Malta and in other archaeological contexts around the Mediterranean compel me to assign them to the following periods, namely, from the Phoenician colonization to the end of the Roman period. It is for this reason that I prefer to discuss them at this point in the sequence of this chapter.

Although they do occur in the rocky landscape of other countries bordering the Mediterranean, in no other place do they occur with such intensity and persistence as in Malta. The reason for this may lie in the fact that it has been easier for them to be covered over by soil and vegetation abroad than it has been in Malta. I have personally observed their existence abroad in archaeological sites of the Classical age, such as in the vicinity of the amphitheatre of the ancient town of Caralis (Cagliari) in Sardinia; close to one of the gates of the Castello Eurialo, and on several spots near the necropolis of Syracuse; and on one of the main thoroughfares winding its way between the monumental tombs of Etruscan Cerveteri. Besides, my attention has on several occasions been drawn to the presence of clusters of other tracks with the same gauge as the Maltese ones elsewhere, including a large concentration of them observed by David Trump in southern France, not far from Marseille. In practically each case these ruts occurred in close association with ancient quarries.

In Malta, ancient quarries are quite easily identifiable from the dimensions between the remaining traces of the narrow trenches that were dug vertically in the quarry face prior to the extraction of the stone blocks. Occasionally, the actual blocks that have remained undetached from their bed can be measured. Although such quarries can be observed in many parts of Malta, where the rock surface has remained uncovered since their creation, I have not yet identified any in Gozo. As for the cart tracks themselves, I know only of four places in Gozo where they occur: at Ta' Lambert, Ras il-Qala, Ta' Ċenċ and Dwejra. Of these only the ones at Dwejra are cut in the soft Globigerina bedrock and large sections of the set are missing. In Malta they have been preserved almost exclusively on Coralline surfaces. They are still preserved in a substantial group at Mensija, but their counterparts at Magħtab have now been lost forever beneath the huge rubbish tip, together with the quarries associated with them.

I should confess that interest in the cart tracks was forced upon me because originally I was really interested in recording ancient quarries. But each time I detected a quarry, there was almost always a set or more of cart tracks close by or even touching on it. The greatest concentration of both quarries and cart tracks is on the Upper Coralline zone around Rabat, the ancient urban centre of ancient Malta. These can be seen in close relation in areas like Baħrija, near the church of the Maddalena near Dingli Cliffs, and Girgenti. Sometimes, as at Salina, the disused quarries were turned into cemeteries by cutting tombs, even elaborate early Christian hypogea, in their vertical faces. The most spectacular concentration of both quarry marks and cart tracks can be observed just south of Buskett, not far from Għar il-Kbir. The group of cart tracks here is better known among British visitors as 'Clapham Junction' because of the great number of intersections that remind one of similar intersections of railway lines in the station by that name south of London.

Away from Rabat, the most suggestive combination of quarry, cart track, and Roman villa I have ever come across was at Il-Brolli, near Birżebbuġa. Here one can trace one's way along some twenty metres of cart tracks from a small quarry to a large cistern which is still used as a reservoir and which once served the water requirements of a typical Roman country house, of which only sporadic traces survive in the field walls.

Cart tracks have been most frequently associated with Bronze Age settlements, in my view on rather weak grounds. Admittedly, they are sometimes found in the vicinity of Bronze Age settlements. At Borġ in-Nadur a solitary set seems directed towards the Bronze Age fortification but it does not in actual fact reach that far. In the case of Ta' Ċenċ, Gozo, the two sets are within a short distance from the Bronze Age dolmens although the earlier temple ruins of L-Imramma are even closer. The argument that the cart tracks have to be earlier than Phoenician, that is, Bronze Age at the latest, because in one or two places they are cut by the shafts of 'Punic' tombs does not hold water: firstly, because it is not quite certain that these particular tombs were in fact Punic, let alone Phoenician; secondly, Punic tombs could have quite possibly been inserted in Punic, or Phoenician, abandoned quarries and need not denote an earlier age. In fact, we have several examples of ancient tombs, even whole necropoleis, of the Classical age planted in abandoned quarries both in Malta and in other Classical sites in the Mediterranean.

In my view these ancient cart tracks – to be distinguished from those more recent ones found along old country paths – served simply as guides, like rails, for some sort of vehicle on which quarried blocks of stone were transported downhill over short distances, either to the building site or as far as the normal made-up road. This connection with quarrying is not such a novel theory anyhow; Gian Francesco Abela, the seventeenth century historian, was already suggesting that they had been used to transport quarried stone, though we should not take too seriously his view that the stone was carried to the sea-shore for exportation.

The Phoenician Traders and their Successors

"For to the south of Sicily three islands lie out in the sea, and each of them possesses a city and harbours which can offer safety to ships in rough weather.

The first one is called Melite, which lies about 800 stades from Syracuse and possesses many harbours which offer exceptional advantages, and its inhabitants are blest in their possessions; for it has artisans skilled in every manner of craft, the most important being those who weave linen, which is remarkably sheer and soft. The dwellings on the island are worthy of note, being ambitiously constructed with cornices and finished in stucco with unusual workmanship.

This island is a colony planted by the Phoenicians, who, as they extended their trade to the western ocean, found in it a place of safe retreat, since it was well supplied with harbours and lay out in the open sea; and this is the reason why the inhabitants of this island, since they received assistance in many aspects through the sea-merchants, shot up quickly in their manner of living and increased in renown.

After this island there is a second one which bears the name of Gaulos, lying out in the open sea and adorned with well situated harbours, a Phoenician colony."

(Diod. Sic. V, 12)

In this passage of his *Universal History* the Sicilian Greek historian, Diodorus, writing in the first century B.C., described Malta and Gozo as Phoenician colonies. As the Maltese islands had become a Roman possession more than a century and a half before, Diodorus was certainly referring, in so far as the Phoenician identity of the islands is concerned, to a past age, to a historical reality that had started to come about around the beginning of the seventh century B.C. at the latest.

Diodorus further tells us that the Phoenicians set up a colony in Malta as they extended their trade to the western Mediterranean basin precisely because they found in it good harbours that offered safe shelter and because it was situated out in the open sea, that is, away from the bases of their Greek rivals and on the direct sea route that connected Phoenicia with its western colonies. We are also told that through their contact with the Phoenicians, the Maltese inhabitants strengthened their economy, particularly by textile production, raised sensibly their standard of living, as well as established a good reputation for themselves.

The Phoenicians were a semitic people living in a group of autonomous cities on the coast of present-day Lebanon. Although some of these cities had been in existence a long time before, most historians agree that we can really speak of Phoenicians only from the twelfth century B.C., that is, after a series of upheavals that occurred in the region following the invasions of the enigmatic "Sea Peoples". Being hemmed in on the coast by the mountains their only outlet for commerce was the sea. They thus became seasoned sea-farers and renowned traders throughout the Mediterranean, and by the end of the ninth century B.C. had secured a foothold by means of colonies in a number of areas in the western Mediterranean.

The earliest evidence of their presence on the Maltese islands goes back to the beginning of the seventh century B.C. and consists of a rock-cut tomb containing typically Phoenician pottery and some items of luxury Greek pottery. This is followed by other tombs of the same type datable to the seventh and sixth century B.C. mostly concentrated around Rabat, Malta, and Rabat, Gozo; which tends to suggest that these two areas were already by then taking shape as the main urban settlements of the two islands, even though no archaeological remains of such an early date have been found inside them. Some distance away from Rabat, Malta, on the other hand, the standing ruins of a prehistoric megalithic temple had already been converted into a Phoenician temple. This temple, situated on the top of the Tas-Silġ hill, commanding the strategic Marsaxlokk harbour, was soon to develop into a sanctuary of universal fame dedicated to Astarte, the Phoenician goddess equivalent to the Greek Hera and the Roman Juno. Numerous inscriptions with the name of Astarte incised on votive cups were found during the archaeological exploration of the site in the 1960s. Much fewer, and of a later date, were those with a dedication to Hera. It was the Latin orator Cicero who, later on, revealed in no uncertain terms the international fame of this sanctuary which had been revered by pirates and Numidian princes, but which the covetous Roman governor of Sicily, Caius Verres, had despoiled of certain treasures.

So far it is not possible to trace the process by which the Phoenicians took possession of the Maltese islands. It was probably a slow and gradual process, starting with simple bartering arrangements on the sea shore with the prehistoric natives of the islands, like the one vividly depicted by the Greek historian Herodotus. It later developed as a modest settlement of trading agents, possibly accompanied by their families, eventually growing into a fully fledged colony. The systematic political control of the archipelago by the semitic newcomers probably did not take place before the mid-sixth century B.C. when, as a result of the loss of political autonomy of the Phoenician fatherland in the east, the western Phoenician colonies rallied under the protectorate of Carthage, the most powerful and prosperous of them, to face the threat of the common enemy, the western Greeks.

The religious rites and beliefs that were introduced in Malta by the Phoenicians can best be gleaned from inscriptions found in various localities. I shall limit myself to mentioning a few. The earliest two inscriptions, datable to the sixth century B.C., reveal the worship of Baal Hammon, the highest male divinity in the Phoenician pantheon, to whom human child sacrifice (the *molk*) was regularly offered, later substituted by the sacrifice of a lamb (the *molk omor*). Another short text, this time written on a tiny fragment of papyrus enclosed in a hollow bronze amulet, contains an imprecation against the evil spirits that beset the soul of the dead on its

journey to the world beyond. The text probably reproduces the words uttered by the goddess Isis whose image accompanies the text. Yet another inscription, found in Gozo, records the restoration of temples or shrines to various other Phoenician divinities, while the well-known identical pair of marble candelabra contain a bilingual dedication to the god Melqart/ Herakles, the protector of the Phoenician city of Tyre. Furthermore, it seems that this semitic people was much inclined to adopt religious iconography and magico-superstitious contraptions from its oriental neighbours, particularly the Egyptians. These are documented by the many amulets and necklace components of Egyptian typology found buried in rock-cut tombs, especially in Gozo.

Besides the hundreds of rock-cut tombs which belong to this period the architectural remains of a religious nature that survive are those associated with the sanctuary at Tas-Silġ – which after the fourth century B.C. was further enlarged and enhanced with architectural features of Hellenistic influence – and those of a partially rock-cut religious complex perched most suggestively right on the edge of precipitous cliffs at Ras Il-Wardija in Gozo, which seems to have had a rather short life-span of a couple of centuries between the third and first centuries B.C. The most outstanding structure of the late Punic period is, however, the square tower enclosed inside a private garden in Żurrieq. It stands about five metres high and preserves a crowning cornice of Egyptian pedigree. It could also have belonged to a religious building the rest of which has unfortunately been destroyed.

The Roman Imperialists

The Maltese islands were taken over by the Romans as a result of an expedition made in 218 B.C. by the Roman fleet under the command of Tib. Sempronius Longus, right at the beginning of the second Punic War, for the purpose of seeking out and attacking the enemy fleet. Another historian, this time a Roman writing towards the end of the first century B.C., gives us a few details of the expedition. No battles were fought, says Livy. Instead, at the approach of the Roman fleet, the commander of the Carthaginian garrison, · together with a little less than 2000 soldiers, the town and the rest of the island surrendered — a historical episode which has a close parallel in the French occupation some 2000 years later. When the consul returned to Lilybaeum, in Sicily, the prisoners — the historian does not specify who they were — were sold into slavery, except for men of noble birth. After this episode Malta remained part of the Roman commonwealth till the first third of the sixth century A.D. At the end of the second Punic War it was incorporated for administrative purposes with the province of Sicily.

We are not sure what type of government the islands had during the first two centuries of Roman rule. They certainly fell under the jurisdiction of the procurator (or governor) of the province of Sicily, as the Verres affair and Cicero's correspondence seem to imply. But a bronze inscription found in Rome in the sixteenth century clearly states that Malta had its own senate and people's assembly, although it probably reflects the situation in the first century B.C. The issue of local coinage, although based on Roman weight standards, further confirms a certain degree of autonomy in the internal administration. As Gozo was later on also allowed to coin its own money, it would seem that from around the first century B.C. Gozo started to have its own administrative set-up.

Coin minting suggests a thriving economy which finds further confirmation both in the written and in the archaeological documentation. Several writers speak highly of a kind of Maltese drapery which seems to have been much admired and sought after throughout the Roman period. Besides the two main towns of Melite and Gaulos with their temples and public buildings, some adorned with marble architecture of the highest quality, the Maltese landscape was marked by scattered agricultural estates several of which comprising sizeable olive-groves attached to farmsteads, better known as villas.

The most important town building ever to be discovered and excavated is the *domus* whose remains are now attached to the Museum of Roman Antiquities in Rabat, just outside Mdina. It was provided with a pleasant Doric peristyle and decorated with floor mosaics of the highest quality, among which small but exquisite pictures (*emblemata*) and borders with festoons and theatre masks, all crafted in *opus vermiculatum*. Only small detached fragments survive of the painted wall plaster. These features date the construction of the house to the first half of the first century B.C. Moreover, towards the middle of the first century A.D., the house was furnished with a set of portrait statues of members of the ruling imperial family. The foremost of these statues was that of the emperor Claudius himself: the separate head was carved from Parian marble while the togate statue was sculpted on richly veined *pavonazzetto* marble. Next to it was a draped statue of a young girl, originally identified as Antonia the Younger, mother of Claudius, now considered to be more likely a daughter of the same emperor.

Not less than thirty Roman villas have been identified, from remains of varying extent, throughout the Maltese countryside. The most extensive remains of the agricultural type of villa is that of San Pawl Milqi in the northwest part of Malta, but those of Ta' Kaċċatura and Żejtun, close to the southeastern harbour of Marsaxlokk, are also considerable. The distinctive features in these buildings are the surviving stone elements of the apparatus used for the pressing of olive oil. Other villas seem to be of the purely residential type, like the one close to the sea shore at Ramla Bay in Gozo, since they lack traces of agricultural activity.

From a number of inscriptions found in Malta and Gozo it appears that by the second century A.D., if not before, both Malta and Gozo had their own *municipium* and some individuals not only obtained Roman citizenship but even attained imperial honours. Some became great benefactors of their respective *municipium* and funded the erection of statues and restoration of buildings. Others enjoyed the title of patron (*patronus*) of the *municipium* or that of the first citizen (*primus* in Latin, or *protos* in Greek). Inscriptions mention also the existence of special priesthoods set up to look after the worship of the emperor or that of his wife. The inhabitants of the Maltese islands as a whole, however, do not seem to have become full Roman citizens until emperor Caracalla's final enfranchisement of the empire's provinces in A.D. 212 when that emperor extended Roman citizenship to all free-born men and women within the empire.

After Livy's account of the initial capture of Malta by the Romans, the only important historical episode connected with Malta mentioned in ancient literature is that of Saint Paul's shipwreck on the island in 60 A.D. described in the *Acts of the Apostles*. Several attempts made over the centuries to transpose the shipwreck to other islands in the Adriatic have not proved at all convincing. On the other hand, the traditional belief that the whole Maltese population was converted to Christianity during Saint Paul's three months' stay on the island does not find any support either in St Luke's account or in the archaeological record. The strongest argument in favour of this belief is, in my view and in that of many others, the Apostle's personality which would certainly not have allowed him to remain confined for such a long time in such a restricted space without doing his utmost to convert the inhabitants who saw him, after all, heal their sick.

The Early Christians and the Rule of Byzantium

The question of Christianization brings us to the time following the division of the Roman empire in two parts, the western one – on the decline from the beginning of the fourth century till its final collapse with the death of the last emperor of the west, Romulus Augustulus, in A.D. 476 – and the eastern part, converging on Byzantium which was turned into the new capital of the empire by Constantine in A.D. 330.

The literary sources do not throw much light on the vicissitudes of Malta and Gozo during this period but there is reason to believe that both found themselves under the jurisdiction of the Byzantine empire around A.D. 535 when Sicily was conquered by Belisarius, the general of Emperor Justinian. Before that date it is also possible that the two islands were taken over by Vandals and then by the Osthrogoths.

The fact that in certain Byzantine sources the names of both islands are combined in one word, Gaudomelete (the Patriarch Nicephorus), and that the name of Gozo precedes the one of Malta (Procopius) implies that although the two islands were treated together as one geopolitical entity, the previous juridical separation of Gaudos left some repercussions even in Byzantine times. Nicephorus informs us that the Byzantine emperor Heraclius (610-641) sent his nephew Theodorus, who had conspired against him, to Gaudomelete, ordering the military governor (*dux*) of the islands to amputate one of his feet on arrival. Procopius, the chronicler of Belisarius, records that the latter sailed from Sicily to North Africa and on the way "touched at Gozo and Malta" in 533.

Early Christianity in Malta is testified by the Palaeochristian underground cemeteries (or 'catacombs', as they are more commonly known), which date from the fourth century onwards, and by the remains of the basilican church built probably in the sixth century on the site of a previous Roman religious complex at Tas-Silġ. Catacombs of various sizes are quite abundant and widely scattered in Malta, suggesting that a considerable proportion of the population must have been christianized from about the fourth century. A small one, probably intended for a family, is still preserved in the vicinity of St Thomas' Tower, in Marsascala. It contains an inscribed invocation in Latin. Other small groups can be visited at Salina, near the salt pans, while those discovered on different occasions on Jesuits' Hill in Marsa were destroyed to make way for the electricity generating station. The largest concentrations are found, as to be expected, outside the boundary of the ancient town of Melite, in Rabat. The most extensive examples are St Paul's and St Agatha's catacombs. It is surprising that, apart from a suspected specimen at Għajn Gerduf near Rabat, catacombs are totally absent in Gozo.

Perhaps the most characteristic feature of these catacombs is the *mensa*, or *agape* table, that seems to have been introduced at some stage in the funerary ritual. It consists of a table, in general round, hewn out of the living rock together with a raised, sloping floor surrounding the best part of it. It is thought that our early Christian ancestors reclined on this floor, presumably on cushions, to celebrate a fraternal meal laid out on the table in commemoration of the dead.

Several catacombs preserve figurative paintings, such as those of a seated man labelled EYTUCHION inside St Paul's catacombs, a Chi-Rho monogram flanked by doves below a scallop-shell in St Agatha's catacombs, and exquisitely modelled birds decorating a canopied tomb in the smaller catacomb of St Catald. One of the small catacombs of Salina Bay is decorated with attractive but very provincial relief carvings. The carvings

inside the hypogeum at Ħal Resqun portray the story of the creation in a very primitive and spontaneous style. Inscriptions are engraved in both the Greek and Latin languages in a few of these early Christian and Byzantine burial places.

The presence of a Hellenized Jewish community living in the ancient town of Melite at this time is testified by several hypogea amidst the early Christian ones, bearing Jewish symbols and epigraphs, some of which referring to typically Jewish religious offices. One such inscription, referring to a *presbytera* named Eulogia, provides new evidence for the likelihood that women held high offices in ancient Jewish synagogues. Even if these hypogea should perhaps be dated to the fourth century or later, one could safely assume that this small but significant community was already established in Malta as early as the third century.

In Gozo, as already noted, there are virtually no catacombs and it seems as if the island was completely deserted in this period. But that life continued, even if to a greatly reduced degree, is witnessed by the number of coins of the time found there and by an eighth-ninth century lead seal inscribed with the name of Theophylact, the governor (*archon*). The seal, found in Gozo around 1960, carries a cruciform monogram on its obverse.

The Muslim Arabs and the Christian Heirs of The Roman Empire

At this stage it needs to be made clear that, in contrast with the previous sections of this chapter, the following section will be concerned exclusively with the very few archaeological tesserae that make up a very small portion of the fragmentary historical mosaic of this period. The rest of the picture falls outside the competence of the present writer. Consequently, for the historical discussion of the various episodes that constitute this and the following periods, some of which are of a quite controversial nature, such as the continuity or otherwise of Christianity under Arab rule, the reader is referred to the recent writings by Medieval historians listed in the bibliography at the end of this chapter.

Whereas it is a real wonder, and a fact established beyond any shadow of doubt, that the language spoken today by the Maltese is a legacy of the Arab occupation of the islands between 870 and 1224, the student of Maltese archaeology cannot but be negatively impressed by the almost total absence of archaeological relics of this period. For the whole of the Arab period there survive absolutely no architectural remains, not even foundations. The alleged evidence of the existence of a mosque at the site of Tas-Silġ cannot be taken seriously and the few archaeological objects that have come to light so far, namely, the graves from Rabat and the respective inscriptions, strictly speaking belong to the period of Norman conquest. This state of affairs could be attributable to a number of reasons, but the main one seems to be the fact that previous generations of Maltese archaeologists and antiquarians have either wilfully neglected this period out of religious or cultural prejudice, or else have not looked specifically for the material remains of this period, and whenever they found them they were too much concerned with earlier antiquities to give them much attention. In all fairness it should be noted that this situation has been prevalent even abroad, but there things started to move more than thirty years ago and by now have gathered an impressive momentum whereas in Malta they have not. It is only now that the Maltese archaeological establishment is provided with personnel qualified to start scratching the surface of the problem.

Gian Francesco Abela in 1647 referred to Fort St Angelo and the Gozo Castello as examples of fortifications built by the Arabs and rebuilt in later times. He claimed that circular towers of this period

were still preserved both in St Angelo and on top of the Castello in his time. Whereas on St Angelo there still exists a round tower with the lower courses consisting of blocks of stone that are larger than normal, no trace of such a tower has survived on the Castello.

After the much mythicised and inflated incursion of Count Roger of 1091, the Maltese islands remained to all intents and purposes a Norman fief under immediate Arab occupation. This is evidenced in the most glaring way by the few unmistakable archaeological remains of the period that have come down to us. These consist of a cemetery of considerable extent that was inserted in the debris that had accumulated over the centuries above the ruins of the Roman *domus* just outside the walls of the Arab city of Mdina. The position of the cemetery indicates clearly that the main town of Malta had by that time reduced itself to its present size.

Excavated by A.A. Caruana in 1881 and Temi Zammit in the 1920s all the graves were oriented in an east-west direction with the head of the corpse facing southeast, in the Muslim tradition. In most cases the graves consisted of stone 'coffins' constructed with, and covered by, thin 'sawn' slabs and containing nothing but the skeletons themselves. A score of prismatic-shaped stele in Globigerina limestone, some of which bearing the date of death and name of the deceased or citations from the Koran incised or engraved in elaborate Cufic characters, were found along with the graves. A gravestone of a different type, with an inscription commemorating the untimely death of Majmuna, daughter of Hassan, on 21 March 1174, was reputedly discovered in Gozo, 'between Xewkija and Sannat', sometime before 1809, the year of its first publication. Though some doubts have been raised recently as to its Gozitan provenance, the documentation of the placename Ta' Majmuna already by the end of the fourteenth century seems to confirm it. The epitaph is inscribed in shallow relief within and outside an elaborate geometric design on a square marble slab which carries a carved Roman architectural decoration at the back.

It is still not possible to identify properly a sequence of pottery for Malta from Arab times to the nineteenth century and much of the pottery traditionally assigned to the Arab period is now known to be later. The pottery exhibited in the same small room as the Majmuna stone in the Gozo Archaeological Museum was, in fact, previously labelled 'Arab', but is now known to be fourteenth century or later. Some glazed pottery unearthed during the excavations conducted by Italian archaeologists from the University of Rome in the 1960s at Tas-Silġ and at San Pawl Milqi are, on the other hand, securely dated to the Arab period.

After the expulsion of the Muslims from Malta in 1224 the Maltese islands fell under the rulers of Sicily – Swabian, Hohenstaufen, Angevin and Aragon. The end of Medieval Malta is marked by the ceding of the islands to the Knights of St John by Charles V of Spain in 1530. The process of Christianization and Latinization, which presumably had already started after the Norman invasion, must have been by then complete.

The study of the abandoned Maltese village of Ħal Millieri published by A. Luttrell in 1976, followed by scientific excavations inside two of its churches the following year, opened a new chapter for Maltese archaeology. For the first time a research oriented excavation was undertaken specifically on an exclusively Medieval site. This excavation brought to light for the first time a sequence of pottery types ranging from Roman to modern times. It also threw light on social aspects of the life in a small Maltese village in the fifteenth century, besides revealing the foundations of a previous, possibly thirteenth-century, church underneath the foundations of the present Annunciation one. The latter dates back to the mid-fifteenth century and preserves an almost complete cycle of frescoes that constitute a unique treasure of late-medieval painting for the islands.

The occupation of Malta by the Order of St John hails in a new chapter in the history of Malta, the beginning of the Early Modern Age, for which the role of archaeology has not even been conceived except in some courses conducted by the present writer at the University of Malta over the last twenty years. Whereas medieval archaeology has started to be practised in earnest on some Maltese sites, like Ħal Millieri, post-medieval archaeology has yet to affirm itself. The only timid attempt at post-Medieval archaeology I know of was undertaken, as a rescue operation, during the digging for the foundations of the present Law Courts in Valletta. It is hoped that with the supply of more archaeologists with a proper university training this specialization will also be catered for.

Bibliography

Introduction

ANATI, E., 'Considerazioni sulla preistoria di Malta. Nota preliminare', Fradkin Anati A. and Anati E., *Missione a Malta*, Jaca Book, Milano, 1988, pp.11-49.
'Arte parietale a Malta (Relazione preliminare)', *Bollettino del Centro Camuno di Studi Preistorici* 25-26, 1990, pp.166-172.
FEDELE, F., 'Malta: origini e sviluppo del popolamento preistorico', Fradkin Anati A. and Anati E., *Missione e Malta*, Jaca Book, Milano, 1988, pp.51-90.

The Natural Setting

ADAMS, A.L., *Notes of a Naturalist in the Nile Valley and Malta*, Edmonston & Douglas, Edinburgh, 1870.
ALEXANDER, D., 'A review of the physical geography of Malta and its significance for tectonic geomorphology', *Quaternary Science Reviews* VII.1, 1988, pp.41-53.
BOWEN-JONES, H.; DEWDNEY, J.C. and FISHER, W.B. (Eds): *Malta: Background for Development*, Department of Geography, Durham Colleges, Durham, 1961.
PEDLEY, H.M.; HOUSE, M.R. and WAUGH, B., 'The geology of Malta and Gozo', *Proceedings of the Geologists' Association* 87,3, 1976, pp.325-341.
SHACKLETON, J.C.; VAN ANDEL, T.H. and RUNNELS, C.N., 'Coastal palaeogeography of the central and western Mediterranean during the last 125,000 years and its archaeological implications', *Journal of Field Archaeology* 11, 1984, pp.307-314.
ZAMMIT-MAEMPEL, G., *An Outline of Maltese Geology*, The Author, Malta, 1977.

Archaeology of Malta and Gozo in General

ABELA, G.F., *Della Descrittione di Malta. Isola del Mare Siciliano con le sue Antichità ed altre Notizie*, Paolo Bonacota, Malta, 1647.
ABELA, G.F.; CIANTAR, G.A., *Malta Illustrata*, G. Mallia, Malta, 1772-80.
AGIUS DE SOLDANIS, G., *Il Gozo Antico-Moderno e Sacro-Profano*, NLM Bibliotheca Ms. No. 145, published in translation by G. Farrugia as *Għawdex bil-Ġrajja Tiegħu*, 2 vols., Stamperija tal-Gvern, Malta, 1936-53.
BONANNO, A., *Malta, An Archaeological Paradise*, M.J. Publications, Malta, 1986.
CARUANA, A.A., *Report on the Phoenician and Roman Antiquities in the Group of the Islands of Malta*, Government Printing Office, Malta, 1882.
MAYR, A., *Die Insel Malta im Alterum*, Oskar Beck, Munich, 1909.
Museum Annual Reports 1903 – , Malta 1905 – .
TRUMP, D.H., *Malta, an Archaeological Guide*, Faber and Faber, London, 1972.

Prehistory

BONANNO, A., 'A socio-economic approach to Maltese prehistory: the Temple Builders', *Malta: Studies of its Heritage and History*, Mid-Med Bank, Malta, 1986, pp.17-45.

An Illustrated Guide to Prehistoric Gozo, Gaulitana, Malta, 1986.
(Ed.), *Archaeology and Fertility Cult in the Ancient Mediterranean*, Grüner, Amsterdam, 1986.
'Techniche costruttive dei templi megalitici maltesi', Fradkin Anati, A. and Anati, E. (Eds), *Missione a Malta*, Jaca Book, Milano, 1988, pp.101-111.
EVANS, J.D., *Malta*, Thames and Hudson, London, 1959.
The Prehistoric Antiquities of the Maltese Islands, a Survey, Athlone, London, 1971.
FRADKIN ANATI, A. and ANATI E., *Missione a Malta. Ricerche e Studi sulla Preistoria dell'Arcipelago Maltese nel Contesto Mediterraneo*, Jaca Book, Milano, 1988.
MALONE, C., STODDART, S. and TRUMP, D., 'A house for the temple builders: recent investigations on Gozo, Malta', *Antiquity* 62, 1988, pp.297-301.
NEUBERT, S., *Die Tempel von Malta*, Gustav Lübbe, Bergisch Gladbach, 1988.
RENFREW, C., *Before Civilization*, Jonathan Cape, London, 1973.
RIDLEY, M., *The Megalithic Art of the Maltese Islands*, Dolphin Press, Christchurch, Hampshire, 1976.
TRUMP, D.H., *Skorba*, Society of Antiquaries, London, 1966.
'The collapse of the Maltese temples', Sieveking, G. de G.; Longworth, I.H. and Wilson K.E. (Eds), *Problems in Economic and Social Archaeology*, Duckworth, London, 1977.
'I primi architetti del mondo, i costruttori dei templi maltesi', Fontana, M.J., Manni Piriano, T. and Rizzo, F.P. (Eds), *Miscellanea di Studi Classici in Onore di Eugenio Manni*, Giorgio Bretschneider, Rome, 1979, pp.2113-2124.
The Prehistory of the Mediterranean, Allen Lane, London, 1980.
'Megalithic architecture in Malta', Evans, J.D. *et al.* (Ed), *Antiquity and Man*, Thames and Hudson, London, 1981, pp.128-140.
'The Maltese temples: function, development and social implications', *Bollettino del Centro Camuno di Studi Preistorici* 25-26, 1990, pp.161-166.

Cart Tracks

GRACIE, H.S., 'The ancient cart-tracks of Malta', *Antiquity* 28, 1954, pp.91-98.
PARKER, R. and RUBINSTEIN, M., *The Cart-ruts on Malta and Gozo*, Gozo Press, Gozo, 1984.

Phoenicio-Punic Period

BONANNO, A., 'The tradition of an ancient Greek colony in Malta', *Hyphen* IV,1, 1983, pp.1-17.
'Malta's role in the Phoenician, Greek and Etruscan trade in the western Mediterranean', *Melita Historica X*, 3, 1991, pp.209-224.
DIODORUS SICULUS V.12.1-4.
GOUDER, T.C., *Malta and the Phoenicians*, Lombard Bank (Malta) Ltd, Malta, 1991.
GOUDER, T., 'Fuq xi amuleti minn Malta Feniċjo-Punika', Cortis, T. (Ed), *Oqsma tal-Kultura Maltija*, Ministry for Education and the Interior, Malta, 1991, pp.67-82.
HECATAEUS, *FHG* I, 24, frag. 313.
HÖLBL, G., *Ägyptisches Kulturgut auf Malta und Gozo*, Österreichischen Akademie der

Wissenschaften, Vienna, 1989.

Missione Archeologica Italiana a Malta 1963-70, Istituto di Studi del Vicino Oriente – Università di Roma, Rome, 1964-73.

MOSCATI, S., *Il Mondo dei Fenici*, Il Saggiatore, Milan, 1966.

et al. (Eds), *I Fenici*, Bompiani, Milan, 1988.

RIZZO, F.P., 'Malta e la Sicilia in età romana: aspetti di storia politica e costituzionale', Kokalos 22-23, 1976-77, pp.173-214.

SKYLAX in MÜLLER, K., *Geographi Graeci Minores*, I, Georg Olms, Hildesheim, 1965, Not.111.

Roman Period

ACTS OF THE APOSTLES, xxvii. 37-44, xxviii, 1-11.

ASHBY, T., 'Roman Malta', *Journal of Roman Studies*, 5, 1915, pp.23-80.

BONANNO, A., 'Distribution of villas and some aspects of the Maltese economy in the Roman period', *Journal of the Faculty of Arts* VI, 4, 1977, pp.73-81.

'Malta in the third century', King, A. and Henig M. (Eds), *The Roman West in the Third Century*, B.A.R., Oxford, 1981, pp.505-513.

Roman Malta, World Confederation of Salesian Past Pupils of Don Bosco, Rome, 1992.

CAGIANO DE AZEVEDO, M., *Testimonianze Archeologiche della Tradizione Paolina a Malta*, Istituto di Studi del Vicino Oriente, Università di Roma, Rome, 1966.

CICERO, *Verr.* ii.2.176, 183; ii.4.38-39, 103-104; ii.5.27, 184.

COLEIRO, E., 'Malta nelle letterature classiche', *Missione Archeologica a Malta 1963*, Rome, 1964, pp.25-38.

'Maltese coins of the Roman period', *The Numismatic Chronicle* Se.VII.11, 1971, pp.67-71.

CORPUS INSCRIPTIONUM LATINARUM X, nos. 7501-7508.

LIVY, xxi. 51.

NAEVIUS, *Bellum Punicum* iv. 37.

PTOLEMY, *Geog.* 4.3.13.

Early Christian and Byzantine Period

BECKER, E., *Malta Sotterranea. Studien zur altchristlichen und jüdischen Sepulkralkunst*, J.H.E. Heaitz, Strassburg, 1913.

BROWN, T.S., 'Byzantine Malta: a discussion of the sources', Luttrell, A. (Ed), *Medieval Malta: Studies on Malta before the Knights*, British School at Rome, London, 1975, pp.71-87.

BUHAGIAR, M., *Late Roman and Byzantine Catacombs and Related Burial Places in the Maltese Islands*, B.A.R., Oxford, 1986.

MAYR, A., 'Zur Geschichte der älteren christlichen Kirche von Malta', *Historische Jahrbuch* XVII,3, 1896, pp.475-96.

NICEPHORUS, *Historia Syntomos*, (ed. C. de Boor), Leipzig, 1880, p.25.

PROCOPIUS, *Bellum Vandalicum*, I. 14. 15-16.

Arab and Medieval Period

BLAGG, T.F.C., BONANNO, A. and LUTTRELL, A.T., *Excavations at Hal Millieri, Malta*, University of Malta, Malta, 1990.

BRINCAT, J.M., *Malta 870-1054. Al-Himyarī's Account*, Said International, Malta, 1991.

GRASSI, V., 'Materiali per lo studio della presenza araba nella regione italiana, I. L'epigrafia araba nelle isole maltesi', *Studi Magrebini* 21, 1989, pp.9-92.

LUTTRELL, A., *Medieval Malta. Studies on Malta before the Knights*, The British School at Rome, London, 1975.

'L'abitato medievale a Malta: un approccio archeologico', *Atti del Colloquio Internazionale di Archeologia Medievale, Palermo-Erice 20-22 settembre 1974*, Palermo, 1976, pp.3-12.

(Ed), *Hal Millieri, a Maltese Casale, its Churches and Paintings*, Midsea, Malta, 1976.

MAYR, A., 'Zur Geschichte der alteren christlichen Kirche von Malta', *Historische Jahrbuch* XVII,3, 1896, pp.475-96.

ROSSI, E., 'Le lapidi sepolcrali arabo-musulmane di Malta', *Rivista degli Studi Orientali* 12, 1929, pp.428-444.

WETTINGER, G., *The Jews of Malta in the Late Middle Ages*, Midsea, Malta, 1985.

'The Arabs in Malta', *Malta, Studies of its Heritage and History*, Mid-Med Bank, Malta, 1986, pp.87-104.

Acknowledgements

Photos by courtesy of the Director, Museums Department, Valletta.

Natural Heritage

Patrick J. Schembri

Introduction

Malta[1] is justifiably renowned for its rich archaeological, historical and cultural heritage. However, the islands are generally thought of as having little to offer in terms of natural history, that is, natural objects and events, including plant and animal life, fossils, rocks, landscape features and climate. This is far from the truth. In spite of their small size, the Maltese Islands are endowed with a variety of habitat types, a diverse fauna and flora, and an interesting geology. These constitute the natural heritage of the Maltese Islands, which is just as worthy of study and preservation as the rest of the nation's patrimony.

Apart from their local importance, some elements of Malta's natural heritage have a wider regional importance. For example:

- A number of Maltese endemic (i.e. found only in a particular region and nowhere else) plants and animals are relics from the pre-glacial Mediterranean flora and fauna and some have no close relatives anywhere else in the world.
- Numerous endemic species and subspecies of plants and animals have been described from the Maltese Islands and these are of evolutionary and biogeographical interest.
- Numerous species of Maltese flora and fauna have a restricted Mediterranean distribution. Some locally relatively common species are endangered on a European scale.
- The island of Filfla situated some

4.5 km off the southern coast of mainland Malta, supports one of the largest known breeding colonies of the Storm Petrel *Hydrobates pelagicus* in the Mediterranean.

- The Mediterranean is divided into two major subregions, the East Basin and the West Basin, each with its own characteristic species. Additionally, there are differences in species diversity between the northern (European) shores and the southern (North African) shores of the Mediterranean. Being situated in the centre of the Mediterranean, the Maltese Islands are at the meeting point of these four regions, and therefore the marine biota of the islands is of biogeographical interest.
- The Maltese Islands include the only part of an extensive central Mediterranean rift system (the Pantelleria Rift) currently to be exposed and as such provide an insight into the processes associated with development of this rift.

This article briefly reviews the main elements of Malta's natural heritage and discusses their cultural and scientific importance. There exists an extensive literature on Maltese natural history, however, there are very few synthetic works. For reasons of space, it was not possible to include a full bibliography, therefore, the works listed in the Bibliography were selected mainly on the basis of their seminality and availability, and on whether they summarise previous

---

1. In this work, Malta means the Republic of Malta as a whole, while the island of Malta is referred to as 'mainland Malta'.

work and include extensive bibliographies. Preference was given to books and book chapters, however, a fair number of primary research papers published in learned journals had to be included as, in many cases, these represent the only available works on the subject.

Geography, Geology and Palaeontology

Geography

The Maltese Islands are a group of small, low islands aligned in a NW-SE direction and located in the central Mediterranean at:

latitude: 35°48'28" - 36°05'00" North
longitude: 14°11'04" - 14°34'37" East

They are situated on a shallow shelf, the Malta-Ragusa Rise, part of the submarine ridge which extends from the Ragusa peninsula of Sicily southwards to the African coasts of Tunisia and Libya. Geophysically, the Maltese Islands and the Hyblean Plateau of southeastern Sicily are generally regarded as forming part of the African continental plate. The islands lie approcimately:

96 km from Sicily (Italy)
290 km from North Africa
1836 km from Gibraltar
1519 km from Alexandria (Egypt)

The sea between the islands and Sicily reaches a maximum depth of not more than 200m and is mostly less than 90m; that between the islands and North Africa is much deeper, in places reaching more than 1000m.

The Maltese archipelago consists of three inhabited islands: Malta, Gozo (in Maltese "*Għawdex*"), and Comino (in Maltese "*Kemmuna*") and a number of small uninhabited islets: Cominotto (in Maltese "*Kemmunett*"), Filfola (better known by its Maltese name "*Filfla*"), St Paul's Islands (in Maltese "*Il-Gżejjer ta' San Pawl*", also known as Selmunett Islands),

Fungus Rock (also known as General's Rock; in Maltese "*Il-Ħaġra tal-Ġeneral*" or "*Il-Ġebla tal-Ġeneral*"), and a few other minor rocks. The land area of the various islands is:

mainland Malta: 245.7 km²
Gozo: 67.1 km²
Comino: 2.8 km²
St Paul's Islands: 10.1 ha
Cominotto: 9.9 ha
Filfla: 2.0 ha
Fungus Rock: 0.7 ha

Geology and Palaeontology

Geologically, the islands are composed almost entirely of marine sedimentary rocks, mainly limestones of Oligo-Miocene age (30-5 million years BP). In many respects these resemble the mid-Tertiary limestones occurring in the Ragusa region of Sicily, in the Pelagian Islands, and in the Sirte Basin of Libya, suggesting that all these localities formed part of the same unit during their formation. There are also some minor Quaternary deposits of terrestrial origin. Although the geology of Malta is overall quite simple in that it consists only of sedimentary rocks in a basic layer-cake arrangement, yet in detail it is remarkably complex. Because of the very good exposures available, the Maltese strata have been the subject of numerous studies by geologists and are frequently the subject of field-trips organized by learned societies and educational institutions.

The five main rock types are (in order of decreasing age):
- Lower Coralline Limestone which is exposed to a thickness of 140m. This is the oldest exposed rock type in the Maltese Islands and it started being laid down between 30 and 25 million years ago. The coralline algae *Lithothamnium* and *Archaeolithothamnium* (from which the formation gets its name) are locally abundant, and corals, bivalves and gastropods are characteristic fossils.

The upper part of the formation consists of a c.1m thick bed especially rich in fossils of the sea urchin *Scutella* and is thus often referred to as the Scutella Bed.

- Globigerina Limestone is exposed to a thickness ranging from 23m to 207m and is subdivided into three units (Lower, Middle and Upper Globigerina Limestones) by two ubiquitous pebble beds. Apart from microfossils (e.g. the foraminiferan *Globigerina* from which the formation gets its name), common fossils of the Globigerina Limestone include bivalves, gastropods and sea urchins. Remains of turtles, crocodiles, a sirenian, and a seal have also been found. The pebble beds are rich in fossil bivalves, gastropods, sea urchins, corals and shark teeth (e.g. of the giant shark *Carcharodon megalodon*, estimated to have attained a length of some 25m).
- Blue Clay is exposed to thicknesses of up to 65m. The upper reaches of this formation are rich in fossils of cephalopods (cuttlefish), bivalves, gastropods, sea urchins and corals. Vertebrate remains including fish teeth, cetaceans and sirenians have also been found.
- Greensand is exposed to a maximum thickness of 12m, however, in most places this formation only attains a thickness of some 1m. The name derives from the abundant dark green grains of the iron mineral glauconite. This horizon is very rich in fossils, especially foraminifera (e.g. the giant *Heterostregina*, sometimes so abundant as to give a 'Heterostregina Limestone'), gastropods, bivalves and sea urchins.
- Upper Coralline Limestone is exposed to a thickness of 162m. This formation is a complex association of limestones. In some areas, the uppermost parts show evidence of an intertidal or even supratidal depositional environment and probably represent the point at

which Malta first became dry land, late in the Miocene, some 10 million years ago.

Localised Quaternary deposits of Pleistocene age (1.9-0.01 million years BP) occur and comprise 'fossil' soils (palaeosols), fluvial gravels, coastal conglomerates and breccias, dunes and infillings of caves and fissures.

The more ancient deposits (such as those of the lower beds in the Għar Dalam Cave sequence) have yielded the remains of hippopotami (*Hippopotamus*), dwarf elephants (*Palaeoloxodon*), bats, swans (*Cygnus*) and other birds. Younger deposits have yielded copious remains of deer (*Cervus*). Other fossils found in this and other cave and fissure infills from various parts of the islands include dormice (*Leithia, Eliomys*), voles (*Pitymys*), shrews (*Crocidura*), bats (*Rhinolophus*), an otter (*Nesolutra*), a bear (*Ursus*), a fox (*Vulpes*), a wolf (*Canis*), a small horse (*Equus*) as well as various bird, turtle, toad and lizard remains.

Many Quaternary deposits, especially the younger red-coloured ones (so coloured by the oxidation products of iron minerals) are rich in the fossil and subfossil remains of brackish water, freshwater and terestrial molluscs.

The Pleistocene sediments and their faunas indicate an overall wetter climatic regime than that at present. They also indicate that after a brief period of connection with the Sicilian/Italian mainland, during which there was an influx of European fauna and flora, the land connection between Malta and Sicily was severed and the Islands underwent a period of isolation sufficiently long for an endemic island biota to evolve. Much of this biota became extinct before the end of the Pleistocene, most probably as a result of changes in the climate. At present there is no very strong evidence for a land connection with the North African mainland.

Soils

Maltese soils are characterised by their close similarity to the parent rock material, their relatively young age, the ineffectiveness of the climate in producing soil horizon development, and the great importance of human activities in modifying them. Using the Kubiëna classification system, Maltese soils are of three main types:

- Terra Soils (or Red Mediterranean Soils) which are relic soils formed during the Pleistocene probably under Mediterranean woodland or scrubland and which are little affected by the present climate. They are mature and extensively weathered, have a low calcium carbonate content, and are also low in organic matter. Terra soils develop on karstland (see below).

- Xerorendzinas which are immature soils with a high calcium carbonate content and low in organic matter. These develop on weathered Globigerina Limestone and on valley deposits.

- Carbonate Raw Soils which are also immature and which have a very high calcium carbonate content and are very low in organic matter. These develop on weathered Quaternary sandstones, Greensand, the lower beds of the Upper Coralline Limestone, Blue Clay and on Globigerina Limestone.

Saline soils and alluvial soils also exist in some areas. In addition there are soil complexes formed through human agency: either by mixing of powdered rock with already existing soil at the time fields were laid out, or by addition of rock debris to soil during reclamation of disused quarries, or by mixing domestic waste with soil for use in land reclamation, or by mixing of different soil types transported from different localities.

Geomorphology

Erosion of the different rock types gives a characteristic topography. Lower Coralline Limestone forms sheer cliffs which bound the islands to the west; inland this rock type forms barren grey limestone-platform plateaux on which karstland develops. Karst is a terrain created by the solution of limestone rock and is characterised by a series of surface hollows, depressions and fissures and a subterranean drainage network. The Globigerina Limestone, which is the most extensive exposed formation, forms a broad rolling landscape. Blue Clay slumps out from exposed faces to form taluses, sometimes with slopes of up to 45°, over the underlying rock. Upper Coralline Limestone forms massive cliffs and limestone-platforms with karstic topography similar to the Lower Coralline Limestone.

Both main islands are tilted seawards to the northeast. This is interpreted as being a result of upwelling which started in late Miocene times as a result of formation of the Pantelleria Rift. There are no mountains, the highest point is at Ta' Zuta on Dingli Cliffs (SW mainland Malta) which is 253m above sea level; the highest point on Gozo is at Dbiegi (191m). There are also no lakes, rivers or streams but only minor springs.

The islands are riven by normal faults grouped in two main families: those trending NE-SW which predominate, and those trending NW-SE. The principal faults of the NE-SW system are the Great Fault on mainland Malta and the South Gozo Fault. The Great Fault bisects the island of Malta perpendicular to its long axis from Fomm ir-Riħ on the southwest coast to Madliena on the northeast coast. In places, the vertical throw of the Great Fault is between 90m and 180m, and produces steep escarpments. The South Gozo Fault runs parallel to the Great Fault and crosses the island of Gozo from Ras il-Qala on the east coast to Mġarr ix-Xini on the southeast coast. Between these two master faults there is a system of ridges and valleys (see below). The principal member of the family of NW-SE trending faults is the Magħlaq Fault along the southern coast of mainland

Malta. This fault shows a vertical throw of some 250m and slickensides (polished and scratched surfaces at the fault plane produced by friction between the opposing sides of the fault) are very evident (e.g. at Ix-Xaqqa). South of the Great Fault, much of the Upper Coralline Limestone, Greensand and Blue Clay strata have been eroded away, leaving the Globigerina Limestone exposed. Here, large scale gentle folding is an important structural feature and this gives southern mainland Malta its characteristic topography of plains and shallow depressions separated by low hills. South of the Great Fault it is only in the Rabat-Dingli plateau that all five strata still remain. Much of the surface of this plateau is typical karstic limestone-platform.

Block faulting north of the Great Fault gives rise to a sequence of horsts (ridges) and grabens (valleys) which, proceeding from the Great Fault are: the Binġemma Basin, Wardija Ridge, Pwales Valley, Bajda Ridge, Mistra Valley, Mellieħa Ridge, Għadira Valley and Marfa Ridge. The next graben in the sequence is inundated by sea water and forms the South Comino Channel separating mainland Malta from the island of Comino. The highest part of the next horst is exposed above sea level as the island of Comino and the next graben is again under water and forms the North Comino Channel.

Topographically, Gozo consists of a series of hills, each topped by an Upper Coralline Limestone plateau, and separated by low-lying plains where the rock has been eroded down to the Globigerina stratum. The plateaux are karstic, the hillsides are covered with clay taluses, and the plains between the hills roll gently.

Characteristic topographic features of particular importance are the *rdum, widien* (singular *wied*), and solution subsidence structures. *Rdum* are near vertical faces of rock formed either by erosion or by tectonic movements. Their bases are invariably surrounded by screes of boulders

eroded from the *rdum* edges. Because of the shelter they provide and their relative inaccessibility, the *rdum* sides and boulder screes provide important refuges for many species of Maltese flora and fauna, including many endemics. *Widien* are drainage channels formed either by stream erosion during a previous (Pleistocene) much wetter climatic regime, or by tectonism, or by a combination of the two processes. Most *widien* are now dry valleys, that is, they only carry water along their watercourses during the wet season; a few *widien* drain perennial springs and have some water flowing through them throughout the year, attaining the character of miniature river valleys. By virtue of the shelter provided by their sides and their water supply, *widien* are one of the richest habitats on the islands; they are also extensively cultivated.

Changes in sea level have submerged the mouths of some of these *widien* where they exit on the coast, giving rise to headlands, creeks and bays. This is especially evident on the northeastern coast because of the islands' seawards tilt in this direction. Especially important are the systems of drowned valleys which form the creeks of Malta's two main harbours: Marsamxett Harbour and Grand Harbour, separated by the Valletta headland. Important examples of inundated river valleys in Gozo include Mġarr ix-Xini Bay and Xlendi Bay.

A solution subsidence structure results when the surface collapses into a circular crater-like hollow due to removal by solution of the underlying limestone. There are two families of such structures in the Maltese Islands: those formed underwater due to seafloor collapse during the Miocene, and those formed on land during the Quaternary. The former are only found in Gozo, and the best examples are Dwejra Bay and Qawra (the 'Inland Sea'). The terrestrial structures are termed dolines and result from cavern roof collapse following enlargement of an underground cavern by groundwater. The best known example of this type of structure is Il-Maqluba on the outskirts of Qrendi on mainland Malta.

One particular feature of regional importance is the Upper Coralline Limestone outlier located in the Għar Lapsi area on the southwestern coast of mainland Malta. An outlier is an outcrop of rock occurring in a detached location from the main body of similar rock. In the case of the Għar Lapsi outlier, the nearest outcrop of Upper Coralline Limestone occurs some 1km to the northwest. This outlier is the only part of the extensive Pantelleria Rift system which is currently exposed above sea level and as such it provides a unique opportunity for study of the syntectonic depositional processes associated with rift development; additionally, the younger parts of the deposit record a Late Miocene emergence of the Maltese Islands better than that seen in any other Maltese locality.

Climate

The Maltese climate is characterised by moist winters during which the bulk of the annual rainfall is deposited, air temperatures which never fall below zero, and a long hot and dry summer. This climatic regime is typical of the central Mediterranean. The table below gives the mean monthly values of selected climatic parameters (based on data from the Meteorological Office of the Department of Civil Aviation).

The average annual precipitation is 530mm (mean for period 1951-1990). Rainfall is highly variable from year to year; some years are excessively wet while others are extremely dry (extreme minimum for period 1854-1990, 191.3mm; extreme maximum for period, 1031.2mm). However, no trend in the annual rainfall appears to exist. The seasonal distribution of rainfall defines a wet period (October to March with c.85% of the total annual rainfall) and a dry period (April to September). Even within the wet period, rain is not evenly distributed. A large amount of rain may fall in a short period of time during a single storm, and the mean annual rainfall may in fact represent three or four short torrential downpours. The most intense outbursts occur during the often violent storms which characterise the transition from the dry to the wet period.

Air temperatures are moderate (mean annual temperature for period 1951-1990, 18.6°C; mean monthly range, 12.3-26.3°C). The reduced temperature difference between the warmest and the coldest months of the year is due to the moderating effect of the sea coupled with the lack of very high ground on the islands. The islands are small enough for the influence of the sea to be felt strongly even in inland sites. Temperatures never fall too low for adequate plant growth. Grass temperatures may fall below zero for a few hours at night

Month	Rainfall (mm)	Max.Temp. (°C)	Min.Temp. (°C)	Sea Temp. (°C)	Sunshine (h)
Jan	86.4	14.9	10.0	14.5	5.3
Feb	57.7	15.2	10.0	14.5	6.3
Mar	41.8	16.6	10.7	14.5	7.3
Apr	23.2	18.5	12.5	16.1	8.3
May	10.4	22.7	15.6	18.4	10.0
Jun	2.0	27.0	19.2	21.1	11.2
Jul	1.8	29.9	21.9	24.5	12.1
Aug	4.8	30.1	22.5	25.6	11.3
Sep	29.5	27.7	20.9	25.0	8.9
Oct	87.8	23.9	17.7	22.2	7.3
Nov	91.4	20.0	14.4	19.5	6.3
Dec	104.3	16.7	11.4	16.7	5.2

during the period December to April. During the summer months, grass temperatures may reach values in the upper 40s.

Because of the maritime nature of the islands, relative humidity is consistently high throughout the year, being mostly in the range 65-80%. The high relative humidity even during the hot, dry period results in heavy dewfalls when the temperature falls slightly during the night. These dewfalls are of extreme importance as they represent the only reliable source of water for numerous biota during the arid summer months. The Maltese Islands receive a great deal of sunshine all the year round (mean for period 1951-1990, 8.3h of bright sunshine per day). The islands are windy, only some 8% of the days of the year are calm. The predominant wind is the northwesterly which on average blows on 19% of windy days. The other winds are all nearly equally represented. Southwesterly winds (known locally as *Xlokk*) bring damp oppressive weather and often copious red dust from the Sahara.

The climate of the Maltese Islands has a profound influence on the vegetation, and consequently, on the islands' fauna, landscape and ecology, including that of the human population. The hot, arid summer months are very stressful to plant growth and the natural vegetation is therefore characterised by evergreen trees and shrubs which resist the adverse summer heat and drought, and a very large number of herbaceous plants which grow and flower during the wet period, but which spend the dry period in the form of seeds or perennating organs (e.g. bulbs, rhizomes etc.) below ground. The main periods of plant growth are autumn and spring, when temperature and rainfall are optimal.

Flora and Fauna

The Maltese Islands are popularly regarded as having an impoverished flora and fauna. This view was probably handed down by casual visitors in colonial times who, more accustomed to northern latitudes and mainland biotas, drew wrong conclusions about the totally different environment of the central Mediterranean. In actual fact, the Maltese Islands harbour a very diverse array of plants and animals, especially when considering the relatively small land area, the limited number of habitat types and the intense human pressure.

The table below gives estimates of the number of species of selected groups of plants and animals which occur in the Maltese Islands.

The number of species of representative groups of plants and animals in the Maltese Islands. Only terrestrial and freshwater species are considered. In some cases the numbers given are only estimates as the groups concerned have not been adequately studied.

PLANTS

Algae	c.200+
Large Fungi	c.200+
Lichenes (lichens)	c.300
Bryophyta (mosses and relatives)	c.130
Pteridophyta (ferns and relatives)	11
Gymnospermae (conifers)	2 indigenous species
Angiospermae (flowering plants)	c.1000

ANIMALS

Hydrozoa (hydras)	1 species recorded
Turbellaria (flatworms)	at least 10 species

Annelida (earthworms and leeches)	at least 15 species
Mollusca (snails and slugs)	c.67
Arachnida (spiders and relatives)	at least 200 + species
Branchiopoda (fairy shrimps, water-fleas and relatives)	at least 10 species
Ostracoda (seed shrimps)	at least 7 species
Amphipoda (sand-hoppers and beach-hoppers)	c.9 recorded
Isopoda (woodlice)	c.49
Decapoda (crabs)	one freshwater species
Odonata (dragonflies and damselflies)	c.10 recorded
Dictyoptera (mantises and cockroaches)	c.11
Orthoptera (grasshoppers and relatives)	c.48
Coleoptera (beetles)	c.600 recorded; probably 2000 + occur
Heteroptera (true bugs)	209 recorded; more occur
Lepidoptera (butterflies and moths)	c.590
Neuroptera (lacewings)	c.12 recorded
Diptera (flies)	c.200 recorded probably 500 + occur
Hymenoptera (bees, wasps and ants)	c.150 recorded probably 500 + occur
Diplopoda (millipedes)	c.14
Chilopoda (centipedes)	c.15
Amphibia (frogs)	1 species
Reptilia (reptiles)	9 species
Aves (birds)	c.13 resident (c.57 regular visitors and c.112 regular migrants)
Mammalia (mammals)	c.20 species

As might be expected, the main affinities of the Maltese biota are with Sicily, the closest landmass of any size. However, the Maltese biota is not merely an appendage to that of Sicily. To illustrate this let us consider vascular plants (Tracheophyta) which are much better known than any other group. The bulk of Maltese vascular plants also occur in Sicily, and indeed some species are Siculo-Maltese endemics, that is, they are found only in Sicily and Malta, for example: Sicilian Squill (*Scilla sicula*), Sicilian Iris *(Iris sicula)*, Pygmy Groundsel (*Senecio pygmaeus*), Pignatti's Fern-grass (*Desmazeria pignattii*) and Late Spider-orchid (*Ophrys oxyrrhyncos*). Nevertheless, several Maltese species are absent from Sicily, for example: Aleppo Spurge (*Euphorbia aleppica*) and Olive-leaved Bindweed (*Convolvulus oleifolius*). The Maltese Islands' position in the centre of the Mediterranean results in the presence both of western elements such as Mediterranean Willow (*Salix pedicellata*), African Tamarisk (*Tamarix africana*) and Sandarac Gum Tree (*Tetraclinis articulata*, the national tree of Malta), and of eastern elements such as Thorny Burnet (*Sarcopoterium spinosum*) and Olive-leaved Bindweed (*Convolvulus oleifolius*). There is also a fairly strong North African element represented by such species as Egyptian St John's Wort (*Triadenia aegyptica*), Rock Crosswort (*Crucianella rupestris*) and perhaps such Pelago-Maltese endemics (i.e. found only in Malta and the neighbouring Pelagian Islands) as Cliff Carrot (*Daucus rupestris*), Maltese Toadflax (*Linaria pseudolaxiflora*) and Maltese Waterwort (*Elatine gussonei*). Similar patterns of biogeographical affinity are also shown by certain animal groups, although for these the data are still incomplete.

The Maltese Islands support a number of species of plants and animals which are found only here and nowhere else in the world. The number of such endemic species from those groups which have been adequately studied are given in the table below.

Some of the endemic plants of the islands are relics from the pre-glacial Mediterranean flora (these are called palaeoendemics) and have no close relatives anywhere else in the world. The principal palaeoendemics are Maltese Cliff-orache (*Cremnophyton lanfrancoi*), Maltese Rock-centaury (*Palaeocyanus crassifolius*, the national plant of Malta), Maltese Salt-tree

The number of endemic species occurring in the Maltese Islands. Only those groups which have been adequately studied taxonomically are included and only freshwater and terrestrial species are considered.

Group	Number of endemic species
Tracheophyta (higher plants)	21
Bryophyta (mosses and relatives)	2
Mollusca (snails and slugs)	8
Pseudoscorpiones (false scorpions)	3
Palpigradi (micro-whipscorpions)	1
Isopoda (woodlice)	5
Decapoda (crabs)	1
Thysanura (silverfish)	1
Orthoptera (grasshoppers and relatives)	1
Heteroptera (true bugs)	1
Coleoptera: Staphylinidae (rove beetles)	4
Coleoptera: Elateridae (click beetles)	1
Coleoptera: Tenebrionidae (darkling beetles)	5
Coleoptera: Curculionidae (weevils)	2
Lepidoptera: (butterflies and moths)	17
Hymenoptera: Formicidae (ants)	2
Hymenoptera: Mutillidae (velvet ants)	1
Reptilia (reptiles)	1
Mammalia (mammals)	1

Endemic species are of great cultural and scientific importance. Culturally they are important because such species are unique to the Maltese Islands and therefore a valuable part of the national heritage. Scientifically they are important because of their intrinsic interest with respect to phylogeny, biogeography and evolution of their group, and for the wider evolutionary processes they demonstrate. Three cases will suffice to show this: the endemic vascular plants, the endemic lizard, and the endemic shrew of Gozo.

(*Darniella melitensis*), Maltese Fleabane (*Chiliadenus bocconei*), Maltese Hyoseris (*Hyoseris frutescens*), and Maltese Dwarf Garlic (*Allium lojaconoi*). The genera *Cremnophyton* and *Palaeocyanus* are monotypic, that is, represented by a single species only, and therefore, these are also endemic to the Maltese Islands. *Palaeocyanus* is most closely related to the genus *Centaurea* but is more primitive than this and related genera. *Cremnophyton* is related to the ancestors of *Atriplex*. These species are therefore of interest from the evolutionary point of view since they throw light on the evolution of certain plant groups. Other endemic plants evolved more recently, following final separation of the Maltese Islands from the Sicilian and European mainlands (these are called neoendemics). The neoendemics include Maltese Sea-lavender (*Limonium melitense*), Zerapha's Sea-lavender (*Limonium zeraphae*), Maltese Pyramidal Orchid (*Anacamptis urvilleana*), and Maltese Sea-chamomile (*Anthemis urvilleana*). These are closely related to mainland species but differ due to their reproductive isolation. Such species therefore illustrate evolutionary processes at work.

These processes are also illustrated by the endemic lizard and the shrew of Gozo. The Maltese Wall Lizard, *Podarcis filfolensis*, is a species endemic to the Maltese Islands and the Pelagian Islands of Linosa and Lampione. Four races have been named from the various islands of the Maltese group (*filfolensis* from Filfla; *maltensis* from mainland Malta, Gozo and Comino; *kieselbachi* from St Paul's Islands; and *generalensis* from Fungus Rock) and one race from the Pelagian Islands (*laurentiimuelleri*). *Podarcis filfolensis* is closely related to *Podarcis sicula*, a southern European species, and to *Podarcis melisellensis*, a species of the East Adriatic coast.

Two species of shrew currently occur in the Maltese Islands: the Pygmy Shrew (*Suncus etruscus*) which is known to have been introduced into the islands in historic times and a White-toothed Shrew (genus *Crocidura*) which is only found on Gozo and which has been assigned different names by different workers. Another species of White-toothed Shrew (equated with the extinct Pleistocene *Crocidura esuae* of Sicily by some workers) pre-dated human occupation of the islands. A recent re-evaluation of the living Maltese *Crocidura* species has shown that this is actually *Crocidura sicula*, a Sicilian species. The present day Sicilian and Maltese

species evolved from the Pleistocene *Crocidura esuae* and the only real difference between the two is a reduction in size. *Crocidura sicula* is a Siculo-Maltese endemism and one of the few survivors of the Pleistocene fauna of the region. The Gozitan population has been named as an endemic subspecies, *calypso*; the other living subspecies are *C.s. sicula* of Sicily and *C.s. aegatensis* of the Egadi Islands. According to some workers, *Crocidura sicula* is closely related to North African species of the genus.

In passing one can mention that many endemic species have been named after the Maltese naturalists who discovered them. In this way Maltese pioneers of the study of the natural history of Malta, such as Stefano Zerafa, Gavino Gulia, Giovanni Gulia, Giuseppe Mamo, Antonio Schembri, Alfredo Caruana Gatto, Giuseppe Despott, Carmelo De Lucca and Anthony Valletta, are commemorated.

Biocoenoses

Biocoenosis is a general ecological term for any naturally occurring group of organisms inhabiting a common environment. The terrestrial biocoenoses of the Maltese Islands may be grouped in two categories: (i) major communities that are part of the successional sequence towards the climatic climax; and, (ii) minor communities which are either specialised to occupy particular habitats, or occupy habitats that are rare in the islands, or are relics from a previous ecological regime, now surviving in a few refugia. Descriptions of Maltese biocoenoses are based mainly on vegetation.

• Woodland

It is thought that before man colonised the Maltese Islands, large areas were covered with Mediterranean Sclerophyll Forest, which is the highest type of vegetation that can develop in the Mediterranean climatic regime. In the central Mediterranean this forest is characterised by Holm Oak (*Quercus ilex*) and Aleppo Pine (*Pinus halepensis*) with an undergrowth of smaller trees, shrubs and climbers. The early settlers cut the trees for their wood and to clear the land for agriculture and buildings. Additionally, these colonisers introduced sheep and goats to the islands, whose grazing causes some damage to mature trees but more importantly prevents them from regenerating. In the Maltese Islands, the native forest is all but extinct and only remnants remain at four localities, all on the island of Malta. These forest remnants take the form of small copses of Holm Oak where the total number of trees is less than thirty. Some of these trees are estimated to be between 500 and 900 years old.

Buskett (mainland Malta) was originally planted by man but is now self-regenerating and has the character of the natural climax community and may be described as a semi-natural woodland. Here the wood is dominated by Aleppo Pine (*Pinus halepensis*) with various other trees being sub-dominant (e.g. Olive, Carob, Holm Oak) and there is an extensive undergrowth of shrubs (e.g. Lentisk, Buckthorn and Hawthorn), herbs and climbers. This semi-natural wood is very important since it represents the only woodland ecosystem on the islands and consequently harbours a large number of woodland plants and animals which, because of the lack of suitable habitats in Malta, are locally very rare. Particularly important woodland species are fungi which are symbiotic with trees, insects which feed, breed or live in trees and dead wood, and leaf-litter inhabiting invertebrates.

Many other wooded areas exist in the islands, however, all are man-made (e.g. public/private gardens, afforestation sites, orchards, etc.) and do not possess the character of the native climax forest ecosystem nor are they self-maintaining and self-regenerating, and therefore do not qualify as semi-natural woodlands.

• Maquis

Maquis is a more or less dense, mostly evergreen shrub community where the individual shrubs reach a height of between 1m and 3m. In Malta, a semi-natural maquis develops in relatively inaccessible sites such as the sides of steep valleys and at the foot of inland cliffs (*rdum*), while a secondary maquis develops round trees, mainly olives and carobs, planted by man.

The local maquis is characterised by a number of large shrubs and small trees principally Carob (*Ceratonia siliqua*), Olive (*Olea europaea*), Lentisk (*Pistacia lentiscus*), Buckthorn (*Rhamnus oleoides*), Yellow Germander (*Teucrium flavum*), Hedge Nettle (*Prasium majus*) and others.

• Garigue

Garigue is a community of low (less than 1m) scattered, often spiney and aromatic shrubs with a herbaceous undergrowth. This is the most common natural vegetation type present in Malta. Some garigue communities are natural, others result from degradation of forest and maquis. Garigues are typical of rocky ground, particularly karstland, and are characterised by such species as Mediterranean Thyme (*Coridothymus capitatus*), Yellow Kidney-vetch (*Anthyllis hermanniae*), Evergreen Germander (*Teucrium fructicans*), Mediterranean Heath (*Erica multiflora*) and the endemic Maltese Spurge (*Euphorbia melitensis*), accompanied by numerous geophytes (herbs with perennating buds below soil level) and therophytes (herbs which survive the unfavourable season as seeds). Many subtypes of garigue exist.

• Steppic grassland

This is a treeless grassland dominated by grasses, umbellifers, thistles and geophytes. Steppic grasslands are widespread and result from degradation of the maquis and garigue, mainly due to grazing (goats are capable of cropping plants very close to their base thus destroying them and are also able to chew and eat spiney xerophytic vegetation), but also in response to other factors. Some steppic communities are, however, climatic or semi-climatic, for example, those dominated by Esparto Grass (*Lygeum spartum*) which develop on clay slopes. The more degraded steppes are characterised by Common Awn-grass (*Stipa capensis*), Goat grass (*Aegilops geniculata*) and a variety of thistles (e.g. Clustered Carline Thistle *Carlina involucrata*, Horse Thistle *Notobasis syriaca*, Mediterranean Thistle *Galactites tomentosa*) and geophytes (e.g. Asphodel *Asphodelus aestivuus*, Seaside Squill *Urginea pancration*). Steppic communities may also develop on abandoned agricultural land.

- Communities of disturbed ground

Given the islands' high human population and its considerable land use, this biocoenosis has a large coverage. It is dominated by a variety of plant species, many of which are aliens. Sub-types occur in abandoned fields, along roadsides and in disturbed seaside habitats.

- Coastal communities

Saline marshlands form an interface between the marine, freshwater and terrestrial environments. Maltese coastal marshes are characterised by a muddy substratum on which a pool of brackish water collects in the wet season. During the dry season this water becomes progressively more brackish until it finally disappears completely, leaving the marsh dry until the following wet season. Because of these harsh environmental conditions, saline marshlands support a highly specialised biota which is only found in this type of habitat. Although several species are common to all local marshlands, yet each

site has its own peculiar habitat characteristics and suite of species.

Many local sandy beaches were backed by dune systems, but at present only very few still persist and even these have been much degraded due mainly to human activities connected with beach development for touristic purposes and with recreational use. Sand dune ecosystems are thus amongst the rarest and most threatened of local ecosystems. Local dunes are dominated by the dune grasses *Elymus farctus* and *Sporobolus arenarius*, and, until recently, also by Southern Marram Grass (*Ammophila australis*) which has now been totally extirpated.

On gently sloping rocky shores, halophytic vegetation grows in isolated patches in the shallow saline soil which accumulates in pockets in the rock. The species present are typical of this type of habitat and mainly form part of the Mediterranean vegetational community called the *Crithmo-Limonietum*. In the Maltese variants of this biocoenosis, two endemic plants are found only in this community type and a third also occurs, although it is not exclusive to low-lying maritime rock. The former are Zerapha's Sea-lavender (*Limonium zeraphae*) and Maltese Sea-chamomile (*Anthemis urvilleana*); the latter is Maltese Dwarf Garlic (*Allium lojaconoi*). Other characteristic plants of scientific importance include: Pignatti's Fern-grass (*Desmazeria pignattii*) and Pygmy Groundsel (*Senecio pygmaeus*), which are Hybleo-Maltese endemics. Although the fauna of low-lying coastal rock is much less well known, several species seem to be more or less exclusive to this habitat type.

- Rupestral communities

These grow on cliff faces and high walls. The south, southwest and west coasts of mainland Malta consist of vertical cliffs rising from the sea to heights of c.70-130m. In the Dingli Cliffs area, these cliffs give way to a steeply sloping substraum.

This sloping ground is terraced and partly under cultivation. Further inland there is a second tier of vertical cliffs (*rdum*). The south and southwest coasts of Gozo consist of sea-cliffs similar to those of southern Malta. Because of the shelter they provide and their relative inaccessibility, both the sea cliffs, and the second tier of *rdum* with the boulder screes which form beneath them, provide important refuges for many species of Maltese flora and fauna, including many endemics.

The fauna of coastal cliffs includes some of the rarest of Maltese animals; for example, the endemic Maltese Door-snail (*Imitatrix melitensis*) occupies a very precarious habitat of a few tens of square metres only on the southwest cliffs of mainland Malta, while two other rare endemic snails are found in a few cliffside localities only. Cliff-side communities are dominated by shrubs and are especially significant due to the presence of a large number of endemic plant taxa including the two (*Palaeocyanus crassifolius* and *Cremnophyton lanfrancoi*) belonging to monotypic genera already mentioned.

- Freshwater communities

During the wet season, rainwater collects in natural depressions and hollows on Coralline Limestone karstland to form temporary rainwater pools. These pools are usually very transient and rapidly dry up, especially with onset of the dry season. These natural freshwater pools house many freshwater species which are overall rare in the Maltese Islands. A few pools which form in natural depressions are more or less permanent either because of their physical size or because they receive water from sources other than rainwater, usually from springs. These pools are of great local interest since they represent the only natural standing water bodies in the islands. Because of the dearth of freshwater in the islands, freshwater plants and animals are overall rather rare, and this is especially true for those species which require a more or less year-round supply of water.

The bulk of Maltese plants and animals associating with freshwater are found in *widien* watercourses when these are filled with water during the wet season. One of the most conspicuous species of these habitats is the Painted Frog (*Discoglossus pictus*), Malta's only amphibian. Apart from freshwater species, watercourses support a rich fauna of terrestrial organisms associated with the luxuriant vegetation that grows along the *widien*. The few remaining permanent springs support a distinctive flora and fauna many species of which, since they require a year-round supply of running freshwater, are limited to this habitat type and are therefore very rare and have a restricted distribution. One such species is the endemic local race of the Mediterranean Freshwater Crab (*Potamon fluviatile lanfrancoi*). Along a few watercourses there are still remnants of broad-leaved deciduous woodland with White Poplar (*Populus alba*), Mediterranean Willow (*Salix pedicellata*), and Grey-leaved Elm (*Ulmus canescens*), sometimes accompanied by Bay Laurel (*Laurus nobilis*).

- Caves

In spite of being made up almost exclusively of limestone, the Maltese Islands have surprisingly few deep caves. It is only recently that the biology and ecology of Maltese caves has started being investigated. These studies have shown that Maltese caves are inhabited by organisms which are adapted to live in such habitats and therefore have a very restricted distribution. The best known cave-dwellers are bats but there are many other species, particularly invertebrates. Moreover, a number of these species are endemic to the Maltese Islands and therefore of great scientific interest. They are also highly vulnerable, both because of the limited habitat available and because of their poor dispersive ability. Additionally, many caves

117

have deposits of Quaternary age, study of which is expected to throw light on the islands' palaeoenvironment and biogeography. One cave, that at Għar Ħarq Ħamiem at St Georges Bay (mainland Malta) is unique in that it houses a deep pool of freshwater, the only such body known in the Maltese Islands.

- Marine biocoenoses

The marine biocoenoses of the Maltese Islands are mostly similar to those found in other parts of the Mediterranean. Only the most interesting locally occurring ones of the shore and shallow water off it are discussed below.

Supralittoral biocoenoses are those which occur high up on the shore where the substratum is only wetted by sea spray and the very highest waves. Supralittoral communities of rocky substrata are by far the commonest given that most of the islands' coastline is of this type. Those of soft substrata are to be found on the few sandy beaches, however, these communities have been little studied locally. A very distinctive supralittoral biocoenosis is that of the so called "banquettes", consisting of masses of drying and decaying plant debris deposited on the shore by wave action. These specialised communities are composed of an assortment of semi-terrestrial marine species and semi-aquatic terrestrial species.

Mediolittoral biocoenoses are those which occur in that part of the shore continuously covered and uncovered by the sea. One such type of biocoenosis which is considered valuable on a Mediterranean scale and which also occurs locally, is the vermetid/coralline algal "trottoir" (or 'rim'). This consists of dense aggregations of vermetid gastropods (*Dendropoma* sp.) whose uncoiled shells are cemented to the rocky substratum and to each other, and where the interstices are filled by the coralline alga *Neogoniolithon*. A second type of threatened rim, that formed by the coralline alga *Lithophyllum lichenoides* may also occur.

Infralittoral biocoenoses are those occurring under the sea, from mean sea level down to a depth where there is sufficient light for photosynthesis. In the Maltese Islands this is down to a depth of c.45m. The main community developing on infralittoral rocky substrata is that dominated by attached macroalgae. Many subtypes are known, depending on shelter, light penetration, nature of the substratum, water movement etc. The most widespread are those dominated by species of the brown seaweed *Cystoseira* which grow on exposed rocky shores starting from very shallow water. Another type of *Cystoseira* community grows in deep water and is based on the species *Cystoseira spinosa, Cystoseira dubia* and *Cystoseira zozteroides*. Most of the Mediterranean species of *Cystoseira* are endemic to the region.

Sea-grass meadows are perhaps the most important sublittoral biotic communities in the Mediterranean. Sea-grass meadows are highly productive ecosystems on which a large number of other ecosystems, and individual species, depend; for example, many fish and cephalopods use these meadows as breeding and nursery grounds. Although common and widespread round the Maltese Islands, sea-grasses are very sensitive to pollution and habitat modification. In many parts of the Mediterranean, these meadows have regressed and eroded away, leaving in their place much impoverished thanatocoenoses (i.e. communities based on dead or dying organisms). The same is likely to happen to Maltese sea-grass meadows in enclosed or semi-enclosed coastal areas receiving a variety of effluents or subject to certain activities (for example, dredging, dumping, aquaculture operations etc.). Several types of sea-grass meadows exist. In deeper water these are formed mainly by Neptune Grass (*Posidonia oceanica*), a species endemic to the Mediterranean. In more sheltered localities and in shallow water, the meadows are based on Lesser Neptune Grass (*Cymodocea nodosa*), Red Sea Grass (*Halophila stipulacea*) and the alga *Caulerpa prolifera*.

Acknowledgements

I wish to thank Mr Edwin Lanfranco (Department of Biology, University of Malta) for his help and advice during the preparation of this article, particularly concerning botanical matters; Mr John A. Schembri (Mediterranean Institute, University of Malta), Mr Stephen Schembri (National Museum of Natural History, Malta) and Mr Frank Ventura (Faculty of Education, University of Malta) for their help with various aspects of this work, and the Meteorological Office of the Department of Civil Aviation for supplying meteorological data.

Bibliography

ALEXANDER, D., A review of the physical geography of Malta and its significance for tectonic geomorphology. *Quaternary Science Reviews* 7, 1988, 41-53.

ANDERSON, E.W. & SCHEMBRI P.J., *Coastal zone survey of the Maltese Islands report*, Beltissebh, Malta, 1989. Planning Services Division, Works Department; xii + 121pp + 100 hand-drawn colour maps + 19 synoptic maps.

BACETTI, B., Notulae orthopterologicae XXX. Gli ortotteroidei dell'arcipelago Maltese. *Lavori della Società Italiana di Biogeografia* n. ser., 1972, 3: 605-608.

BALDACCHINO, A.E.; Dandria, D.; Lanfranco, E. & Schembri, P.J., Records of spiders (Arachnida: Araneae) from the Maltese Islands (Central Mediterranean). *The Central Mediterranean Naturalist* 2(2), 1993, 37-59.

BALDACCHINO, A.E., Lanfranco, E. & Schembri, P.J., *Discovering nature in the Maltese Islands*. Blata l-Bajda, Malta, 1990, Merlin Library Ltd.; 104pp..

BANNERMAN, D.A. & Vella Gaffiero, J.A., *Birds of the Maltese Archipelago*, Valletta, Malta, 1976: Museums Department; xxi + 550pp. + map.

BECKMANN, K.H., Land- und Süßwassermollusken der Maltesischen Inseln. *Heldia* 1 (suppl.), 1987, 1-38.

BIAGINI, E., *Le isole maltesi*. Genova, 1974. Accademia Ligure di Scienze e Lettere; 223pp.

BORG, John, *Descriptive flora of the Maltese Islands*. Valletta, Malta, 1927: Government Printing Press; 846pp. (reprinted 1976 as *Floras of the World* Vol.2 by Otto Koeltz Science Publishers, Germany).

BORG, Joseph, *The public gardens and groves of Malta and Gozo*. (3rd ed.) Malta, 1990: (the author); xii + 149pp.

BORG, P., *The scale insects of the Maltese Islands*. Malta, 1932: Government Printing Office; 67pp.

BOSENCE, D.W.J. (ed.), *Field guide to the Cenozoic platform carbonates of the Maltese Islands*. Nottingham, 1990: International Sedimentological Congress 1990; 111pp.

BOSENCE, D.W.J., Pedley, H.M. & Rose, E.P.F., *Field guide to the mid-Tertiary carbonate facies of Malta*. London, 1981: The Palaeontological Association; 88pp.

BOWEN JONES, H., Dewdney, J.C. & Fisher, W.B. (eds.), *Malta, a background for development*. Durham, 1961: Durham University Press, 356pp.

BUSUTTIL, S., Lerin, F. & Mizzi L. (eds), *Malta: food, agriculture, fisheries and the environment*. (Options Méditerranéennes ser.B: Etudes et Recherches No7), Paris, France, 1993: CIHEAM (Centre International de Hautes Etudes Agronomiques Méditerranéennes); 192pp.

CAMERON, M. & Caruana Gatto, A., The Coleoptera of the Maltese Islands.

Transactions of the Entomological Society of London 59, 1907: 383-403.

CARUANA GATTO, A., *Common beetles of the Maltese Islands*, Malta, 1894: G. Muscat; 14pp.

CARUSO, D. & Lombardo, B.M., Isopodi terrestri delle Isole Maltesi. *Animalia* 9, 1982: 5-52.

CHETCUTI, D.; Buhagiar, A.; Schembri, P.J. & Ventura, F., *The climate of the Maltese Islands: a review*, Msida, Malta, 1992: Malta University Press; vi + 108pp.

CILIA, J.L., Coleoptera. In: Schembri, P.J. & Sultana, J. (eds) *Red data book for the Maltese Islands* pp.105-128; Valletta, Malta, 1989: Department of Information.

ELLENBERG, L., Die küsten von Gozo. *Essener Geographische Arbeiten* 6, 1983: 129-160.

ENGHOFF, H. & Schembri, P.J., The millipedes of the Maltese Islands (Central Mediterranean) (Diplopoda). *Bollettino della Società Entomologica Italiana* 120, 1989: 164-173.

FELIX, R., *Oligo-Miocene stratigraphy of Malta and Gozo*. Medeelingen Landbouwhogeschool Wageningen Nederlands 73 (20), 1973; 104pp.

FRANCINI CORTI, E. & Lanza, B., XVIII Congresso della Società Italiana di Biogeografia: note conclusive sulla storia del popolamento animale e vegetale delle isole circumsiciliane. *Lavori della Società Italiana di Biogeografia* n.ser., 3, 1972: 911-918.

GIUSTI, F.; Manganelli, G. & Schembri, P.J., *The non-marine molluscs of the Maltese Islands*. Torino, Italy: Museo Regionale di Storia Naturale (in preparation).

GRIMM, R., Tenebrionidae vom Maltesischen Archipel (Insecta: Coleoptera). *Stuttgarter Beitraege Naturkundliche* ser. A. 392, 1986: 1-17.

GUILCHER, A. & Paskoff, R., Remarques sur la geomorphologie littorale de l'archipel maltais. *Bulletin de l'Association Geographique de France* 427, 1975: 225-231.

GULIA, G., Uno sguardo alla zoologia delle 'Isole Maltesi'. *IX° Congrès International de Zoologie (Monaco, 1913)* sect. 4: 545-555, Rennes, France, 1914.

HASLAM, S.M., *Malta's plant life*. Malta, 1969: (the author); viii + 129pp.

HASLAM, S.M. & Royle, P.Y., *Buskett and its natural history*, Msida, Malta, 1968: Malta University Press; 52pp.

HASLAM, S.M.; Sell, P.D. & Wolseley, P.A., *A flora of the Maltese Islands*, Msida, Malta, 1977: Malta University Press; lxxi + 560pp + plates I-LXVI.

HOUSE, M.R.; Dunham, K.C. & Wigglesworth, J.C., Geology and structure of the Maltese Islands. In: Bowen Jones, H.; Dewdney, J.C. & Fisher, W.B. (eds) *Malta, a background for development*. pp.25-47; Durham, 1961: Durham University Press.

HUTTERER, R., Temporal and geographical variation of shrews of the Sicilian-Maltese archipelago since the Pleistocene. *Vie Milieu* 40, 1990: 213-217.

Variation and evolution of the Sicilian shrew: taxonomic conclusions and description of a possibly related species from the Pleistocene of Morocco (Mammalia: Soricidae). *Bonner zoologische Beitraege* 42, 1991: 241-251.

HYDE, H.P.T., *Geology of the Maltese Islands*, Malta, 1955: Lux Press, 135pp.

LANFRANCO, E., *Guida alle escursioni a Malta; Aprile 1984*. Società Botanica Italiana sezzione Siciliana, 1984; 10pp. (mimeographed).

Jewels of the Maltese flora: plants endemic to the Maltese Islands. *Spectra, New Lyceum Science Magazine* (Malta) 5, 1987: 2-11 + cover.

Il-pjanti vaskulari endemiċi tal-Gżejjer Maltin. In: Cortis, T. (ed.) *L-identità kulturali ta' Malta*, pp.141-164; Valletta, Malta 1989: Dipartiment ta' l-Informazzjoni. (in Maltese).

The flora. In: Schembri, P.J. & Sultana J. (eds) *Red data book for the Maltese*

Islands. pp.5-70; Valletta, Malta, 1989: Department of Information.

LANFRANCO, E. & Schembri, P.J., Maltese wetlands and wetland biota. *Potamon* (Malta) 15, 1986: 122-125.

LANFRANCO, G.G., *Maltese mammals*. Valletta, Malta, 1969: Progress Press; 28pp. + plates 1-8.

Field guide to the wild flowers of Malta, Valletta, Malta, 1969: Progress Press; viii + 83pp. + plates 1-65.

The fish around Malta (central Mediterranean), Valletta, Malta, 1993: Progress Press; xi + 132pp.

LANFRANCO, G.G. & Schembri, P.J., Vertebrates other than birds. In: Schembri, P.J. & Sultana, J. (eds) *Red data book for the Maltese Islands* pp.129-137; Valletta, Malta, 1989: Department of Information.

LANG, D.M., *Soils of Malta and Gozo*. (Colonial Research Studies 29) London, 1960: Her Majesty's Stationary Office; 122pp. + map.

LANZA, B., Gli anfibi e i rettili delle isole circumsiciliane. *Lavori della Società Italiana di Biogeografia* n. ser., 3, 1972: 755-804.

LORENZ, C. & Mascle, G., Le point sur la geologie de l'archipel maltais. *Revue de Géologie Dynamique et Geographie Physique* 25, 1984: 63-68.

MAHNERT, V., Pseudoscorpione von den Maltesischen Inseln. *Fragmenta Entomologica* 11, 1975: 185-197.

MATIC, Z.; Darabantu, C. & Clichici, M., Contributo alla conoscenza dei chilipodi di Spagna e di Malta. *Bollettino delle Sedute della Accademia Gioenia di Scienze Naturali in Catania*, ser.4, 9, 1967: 175-199.

MICALLEF, H. & Evans, F., *The marine fauna of Malta*, Malta, 1968: Biology Department, The Royal University of Malta; vi + 26pp.

MIOSSEC, J.M., L'archipel maltais. *Bulletin de la Société Languedoc. de Géographie* 14, 1980: 43-96.

MITCHELL, P.K. & Dewdney, J.C., The Maltese climate and weather. In: Bowen Jones, H.; Dewdney, J.C. & Fisher, W.B. (eds) *Malta, a background for development*. pp.48-82; Durham, 1961: Durham University Press.

MURRAY, J., The Maltese Islands, with special reference to their geological structure. *Scottish Geographical Magazine* 6, 1890: 449-488 (+ plates I and II).

NEHRING, B., Die maltesischen Inseln. *Tübinger Geograph. Std.* 19, 1966: 1-172.

PASKOFF, R. & Sanlaville, P., Observations geomorphologiques sur les cotes de l'archipel maltais. *Zeitschrift für Geomorphologie* N.F., 22, 1978: 310-328.

PEDLEY, H.M., Miocene seafloor subsidence and later subaerial solution subsidence structures in the Maltese Islands. *Proceedings of the Geologists' Association* 85, 1974: 533-547.

The occurrence and sedimentology of a Pleistocene travertine in the Fiddien Valley, Malta. *Proceedings of the Geologists' Association* 91, 1980: 195-202.

Controls of Cenozoic carbonate deposition in the Maltese Islands: review and reinterpretation. *Memorie della Società Geologica Italiana* 38, 1987: 81-94.

The Ghar Lapsi limestones: sedimentology of a Miocene intra-shelf graben. *Centro* (Malta) 1 (3), 1987: 1-14.

PEDLEY, H.M., House, M.R. & Waugh, B., The geology of Malta and Gozo. *Proceedings of the Geologists' Association* 87, 1976: 325-341.

The geology of the Pelagian Block: the Maltese Islands. In: Nairn, A.E.M.; Kanes, W.H. & Stehli, F.G. (eds) *The ocean basins and margins. Vol. 4B the western Mediterranean*. pp.417-433, London, 1978: Plenum Press.

POGGI, R., Appunti su alcuni Pselaphidae e Scydmaenidae di Malta (Coleoptera).

Bollettino della Società Entomologica Italiana 112, 1980: 167-170.

RANSLEY, N. & Azzopardi, A., *A geography of the Maltese Islands* (4th ed.) Malta, 1988: St Aloysius College Publ., x + 150pp.

REUTHER, C.D., Tectonics of the Maltese Islands. *Centro* (Malta) 1 (1), 1984, 1-20.

RICCARDI, R., Aspetti geografici di Malta. *Bollettino della Regia Società Geografica Italiana* 7/8, 1943: 193-207.

RIEGER, C., Wanzen aus Malta (Insecta, Heteroptera). *Carolinea* 44, 1986: 87-90.

SABATINELLI, G. & Schembri, S., Gli scarabeidi floricoli delle Isole Maltese (Coleoptera Scarabaeidae). *Bollettino della Società Entomologica Italiana* 122, 1990: 31-36.

SAMMUT, P.M., A systematic and synonymic list of the Lepidoptera of the Maltese Islands. *Neue Entomologische Nachrichten* 13, 1984; 124pp.

Il-Lepidoptera Maltija. In: Cortis, T. (ed.) *L-identità kulturali ta' Malta*. pp.117-139; Valletta, Malta, 1989: Department of Information. (in Maltese)

SAMMUT, P.M. & Valletta, A., Lepidoptera. In: Schembri, P.J. & Sultana, J. (eds) *Red data book for the Maltese Islands* pp.97-104; Valletta, Malta, 1989: Department of Information.

SAVONA VENTURA, C., The fossil herpetofauna of the Maltese Islands; a review. *Naturalista Siciliano* ser.4, 8, 1984: 93-106.

SCHEMBRI, P.J., *Report of survey: natural resources.* (Malta Structure Plan Technical Report 5.4) Colin Buchanan and Partners/Generale Progetti SpA/Planning Services Division, Government of Malta, 1991; vii + 138pp.

Ekoloġija tal-Gżejjer Maltin: ħarsa ġenerali. In: Cortis, T. (ed.) *Oqsma tal-kultura Maltija*. pp.5-37; Beltissebħ, Malta, 1991: Ministeru ta' l-Edukazzjoni u ta' l-Intern. (in Maltese)

Physical geography and ecology of the Maltese Islands: a brief overview. In: Busuttil, S.; Lerin, F. & Mizzi, L. (eds) *Malta: food, agriculture, fisheries and the environment.* (Options Méditerranéennes ser.B: Etudes et Recherches No7) pp.27-39; Paris, France, 1993: CIHEAM (Centre International de Hautes Etudes Agronomiques Méditerranéennes).

The fauna of the Maltese islands: a review and analysis. In: Ellul-Micallef, R. & Fiorini, S. (eds) *Collegium Melitense quatercentenary celebrations (1592-1992): collected papers contributed by members of the academic staff of the University of Malta.* pp.541-573; Msida, Malta, 1993: University of Malta.

SCHEMBRI P.J.; Lanfranco, E.; Farrugia, P.; Schembri, S. & Sultana, J., *Localities with conservation value in the Maltese Islands*. Beltissebħ, Malta, 1987: Environment Division, Ministry of Education; iii-27pp.

SCHEMBRI, P.J. & Sultana, J. (eds), *Red Data book for the Maltese Islands*. Valletta, Malta, 1989: Department of Information; viii + 142pp. + plates I-VIII.

SCHEMBRI, S., Vespoidea from the Maltese Islands (Hymenoptera Aculeata). *Bollettino della Società Entomologica Italiana* 112, 1980: 90-93.

Recent records of Hymenoptera Apoidea from the Maltese Islands. *Bullettin of the Amateur Entomologists' Society* 41, 1982: 25-30.

The Vespoidea of the Maltese Islands: remarks and additions (Hymenoptera Aculeata). *Bollettino della Società Entomologica Italiana* 117, 1985: 115-116.

Insects excluding Coleoptera and Lepidoptera. In: Schembri, P.J. & Sultana, J. (eds) *Red data book for the Maltese Islands* pp.90-96; Valletta, Malta, 1989: Department of Information.

Sphecid wasps of the Maltese Islands: a review (Hymenoptera Spechidae). *Bollettino della Società Entomologica Italiana* 122, 1991: 175-184.

The Anthicidae of the Maltese Islands (Coleoptera). *Bollettino della Società Entomologica Italiana* 123, 1991: 32-38.

An annotated catalogue of the heteropteran bugs of the Maltese Islands (Heteroptera). *Memorie della Società Entomologica Italiana*, 71, 1992: 467-503.

SCHEMBRI, S. & Collingwood, C.A., A revision of the myrmecofauna of the Maltese Islands (Hymenoptera, Formicidae). *Annali del Museo Civico di Storia Naturale, Genova* 83, 1981: 417-442.

SCHEMBRI, S. & Ebejer, M.J., A review of the Tettigoniidae of the Maltese Islands. *Bollettino della Società Entomologica Italiana* 115, 1983: 135-138.

SCHEMBRI, S.; Gatt, P. & Schembri, J.L., Recent records of flies from the Maltese Islands (Diptera). *Memorie della Società Entomologica Italiana* 70, 1991: 255-277.

SCHEMBRI S. & Sama, G., The Cerambycidae of the Maltese Islands (Coleoptera). *Bollettino della Società Entomologica Italiana* 118, 1986: 93-100.

SCHEMBRI, S. & Schembri, J.L., A preliminary report on the Dermaptera of the Maltese Islands. *Annali del Museo Civico di Storia Naturale, Genova* 82, 1978: 329-332.

Recent records of Coleoptera Staphylinidae from the Maltese Islands. *Lavori della Società Veneziana di Scienze Naturali* 7, 1982: 45-53.

SIVARAJASINGHAM, S., *The soils of Malta*. (UNOP/SF Project MAT/5, Water disposal and water supply) Rome, 1971: Food and Agriculture Organisation of the United Nations; 82pp.

SOMMIER, S. & Caruana Gatto, A. *Flora Melitensis nova*. Firenze, Italy, 1915: Stab. Pallas; viii + 142 pp.

SOÓS, L., A systematic and zoogeographical contribution to the mollusc fauna of the Maltese Islands and Lampedusa. *Archiv für Naturgeschiche* 2, 1933: 305-353.

STORCH, G., Holozäne Kleinsäugerfunde aus der Għar Dalam-Höhle, Malta (Mammalia: Insectivora, Chiroptera, Rodentia). *Senckenbergiana Biologica* 51, 1970, 135-145.

STRUMIA, F., Imenotteri crisididi delle Isole Maltesi (Hymenoptera Chrysididae). *Bollettino della Società Entomologica Italiana* 113, 1981: 167-168.

SULTANA, J. & Gauci, C., *L-agħsafar*. Valletta, Malta, 1979: The Ornithological Society; 190pp (in Maltese).

A new guide to the birds of Malta, Valletta, Malta, 1982: The Ornithological Society; 205pp.

TAMANINI, L., Eterotteri delle Isole Maltesi (Hemiptera, Heteroptera). *Bollettino delle Sedute della Accademia Gioenia di Scienze Naturali in Catania* ser.4, 8, 1966: 679-697.

THAKE, M.A., The biogeography of the Maltese Islands illustrated by the Clausiliidae. *Journal of Biogeography* 12, 1985: 369-287.

THAKE, M.A. & Schembri, P.J., Mollusca. In: Schembri, P.J. & Sultana, J. (eds) *Red data book for the Maltese Islands*. pp.79-89; Valletta, Malta, 1989: Department of Information.

TRECHMANN, C.T., Quaternary conditions in Malta. *Geological Magazine* 75, 1938: 1-26 (+ plates I and II).

VALLETTA, A., *The butterflies of the Maltese Islands*, Valletta, Malta, 1971: Giov. Muscat; 64pp.

The moths of the Maltese Islands. Valletta, Malta, 1973: Progress Press; 118pp.

VOGEL, P.; Schembri, P.J.; Borg, M. & Sultana, J., The shrew (*Crocidura* sp.) of Gozo, a probable survivor of the Pleistocene fauna of Mediterranean islands. *Zeitschrift für Säugetierkunde* 55, 1990: 357-359.

VOSSMERBÄUMER, H., Malta, ein Beitrag zur Geologie und Geomorphologie des
    Zentralmediterranen Raumes. *Würzburger Geographische Arbeiten* 38, 1972: 1-213.
ZAMMIT MAEMPEL, G., *An outline of Maltese geology*. Malta, 1977: Dr G. Zammit
    Maempel; 44pp.
    Ghar Dalam cave and deposits. Malta, 1989: Dr G. Zammit Maempel; 74pp.
    Pioneers of Maltese geology. Malta, 1989: Dr G. Zammit Maempel; 302pp.

Architecture

Leonard Mahoney

It was at the height of the Renaissance, in 1530, when Charles V handed over the two small islands of Malta and Gozo to the Knights of St John. The momentous event was to usher in a long period of building activity which produced some of the island's finest architectural monuments, but it was not the first time that Malta had stood at the peak of architectural achievement. Prof. Colin Renfrew, the famous archaeologist describes the Maltese neolithic temples (ca. 3000 B.C.) as "the earliest free-standing monuments in stone in the world" and the "memorably imposing' facade of the Ġgantija temple, in Gozo, as "perhaps the earliest architecturally conceived exterior in the world".

Very much later, during the days of antiquity, the excellence of Maltese houses, "very beautiful and ambitiously adorned with cornices and stucco works", caught the attention of the Sicilian Greek historian Diodorus Siculus (80-20 B.C.). At the time Malta was ruled by the Romans and, as elsewhere, these built temples, town houses, baths and villas. Malta had an active harbour where, today, there is the Marsa basin, quays built with massive masonry blocks perfectly cut and jointed, and many warehouses. Melita, the capital of the island (the present Mdina and Rabat) was a sprawling city with well built houses, paved streets, and an underground sewage system. The Dark Ages came over Malta as they did over the rest of Europe, but whilst the latter emerged triumphantly out of its torpor to beget the great monuments of the Romanesque and Gothic periods, the Maltese islands slumbered on. All through the Middle Ages, Malta was a desolate, sparsely inhabited island, because Mediterranean shipping tended to hug the continental coastline, shying away from Malta to avoid shipwreck or pirates that could be lurking in its coves and bays.

Maltese architecture of the medieval period is almost non-existent. Such buildings as there were, were strongly influenced by the Arab tradition, the island having been subjected to Arab domination from 870 A.D. to 1090 A.D., and to a further period of Muslim preponderance which only came to an end in 1127 A.D. with the reconquest of the island by Roger II of Sicily. The island had a number of troglodytic churches with Byzantine figures which probably date from the post-Arab period. Free-standing churches consisting of small flat-roofed cubical structures terminating at their eastern end in an apse, also date, at the earliest, to this period. The system of construction of these churches was conditioned by the fact that the only available building material was the soft, fine-grained limestone, easily quarried and worked. Driven by necessity, the Maltese stonemason learned to make everything of stone, not only walls, but roofs as well. Arches played a principal part, and interior spaces were covered with slabs laid across slightly-pointed transverse arches. These arches divided the interior into bays of about two metres, which is the maximum space that a slab of soft limestone can span. Internally the walls were plastered over and covered with painted murals in gay colours of red and yellow ochre, verdigris and a dark blue-grey. Only a few of these late medieval churches survived — the Annunciation at Ħal Millieri, Sta. Maria of Birmiftuħ, old St Gregory, at Żejtun, and a few others. Externally these churches were very plain, the only ornamental feature consisting of a deep hood mould over the small, slightly pointed doorway with, sometimes, a small circular window above. In Mdina, at Birgu (Vittoriosa), and in the citadel of Gozo, there are some late medieval houses with windows in the first floor of characteristically Catalan inspiration, with round-headed double lights separated by an excessively slim colonette; the two windows being sometimes contained under a wide, slightly pointed hood mould. There was a Cathedral at Mdina, dating from the thirteenth century, with a three-aisled, five-bayed basilican plan. This church was later enlarged by the addition of transepts and a choir, whilst the roof was raised by the addition of a clerestory.

With the arrival of the Knights, Malta suddenly found itself, once more, linked to the main international currents, and with an owner, to booth, representing, then, a concentration of international wealth combined with an incredible reserve of human resources. The time was soon to come when the wealthy aristocratic Knights, and especially their Grandmasters, would shower their riches on the Maltese islands, endowing them with fine works of art and architecture. Eminent artists, military and civil engineers, architects, doctors and artisans would be 'lured' to Malta by one or other of the Knights or Grandmasters; the Order of St John was a good paymaster and painters (like Mattia Preti and Antoine de Favray) and engineers and architects (like Francesco Buonamici, Mederico Blondel, Charles François de Mondion and others) who called at Malta for a few days would remain for many years to the benefit of the whole island.

The Knights chose Birgu (Vittoriosa) as their residence because of its position athwart a peninsula in the Grand Harbour, with deep creeks on either side providing shelter for their fleet. The immediate task was to secure their base. As they had never paused in their campaign against the Turks they were fully conscious that their new headquarters was regarded as a centre of

Christian piracy calling for a hostile response from the mighty Ottoman. Defence-wise their position was, at first, untenable, but with the help of some of the foremost military engineers that were provided by the Christian states, it was rendered sufficiently strong to withstand repeated attacks by a great Turkish force which was sent to dislodge the Knights by Suleiman the Magnificent. After the Great Siege of 1565 the Order decided to build a new fortified town on the high promontory (Mount Sciberras) which straddled and dominated the island's two main harbours, viz., the Grand Harbour and Marsamxetto Harbour. Pope Pius IV sent to Malta Francesco Laparelli da Cortona, one of his best engineers and an assistant to Michelangelo at St Peter's, to advise on, and supervise, the project. The first stone was laid on March 28, 1566, and the city was named "Valletta" after the hero of the Great Siege. The fortifications which encircle Valletta were completed in less than five years – the local labour force being augmented by foreign labour from Italy. When, in 1569, or the beginning of 1570, Laparelli left the island, the task of completion was left in the hands of his able assistant, the Maltese architect Gerolamo Cassar (ca. 1520-1592). It was this architect who subsequently designed the principal buildings of Valletta, comprising the Grand Master's Palace, the Conventual Church of St John's, the seven auberges of the Knights, the Hospital of the Order, the slaves' prison, the Ferreria or arsenal, the orphan asylum, the bakeries and several churches and monastic buildings.

Before embarking on his task Cassar had been sent on a short tour of the principal cities of Italy, and the buildings designed by him rose up in a severe variant of Italian Mannerism. The austere military style of the Valletta buildings, it should be emphasised, had been adumbrated by the rigid grid-iron layout of its street plan which had been designed by Laparelli. It was Laparelli also who had chosen the severe Palazzo Farnese, Rome, as a model for the Magisterial Palace. Gerolamo Cassar's buildings which, as it happened, perpetuated many features which had appeared in late fifteenth century and earlier sixteenth century buildings in Mdina and Birgu, were to set the character of all the buildings of Valletta and influenced, to a great measure, all subsequent buildings in the following centuries. Cassar's façades were all astylar (ie. without pilasters or columns), single or double-storied, with an exceedingly high upper floor, a long uniform row of widely-spaced, straight-headed windows, and a shallow crowning cornice. The emphasis was strongly horizontal with huge masses of plain masonry predominating; the whole tied in with rusticated corners. These rusticated corners finally became the hallmark of Cassar's façades and, as he progressed, the rusticated quoins became wider, more ponderous in character, and more deeply cut and powerful than any example he might have seen abroad. The church of St John is Cassar's masterpiece, and there, in its monumentality, its simplicity, its deep solemnity, and its many Mannerist features, one can appreciate the strong personality of its architect. Cassar's church was originally as severe internally as it is externally, a severity which was intended to express the character of the Order whose church it was, as well as the surrounding fortifications of Valletta. Cassar felt that all his buildings should reflect the fact that they were built in a fortified city, and therefore have a military cast. Subsequently the interior of the church of St John was transformed, mainly by the Calabrese painter Mattia Preti, into the magnificent Baroque interior that it is today.

During the first half of the seventeenth century a number of village parish churches were built in a style strongly reminiscent of the Italian Quattrocento; with elements recalling, as well, the Maltese late medieval churches, particularly in their roofing with serried transverse arches. These churches which had a cruciform plan and a three-bayed unaisled nave seem to have been inspired by the church of Sta Maria del Calcinaio, in Cortona (1484-1502). Another church, that of St George, Qormi, has a basilican plan recalling a very similar plan which is to be found in Francesco Laparelli's collection of drawings, the so-called *Codex Laparelli*. As Laparelli hailed from Cortona it is quite possible that all these churches owe their origin to this engineer. Most of these churches were later enlarged and, in the process, partly spoilt. One of them, however, the parish church of Attard, was left practically untouched, and it is still one of the best examples of a Renaissance church in the island. Another church, Sta Maria, in Birkirkara, was saved through the accidental collapse of its vault. This church, which seems to be influenced by the Spanish Plateresque style, is remarkable for the crispness and richness of its carving.

The Baroque style came to Malta quite early: it is said with the water that, in 1615, flowed to Valletta – by means of an aqueduct – all the way from the aquifers of Mdina. An archway at Fleur-de-Lys (now demolished), a watering station at Floriana, and some fountains in Valletta, were designed in the new Baroque style, presumably by Bontadino de Bontadini, the engineer responsible for the water project. However it was Francesco Buonamici, an architect from Lucca, who built the first important Baroque buildings in Valletta and in other parts of the island, and who was largely responsible for the sober Roman character of Maltese Baroque architecture. Buonamici was the Order's resident enginer from 1634 to 1659, and his primary duties were those of overseeing the extension of the Order's fortifications (notably the fortifications of Floriana), and the maintenance of all the other fortifications. His designs in the then current Baroque style include the church of St Nicholas in Valletta, the remodelling of the Jesuit church, Valletta, the plan of the church of St Paul at Rabat, the adjoining church of St Publius, part of the façade of Żebbuġ parish church, and several altar retables. His civil buildings include the Jesuit College, Valletta, the Hostel de Verdelin, also in Valletta, Wignacourt's College, at Rabat, and perhaps the façade of the Inquisitor's Palace, in Vittoriosa, as well as some palaces on the Vittoriosa waterfront. In the first two façades Buonamici showed how a long façade could be articulated by means of panelling, retaining at the same time the astylar treatment of Valletta's earlier palaces.

Another architect who worked in Malta in the mid-seventeenth century was the Frenchman Mederico Blondel who succeeded Francesco Buonamici as the Order's resident engineer. Blondel is only recorded as the designer of the splendid Baroque façade of the church of St Mary of Jesus (1689), Valletta, but the Valletta churches of St Rocco (1681) and St Francis (1681) are also thought to be his, whilst he was probably also involved in the Carmelite church (1650-72) at Mdina. This centralised church, with an oval plan similar to Vignola's S. Anna dei Palafrenieri, was built by Francesco Sammut and completed by Lorenzo Gafà. Gafà is Malta's greatest Baroque architect. Like Buonamici's and Blondel's, Gafà's Baroque was a sober, classical kind of Baroque, with straight façades and large areas of undecorated wall surfaces employed both for the sake of contrast as well as that of gravity; a gravity that was usually tempered by the liveliness of the skylines. Beginning life as a sculptor, he later turned to architecture and was responsible for a number of churches including St Nicholas (1676-93), Siġġiewi; St Lawrence (1681-97), Vittoriosa; Sta Maria (1685-1712), Qrendi; St Catherine (1692-1778), Żejtun; the Matrice (1697), Gozo; and the Cathedral (1697-1702), Mdina. The latter is Gafà's masterpiece and establishes the apex of the Baroque in Malta. For its dramatic position on the ramparts of Mdina, Gafà's Cathedral has

been said to recall the Baroque monastery of Melk, in Austria, and rightly so, particularly to anyone who approaches Mdina from Valletta. The encircling walls of the old hill town look like parts of the Cathedral building itself, and the whole is surmounted by a beautiful, plastically conceived dome such as only a Baroque sculptor could have fashioned.

Gafà built few secular buildings because churches were his forte. However it is documented that the bishop's palace, in Mdina, Villa Bighi (later screened with a Neo-classical portico on the seaward side and incorporated in the British designed Bighi Hospital) and the Palace of the General of the Galleys, in the Vittoriosa Marina, were designed by him. The last – unfortunately badly battered in World War II but which is still repairable – had a magnificent set of rooms planned symmetrically in the Palladian manner.

Many books have been written to explain how the Baroque style came about and why it became so popular in Roman Catholic countries. Here it is sufficient to say that as this architectural style gained popularity in Malta the Knights tried to transform the austere military character of their city by replacing the original buildings with others in the new flamboyant style, and hence the spate of new churches, new auberges and public buildings in the Baroque style. This transformation was most successful in the two main streets of Valletta, especially so in Merchants Street. The Maltese church had adopted this style before the Knights, and many of the older churches were either remodelled, as, for example, the church of the Annunciation at Tarxien, and the church of the Madonna tal-Għar, Rabat, or demolished and rebuilt, as in the case of the old Cathedral, at Mdina, and the Matrice, in Gozo.

In keeping with the principles of the Baroque style the austerity of the network of fortifications girdling the harbour towns was interrupted with military gateways communicating the splendour and power of the reigning princes, whilst the sea approach to Valletta was made to express the opulence of the city by a series of magnificent magazines along the waterfront of Valletta facing the Grand Harbour balanced, on the opposite side, along the Vittoriosa Marina, by a breath-taking succession of splendid palaces ostensibly meant as residences for the galley captains with warehouses on the ground floor.

The Order's architects who were chiefly responsible for the transformation of Valletta and Mdina, during the first decades of the eighteenth century, into the Baroque cities which they are today were Roman-born Romano Fortunato Carapecchia, who worked in Malta from 1706 to 1738, the Frenchman Charles François de Mondion, who was the Order's resident engineer from 1715 to 1733, and the Valletta-born architect Andrea Belli (1703-1772).

Carapecchia had studied under Carlo Fontana, one-time assistant to those Baroque giants Cortona, Rainaldi and Bernini. Fontana's work has been described as accomplished but derivative and it has been said that he was largely responsible for the classicizing bookish academism into which the Baroque style declined. Nonetheless his studio was the forcing ground of such formidable architects as Ferdinando San Felice (1675-1748), Filippo Juvarra (1678-1736), Johann Bernhard Fischer von Erlach (1656-1723), Johann Lukas von Hildebrant (1668-1745), James Gibbs (1682-1754), and Matheus Daniel Popplemann (1662-1736). Certainly no other architect practising in Malta had such impressive credentials as Carapecchia. As ill-luck would have it no opportunity presented itself for a really great building. The small jobs which came his way, polished, elegant and sometimes ingenious, brought a new air of sophistication to the streets of Valletta. These included the remodelling or outright rebuilding of the national churches of the various langues — the church of St James (1710) for the Langue of Castille,

the church of St Catherine of Italy (1713) for the Langue of Italy, the church of Our Lady of Pilar (1718) for the Langue of Aragon and the church of St Barbara (1739) for the Provençal Langue — as well as the church and convent of St Catherine in lower Republic Street, the Municipal Palace (1720) (today the Public Registry), the Manoel Theatre (1731) and three houses in South Street (Maison Demandolx). Spinola Palace, in St Julians, was also remodelled after a design by Carapecchia.

Charles François de Mondion who had, from 1701, served his apprenticeship under a renowned military engineer, the field marshal Sebastian le Prestre de Vauban, and then served the French Crown until 1720, was a very versatile man. His architectural designs are characteristic of his age: polished, eclectic and impressively elegant. The crispness of the carving and the contrasting texture of the surfaces of his façades are other qualities which are responsible for the outstanding character of his creations. Mondion's chance came when, in the wake of the 1693 earthquake which shook Mdina and demolished its decrepit houses, Grand Master Manoel de Vilhena decided to replan salient sections of the old capital, update the retrograde design of the fortifications and rebuild a number of official edifices. It is thought that in this way Vilhena sought to impress the might of the Order upon a city which had remained a stronghold of the proud Maltese nobility. The buildings designed by Mondion, the Magisterial Palace, which is right at the entrance to Mdina, the Law Courts, and the Banca Giuritale (or Town-House) contribute in no small way to the Baroque character of present-day Mdina but more impressive, perhaps, than these buildings are the city gates which Mondion designed not only for the main entrance to Mdina, but also for Floriana (Portes des Bombes) and Fort Manoel, this fort having been also constructed under his supervision.

The edifices designed by Mondion and Carapecchia are all fine buildings and on a par with those that were being produced on the mainland of Europe. However, the Auberge de Castille (1741-1745), the major baroque palace in Valletta, and the most splendid of all, was designed by a Maltese architect, Andrea Belli. Belli, who was born in Valletta, had spent many years together with his family, in Venice. Thence it is possible that he had visited Austria and southern Germany because some features of his buildings have close parallels with buildings in those countries. Belli was certainly in Italy when the Palazzo della Consulta, in Rome, was completed (1737). This palace was the source of inspiration of the Auberge de Castille although the Maltese building is no blind copy. Belli was responsible for a number of other splendid Baroque buildings whose paternity had been forgotten. The Bishop's Seminary at Mdina (today the Cathedral Museum), a veritable Baroque jewel, was largely designed by him. Belli's design for the Augustinian priory, a stone's throw away at Rabat, was chosen as the winning design in a competition held for this edifice, by none less than Gabriele Valvassori, one of the great masters of the late Roman Baroque. Belli's, as well, is the Museum of Fine Arts, in Valletta, with its magnificent *treppenhaus* staircase, and the Bishop's Curia in Floriana (originally a Jesuit house of retreat) with its charming chapel which seems to have been inspired by Cosmos Damian Asam's Abbey church in Weltenburg (1716-25).

The last eighteenth century architect to practise in Malta was the Sicilian Stefano Ittar (died Jan.18, 1790) who designed the Neo-classical National Library (1786-1796), in Valletta, and presumably finished the Customs' House, another striking Neo-classical building, which had been commenced in 1774 by Giuseppe Bonnici.

So far we have said very little about the plans of these buildings. As in other Mediterranean countries Maltese houses were centred upon the courtyard. At first they were single-storied with hardly any openings on the outside. It seems that there was a time in the late Middle Ages when it was touch-and-go whether our houses would have tiled sloping roofs, as in Sicily, or flat roofs as in North Africa. By the time the Knights came to Malta, in 1530, flat roofs had become general. These were made water-proof, as they were until recently, with a fine layer of 'diffone' — a substance consisting of lime mixed with small pieces of pottery and powdered earthenware. Due to the high cost of land, houses in cities like Valletta and Vittoriosa were multi-storied, with a relatively small internal yard, whilst the plan was very often U-shaped or L-shaped, i.e. the rooms did not quite surround the courtyard. In palaces, however, the *cortile* was fairly spacious with rooms all around and generally with an arcaded gallery between the courtyard and the surrounding rooms. Because of its size the Grand Master's palace had two courtyards but only one has a surrounding arcade. Some of the auberges were originally single-storied but most, very soon, had an extra floor, or more, added to them. At first the staircase was tucked unobtrusively in some angle of the palace so that the entrance vestibule was connected directly to the *cortile*. In the Auberge de Provençe, however, perhaps in 1638 or so, the staircase leading to the main floor above was placed between the courtyard and the entrance vestibule. About a century later this arrangement was repeated but with greater scenographic effect in the Inquisitor's Palace, in Vittoriosa, in the Auberge de Castille (1741) and the Museum of Fine Arts (1761). In the last two the staircase branches out into two parallel flights and is of a type which is called imperial.

Very few of these palaces (town houses) had a manifestly symmetrical plan but when it came to the design of country-houses (villas) many had a characteristic plan which was repeated time and again. This consisted of a long central hall with three approximately equal rooms on each side. The second room was usually taken up by the staircase whilst the room on the opposite side was often turned into a vestibule leading to a side-entrance. This is the plan, for example, of Villa Bologna, Attard (ca. 1747) and Villa Gourgion, Lija (ca. 1700). Sometimes the central hall is preceded by a lobby as at Verdala Palace and Selmun Palace, and sometimes, as at Palazzo Marnisi, Marsaxlokk, an external staircase leads directly to the first floor. This kind of layout fitted well within a square site and thus we find the cubical tower at Bubaqra with a ground floor plan almost identical to that of Villa Bologna and Villa Gourgion. In the first floor, Bubaqra tower has a two-storey high cruciform room with four smaller rooms tucked away in each corner. This layout recalls the perfectly symmetrical layouts of Palladio's villas which also occupied a squarish site. Mamo Tower has a circular central chamber, radiating arms on the main axes and a square room at each of the four ends of the diagonal axes, approaching very nearly, in plan, to Palladio's Villa Rotunda. These country-houses were originally fortified and their façades were necessarily plain. Many had the external appearance of towers — Malta's mini-castles. In due course the danger of corsair attacks subsided and the Maltese nobility and the nouveau riche started building country houses in an even greater number, some clustered in the Three Villages — Lija, Balzan and Attard — and others scattered in various parts of the island, at Gudja, Tarxien, Wardija, Floriana, etc. These country-houses were unfortified although Selmun Castle and some others had the semblance, one imagines for romantic reasons, of the earlier fortified houses.

Up to the mid-eighteenth century most of these country-houses continued the tradition of external simplicity which made them fuse happily with their rustic settings. Some pertinent examples are Palazzo Marnisi at Birżebbuġa, Palazzo Gomerino at Għemieri, Aedes Danielis at Żejtun, the country-house at Djar il-Bniet, the Inquisitor's Palace at Girgenti, Villa Abela at Tarxien, and Gourgion tower in Gozo. After the mid-eighteenth century these villas were often very ostentatious, e.g. Villa Bologna, in Attard, Villa Preziosi (now Francia), in Lija, and Villa Agata in Floriana. Some of these villas cost so much to build that their ambitious owners ended up bankrupt. Most had very big gardens, some as big, or even bigger, than San Anton, and were generally planned with a strong central axis, and divided by low walls into compartments as a protection against strong winds. Many of these gardens have disappeared but one of the most interesting (Palazzo D'Aurel, Gudja) still survives although its old olive groves were destroyed during World War II when it was occupied by the military. This garden, like the plan of the villa itself, has striking similarities to that of Palazzo Leone, Sta Venera, which had been built by Mondion in 1730 for Grand Master Manoel de Vilhena. It has a well-enclosed open court at the back of the house, with an archway centring on a curious temple-like structure at the far end of the main axis. Another walk in the garden of this country-house was flanked with stone vases and statues of elephants, giraffes, dogs and cats, all about the same size. The owner of this country-house, the Marchesa Bettina Dorell, had been a lady-in-waiting in Naples to Carolina, Queen of the Two Sicilies, sister of Marie Antoinette, and had brought with her the romantic ideas of that court. One of the follies in this garden is a mock *girna* inside which a life-like stone "hermit" gazes stonily at his visitors. The most striking of these romantic follies was a "ruined" tower — tall, circular, and rustic-looking — which glistens in the sun, because pieces of glass were embedded in the mortar. It dates from about 1780 and was built, it is said, around an old watch-tower. The rooms in this tower were frescoed, walls, ceilings, and floors also; whilst one of them had a stone table laid out with typically Maltese dishes, all made of stone and painted to look "natural".

Late Medieval churches had the simplest plan possible, consisting of a rectangle with a semicircular apse at the eastern end where the high altar was situated. Devout people sometimes built other box-like churches next to the first one. If two such churches were placed end to end and the separating walls were removed a longish church would be formed. The second box was sometimes built parallel to the first one with a common side-wall and the churches connected, each to the other, by an opening formed between the piers supporting the transverse arches. The same operation was then repeated on the other side of the church. Sometimes chapels were built with their inner end touching the side of the original church. When a church was sufficiently long a nave with accompanying side chapels might have resulted. The obstacle to this kind of plan lay in the piers supporting the transverse arches because the Maltese roofing technique demanded that the distance between them could not exceed two metres. When the Dominicans settled in Malta, in the mid-fifteenth century, they brought with them just such a plan. To provide a good view into the side chapels they did away with the restricting transverse arches and roofed the nave with wooden beams. As this type of plan was, in Italy, favoured mostly in churches run by friars it is known as a "friary church plan". For an island without a natural supply of timber, or to provide a fire-proof structure, this was not the ideal solution. Gerolamo Cassar adopted this plan on a bigger scale for the Conventual church of St John and solved the problem of the timber roof by spanning the nave with a great barrel-vault which was supported at the sides by buttresses rising from the walls of the side chapels. Some of his churches for the religious orders, however, were still roofed with timber trusses. Vignola's Gesù, the prototype of almost every Cruciform Baroque church, with a barrel-vaulted nave with side-chapels, a domed crossing, and a deep choir, appeared in Malta in about

1600 with the building of the Jesuit church to the design of Fra Giuseppe Valeriano, the official architect of the Jesuit Order, but this type of church was too big for most of the village parish churches. As already stated these adopted a cruciform plan with a three-bayed unaisled nave and square-ended transepts and choir similar to that of Francesco di Giorgio Martini's Sta Maria del Calcinaio, in Cortona. The architect of these churches was possibly Vittorio Cassar but they are generally attributed to Tommaso Dingli, who is known to have carved the stonework of Sta Maria of Attard, the new Dominican church at Rabat, and several others. It is known for a fact that he completed, as an architect, a number of churches which were possibly designed by Vittorio Cassar (viz. Sta Maria of Birkirkara and St Philip of Żebbuġ) whilst other churches, e.g. Sta Maria of Mosta, St Bartholomew of Għargħur, Our Lady of Graces of Żabbar, and Sta Maria of Gudja, were probably designed by him.

A number of centralised churches were oval (the Carmelite church, Mdina), circular (Our Lady of Sarria, Floriana), octagonal (St Catherine of Italy, Valletta), or in the form of a Greek Cross (St Nicholas church, Valletta). The church of Our Saviour, Lija (1694-1709) had a plan which was identical to that of the hundred-years earlier church of Attard, except that all the four arms (choir, transepts and nave) ended in apses, and the vault rose from attic pedestals. In fact the apsed ends, the attic, and a vault pierced with high vertical windows, were the principal features which differentiated late seventeenth and eighteenth century Baroque churches from the churches of the early seventeenth century. As in the earlier churches vaults were articulated with transverse ribs but instead of being coffered, vaults were now decorated with paintings.

The church of St Lawrence, Vittoriosa (1681-1697), was built from the beginning with wide ambulatories so that space

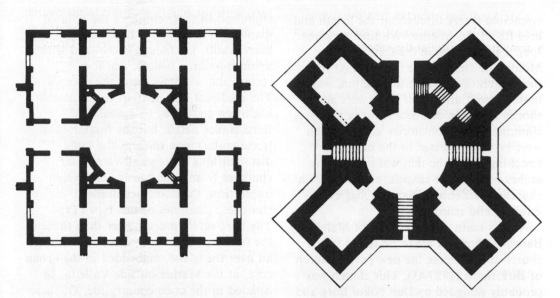

Andrea Palladio: Villa Rotonda, Vicenza.
Perfectly symmetrical layout occupying a
squarish site.

Mamo Tower: very similar in plan to
Palladio's Villa Rotunda. Many country
houses had a characteristic symmetrical plan.

Bay windows on the Sliema promenade during the British period.

circulated freely throughout the length and breadth of the interior. We find the same spatial integration in the Cathedral at Mdina and the Matrice in Gozo. At first the church of St Catherine, Żejtun, was built without aisles, but these were added shortly after. In due course many aisle-less churches had ambulatories added, which were easily connected to the nave by knocking down the thin walls below the arches of the nave chapels, e.g. the parish churches of Żebbuġ, Naxxar, Siġġiewi, Żabbar, and many others.

All the main characteristics of Maltese Baroque churches are to be found in the church of St Helen, the new parish church of Birkirkara (1727-45). This church was probably designed by Dun Nikol Borg and his kinsman, Salvu Borg, who was the Capomastro, or master mason. These ambitious men had the idea of copying the Cathedral at Mdina, "improving" on that church in the process. Thus in the interior, all the ends were made apsidal – in the Cathedral only the choir finished with an apse – whilst, in the façade, the clock faces were placed in the middle of the upper panels. A number of other adjustments followed in the heavier, more plastic, modelling of the eighteenth century, a little more ornament was added here and a little there, the triangular pediment at the top was replaced with something lighter and more florid, and statues were added on the skyline. With the incorporation of these elements a new façade was created, monumental, like that of Mdina, but gay and festive, where that had been properly grave.

A class of church which is encountered all over the island is the so-called "wayside chapel". These chapels are small, single-cell structures and may be found anywhere, in isolated and desolate places, some overtaken by urban sprawl, others magnificent little jewels, cherished by the community they serve. These churches belong to two distinct types. Churches of the first type (Type One) are the direct descendants of the late-medieval cubical churches. In these churches the pointed diaphragm arches have been replaced by a barrel-vault, the façade is crowned with a Spanish-looking bellcot, and low rectangular windows flank the doorway. The medieval simplicity of their ancestors has often given way to a wealth of Renaissance detail, but the fundamental (rectangular) plan remains the same, distinguishing these small vernacular churches from their cousins of foreign inspiration, the domed centralised churches. Churches of this type (Type Two) are rarely much bigger than those of the first type and these, also, are scattered all over the island, embedded in the urban core, at the Marina outside Valletta, or isolated in the open countryside. Of these the most memorable are the churches of Sarria, at Floriana, of Ta' Liesse as seen from the Upper Barrakka Gardens, and of Tal-Providenza in the fields between Siġġiewi and Għar Lapsi. However there are many others which are almost as striking.

During the first fifty years of British rule there was hardly any building activity in the island. The British found themselves well-provided for as regards building. The fortifications could still withstand attack as they had proved during the siege against the French, whilst the palaces and auberges provided all the accommodation that was necessary for the British Civil and Imperial Government. This period coincided with the artistic reaction abroad against the ornateness and frivolity of the Baroque-Rococo style. The return to classical severity, known as the Neo-classical style, did not stop at a revival of the architecture of Ancient Rome but architects went to the original sources of the classical style, that is, to Greece and to the Greek remains of Southern Italy and Sicily. This revival of Greek architecture, primarily of the use of the Greek Doric order gained great popularity in Britain, as it seemed to the British that it represented the purest style of architecture. Thus it was that the Doric Revival was used by the British to assert their presence in the island and as a symbol of their imperial might and glory. The Main Guard rose in the centre of Valletta, Sir Alexander Ball's monument in the Lower Barrakka and, across the harbour, the Bighi Naval Hospital. Many monuments were built at this time, ostensibly to the memory of naval and army officers, but actually as an excuse by the British to leave an impact on the island's landscape, especially on Valletta and its surroundings; eliciting the remark by an English visitor that "since the English became masters the proud bastions of Valletta have become sepulchral."

These artifacts were mostly designed by British architects, but Giorgio Pullicino, from 1803 Professor of Drawing at the University, had studied at the Accademia di San Luca, in Rome, and is reputed to have designed the entrance of the old University in Valletta, the pavilion at Villa Frere, Pietà, the exedra surrounding Perello's Fountain in Fort St Elmo, Sir Alexander Ball's monument in the Lower Barrakka, and Spencer's obelisk. On documentary evidence, however, only the last one can be definitely established as his.

The first stone of the present Anglican Pro-Cathedral in Valletta was laid in 1842 on the site of Gerolamo Cassar's old Auberge d'Auvergne. This was the third design for this Anglican building. In 1825 Col. Whitmore had prepared a design but nothing came of it. Then, in 1838, Queen Adelaide, who was recuperating in Malta, donated £10,000 for the new cathedral. The building was commenced in 1839 to the design of Richard Lankersheer who was the English Director (then called Superintendent) of Public Works between 1 March 1830 and 13 August 1841. As an architect Lankersheer had considerable talent but unfortunately was unversed in local building construction and, soon after the foundation stage, "cracks, splits, and crushings" in the structure began to appear. The anti-British press capitalised on this incident to attack the occupation of all high posts by Englishmen and, in

particular, the post of Director of Public Works. Lankersheer, disgraced, died of a broken heart at the age of 38. The work was finally entrusted to William Scamp, a young naval architect who had already distinguished himself in the construction of a dry-dock and the Naval Bakery at Vittoriosa. This building, the first and finest example of British industrial architecture in the island, was externally inspired by Kent's Horse Guard in London, and is as Baroque as British architecture was in the mid-eighteenth century (i.e. when the Horse Guards was built).

With such precedents one hardly expected that overnight William Scamp would turn to classical purity. And yet he did, to produce one of the neatest and coldest examples of Neo-classicism in Valletta. But the tower and spire of this church; unclassical and quintessentially English, struck the right vertical note to the emphatical horizontality of the curtains, bastions and buildings of Valletta – which is more than can be said for the Royal Opera House.

This building, of which the Maltese were so proud, was designed by a British architect, in his British studio, principally for the social delectation of British service officers stationed in the island. Columnar façades are foreign to the architecture of Valletta which is overwhelmingly astylar, but the architect of the Royal Opera House – Edward Middleton Barry, the architect of the Royal Opera House of Covent Garden – estranged from everything else that is Maltese struck a sympathetic chord in the common people by endowing it with a massiveness, vigour and floridity, which can only be described as Neo-Baroque. At the time that it was built (1860) there had been a shift in this direction everywhere, e.g. the Operà, Paris (1861-74), the Exchange (1876) and Palais de Justice (1866-83), Brussels, etc. Classical façades are grave and static. Columns breaking forward from their fellows, column clusters, and vital dynamic skylines, such as we find in Barry's Opera House, are unclassical. The best view of Barry's Opera House was diagonal and, had it been finished as designed by Barry, the skyline of the Opera House would have been even livelier with its flourish of vases and statues.

Grongnet's Mosta Dome (1833-1860) the only ostensibly Neo-classical building designed by a Maltese architect, won popular approval for the same reason. It was monumental, it was rich with coarsely detailed, excessive, ornament, and it was vital. In the Mosta church the static classical dome of the Pantheon (the original classical model) was enlivened by a dynamic catenary curve and the static centralised plan was given directional emphasis by the addition of a deep eastern choir. This dynamic Baroque vitality is emphasised by the coffering in the dome. In the Pantheon the coffering consists of horizontal bands of gradually diminishing squares. In the Mosta dome these turn into diagonal bands of lozenge-shaped panels which spiral upwards with a whirling movement. The Maltese, who have never taken to the Neo-classical style, took this church to their hearts and, as soon as the stonework was finished, started to decorate it and have continued ever since, in the same way that they have decorated and continue to load with ornament their other Baroque churches.

It was at about this time (ca. 1835) that there appeared a type of villa, or country-house, which was new to Malta. Villa Portelli, at Kalkara, and Capua Palace, in Sliema, were apparently designed by the same architect. Their inspiration was probably British because verandahs on external façades are not a Maltese device. On the other hand, in every part of the Empire, Britons built colonnaded or arcaded porticos to ward off the strong direct sun. These two villas had a progeny of a sort — e.g. Dragonara Palace, Villino Chapelle, and a number of smaller villas but, more often, Maltese architects preferred to combine external colonnaded,

or arcaded, porticos with larger areas of solids.

Verandahs or porticos were popular with the designers of Military Barracks, an important aspect of Maltese architecture during British rule, and a number of Maltese schools with long colonnaded façades, like, for example, the Government Schools of Sliema, Żejtun, etc. (built in the early decades of the twentieth century) may not have been uninfluenced by these military buildings, but the most successful secular, arcaded and porticoed building was designed by British, probably naval, architects. The Dockyard Terrace on the Senglea Marina was originally the Palazzo dei Capitani delle Galere, erected by the Knights of St John as a residence for the Order's Galley Captains. The British put up a screen of arcades and light columns on the façade and converted it into a residence for high-ranking Dockyard officials. During World War II the light Upper Gallery was destroyed and has remained unreplaced. On the opposite side, in the Vittoriosa Marina, the British repeated the same idea but with much less success. In fact they did more harm than good by mutilating some very fine palaces in the process.

After about the mid-nineteenth century architects abroad had grown tired of the Greek revival and eclecticism had set in. The same thing happened in Malta where the local temperament had never favoured classical purity. Soon "the fancy dress ball of architecture" was in full swing with three Maltese architects, in particular, holding the scene during the second half of the nineteenth century. The eldest of these three architects, Nicola Zammit (1815-1889) was a medical doctor by profession and a philosopher by inclination. As an architect Zammit's forte was the designing of new church façades for old churches. These include St Catherine, Żurrieq (1861); St Nicholas, Siġġiewi (1862); St Publius, Floriana (1885); and St Paul Shipwrecked, Valletta (1885).

The predominant character of these

façades is Baroque with motifs inspired by Ferdinando Fuga's Sta Maria Maggiore and Christopher Wren's St Paul's Cathedral. Columns are used with monumental effect in sharp contrast to the characteristic Baroque church façade (of the seventeenth and eighteenth centuries) in which columns are conspicuously absent. Zammit's influence through his writing extended beyond his excursions in architecture but perhaps his most outstanding success was his introduction of one of the basic tools of the Maltese mason — the stone-scraper (raxketta), used for the first time in the façade of Zammit's village parish church of St Nicholas. It is a pity that hardly anyone associates this tool with his name.

The second of the three major architects practising in the second half of the 19th century was Giuseppe Bonavia (1821-1885). Bonavia was born in Valletta and his most important buildings are actually there. The façade of the Carmelite church, rebuilt in 1852 to Bonavia's design, an academic composition remarkable mainly for the unusual double windows which formed its central feature. To Bonavia, then employed as Clerk of Works with the Royal Engineers, goes the distinction of being the author of the first Gothic church in Malta — in an island where this style, in its historical period, had manifested itself in isolated features, in windows, in a Gothic system of roofing, etc., but never in an entire building. This Gothic building, commenced in 1854, was the Presbyterian church of St Andrew, which is in South Street corner with Old Bakery Street, and its style and architecture were greatly dictated by Bonavia's client, the Scottish Minister Rev. George Wisely who took great pains to give the building a consistently British look. Two years later Bonavia designed the Carmelite church at Balluta. Here Bonavia was given an entirely free hand and the result was a rather qualified sort of Gothic. Bonavia's best known building was the Borsa, or Exchange Building, in lower Republic Street (completed in 1857). The façade of this building is in the Neo-classical style; but in a style so light that it is nearer to the Rococo-Classical of Robert Adam. The low-relief sculpture, the cornucopia in the spandrels of the arched doorways, the medallions over the windows in the first floor, and the garlands in the wide frieze above, as well as the characteristic cast-iron railings in the long open balconies, are all typical of this light elegant style.

In the records office of the P.W.D. there is a project by Bonavia, dated 1859, for the proposed Royal Opera House, in the same light Neo-classical style as for his Borsa. Bonavia's façade had three storeys, or rather two and a high attic, but otherwise it was typical of Valletta's architecture — astylar, with arcading on the ground floor, straight-headed windows on the other floors, and robust corner pilasters characteristic of Valletta. Unfortunately Bonavia's design was rejected for that by Barry. A decade and a half after the rejection of Bonavia's project this Maltese architect built the palace or rather twin palaces — opposite the Royal Opera House. This time Bonavia was as effusive as his supplanter had been in the Royal Opera House. For his palace Bonavia went to Venice for inspiration, to produce a façade which, for its richness, is worthy even of that city of rich façades. Bonavia's façade was almost as alien to the Valletta scene as Barry's had been. However Bonavia's palace was astylar, like the other Valletta houses, and, with the addition of the oriental-looking "Maltese" balconies — then in their heyday — the architect established an acceptable compromise — a façade which for all its foreignness was somehow familiar. Soon semicircular-headed binary windows sprouted all over the island, consolidating the "Malteseness" of Bonavia's façade. Of Bonavia's other buildings, which included the church of Stella Maris at Sliema (almost totally rebuilt soon afterwards) the most noteworthy is perhaps one of the best examples of Romanticism in Malta — a combination of a staged tower and a Roman circular temple which was built, as an embellishment, in the garden of Villa Depiro, Lija. This exquisitely proportioned little structure, partly derived from Bramante's Tempietto of S. Pietro in Montorio, and almost as bare of ornament, is now entirely out of context, standing as a traffic island in a vast open space for which it was not meant originally.

The third and most prolific of the major architects of the nineteenth century was Emmanuele Luigi Galizia (1830-1906) who made his mark as an architect in the Public Works Department, of which he was Superintendent (or Director) from 1880 to 1888. Galizia's first important work came in 1855 when, at the age of 25 years, he got the prestigious commission to design the chief Protestant cemetery at Ta' Braxia, outside the Floriana fortifications. The Neo-Romanesque chapel of this cemetery is mainly of interest because it signals the appearance in the Maltese architectural scene of yet another period style which was later to become fairly popular in ecclesiastical quarters through its patronage by a Maltese Benedictine monk, Dom Maurus Caruana, who was bishop of Malta from 1915 to 1943.

Galizia's big chance came shortly after, when he was commissioned to design a big Catholic burial ground on Tal-Ħorr hill outside the village of Tarxien. Recognition of Galizia's masterpiece was immediate. When the cemetery, which was dedicated to the Addolorata, was solemnly consecrated on May 9, 1869, newspaper reports were enthusiastic about the beauty of its architecture, its meticulous planning and the decorative aspect of the small Gothic church crowning the summit of Tal-Ħorr hill. It is to Galizia's credit that he had identified the potentialities of the site and risen to the occasion. Galizia's success brought him a commission (in 1874) for yet another cemetery; this time for the Muslim community. For this cemetery Galizia sought inspiration in the architecture of Muslim India, which was at hand, or very

nearly, in the Royal Pavilion at Brighton. Galizia's cemetery won the admiration of Abdul-Aziz Khan, the visiting Sultan of Constantinople, who conferred the Order of the Mejidie, in appreciation, on its architect. This excursion in Saracenic architecture produced, at about this time, those quaint "Moorish" houses in Rudolph Street Sliema, which with their horseshoe arches and characteristic fretwork-type carving bring a delightfully exotic touch to one of the oldest corners of Sliema. For the Carmelite church at Balluta (1871) Galizia reverted to Gothic. This church, with its interesting Neo-Gothic rendering of the traditional two-towered Maltese church façade, was particularly remarkable for the rightness of its scale in relation to the flanking row of low terrace houses and for its poly-chromatic touches so harmoniously complementary to the azure waters of the bay fronting it. This church was replaced by another "Gothic" structure in the 1950's but with less satisfying results.

Galizia's sense of the rightness of his architecture in relation to its setting is again evident in the Gothic chapel of Our Lady of Lourdes at Mġarr, Gozo, which was built between 1888 an 1893. Overlooking a bay, like his church at Balluta, this chapel is isolated and stands on top of a hill. Thus a façade with a single steeple as the crowning feature was just right.

The Gothic style which had been introduced by the British for its Britishness — the church of St Andrew in Valletta (1854), the Trinity Church and adjoining rectory in Sliema (1866), Sliema Point Battery at Għar id-Dud, Sliema (1872-77), and the Methodist church in Floriana (1881) — had been accepted and became even popular in Maltese ecclesiastical circles for its association with Pre-Reformation Society. In the last decades of the nineteenth century it was adopted for its picturesque qualities by the noble and wealthy Maltese families who built turretted and battlemented country villas at

Wardija, Mġarr, Rabat and Lija and elsewhere. But the most fantastic manifestation of the Romantic movement was a public utility building, the mock Neo-Gothic villa which houses the sewage pumping station in Rue d'Argens, Gżira. In domestic architecture the revivalist styles remained in vogue for a considerable time, not only in country villas but, sometimes even in crowded city-scapes where some pretentious façades included not only pointed windows, hood-mouldings, crockets and similar Gothic motifs, but battlements and on occasional corbelled turret as well.

Some Maltese architects amalgamated Gothic and classical motifs to produce refreshingly new combinations. The most interesting example was the church of San Gaetano, Ħamrun, built by George Schinas between 1869 and 1875 with medieval elements internally and a façade hailing from Longhena's Baroque Sta Maria della Salute and towers from Laon's Gothic cathedral. The crossing had to be crowned with a Romanesque lantern — such as those of Mayence cathedral and of St Sernin, Toulouse — which would have been a total alien in the Maltese scene. Fortunately this was never built, the present dome being built in 1953-55 by Chev. Gużè Damato to the design of Andrea Vassallo (1856-1928). Taking his cue from the façade, Vassallo had very wisely modelled his dome on that of Sta Maria della Salute, in Venice.

It is no accident that near the end of this article we should meet with the architects Vassallo and Damato associated together in the design and construction of this, the most beautiful dome in Malta, because these two men were, without doubt, the last two great architects of an island which has produced many illustrious architects. Both, as it happens, were self-taught men without any formal training in architecture. Architecture was in their bones. To Vassallo we owe the dome of St Nicholas, Siġġiewi, "the most graceful dome in Malta", the dome of St Gaetano, Ħamrun,

the church of Ta' Pinu, in Gozo, the government school, Sliema, the church of Tal-Ħerba in Birkirkara and innumerable interventions in other churches. Vassallo was an eclectic, designing in the different period styles with the same ease. Two of his last works are in the Art Nouveau: the Casa Said, on the Sliema front, which has been demolished recently, and Villa Rosa, in St Andrew's; this last crowning the brow of a hill which was terraced, laid out with exotic trees, walks, pergolas and a nymphaeum.

In Maltese history Ġużè Damato will be identified as the architect who was mainly responsible for the prolongation of the Renaissance form-language well beyond its natural historical limits. He will be remembered as the architect chiefly responsible for the perpetuation of a tradition which, to an observer coming to Malta from countries were other conceptions of architectural history apply, may seem absurd and even inconceivable. Damato thought big, and all his churches — like Gafà, Damato was mainly a builder of churches — are big, sometimes enormous, often provoking harsh criticism for their obtrusive impact on their environs. Nonetheless for his churches of Casal Paola, the Carmelite church, in Valletta, and the rotunda of Xewkija, Gozo, Damato deserves a secure place in the Hall of Fame.

It is rather sad that this study has to end on a very pessimistic note. Since Independence the Maltese nation has become affluent with the consequence that the island was witnessed a building boom out of all proportion to its size. Already large tracts of countryside, both in Malta and Gozo, have disappeared. Soon there will be no countryside left at all. There cannot be architecture without building but even great architecture is no substitute for the grandeur of nature. Would that the Maltese nation wake up to the impending doom before it is too late! But I have little hope.

Bibliography

ABELA, G.F., *Della Descrittione di Malta*, Malta, 1647.

ASHBY, T.H., "Roman Malta", in *Journal of Roman Studies*, V, 1915, pp.28-80.

AZZOPARDI, J., *The Church of St John in Valletta: 1578-1978*, edited by Fr John Azzopardi, Malta, 1978.
　St Paul's Grotto, Church and Museum at Rabat, Malta, edited by J. Azzopardi, Malta, 1990.

BECKER, L., *Malta Sotterranea − Studien zur Altchristlichen und Jurichen Sepulkralkunst*, Strassburg, 1915.

BINNEY, M., "Baroque Architecture in Malta" in *Country Life*, 30 Oct. 1969.

BLOUET, B.W., "The impact of armed conflict, in the rural settlement patterns of Malta, A.D. 1400-1800", in *Institute of British Geographers*, Transactions N.S. Vol.3, No.3, 1978.

BONANNO, A., "Quintinus and the location of the Temple of Hercules at Marsaxlokk", in *Melita Historica*, Vol.VIII, 3, 1982, pp.190-204.

BONELLO, V., "Posizione Storica Dell'Architettura Maltese"; and "Mattia Preti", in *Atti del XV Congresso di Storia dell'Architettura*, Rome, 1970.

BORG, K., "Neo-Gothic Architecture in Malta in the nineteenth century", unpublished B.E.&A. dissertation, University of Malta, 1982.

BORG, V., "Maltese Churches" in *Maltese Baroque*, edited by G. Mangion, Malta, 1989.

BORG, V., with R. Bonnici Calì, *Il-Knisja ta' Ħal Tarxien*, Malta, 1973.

BOWERMAN, H.G. *The History of Fort St Angelo*, Malta, 1947.

BRAUN, H., *Works of Art in Malta: Losses and Survivals*, London, 1946.
　An Introduction to Maltese Architecture, Valletta, 1944.

BUHAGIAR, M., DENNIS DE LUCCA, A. LUTTRELL, "The Tal-Baqqari churches", in *Hal Millieri: A Maltese Casale and its Churches*, edited by A. Luttrell, Malta, 1976.

BUHAGIAR, M., "Medieval churches in Malta", in *Medieval Malta*, London, 1975.
　Late Roman and Byzantine Catacombs and related Burial Places in the Maltese Islands, Oxford, 1986.

BUHAGIAR, M., and SERAPHIM ZARB, *St Catherine of Alexandria: Her churches, paintings and statues in the Maltese Islands*, Malta, 1979.

CAGIANO DE AZEVEDO, M., "Medieval Buildings at Tas-Silġ and San Pawl Milqi", in *Medieval Malta*, edited by A. Luttrell, London, 1975.

CROCKER, J., *History of the Fortifications of Malta*, Malta, 1920.

DARMANIN, J.F., "The Buildings of the Order of H.M. Victualling Yard, Malta", in *Melita Historica*, Vol.II, 1957, pp.66ff.
　The Phoenico-Graeco Roman Temple and the origin and Development of Fort St Angelo, Malta, 1948.

DARMANIN DEMAJO, G., A series of articles (based on primary sources) on the Valletta Auberges, in the *Archivio Storico di Malta*, Vol.1 pp.261ff; Vol.II pp.57ff and pp.213ff; Vol.III pp.70ff and pp.201ff; Vol.IV pp.65ff.
　"Memorie Storiche delle Albergie dei Cavalieri Francesi dell'Ordine Militare di S. Giovanni", in *Archivum Melitense*, Vol.III, Aug. 1929, pp.51ff.

DEGIORGIO, R., *A City by An Order*, Malta, 1985.

DE LUCCA, D., "The Maltese 'Perit' in History", in *Melita Historica*, Vol.VI, No.4, 1975.
　"French Military Engineers in Malta during the 17th and 18th Centuries", in *Melita Historica*, Vol.VIII, No.1, 1980.

"The Contribution of Francois de Mondion in the Architectural Development of 18th Century Malta", in *Proceedings of History Week 1981*, pp.78-81.

"Islamic Architectural Manifestations in 18th Century Malta", in *Hyphen*, Vol.IV, No.5, 1985, pp.159-168.

"British Influence on Maltese Architecture" in *The British Colonial Experience 1800-1964*, edited by V. Mallia Milanes, Malta, 1988.

ELLUL, M., "Francesco Laparelli da Cortona and the Fortifications of Valletta (Malta)", in *Atti del XV Congresso di Storia dell'Architettura*, Rome, 1970.

"Carlo Gimach (1651-1730) – Architect and Poet", in *Proceedings of History Week 1986* of the Historical Society, (Malta).

Fort St Elmo – Malta, a brief history, Malta, 1988.

FERRIS, V.A., *Descrizzione Storica delle Chiese di Malta e Gozo*, Malta, 1866.

FLORENSA, A., "L'Architettura di Spagna a Malta", in *Atti del XV Congressi di Storia dell'Architettura*, Rome, 1970.

HOPPEN, (BUCHAN), A., "Military Engineers in Malta, 1530-1798", in *Annals of Science*, No.38, pp.413-433, England, 1981.

The Fortification of Malta by the Order of St John, Edinburgh, 1979.

HUGHES, J.Q., *The Building of Malta, 1530-1795*, London, 1969.

Fortress: Architecture and Military History of Malta, London, 1969.

LUTTRELL, A.T., "Approaches to Medieval Malta", in *Medieval Malta: Studies on Malta before the Knights*, ed. A.T. Luttrell, London, 1975.

"Malta Troglodytica: Għar il-Kbir", in *Heritage*, No.24.

Hal Millieri: A Maltese Casale and its Churches and Paintings, edit. by A. Luttrell and including contributions by M. Buhagiar, D. De Lucca, G. Wettinger, Tony Mangion, Paola Zanolini and G. Bautier Bresc., Malta, 1976.

"The House of the Castellan of Malta", in *Heritage*, No.9, Jan. 1978.

MAHONEY, L., "The Conventual Church of St John", in *Architecture in Malta*, Malta, 1986.

A History of Maltese Architecture from Ancient Times up to 1800, Veritas Press, Malta, 1988.

"Architect Andrea Vassallo (1908-1928)" in *Melita Historica*, Vol.X, No.3, 1990, pp.225-236.

"17th Century Architecture" in *Maltese Baroque*, edited by G. Mangion, Malta, 1989.

MALLIA-MILANES, V., "In Search of Vittorio Cassar. A documentary approach", in *Melita Historica*, Vol.IX, No.3, Malta, 1986.

MANGION, G., "Malta Barocca" in *Studi Italo-Maltesi*, Malta, 1989.

OCCHINI, P.L.I., *Un grande Italiano dell'500, Francesco Laparelli a Malta*, Arezzo, 1937.

PIRRI, P., *A. Valeriano, S.J., Architetto, Pittore, 1542-1596*, Rome, 1970.

QUINTIN d'AUTUN, J., *Insulae Melitae Descriptio*, Lyons, 1536.

SALOMONE, E., *Grongnet confuta Fergusson, Documenti Inediti*, Malta, 1911.

SAMMUT, E., *Art in Malta*, Malta, 1960.

"Note on Stefano and Sebastiano Ittor" in *Proceedings of History Week*, 1982.

SCHERMERHORN, E., *Malta of the Knights*, London, 1929.

SCICLUNA, H., *St John's Co-Cathedral*, Rome, 1955.

TONNA, J.A., *Tumas Dingli – A study of his architectural works*, Malta, 1966.

"The Evolution of Palace Architecture: Valletta and Mdina", in *Atti del XV Congresso di Storia dell'Architettura*, Rome, 1970.

TONNA, J.A., and DE LUCCA, D., *Romano Carapecchia. Studies in Maltese architecture*, Malta, 1977.

ZAMMIT, T., *Valletta – An Historical Sketch*, Malta, 1929.

*Mdina '93: a re-enactment of the Grand Master's entry into the Città Notabile.
On the arch are Malta's three patron saints: Publius, Paul and Agatha.*

A detail from Antoine Favray's painting of Grand Master Emanuel Pinto de Fonseca at St John's in Valletta.

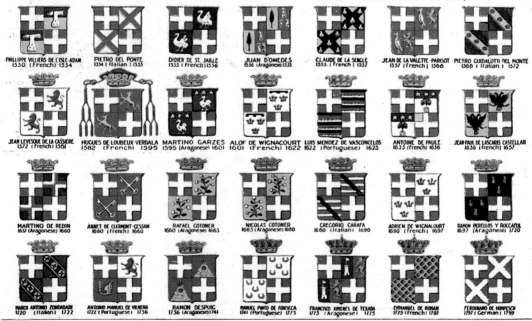

COATS of ARMS of the GRAND MASTERS of the ORDER of ST. JOHN of JERUSALEM who have ruled in MALTA.

PHILLIPPE VILLIERS DE L'ISLE-ADAN 1530 (French) 1534

PIETRO DEL PONTE 1534 (Italian) 1535

DIDIER DE ST. JAILLE 1535 (French) 1536

JUAN D'OMEDES 1536 (Aragonese) 1553

CLAUDE DE LA SENGLE 1553 (French) 1557

JEAN DE LA VALETTE-PARISOT 1557 (French) 1568

PIETRO GUIDALOTTI DEL MONTE 1568 (Italian) 1572

JEAN LEVESQUE DE LA CASSIERE 1572 (French) 1581

HUGUES DE LOUBEUX-VERDALA 1582 (French) 1595

MARTINO GARZES 1595 (Aragonese) 1601

ALOF DE WIGNACOURT 1601 (French) 1622

LUIS MENDEZ DE VASCONCELOS 1622 (Portuguese) 1623

ANTOINE DE PAULE 1623 (French) 1636

JEAN-PAUL DE LASCARIS CASTELLAR 1636 (French) 1657

MARTINO DE REDIN 1657 (Aragonese) 1660

ANNET DE CLERMONT-CESSAN 1660 (French) 1660

RAFAEL COTONER 1660 (Aragonese) 1663

NICOLAS COTONER 1663 (Aragonese) 1680

GREGORIO CARAFA 1680 (Italian) 1690

ADRIEN DE WIGNACOURT 1690 (French) 1697

RAMON PERELLOS Y ROCCAFUL 1697 (Aragonese) 1720

MARCO ANTONIO ZONDADARI 1720 (Italian) 1722

ANTONIO MANUEL DE VILHENA 1722 (Portuguese) 1736

RAMON DESPUIG 1736 (Aragonese) 1741

MANUEL PINTO DE FONSECA 1741 (Portuguese) 1773

FRANCISCO XIMENES DE TEXADA 1773 (Aragonese) 1775

EMMANUEL DE ROHAN 1775 (French) 1797

FERDINAND DE HOMPESCH 1797 (German) 1799

The Coats of Arms of the Grand Masters who ruled Malta between 1530 and 1798.

Festa fireworks and an Easter Sunday festivity.

Presidents Bush and Gorbachev during their "end of the Cold War" meeting at Marsaxlokk, Malta, in December 1989.

Malta prime minister Eddie Fenech Adami talks to European Commission president Jacques Delors, with Malta's full membership of the European Union in the offing.

Għar Dalam cave: deposit of a great quantity of bones of Pleistocene animals, later the abode of Neolithic man.

The Ġgantija temples, now considered to be the earliest example of free standing stone architecture in the world.

A large concentration of cart tracks south of Rabat.

Graves with spiral decorations in relief inside one of the Salina hypogea.

*Square tower (5.60m. high) of ashlar masonry, datable to the late Punic period,
inside a private garden in Żurrieq.*

One of the finest portraits of the emperor Claudius (A.D. 41-54), found during the 1881 excavations of the Roman "domus" outside Mdina.

Il-Kullana cliffs in the Fawwara area of Dingli Cliffs. Here all five rock types forming the stratigraphic sequence of the Maltese Islands are visible. The island of Filfla is in the background.

Sea arches on the northeast coast of the island of Comino. This is one type of marine erosion feature resulting from the action of the sea on the limestone rock of the Maltese Islands.

The watercourse at Wied il-Għasel, limits of Mosta, in winter. Because of their abundant supply of water during the wet season, and the shelter they provide, the "widien" are amongst the richest habitats in the Maltese Islands.

Maltese Everlasting (Helichrysum melitense) growing on the cliff edge at Fungus Rock, Gozo. This plant is endemic to the Maltese Islands, where it is found almost exclusively on the cliffs along the western coast of Gozo.

The endemic Filfla door-snail (Lampedusa imitatrix form gattoi), a terrestrial snail found only on the island of Filfla. The scientific name of this animal commemorates Count Alfredo Caruana Gatto, one of the pioneers of the study of the natural history of the Maltese Islands.

A medieval countryside chapel at Ħal Millieri.

The main altar and interior of the Carmelite Church at Mdina.

The main door of a Norman house at Mdina and its courtyard.

Depictions of the Great Siege of 1565 by Perez d'Aleccio.

Two Maltese artists: a portrait of Giuseppe Calì (1846-1930) by Edward Caruana Dingli (1876-1950).

Detail from "Life under the Soil" by Antoine Camilleri.

Esprit Barthet's "nudi".

Eighteenth century carnival depictions by Antoine Favray, from a private collection.

A folk singer in rustic setting from Caruana Dingli's brush.

A portrait at the Chamber of Commerce of Sir Adriano Dingli (1817-1900): Councillor, jurist and adviser.

The Santo Spirito Hospital, Rabat, now housing Malta's National Archives.

The Holy Infirmary of Valletta, now housing the Mediterranean Conference Centre.

A portrait of the surgeon Michel'Angelo Grima (Museum of Fine Arts).

Seaside and agricultural scenes contrast with one of Malta's industrial estates.

Some Maltese delicacies: "braġoli" (beef olives), "soppa ta' l-armla ("widow's soup"), with fresh "ġbejniet" from Gozo; fish, vegetables, Maltese bread and wine.

Art

Antonio Espinosa Rodriguez

The earliest artistic manifestations in Malta date to prehistoric times. This is testified by a rich archaeological heritage consisting of a variety of decorated clay and stone artifacts and a series of impressive megalithic structures. The potter's craft developed into an expression of cultural vitality materialised through a series of patterns and decorations that reflect successive aesthetic requirements. The *Impressed Ware* of the early neolithic farmers of the *Għar Dalam* phase (5000-4500 B.C.) was superseded by the prosaic forms of the *Grey Skorba* phase (4500-4400 B.C.) and enlivened by a bright red slip in the course of the so called *Red Skorba* phase (4400-4100 B.C.). Meanwhile man discovered the art of modelling anthropomorphic figurines. However it was during the *Temple Period* (4100-2500 B.C.) that prehistoric man in Malta poured forth an extraordinary civilising energy that took the contours of greatness.

Beside the master potter there developed a race of builders and stone carvers whose inspired daring and skill are vouched for by the monumental temples of Ġgantija, Mnajdra, Ħaġar Qim, Tarxien and a string of less known sites. Buildings that are reputedly amongst the finest and oldest stone edifices in the world. Here the sculptor carved into the soft globigerina limestone uncanny abstract and figurative relieves and statuettes in the round that vie with the best of modern art. In the hallowed underground environment of the Ħal Saflieni Hypogeum architecture and stone carving were fused into a single act whilst complex spirals, executed in red ochre, testify inherent painterly practices.

The succeeding Bronze Age people built, at Borg in-Nadur, the earliest fortifications in Malta and produced a number of stylised flat terracotta figures and decorated their pottery with an ornate sharp geometrical motif.

The eclectic Phoenicians made their first appearance in Malta some time round the year 700 B.C. With their trading wares they brought new customs and fashions. At Tas-Silġ, near Marsaxlokk, they erected a sanctuary in honour of the goddess Astartes. With time Malta's link with the Punic world, particularly Carthage, grew closer. Personal jewellery, amulets, ornaments and a few surviving architectural remains betray the egyptianizing forms favoured by this Semitic people. The impressive baked clay anthropomorphic sarcophagus found at Għar Barka near Rabat dating to the fifth century B.C., is illustrative of Egyptian influence. On the other hand a few imported bowls found in tombs, the typology of certain locally manufactured pottery and a pair of marble candelabra, with Greek and Punic inscriptions dedicated to Herakles-Melqart, indicate some form of contact with the Greek world.

In 218 B.C. Rome conquered the Maltese Islands from the Carthaginians. Roman rule was to last some six hundred years. Notwithstanding its provinciality and relative isolation there is evidence of lively artistic activity in Malta. Excavations carried out in 1881, at Rabat, revealed fragments of the rich mosaic pavements of a patrician town house. Dating to the first century A.D. these mosaics are composed in the refined *opus tessellatum* and *opus vermiculatum* techniques and show a high degree of workmanship. The Roman baths at Għajn Tuffieħa were likewise embellished with mosaics. Architectural fragments confirm the former existence of lavish buildings. The tombstone of a musician and comedian and other archaeological evidence indicate that Roman Malta had its own theatre. Notable amongst the extant statuary of the period are the portrait bust of *Antonia the Younger* and the head of *Emperor Claudius*. Cicero in his prosecution against Caius Verres describes the latter's pillage of works of art from the temple of Astartes, which by then had been rededicated to Juno, her Roman counterpart.

Christianity made its first appearance during the Roman domination. Traces of early Christian art are evident in underground cemeteries called Catacombs. Fragments of murals, graffiti and carvings stand witness to the desire of translating into visual forms the prayers of the faithful and the Christian message of eternal life. Unfortunately most of these works are now in a dilapidated state and consequently their artistic evaluation is difficult and problematic. However, their quality appears to range from the purely naive carvings of the Ħal Resqun Catacombs to the ornate sophisticated forms noticed in the decorations at the Abbatija tad-Dejr and Salina Bay Catacombs. Tracts and traces of wall paintings are still visible in St Agatha's Catacombs at Rabat.

The vestiges of an early Christian basilica and baptistery, uncovered at Tas-Silġ, and the above mentioned Catacombs are remnants of palaeochristian artistic practices. On the other hand a few tombstones – of which the elegant *Maimuna's Stone* is the best known example – a silver ring, and some bits of pottery, is all we have to attest to the presence of Islamic art and crafts within the Maltese Islands.

As Mario Buhagiar rightly points out in his authoritative *The Iconography of the Maltese Islands* no painting, excluding fragments extant in Christian catacombs, can be dated to before the late Middle Ages. A common Maltese Mediaeval

practice was the use of underground cavities as dwellings and churches. One of the earliest paintings in Malta is the late thirteenth century image of the *Virgin and Child* in the rock-cut sanctuary at Mellieħa. Of special interest is the *Crucifixion* and *Annunciation*, probably dating to the fourteenth century from the apse of the crypt adjoining the Abbatija Tad-Dejr catacombs now removed and exhibited at the National Museum of Fine Arts. These and other surviving troglodyte murals, notably those in St Agatha's Crypt at Rabat, betray the iconography and formal hieratic composition of the Siculo-Byzantinesque School. Pertaining to the same tradition but dating to the late fifteenth century are the frescoes adorning the wayside chapel of the *Annunciation* at Ħal Millieri near Żurrieq.

The avowed *St Luke Madonna* in the Cathedral at Mdina is a beautiful and refined Byzantinesque panel whose sophisticated execution suggests Sienese and International Gothic influences. Similar artistic traits appear in the superb *Virgin of Mercy with SS. Paul and Augustine* now in the sacresty of the Augustinian Church at Rabat. This was originally a polyptych of which a fourth panel, depicting St Catherine, also survives. Another altarpiece dating to the middle of the fifteenth century and of which four panels are still extant is to be found in the parish church of St George at Qormi. The central scene represents an extraordinary *Lamentation*. Here the painter conveys, through the emaciated body of Christ and the intense doleful expressions of Mary and her companions, a heavy atmosphere charged with strong emotional piety and pathos. The entire pictorial complex which includes St George, St Gregory and a Crucifix encompass Byzantine spirituality with International Gothic narrative zest.

The splendid *St Paul Polyptych*, now at the Cathedral Museum, was the former reredos of the Cathedral Church. It is a work of great beauty attributable to the circle of the Catalan painter Luis Borassa (1360-1426). Nothing is known of its early history but given the subject and iconography it must have been purposely commissioned for Malta. The central panel, representing St Paul in Majesty, is surrounded by ten other smaller panels. Significantly one of the scenes recounts the apostle's shipwreck in Malta. Notwithstanding the loss of its original framework and the damage brought about by the passage of time it still has the power to arrest and impress the beholder.

Throughout the Middle Ages Malta received its artistic stimulus via the nearby larger island of Sicily. The 'Messina' painters, for instance, introduced innovative late fifteenth and early sixteenth century modes. Antonio de Saliba (1466-1535) and Salvo d'Antonio (active 1493-1526) had intimate family links with Antonello da Messina (c. 1430-1479) and their art is closely related to that of the great Renaissance master. Both artists received Maltese commissions. Antonio de Saliba executed in 1517 an altarpiece for the church of Santa Maria de Gesù at Rabat whilst Salvo d'Antonio produced, in 1505, a polyptych for the Benedictine Nuns of Mdina. One other Sicilian painter active in Malta just prior to the coming of the Order of St John was the Syracusan Alessandro Patavino, or Padovano, who from 1520 to 1521 was engaged in decorating the ceiling of the old Cathedral Church of Mdina. In 1529 Patavino was still receiving occasional commissions from the Cathedral Chapter.

The advent of the Knights of St John in 1530 signified the beginning of a new era. Up to the time the Cathedral at Mdina had been the principal artistic hub of the Maltese archipelago. The Knights shifted attention first to the harbour town of Birgu and later to the new city of Valletta. With them they brought from Rhodes their archives and many of their artistic treasures. These included the precious twelfth century Byzantine icon of the *Madonna of Damascus* now extant in the Greek Catholic Church of Valletta and a set of French illuminated choral books commissioned in 1521 by Grand Master Philippe Villièrs de L'Isle Adam.

In the wake of the Order of St John there came a large group of retainers and followers including skilled craftsmen. One was a certain Nicola Caccialepre who in 1535 carved a marble stoup for the chapel of Santo Spirito Hospital. The influential Sicilian sculptor Antonello Gagini (1478/79-1536) had in 1504 produced a fine marble *Madonna and Child* for the Franciscan Church of Santa Maria di Gesù at Rabat. Now at the demise of Philippe Villièrs de L'Isle Adam in 1535 the same artist was commissioned to execute the funeral effigy of the Grand Master. Another work generally attributed to Gagini or his workshop is the fine marble Baptismal Font in the Cathedral at Mdina.

Artistic links with Sicily continued through the early years of the Order's rule. In 1551 Can. Giuseppe Manduca commissioned an altarpiece for the Chapel of St Agatha in Mdina from an unknown painter of Sicilian extraction or training. Thus sifted late Renaissance models percolated into Malta receiving, in the process, a local mannerist twist that resulted in the admixture of retardataire and innovative features. This is very much in evidence in the remaining fragments of the *Last Judgement* in the Church of Bir Miftuħ at Gudja. The 1546 *Santa Scholastica* altarpiece, now in the Monastery dedicated to that Saint at Vittoriosa, is illustrative of the whimsical artistic currents then effecting the Maltese Islands.

Giovanni Maria Abela is one of the earliest recorded Maltese painters. Only one certain painting by his hand is known to have survived the ravage of time. The picture represents the *Virgin of the Rosary surrounded by the Holy Mysteries*. This is a painting, signed and dated 1591, which originally graced the church of Siġġiewi and is now on permanent display at the Cathedral Museum in Mdina. A similar altarpiece, dated 1595, at Naxxar is also generally ascribed to Abela. Both works represent a fair indication of the charms and limits of contemporary local painters.

On the 28 March, 1566 Grand Master Jean Parisot de La Vallette solemnly laid the foundation stone of the fortified city that still bears his name. The city's layout and defences were set by the Italian military engineer Francesco Lapparelli (1521-1570). However it was the Maltese military engineer and architect Geronimo Cassar (1520-1586) who supervised the actual construction of the new city and was responsible for the design of its principal buildings. One of the first edifices to be erected in Valletta was the Magisterial Palace. Here the Italian Matteo Perez D'Aleccio (1547-1616) decorated the throne room or 'Sala del Maggior Consiglio' with an impressive series of frescoes that recount the heroic defence of Malta at the time of the Great Siege of 1565. For the new Conventual Church Perez D'Aleccio executed the large *Baptism of Christ* to serve as its main altarpiece. For the Collegiate Church of St Paul he produced the vast *Shipwreck of St Paul* which established the Apostle's Maltese iconography. Mattia Perez D'Aleccio eventually left Malta and after spending some time in Rome and Seville migrated to Peru where he set up shop in Lima. Other late mannerist painters whose works can be admired in Malta include Antonio Catalano il Vecchio (1560-1606), Francesco Potenzano (c.1540-1599), Giovanni Battista Riccio (1537-1627), Daniele da Monteleone (active 1600-1622) and Filippo Paladini (c.1544-1616).

The painter Filippo Paladini reached Malta chained to a bench of a Tuscan galley in 1588. The previous year he had been condemned to row in a galley for his involvement in a violent fight in Florence. However the then reigning Grand Master Hugues De Loubenx Verdale interceded on his behalf and secured his release and services. The Grand Master soon had him working on the decorations of Verdala

Castle and in the Magisterial Palace at Valletta where he frescoed the Palace Chapel and painted its main altarpiece. His splendid *St James*, in the Church of that saint in Valletta, is an explicit and superb example of Mannerist pictorial art.

Amadeo Perugino painted in 1617 the venerable but mediocre altarpiece of *Our Lady of Ta' Pinu* in Gozo. Compared to this pedestrian work Vincenzo Baiata's *Madonna and Child* of 1611, formerly at Tal-Virtù Chapel and now in the Collegio Wignacourt Museum, appears as a veritable tour de force. Clearly influenced by Filippo Paladini it is a handsome painting whose execution and chromatic values are in the best tradition of late Italian Mannerism. Paladini's art was to have a lingering influence on painting in Malta. Filippo Dingli's attractive canvas, dated 1660, of the *Magdalene* at Madliena harks back to the style introduced by the master at the start of the century.

The Conventual Church of St John, built by Geronimo Cassar, rapidly became a focal centre of art in Malta. It was the main Church of the Knights of St John and the Order and its members vied in its embellishment. Round 1608 the great Michelangelo Merisi da Caravaggio (1571-1610) painted for the Oratory of St John his momentous *Beheading of St John* and for the Chapel of Italy the magnificent *St Jerome*. Caravaggio's triumphant stay in Malta was short-lived for his pesky spirit landed him in trouble and he was imprisoned. Somehow he eluded his guards and made his escape from Fort St Angelo only to die shortly after at Porto Ercole in Italy. Amongst the canvases Caravaggio executed in Malta is the well known '*Louvre*' portrait of Grand Master Alof De Wignacourt accompanied by a page and wearing the Verdelin suit of armour. Caravaggio's revolutionary dramatic realism, tonal values and extraordinary interplay of light and shade turned him into one of the most influential and important European painters of all time.

In Malta the influence of Caravaggio was particularly felt by a painter called Cassarino to whom a number of generally mediocre and inferior paintings have been attributed on stylistic grounds. This enigmatic painter was first identified by the late Dr J.A. Cauchi when his signature was uncovered during the cleaning and restoration of a *St Sebastian tended by the Holy Women* belonging to the Church of St John. The figures appear to emerge from within sombre Caravaggesque tonalities highlighted by flashes of a warm brown light that picks up salient details and accentuates the drama enacted in the painting. However Cassarino's mannered and rigid execution falls short of respectable artistic standards. Notwithstanding a mystifying effort to equate him with a certain Giulio Felici, Cassarino's enigmatic personality still remains a moot point.

Bartolomeo Garagona's (1584-1641) *Deposition*, dated 1627, in the Cathedral sacresty at Mdina, is saturated by Caravaggesque tonal values. However its pathos and expressive religious intensity recalls late Spanish Gothic models. Garagona, who hailed from Senglea, also engaged himself in architectural projects. Fra Lucas Garnier (active 1650-1700) and Gaspare Formica (d.1647) were foreing painters active in Malta. Fra Garnier was a French member of the Order of St John. His works were competently executed but lack the lustre of the real master. His enormous altarpiece of *St Theresa* at Cospicua communicates the peculiar sensation that it is the product of a well exercised dilettante. Gaspare Formica is said to have originated from Piacenza. His works are usually charged with queer unreal chromatic values and contain monumentally conceived figures who are seemingly conscious of the beholder's presence. His talents, however, defaulted through a dearth of originality and his compositions are brazen adaptations of other people's ideas. A case in point is his bizarre *Holy Family* of 1626, in the convent of the Friar Minors of Valletta, which he lifted direct from Luca Cambiaso.

Mario Minniti (1577-1640), Pietro Novelli (1603-1647), Giovanni Battista Caracciolo (1578-1635) and Jusepe Ribera (1591-1652) either worked in Malta or executed their Maltese commissions abroad. As a matter of fact there was a constant flow of fine paintings coming into Malta from overseas. Guido Reni (1575-1642) is not known to have visited Malta and yet his *Christ Holding the Cross*, formerly in the Grand Master's Palace and now in the National Museum of Fine Arts, must have reached Malta at the time. Very active in this respect were some of the Knights themselves. In 1653 Jacques De Cordon D'Evieu, Ambassador of the Order of St John to the Holy See, commissioned his portrait in Rome from Pierre Mignard (1612-1695). The painting was eventually sent to Malta and incorporated into the Palace Collection. At one time it hung at San Anton's Palace from where it was transferred to the National Museum of Fine Arts.

The second half of the seventeenth century was dominated by the presence in Malta of Mattia Preti (1613-1699). Preti's magnificent brand of Baroque resulted from the interpolation of his Neapolitan and Caravaggesque formation with his attraction to the splendid chromatic qualities of Venetian painting. A brilliant draughtsman, his productions mirror a strong and overpowering artistic personality. In 1661 he started work on the ceiling decorations of St John's Church. It was Preti who converted this building's erstwhile unassuming interior into a dazzling Baroque scenario. Preti did not limit his *oevre* to the Conventual Church. In the course of thirty years Preti continued to work in Malta producing countless paintings for both local and foreign patrons.

Mattia Preti's influence was all-pervasive and his paintings are encountered all over the Maltese archipelago. He had several followers, assistants and imitators whose often meek output fell short of the master's high standards. Preti's pupils included the Spanish Knight Don Pedro Nunez De Villavicencio (1640-1698), best remembered as a lifelong friend of Murillo, who in 1668 painted the altarpiece of *St Philip Neri* for the Church of Our Lady of Porto Salvo at Senglea.

Notwithstanding the presence of Mattia Preti the painters Giuseppe D'Arena (1633-1719) and Stefano Erardi (1630-1716) kept a busy workshop and enjoyed a certain amount of prestige. Invariably prompted by the art of the great master their personality were not, however, entirely stifled and managed to steer along parallel artistic courses. Their paintings can be admired in almost every Maltese parish. Both painters received the privilege of painting a picture for the Conventual Church of St John. The former painted the lunette of *St Sebastian before the Pope* in the Chapel of Auvergne whilst the latter did *The Adoration of the Magi* in the Chapel of Germany. Generally D'Arena's compositions tend to be studiously schematic and derivative but he had the ability, on occasions, to impress and rise above average. Erardi was not shy to plagiarise or emulate the work of other masters but his fine articulated compositions are fluid and grand. Alessio Erardi (1617-1727) was the son of Stefano. He was a worthy artist who deserves to be better appreciated. His *Virgin of the Rosary* in the Parish Church of Lija is truly impressive.

In 1693 an earthquake struck Sicily and the Maltese Islands. The Old Cathedral and other mediaeval buildings at Mdina were either destroyed or severely damaged. This gave the excuse to the Cathedral Chapter to embark on the already envisaged plan to erect a new Cathedral. The task of designing and building the new Cathedral was assigned to architect Lorenzo Gafà (1630-1704). This imposing well proportioned building epitomises the sober elegant sculptural quality of Malta's baroque architecture. The skyline and physical character of the country is governed by the baroque imprint left by ingenious Maltese architects and stonemasons, too numerous to enumerate, whose clever use of the local building medium is truly admirable. Romano Carapecchia, on the other hand, came from Rome in 1706 and was not Maltese. Yet, through his ingratiating and elegant form of baroque Carapecchia transformed the face of Valletta giving it its present urbane stamp.

In the realm of sculpture Melchiorre Gafà (1635-1667) stands out at a par with the greatest Italian sculptors of the time. He was the brother of Lorenzo Gafà and his talents must have been nurtured through the direct handling of Malta's soft limestone. Unfortunately he died an untimely death in Rome and his works in Malta are few. The Italian Giuseppe Mazzuoli (1644-1725) followed Melchiorre Gafà's design in his impressive *Baptism of Christ* at the Conventual Church. Maltese ecclesiastic and domestic baroque architecture were enriched with refined sculptural motifs by mostly anonymous local stone carvers. This important aspect of Malta's art has, unfortunately, never been properly studied and only a couple of names such as Pietro Felici (1669-1743) and Paola Zahra (1685-1447) are still vaguely remembered.

In concomitance with baroque taste the interiors of stately houses become showy and elaborate. Niccolo Nasoni (1691-1773) was invited to Malta to paint the soffits above the corridors in the Magisterial Palace at Valletta. He decorated the Chancery's main hall, some of the rooms at the Verdala Castle, the Grand Masters' Crypt at St John and possibly the entrance hall of the Auberge De Provence. Judging from a painted ceiling inside 'Palazzo Spinola' at No.9 Frederick Street, Valletta it seems that Nasoni was also engaged in the decorations of private residences. These decorations usually consisted of *tromp-l'oeil* architectural compositions, with open skies, foliage and floral devices and make-belief medallions and sculptures. The Messinese Antonio Manoel produced, round 1793, the well known "fake" dome in the Cathedral of Gozo. This form of decorative art was carried on into the nineteenth century by the Maltese painter Antonaci Grech. The fashion was revived at the turn of the present century when painters such as Filippo Venuti (fl.1880-1906) were engaged to decorate the homes of the emergent well to do classes.

Gian Nicola Buhagiar (1698-1752) and Francesco Vincenzo Zahra (1710-1773) were two outstanding eighteenth century Maltese artistic personalities. Both of them were sons of gifted stone carvers and must have received the first artistic notions from their respective fathers. They worked mostly for the Ecclesiastical establishment painting grand compositions full of movements and articulated figures. Although they operated within the same environment, kept separate workshops and possibly competed for the same type of commissions, their personal relations appeared to have been cordial. At Żejtun they were respectively commissioned to paint, in a sort of friendly competition, the corresponding transepts apses of the Parish Church of St Catherine. Of the two painters Zahra clearly emerges as the more dynamic and forceful. Zahra was also a successful and highly competent portrait painter.

The second half of the eighteenth century saw the establishment in Malta of the French painter Antoine Favray (1706-1798). He just about became an "official" painter to the Order of St John and through his art he presided over its decadence, reflected in the flamboyant elegance of his portraits. In addition he painted attractive altarpieces of which the admirable *Annunciation* in the Cathedral Museum is a fine example. His charming *Maltese Ladies Paying a Visit* in the National Museum of Fine Arts is emblematic of a fashionable rococo genre that recorded the last vestiges of a vanishing era.

The year 1798 was a watershed and a turning point in the history of the Maltese Islands. The Knights were ignominiously expelled from Malta by the French who were, in their turn, ousted by the British. The new century was inaugurated by a change in status and political regime. British rule remained in vigour up to the attainment of Independence in 1964.

Shortly after taking control of the Maltese Islands Captain Alexander John Ball, the Civil Commissioner, re-established the University of Malta which had been closed by the French. The new Rector of the University, Canon Francesco Saverio Caruana (1759-1847), then founded an Art Class which was incorporated in the Faculty of Architecture. The painter Michele Busuttil (1770-1828) was appointed Professor of Drawing. So it happened that this late Baroque artist became the mentor of the new upcoming generation of Maltese painters.

Towards the close of the eighteenth century Giuseppe Grech (1757-1787) was the most promising Maltese artistic element but his untimely death, whilst studying in Rome, impeded him from acting as a link bridging the passage of art in Malta from the eighteenth to the nineteenth century. However although Busuttil dominated the artistic scene he was not the only painter active at the time. Due consideration should be given to Gaetano Calleja who was commissioned by the 'Università', that is the municipal government, to paint the portrait of King George III now at the Palace in Valletta. Antonaci Grech, brother of Giuseppe Grech, supplemented the income derived from his interior decorations by paintings watercolour Malta views and militiamen.

The exuberant and eloquent Baroque style has left an indelible mark over the Maltese Islands. It is an essential feature of the archipelago's physiognomy and culture. Yet nineteenth century Malta experienced a virulent reaction against the Baroque movement and its manifestations.

The anti-Baroque reaction was essentially

two pronged. 'Neo-classical ideals', expounded by antiquarian Johann Joachim Winckelman (1717-1768), which ostensibly promoted a return to Greek Classical art and architecture was favoured by Malta's new rulers and a section of the local cultured elite. The 'Purist' and 'Nazarene' movements, which promoted a form of Christian art purified from what were considered to be pagan incrustations, was promoted by the Church and the more conservative Catholic intellectuals.

The former is best exemplified in architecture and in some instances in sculpture whilst the latter is best manifested in religious painting. To this must be added an infill of romantic Gothic revival in the form of a few pseudo Gothic Chapels and houses with a marked British accent.

Official preferences are clearly manifested in public monuments and buildings. Ball's Memorial at the Lower Baracca, the portico at the Main Guard, Bighi Naval Hospital and the main entrance to the old University building at Valletta have a definite classical appearance. An important promoter of this style was Col. George Whitmore (1775-1862) of the Royal Engineers who was in charge of the Public Works Department. Certain Maltese gentlemen also developed a linking for Neoclassicism. Sir Agostino Portelli, for instance, introduced doric columns and related architectural features in his Villa at Kalkara. Certainly the most pompous Neoclassical building in Malta is the Mosta Parish Church designed by George Grognet De Vasse (1774-1862).

However the prevailing taste of the populace remained essentially Baroque. Proof of this are the many processional statues produced by sacred image makers and sculptors such as the refined Mariano Gerada (1770-1823) and the ever popular Carlo Darmanin (1825-1905). Illustrative of the artistic dichotomy then existing in the arts is the ouvre of sculptor Vincenzo Dimech (1768-1831). On the one hand he

executed, in collaboration with his cousin Ferdinando Dimech (d.1840), the explicit Neoclassical *Monument to Judge Joseph Nicholas Zammit* erected at the Upper Baracca Gardens in 1824. On the other hand he was the author of the exquisite baroque stone *Annunciation* that still grace the parvis outside the Balzan Parish Church.

Topographical views of Malta and its harbour have always enjoyed a certain amount of favour. In 1749 Alberto Pullicino painted a series of views for the Chevalier De Turgot. In the course of the nineteenth century the genre became increasingly popular. Louis Taffien (1811-1866), the various members of the Schranz and Brockdorff families, Giorgio Pullicino (1779-1851), and Michele Bellanti (1807-1883) were specialists in the genre who made it their metier and main source of revenue. Others like Nicolas Cammillieri (c.1773-1860) and the elusive G. D'Esposito concentrated in ship-portraiture which they sold to seafarers and ship-owners.

Through the good offices of Canon Francesco Saverio Caruana a scholarship was established by Government to permit promising young artists to further their studies in Rome. Pietro Paolo Caruana (1794-1852) and Giuseppe Hyzler (1793-1858) were amongst the first to benefit from this scheme. In Rome they soon absorbed the lessons imparted by the Purists and Nazarene painters.

Pietro Paolo Caruana eventually succeeded Michele Busuttil as Professor at the Art Class. He enjoyed a special relationship with his mentor Tommaso Minardi who, as head of the 'Accademia di San Luca', was the foremost influential artist in Rome. Caruana received important church and state commissions. His ecclesiastical works include the altarpiece of the *Visitation* in the Dominican Church in Valletta. and that of the *Immaculate Conception* in the Collegiate Church at Cospicua. In 1823 he executed the monumental canvasses of *St George* and

St Michael purposely commissioned by Governor Thomas Maitland for the Palace throne room. Caruana also pioneered the art of lithography in Malta. His son Raffaele (1820-1886) was also a talented though less successful painter.

Giuseppe Hyzler (1793-1858), however, was probably the most influential Maltese artist of his age. He was the leading advocate of the Nazarene movement in Malta and was a personal friend of the German painter Friedrich Overbeck (1789-1869). Hyzler became one of the determinant factors that fomented anti-baroque feelings in Malta. His artistic ideals lay in the middle ages, the Umbrian School particularly Perugino and the early Raphael. The emblematic *Our Lady of the Rosary* in the Dominican Church in Valletta and the titular painting in the Chapel of Manresa in Gozo are amongst Hyzler's finest works. The National Museum of Fine Arts has a fine self portrait depicted in 1821 in which he shows himself in the characteristic garb of the Nazarenes. His brother Vincenzo Hyzler (1813-1849) was an artist of great promise. Unfortunately his early demise cut short his career.

The despoliation of baroque carvings and decorations suffered by several Maltese churches are generally attributed to the influence exercised by Giuseppe Hyzler and his followers. Certainly he was responsible for the unhappy modifications carried out in 1838 to the Chapel of France in the Conventual Church of St John. However it is unfair to attribute to him the often senseless mutilations carried out in Churches in later times. Whatever his merits or demerits Giuseppe Hyzler was instrumental in shaping nineteenth century religious painting in Malta. It was through his intervention that important Maltese mediaeval panels and murals were saved from destruction or utter oblivion.

Giuseppe Calleja (1828-1915) was Hyzler's most assiduous and faithful disciple. He continued advocating the Nazarene and Purist philosophy right to

the end of his life. He produced a large number of altarpieces notable amongst which are the main altarpieces of Balzan Parish Church and that of the Franciscan Church of St Joseph in Rabat. Apart from Calleja other painters such as Tommaso Madiona (1803-1864), and Salvatore Micallef (1810-1891) continued to propagate the Nazarene style long after it had become stale and dated. Sadly, few if any of Hyzler's followers or imitators ever managed to rise above mediocrity.

Michele Bellanti (1807-1883) deserves to be singled out as one of the most original and talented painters in Malta at the time. His *Virgin of Mount Carmel* and *Elijah* are truly remarkable works. As already noted he was also a fine watercolourist and lithographer. Can. Giuseppe Bellanti (1787-1861), the Cathedral Dean, was his brother and was himself an amateur painter and art connoisseur.

Several foreign artists, mostly Italian, dominated Malta's artistic scene at the close of the century. Domenico Bruschi (1840-1910) was active in Malta in the 1880's. His most impressive Maltese painting is the large *Annunciation* in the Cathedral at Mdina which is dated 1886. Another Italian painter was Giovanni Gallucci (b.1815) from Ancona who was commissioned to paint the dome of the Cathedral. Francesco Grandi (1831-1891) produced a fine *Descent of the Holy Spirit* also in the Cathedral Church. Pietro Gagliardi (1809-1890), however, was to become the most successful and popular Italian painter in Malta. He was introduced into the local artistic scene by Canon Paolo Pullicino who commissioned him a *Madonna and Child* for the Philermos Chapel in St John's. Gagliardi's popularity grew to the extent that he came to entirely dominate religious paintings in Malta. Attilio Palombi (c.1860-1912), Eliodoro Coccoli (1880-1974), Virgilio Monti (1860-1940), Caffaro Rore (b.1910) and Giovanni Battista Conti (1880-1972) are some of the notable Italian artists who, from the second half of the nineteenth century to the second half of this century, became household names in many Maltese parishes.

Giuseppe Calì (1846-1930) was the most forceful and acclaimed Maltese painter of his age and could not stomach what he considered to be unfair competition from Italian artists. He was born in Valletta of Neapolitan parents. His father was a musician and scenographer, his mother a soprano. He received his artistic training in Naples under Giuseppe Mancinelli (1813-1875) but was greatly attracted by the art of Domenico Morelli (1826-1901). Morelli's influence is clearly manifested in his *St Jerome* at the Sacro Cuor Church in Sliema. His strong personality and great facility with the brush saw no rivals. Avid for work he suffered no qualms in undercutting prices to insure he got commissions that would otherwise have gone to an Italian competitor. He was a fast and prolific painter and his productions encompass a very wide spectrum of subjects and genres. In the field of religious art he produced some of his most remarkable works, foremost amongst which is his splendid *Glory of St Francis* in the Valletta Church of that saint.

Lazzaro Pisani (1854-1932) was some twelve years younger than Giuseppe Calì. He was a gifted painter who has left us some very fine works. However the quality of his productions tend to fluctuate. His moment of glory came when he collaborated with the sculptor Francis Xavier Sciortino (1875-1958) in the decoration of Nadur Parish Church in Gozo. An important decorative scheme, which alas was lost during World War II, was the ceiling decorations in the Dominican Church of Vittoriosa. The main altarpiece in St Ubaldesca Church at Paola is noteworthy for some of its painterly passages and the inclusion of figures in contemporary dress. Although aware of the various revolutionary trends effecting the arts abroad he remained the last of a breed of painters who owed their allegiance to

nineteenth century bourgeois academism marked by a strong dose of sentimentalism and melodrama.

In the wake of Giuseppe Calì's art there was his son Ramiro Calì (1882-1945). Less able than his father he was nonetheless a capable painter. Two of his largest canvases are the allegories of *Melita* and *Britannia*, on display in the Maritime Museum at Vittoriosa, which he painted for the Malta Pavilion at the British Empire Exhibition held at Wemble Park, London in 1924. The contemporary Ġuże Duca (1871-1948) was a copious painter whose numerous altarpieces seldom rose above mediocrity.

With the demise of Giuseppe Calì and Lazzaro Pisani Maltese religious painting fell into the doldrums. The sculptor Antonio Sciortino (1879-1947) became Malta's most significant artistic personality. Sciortino spent a good part of his active life in Rome where he was director of the British Academy of Arts. Stylistically he was abreast with his time and many of his works show clear modernistic tendencies undeniably inspired by 'Art Nouveau' and 'Futuristic' obsessions with speed and movement. Highly respected and esteemed, he became a national celebrity. His impressionistic bronze *Les Gavroches* of 1907 at the Upper Baracca Gardens and his stupendous *Christ the King* at Floriana remain Malta's finest public monuments. Although he did execute some religious works his production was largely secular.

Francis Xavier Sciortino (1875-1958) was Antonio's brother. His talents as a sculptor were considerable and what we have of his in Malta is worthy of admiration. F.X. Sciortino travelled widely and in 1914 settled in Canada. In 1939 he returned to Malta but went back to Canada in 1954 where he died. Edward Galea (1893-1971) was one other gifted sculptor who migrated to Canada in search of work and recognition.

Abram Gatt (1863-1944) was a first rate practitioner of traditional 'papier mache' devotional and processional statues and also provided numerous designs for church silver and furnishing. His only known painting is the attractive *Christ the King* which he did for the Domus Piux IX of Cospicua. The art of popular 'papier mache' devout sacred imagery was perpetrated by the prolific Gozitan Agostino Camilleri (1895-1979) and is now continued by the latter's son Alfred. Paul, another son of Agostino Camilleri, is currently sought for his conservative pseudo baroque church decorations.

In the mean time architecture had been going through various developments that reflect a combination of a traditional mentality and building methods with models or fashions imported from abroad. A fine instance is the remarkable Royal Naval Bakery at Vittoriosa designed by the British architect William Scamp (1791-1871) and built in the period 1842-1845. Giuseppe Bonavia (1821-1885) was the first ever Maltese architect to use the Gothic idiom. This was the Presbyterian Church of St Andrew in Valletta consecrated in 1856. The style became a fad with local anglophiles who introduced it in domestic architecture. Architect Emanuele Luigi Galizia (1830-1907) took the mode to heart and used it in several projects including the Addolorata Cemetery and its Chapel.

At the turn of the century Modernistic trends gradually crept in domestic architecture. In the 1920's Art Nouveau found fertile grounds in the development of Sliema. A number of new houses at Birkirkara and Balzan also followed the fashion. Notwithstanding inherent beauty and elegance these buildings are now falling prey to speculators with disastrous consequences to the general environment and transmutation of Sliema.

After Giuseppe Calì and Lazzaro Pisani the painter Edward Caruana Dingli (1876-1950) became the premier Maltese painter of the pre-war period. A society painter *par excellence*, he excelled in portraiture, landscape and genre subjects with a special Maltese flavour. In 1927 he was appointed head of the Government School of Art. Edward Caruana Dingli distinguished himself for his brilliant palette and great artistic technical abilities. Obfuscated by his brother's shadow, Robert Caruana Dingli (1882-1940) merits better recognition. He was an excellent illustrator and engraver and his paintings are often full of zest and vibrant life. Unlike his brother who hardly ever ventured into sacred art, Robert did produce a few Church paintings for Gozo.

Gianni Vella (1885-1977) was a prolific if somewhat uneven painter. For many years he dominated church painting in Malta and his works tend to be repetitive and stale. His easel paintings, however, are more satisfactory. They show his awareness of modernistic trends and reveal the artist free of the constraint of popular taste imposed on his church commissions.

Joseph A. Briffa (1901-1987) deserves to be remembered and revered as one of Malta's outstanding twentieth century masters. His command of the painting medium was complete and his handling of the brush was superb. His sacred productions are truly impressive, but so are his non religious works. His bozzetti are masterpieces of spontaneity and freshness. Briffa deserves to be properly studied and appreciated. Amongst his many works are the ceiling decorations of the Tal-Ħerba Church, the small Church of St Paul at Birkirkara and the dome of the Parish Church of St George at Qormi.

The years immediately preceding the second world war saw the formation of a group of remarkable Maltese artists. Most of them had received their artistic training at the Government School of Art under the brothers Caruana Dingli and had furthered their studies at the Regia Academia di Belle Arti in Rome. Here their guiding light was Prof. Carlo Siviero. However a few did go to England whilst the remarkable etcher and painter Carmel Mangion (b.1905), for instance, travelled to Paris and New York.

George Preca (1909-1984) returned to Malta on completing his studies in Italy but, after some disappointments, he opted to return to Rome where he worked and lived paying occasional visits to his native country. His little understood *Crucifixion* at Żejtun marks a departure from traditional formulas and paved the way towards a new form of religious artistic sensibility in Malta.

Anton Inglott (1915-1945) had a sensitive and deeply religious personality. He seemed destined to dominate Maltese painting but his untimely death kept him from enriching Malta's artistic heritage. Nonetheless he has left a respectful number of works that attest to his great artistic abilities. The large apse decoration in the Parish Church of Msida representing the Death of St Joseph can be considered as the epitome of Maltese sacred art.

Willie Apap (1918-1970) spent most of his productive life abroad. He was a remarkable and versatile painter and his paintings bear the impression of a strong and original artistic personality. His *Woman taken into Adultery* at the Fine Arts Museum is a moving and powerful work that attests to the superlative level of Willie Apap's art. He was also a refined and accomplished portrait painter.

Whilst studying in Rome Willie Apap shared his apartment with Carmelo Borg Pisani (1914-1942) a Maltese painter of some promise whose blind Fascist ideals led him to an early and tragic death.

Emvin Cremona (1891-1987) was a great decorator and his artistic style bears a strong personal imprint. He did embellish many churches with vast decorative schemes and produced several altarpieces. Cremona engaged himself with equal elan in executing non-religious works of art. His innovative verve led him to experiemtn with new and unusual materials. His abstract and semi-abstract works bear a strong personal mark, as does his art in general, and deserve respect. The designs for his Malta stamps remain to date unsurpassed for their beauty and originality.

George Borg (1906-1983) can be considered as Antonio Sciortino's true successor. His command of the sculpture medium, especially modelling, was complete. His slow and fastidious manner of execution prolonged the completion of his works but the end result can only be described in superlative terms. His portraits are no mere likenesses for they pulsate with life and express incredible internal energy and power. His religious works are also invested with great sensibility and originality. Probably because of his introvert nature George Borg was not popular with the general public who tended to bypass him. Yet he stands like a giant amongst his contemporaries. The portraits of Dun Karm, Princess Poutiantine and many other works are pointers to the rare qualities of this sculptor.

Vincent Apap (b.1909), brother of Willie Apap, is an extrovert. A man of great technical ability and refined artistic sensibility he has great facility in modelling and producing works of art. He has received important commissions and produced the likeness of several famous personalities including members of the British Royal family and Sir Winston Churchill. The *Temptation of St Anthony* is one of his happy ventures into sacred art.

Joseph Kalleja (b.1898) is the current doyen of Malta's artistic community. His peculiarly mystic character made him experiment with the tortured forms of expressionism. His works are marked by great individuality and idiosyncrasy. Slightly older than Kalleja was the sculptor Ignatius Cefai (1894-1981) whose polished sensual figures have distinct Art Deco accent. Other equally valid sculptors of this generation include Emmanuel Borg Gauci (b.1911), Victor Diacono (b.1915), Joseph Galea (b.1910) and John Spiteri Sacco (b.1907).

Pertaining to a younger generation was the sculptor Edward Pirotta (1938-1968) whose rising talents were squashed by a traffic accident. His works are not numerous but what we have testify to the great possibilities this man possessed had he had the chance to develop his talents fully.

Our century has seen the rise of a number of remarkable watercolour painters. Joseph Galea (1905-1985) is perhaps the best remembered of the older generation for his name became a synonym with watercolour Malta views. The latter's son, Edwin Galea, proudly continues the family tradition but with a marked preference for ships and maritime historical scenes. The remarkable Giuseppe Cassar (b.1917) prefers the intimate narrow streets, nooks and corners of his island home with occasional ventures in the depiction of fishing boats and villages capturing in the process the sharp chromatic brilliance of Maltese light. John Martin Borg (b.1953) with his transparent atmosphere handles the medium with great dexterity and effect. The upcoming Debbie Caruana Dingli (b.1962) shows she is a worthy daughter of a family with a strong artistic tradition.

Giuseppe Arcidiacono (b.1908) must be singled out for he belongs to a class of his own. This extraordinary watercolourist handles the medium with incredible ease. His brushstrokes flow to the natural rhythm of water capturing refracted light that render his subjects direct and palpable. Arcidiacono's paintings never date for hidden in them is the secret of eternal youth.

The post war period saw a remarkable revival of the arts for a new generation of artists. Inspired by the innovative spirit of Modern and Contemporary art, they appeared to rebel against academic formalisms. Antoine Camilleri (b.1922) engaged in a continuous process of introspection and experimentation: he has the power to crystallise the breathless energy of a cyclone into reflective stillness. Esprit Barthet (b.1919) is best known for his many portraits yet his female nudes and his studies of rooftops are landmarks in Maltese contemporary art. Alfred Chircop (b.1933) has ventured into a symphony of ever-changing ever-fresh abstract pure forms whose texture and chromatic values are delineated with the consummate hand of an old master. Harry Alden (b.1929) uses the hard edge technique to model his subjects and landscape through clean facets of pure colour. The sculptor Anton Agius (b.1933) releases the fantastic forms he discovers hidden in old and dead tree trunks. The extrovert Gabriel Caruana (b.1929) expresses his creative energy through the bizarre form and glazes of his incredibly beautiful ceramics. Richard England (b.1937) has injected new invigorating concepts into Maltese architecture. Other artists are Joseph Borg Xuereb (b.1928), Samuel Bugeja (b.1921), George Fenech (b.1926), and also John Bonnici, Joseph Mallia, Frank Portelli. Belonging to my own generation are Frans Galea, Lino Borg, Paul Carbonaro, Caesar Attard, Norbert Attard, Marco Cremona, Eman Grima, Salvu Mallia, Luciano Micallef, Raymond Pitre, Mary De Piro, Josette Caruana and Elizabeth Borg. Of course there are others whose passionate dedication to the arts continues to enrich Malta's variegated artistic firmament.

As the older generations of painters, sculptors and architects pass away, fledging new masters take their place. The test of time will select the chaff from the grain and the deserving will emerge to receive lasting recognition.

Bibliography

ATTARD CASSAR, C., *Exhibition of Maltese Art at the British Institute, Valletta, Malta*, 1946.

AZZOPARDI, J., (ed), *Francesco Zahra 1710-1773*, Mdina, 1986.

(ed), *Anton Inglott 1915-1945*, Mdina, 1988.

(ed), *The Schranz Artists: Landscape and Marine Painters in the Mediterranean*, Mdina, 1987.

(ed), *The Order's Early Legacy in Malta*, Valletta, 1989.

(ed), *Giorgio Pullicino 1779-1851: Architect and Painter*, Mdina, 1989.

(ed), *St Paul's Grotto, Church and Museum at Rabat, Malta*, Valletta, 1990.

BONANNO, A., *Malta an Archaeological Paradise*, Malta, 1987.

BONELLO, V., *La Madonna nell'Arte*, Malta, 1949.

BUHAGIAR, M., *St Catherine of Alexandria: Her Churches, Paintings and Statues in the Maltese Islands*, Malta, 1979.

(ed), *Marian Art during the 17th and 18th centuries*, Mdina, 1983.

Late Roman and Byzantine Catacombs and Related Burial Places in the Maltese Islands, Oxford, 1986.

The Iconography of the Maltese Islands 1400-1900, Valletta, 1988.

CAFFARO-RORE, M., *Mario Caffaro-Rore: Pittore Scultore*, 1984.

CALLEJA, J., *Giuseppe Calleja (1828-1915)*, Malta, 1992.

CALLEJA, P., (ed), *Architecture in Malta: Historical Aspects*, Msida, 1986.

CARUANA GATTO, V., *Malta Artistica Illustrata*, Malta, 1906.

CINI, C., *Gozo: The Roots of an Island*, Valletta, 1990.

DYER, S., *Malta Views*, London, 1984.

ELLUL, M., *Heritage of an Island – Malta*, Malta, 1975.

ESPINOSA RODRIGUEZ, A., *Three Artistic links between Malta and Seville*, Malta, 1985.

Paintings at the National Museum of Fine Arts in Malta, Valletta, 1990.

FERRES, A., *Descrizione Storica delle Chiese di Malta e Gozo*, Malta, 1866.

FORMOSA, I., *Dei Libri Corali Antichi del Duomo di S. Giovanni di Malta*, Malta, 1902.

LUTTRELL, A., (ed), *Medieval Malta: Studies on Malta before the Knights*, London, 1975.

(ed), *Hal Millieri: A Maltese Casale, Its Churches and Paintings*, Malta, 1976.

EVANS, J.D., *The Prehistoric Antiquities of the Maltese Islands*, London, 1971.

FIORENTINO, E., & GRASSO, L.A., *Giuseppe Calì 1846-1930*, Valletta, 1991.

GAUCI, G., (ed), *Sacred Art in Malta 1890-1960*, Valletta, 1990.

GOUDER, T.C., *The Mosaic Pavements in the Museum of Roman Antiquities*, Valletta, 1983.

"Malta and the Phoenicians" in *Lombard Bank (Malta) Ltd – Annual Report 1991*, Valletta, 1992.

MAHONEY, L., *A History of Maltese Architecture*, Malta, 1988.

MANGION, G., *Maltese Baroque*, Malta, 1989.

PELLEGRINI PETIT, J., (et al.), *Antoine de Favray (1706-1798)*, Mdina, 1982.

PULLICINO, P., *Antiche Tavole altre volte componenti il Principale Gran Quadro della Chiesa Cattedrale di Malta*, Malta, 1871.

RIDLEY, M., *The Megalithic Art of the Maltese Islands*, Hampshire, 1971.

SAMMUT, E., *Profili di Artisti Maltesi*, Malta, 1937.

SAMMUT, E., *Art in Malta*, Malta, 1954.

    Willie Apap 1918-1970, Mdina, 1984.

SCICLUNA, H.P., *The Church of St John in Valletta*, Malta, 1955.

VELLA, A., *Gianni Vella: Paintings, Watercolours and Sketches of Malta*, Malta, 1979.

ZAMMIT, T., and SINGER, C., "Neolithic Representations of the Human Form from the Islands of Malta and Gozo" in *Journal of the Royal Anthropological Institute*, Vol.LIV, 1924.

XUEREB, D., (ed), *Architecture in Malta: Evolution of a Culture*, Msida, 1990.

ZERAFA, S., *Storia Artistica di Malta*, Malta, 1850.

Music

Joseph Vella

In order to understand properly the Maltese cultural background, one must be aware of the historical associations the island passed through over the centuries and which, in some way or other, left their mark on the Maltese way of life, socially and, at a tangent, also culturally.

Although written evidence about musical activity in Malta throws us back less than four centuries (that is around the year 1600), I think that one can safely assume that these practices have had their roots in the misty dawns of prehistory. When one remembers that archaeological research has placed some of Malta's ancient stone temples as anteceding even the pyramids of Egypt, one can then easily surmise how far back in time this line can stretch.

The Mediterranean region has often been referred to as the cradle of civilization and Malta, being right in the centre of this area, could never escape or be immune to the cauldron of political and cultural upheavals that from time immemorial successively engulfed this region as nation after nation, dynasty after dynasty, creed after creed battled it out for supremacy and assertion. In fact, Malta's geographical position plus an inherent helplessness in its defensive potential due to its size, pre-ordained a pattern of events that can be monotonously traced from the time of the Phoenicians to the tragic days of the second world war – whichever nation or religious faction held the sway of military power along the Mediterranean littoral dominated this small island. In the fashion of the classic Roman dictum *"Veni, Vidi, Vici"*, they came, they saw and they conquered, and some of them even stayed for hundreds of years.

It is in the light of the above that one has to look in order to understand Malta's cultural heritage and to a great extent its musical traditions. History shows us that cult and music-making were not only complimentary but almost inseparable partners. It is, then, not that difficult to imagine that at some point in time in this island of temple worshippers one could hear the pervasive rhythms of the sacrificial drums of the Neolithic peoples in their massive stone temples, the rippling fresh sounds of the Greek lyre, the martial fanfares of the Romans or the mystic chants of the Byzantines and the Arabs.

The year 870 A.D. marks the scene of active history by the advent of a new Mediterranean power which for long had challenged European civilization. F.W. Ryan in his book *Malta* writes that:

"the Arabs inspired by Mohammed roused themselves from their leisured life as mere tent-dwellers in Arabia, and poured in vast numbers out of their country, with the fury of fanatics, carrying their new religion abroad at the point of the sword. They swept westward through Syria, Palestine and North Africa to Spain and also took possession of Malta".

Thus, the authority of the Byzantine Emperor, Basil 1, was declared at an end and the government was assumed by an Arab Emir. It is a curious fact that despite a physical presence on the Island lasting about four centuries, apart from the spoken language, practically nothing is left of the Arab cultural heritage whether this be archaeological, architectural or musical.

When Count Roger of Hauteville wrested the island from the hands of the Arabs, Malta became a feudal fief until the year 1530 and as such was successively subject to the many different holders of the Sicilian crown, namely the Normans, the Hohenstaufens, the Kings of Anjou, of

159

Aragon and of Castille.

From Count Roger's time onwards one can safely say that Malta always looked towards Europe for its cultural inspirations and models.

In his book *Musica e Musicisti a Malta*, Livorno, 1932, Ulderico Rolandi, without however quoting his sources writes: "I have come across here and there names of various cantors, precentors etc who from time immemorial were active in the churches of Malta". He goes on to make a list of some of these, mentioning, for example, *Guido Anselmi, Cantor* in the year 1112; *Magister Philippus, Cantor Tripolitanus* in the year 1124; *Raimondus Provincialis, praecentor* in the year 1170; *Rainaldus, Cantor Tiberiadis* in the year 1174; *Joannes, Praecentor acconiensis* in the year 1200; and *Willelmus, Cantor vallaniensis* in the year 1234. This information attests most vividly not only to a healthy musical life in Malta at such an early age, but is also indicative of an artistic phenomenon valid for most of the successive centuries, namely the musical ties Malta has had on an international level, especially with Italy. Another important point that emerges from Rolandi's writing and which ties closely with the phenomenon just mentioned is the fact that Malta, during this period, not only "imported" musicians, but also had its fair share of "exporting" them. One finds, for example, mention of *Don Luca Vella, Cantore Maltese* and *Giovanni Isconfort, Maltese* who, in 1550, were employed with Cardinal Alessandro Farnese, and the Papal Cappella in Rome respectively.

The first ever known poem written in Maltese belongs to the middle of the 15th century. It is a most interesting and important "*Cantilena*" penned by Pietro Caxaru, discovered in 1966 by Prof. G. Wettinger and Fr Mikiel Fsadni. The structure and rhythm of the poem strongly suggest that it could have been sung, although no hard evidence in this direction is extant. However, the poem could perhaps fit the style of a particular genre of Maltese music, namely the "*Għana*".

"*Għana*" is the major expression (and in many reasons one can say the only expression) of the Maltese folk musical tradition in spite of the fact that the main interest of the "*Għana*" lies more in its literary rather than its musical aspect.

In the field of "*Għana*" singing, one comes across a few melodies, (or better still melodic forms) which serve the "*għannej*" (singer of "*għana*") as a vehicle on which to improvise his verses or else to relate in verse form a pre-established story from the folk literature tradition. As one can easily note, in both cases the musical element is always secondary to the text.

"*Għana*" is invariably sung to an accompaniment of guitars which serve a dual purpose. One is to provide a harmonic basis for the melodic line, and the other is to play interludes between the many verses to give the singer both a period of rest and a short time to think and formulate his next stanza. The played interludes are of an improvisatory nature using the main melodic line as a basis.

The fact that in "*għana*" we find limited use of melodic intervals smaller than the semitone has led some people to associate its roots with North Africa where mono-melodic variations and micro-tonal intervals are an integral part of the musical culture. Personally, I am of the opinion that the spiritual roots of "*għana*" are to be found in the south of Spain, and that they reached our shores via Sicily. If one listens to traditional singing from these places, one can easily associate similarities of construction and performance with Maltese "*għana*". The traditional use of guitars as accompanying instruments is, I feel, a very strong relevant detail in this regard.

Other instruments belonging to our folk musical tradition (some of which are, unfortunately, well on the way to extinction) are the "*fifra*" (reed pipe) and the "*tamburell*" (tambour). A variant of the "*tamburell*" was the "*tamburin*" (tambourine). Another popular percussion instrument was the *"Rabbaba"* also known as the *"Żuvżafa"* (friction drum).

The *"bronja"* and the *"qrajna"* were two primitive, folk instruments. The *"bronja"* (sea-shell trumpet) and the *"qrajna"* (bull's horn trumpet) are well on the way out to disappear completely from the local scene. Malta too had its variant of the Pipes of Pan, locally called *"flejguta"* and *"bedbud"*.

In all the above there are very few things that can be called purely indigenous. As regards "folk instruments", Malta shared most of these with other countries found along the Mediterranean littoral.

However, from this aspect one could make a special reference to the Maltese bagpipe *"żaqq"*. Of all the varieties of bagpipe found all over the world, the Maltese bagpipe seems to be the only one made of an inflated dog's skin, which is held under the left arm with the dog's legs directed upward. There is also a mouthpiece through which the skin is filled with air and a holed reed which produced the required notes.

In the *Galpin Society Journal* published in the UK in 1977, J.F. Partridge and F. Jeal discuss the bagpipe of Malta from a musical, sociological and etnological point of view and they maintain that it seems to have little affinity to the Italian *"zampogna"* or the Sicilian *"cornamusa"* (traditional sources of influence). Rather, they point to an Aegean influence.

The peculiarity of the Maltese bagpipe is that unlike most others it still looks alarmingly like the animal from which it is made. In this respect it has also some resemblance to the *"zukra"* (Turkish bagpipe).

When the Knights of St John arrived on the island in 1530, Malta saw the blossoming of a truly artistic renaissance. Since the Knights represented a very valid cross-section of all the noble houses of Europe, from England to France, to Spain, to Italy, to Germany, it is not surprising that their presence gave the necessary impetus for a wave of cultural experiences hitherto unknown on the island.

However, as events began to take their course, for its culture Malta started to look more and more closely towards Italian ideals and practices. I am inclined to think that there were two reasons for this state of affairs — one was the geographical proximity which made actual physical contact easier than that with any other nation: the other was the influence of the Catholic Church which for its spiritual and artistic inspiration obviously looked towards Rome. From this time onwards, a lot of details about musical practice in Malta started to be documented, and thus one can trace this phenomenon emerging slowly but very clearly.

We know that by the end of the 16th Century there were two established *"cappellas"* on the island .— the one at St John's in Valletta, the seat of the Grandmaster and the one in Mdina, the seat of the Bishop.

Each centre had its group of singers and musicians in order to provide the music during the various types of divine services like matins, masses and vespers. During this time, services were far more numerous and far longer than the ones we find today in the ecclesiastical calendar, and this provided ample scope for the full-time employment of singers and instrumentalists.

Both these centres provided an ideal breeding ground for talented musicians and singers. In them, there was so much scope for music-making, and when one remembers that music, then, was written not for an ideal audience or for posterity as happens nowadays, but for pure everyday consumption, one realizes that talented composers had to churn out new compositions practically every day, all to the benefit of the members of the particular *"cappella"*, singers and musicians.

This was the type of music centre that gave us G.P. da Palestrina (1525-1594) in Italy, William Byrd (1542-1623) in England, T.L. de

Victoria (1594-1611) in Spain and Orlando di Lasso (1532-1594) in the Netherlands and later on Claudio Monteverdi (1567-1643) and Antonio Vivaldi (1676-1741) from St Mark's in Venice, Henry Purcell (1658-1695) from the Chapel Royal in London and later still J.S. Bach (1685-1750) from St Thomas's church in Leipzig.

The two above mentioned nuclei of religious musical culture in Malta were soon vying with each other for artistic excellence. At first, Italian vocalists and instrumentalists were imported by both the Bishop and the Grandmaster to give their services in the respective *"cappellas"*. Because of the existing rivalry, they obviously always aimed at the very best. This factor raised the tone and standard of local music-making to a high degree in a very short time and Malta could then be very well considered as just another centre of Italian musical culture like Palermo, Naples, Rome or Venice.

After a short time, talented young Maltese musicians were sent over to Italy to study at one of the established centres, mostly in Palermo and Naples, where, after spending a few years in apprenticeship they were expected to return to Malta to practice their art.

A very positive step happened during the middle of the 17th century, when the post of organist at Mdina Cathedral was elevated to the one of chapel master (*"maestro di cappella"*) with specific tasks and functions tied to the post, like composing, teaching the organ and training singers. By the end of the century, musical creativity and interpretation had reached the high standards of any typical *"cappella"* on the continent.

Manuscripts and old music books found in the Archives of the Cathedral museum in Mdina attest to the close ties that seem to have been forged between Malta and the better known *"cappellas"* in Italy since most of the great composers from these *"cappellas"* are represented in this collection. The fact that their works are mostly found in hand written anthologies would seem to imply that they were very much in common usage. Some of the big names that were being played in Malta at that time are Ludovico Grossi da Viadana (1564-1645), Claudio Monteverdi (1567-1643), Virgilio Mazzocchi (1597-1646), Bonifacio Graziani (1604-1665), Giacomo Carissimi (1604-1674), Gian Battista Vitali (1644-1692), Gesualdo Principe di Venosa (1560-1613) and Francesco Durante (1684-1755).

These were the trail blazers who beat a distinctive path not only in their native Italy but who influenced the course of music history all over Europe — Carissimi with his Oratorios, Monteverdi with his Operas, da Viadana with his Basso Continuo and Gesualdo with his Madrigal.

As regards secular music in Malta, recent research by G. Wettinger and M. Fsadni has shown that references to this type of activity can be traced as far back as 1419 when nine *"juculari"* (musicians) were employed in the militia at Mdina (see *L-Għanja ta' Pietru Caxaru* p.35). They also note that the authorities in Mdina used to employ musicians to play during the processions of the principal feasts of the town (not unlike modern practice, one may add). Rather more interesting is their reference to a notorial act of 1467 wherein it is stated that two persons by the name of Pietru Muscatu and Mikiel Galdes teamed up to provide musical entertainment during wedding feasts. Also, at about this time, a certain Andreotta de Bisconis used to walk round the streets of Gozo with a group of young men *"cantare e dicere cantilenas alta voce"*. The authors suggest that de Bisconis may have been improvising his cantilenas in the manner of the type of *"Għana"* known as *"spirtu pront"*.

The Italian influence, already referred to as regards Maltese sacred music of the 16th and 17th centuries, can also be traced to secular compositions. As early as 1650, we come across a libretto for an opera with the title *Dafnè, ovvero La Vergine*

Trionfante by Enrico Magi. Magi was born in Valletta on the 4th of December 1630. This libretto was dedicated to Fra Salvatore Imbroll, Prior of the Order (See MS 775, National Library, Valletta).

Unfortunately, no written evidence is extant as to who may have put this text to music or even whether this opera was ever performed in public at all. However, the fact that as early as 1650 we can come across material with connections, (even if at a tangent), to operatic activity shows that in this field Maltese music was not lagging far behind musical events happening on the continent.

Experiments in the birth of opera as a new artistic form of musical expression had started just after the turn of the century in Florence. What has come to be historically known as the Florentine Camerata (a group of people which included such *"litterati"* like Count Giovanni Bardi and Count Corsi and musicians like Vincenzo Galilei (1533c-1591), Giulio Caccini (1546-1618) and Jacopo Peri (1561-1633)) was responsible for the first early crude attempts at opera production.

The Camerata claimed that the music of the 16th century with its diverse contrapuntal devices had literally torn the poetry to pieces (*laceramenti della poesia*). They wanted to do away with all this pedantry and aspired to translate the sense of an entire passage rather than that of a single word into music. Thus, the first attempts at *"recitativo"* were achieved. While the old intermezzo juxtaposed drama and music, the new ideals tried to blend them together as a drama in music, hence *"dramma in musica"*.

Ottavio Rinuccini (1550-1621) fashioned his first libretto after the model of the traditional pastoral intermezzo and not by accident do several early operas carry the subtitle of *favola pastorale*. Not by accident either is the fact that Enrico Magi's *Dafnè* written in Valletta in 1650 carries the subtitle of *favola Boschereccia*.

Ulderico Rolandi in his *Musica e Musicisti a Malta* records that in 1664 an opera by the name of *Annibale in Capua* was performed in Valletta. The authorship of the music is doubtful. In fact, Rolandi attributes the music to the Venetian composer Antonio Ziani (brother of Marc Antonio) while well-known historian Fr John Azzopardi maintains that the music of *Annibale in Capua* was composed by Vincenzo Tozzi, a Sicilian composer.

It could however, very well be that both Ziani and Tozzi set to music a libretto by the name of *Annibale in Capua*. It is well worth the while here to remember that Baroque practice found nothing wrong or ethically wanting to have the same libretto set to music by different composers (witness the libretti of Pietro Anastasio (1698-1782), some of whose operatic texts were set to music by about thirty different composers with the result that the words of his texts were known in advance almost by heart by regular operatic audiences the way church-goers know their book of prayers).

Towards the end of the century this Italian operatic influence started to take deep root with the result that in 1732 Grandmaster Manoel de Vilhena felt the need to build a public theatre in which this new type of music diversion could be produced. The Manoel Theatre is a jewel of our historical/cultural heritage and its date of construction makes it one of the oldest public theatres in Europe. What is even more precious is the fact that it is still functioning the way it was intended to over two hundred and fifty years ago.

After tracing Italian musical influences in Malta during the 17th and 18th centuries, one can perhaps proceed to highlight the effects that these had on the local product, as it were.

The oldest extant musical composition by a Maltese composer dates back to 1652. It belongs to the Cathedral Archives in Mdina and the composer is Giuseppe Balzano who was born in Valletta on September 19th 1616. Ordained priest in 1640, he first served in the church of St Paul's Shipwreck. Twenty one years had to pass before he was finally appointed *"maestro di cappella"* at the cathedral in Mdina, a post he held on and off until his retirement in 1699.

The composition referred to is a motet for two tenors, bass and continuo, entitled *Beatus Vir*. This non-liturgical piece falls into two main sections, the first of which mainly involves the Bass solo. The *"stile rappresentativo"* of the early Italian Baroque style stemming from the Florentine ideals already referred to are very evident here. Mostly, the music makes use of one note per syllable, breaking off into melismatic flourishes on some of the more important words. The second section beginning on *"Cantemus Ergo"* is a rhythmic triple meter piece where a lot of use is made of imitative counterpoint. The last few bars, in quadruple measure, form a kind of Coda where the three voices are brought together for the final cadence.

Unfortunately this is the only known signed complete composition by Giuseppe Balzano. But luckily for us in the Cathedral archives one can also find a contemporary musical repertory which includes the works of Giuseppe Balzano extant there at the time of its compilation. It lists an impressive catalogue of 18 masses, 70 vespers, 36 hymns and 51 motets.

In her dissertation, *Scores Attributed to Giuseppe Balzano*, 1991, Ms Natascha Chircop sets out to trace some of the lost works by Giuseppe Balzano from a number of anonymous compositions still extant in the archives. As Fr John Azzopardi writes in the preface

"an examination of the works listed under Giuseppe Balzano in the old repertory and the group of anonymous scores available today reveals several titles of non-liturgical motets that are common to both, not only as regards the actual title but also as regards details of voices and instruments employed e.g. *'a tre voci con sinfonia'*. These coincidences lead us to suspect that some works by Giuseppe Balzano, Malta's oldest composer with an extant score and some fragments, may still have more compositions which are not signed but are preserved among our anonymous works".

From this critical study, Ms Chircop attributes another seven extant but unsigned compositions to Giuseppe Balzano, namely the cantatas *"Det Tuba"* (MS 152), and *"Ego Ille"* (MS 161), the motets *"Da Pacem Domine"* (MS 159), *"Ecce Servum Dei"* (MS 163), *"Quis Est Hic"* (MS 186) and the hymns *"Te Splendor Et Virtus"* (MS 205) and *"Jesu Redemptor Omnium"* (MS 208).

The next oldest extant signed work is the motet *"Venite Omnes"* scored for Cantus and Altus with continuo dated 1680. It is the work of Domenico Balzano (1632-1707), Giuseppe's younger brother and like him a priest and *"musico salariato"* at St John's, at St Paul's Shipwreck and finally as *"maestro di cappella"* in Mdina.

The dates of these two extant compositions (1652 and 1680) attest to the long line of Maltese compositional activity which until a few years ago was hardly ever thought to extend beyond the works of the well-known Nicolò Isouard.

Aloysio Mataron is another name recently come to light. He was active during the middle of the 17th Century and was the son of a French father (Jacobus Mataron) and Maltese mother (Aloysia Ghimes). There are only two works of his known namely the motets *"Dulcis Amor"* (MS 113) and *"Salve Regina"* (MS 113). The beauty of these works scored for Cantus, Altus, Tenor and continuo makes it even more desirable that someone will research the life and opus of this enigmatic figure in the history of music in Malta, about whom very little is known.

Maltese musical activity of the 18th century opens with an interesting but not so very familiar figure. Pietro Gristi (1696-1738) was born in Rabat and first served as a boy soprano in the *"cappella"* in Mdina. He was the first of a long list of Maltese musicians to be sent to Naples to complete his musical studies. Up to his time, Palermo was usually the place to go to. Financial assistance was provided by the Cathedral Chapter and, as one would expect, when in 1717 he returned to Malta from his studies at the *Conservatorio dei Poveri di Gesu Cristo*, he took up the post of *"maestro di cappella"* at Mdina Cathedral. In 1720 he was ordained priest. Gristi was only 42 years old when he died in 1738.

Very few pieces by Pietro Gristi are extant and most of these can be found in the musical archives of the Collegiate Chapter of Cospicua. However, a close look at these works would seem to indicate that Gristi was an able composer who knew his job very well. His compositions are of quite an acceptable standard and of course betray the Neapolitan influence to the core.

Girolamo Abos, born in Valletta, was a musician of Spanish descent. He died in Naples. Diverse scholars give different dates for the birth and death of this very cosmopolitan musician. As regards his date of birth, Rolandi quotes the year 1706, Eric Blom (Dictionary of Music) the year 1719; Dulfocq the year 1708 while Trecanni and Vallardi (Encyclopedia) limit themselves to say that he was active during the 18th century. Rolandi, Vallardi and Dulfocq give 1786 as the year of his death, Trecanni the year 1760 and Blom the year 1769. From circumstantial evidence I would opt for the dates given by Corbet in the *Grove Dictionary of Music*, namely 1715-1760.

When Abos was still very young, he was sent to Naples to study, never to return to Malta, his birthplace, again. In fact, no archive in Malta possesses any manuscripts by this composer although his music, both printed and in manuscript form can be found in Naples, Bologna, Rome, the National Library in Vienna and the British Museum, amongst other places.

The case of Girolamo Abos represents quite clearly the musical inclination and artistic mentality of 18th century Malta. Abos was not only influenced by the Italian school, but he made it his own in such a way that for all intents and purposes he could be considered as just another Italian musician.

Like Gristi, Abos studied at the *"Conservatorio dei Poveri di Gesu Cristo"*, in turn teaching at the *"Pietà dei Turchini"* where, amongst his pupils, one finds the famous Paisiello (Vallardi, Enciclopedia Moderna Illustrata). Francesco Caruana Dingli writing in 1842 names him as also being for some time *"maestro di cappella"* in the Cathedral in Naples. In this city, Abos presented his first opera *Le Due Zingare Simili*. His career took off quite rapidly and in his capacity as composer and orchestra director he toured the length and breadth of Europe from Vienna to London. For two years (1756-1758) he was musical director of the so-called "Italian Theatre" in London. Abos composed many sacred works and operas, and during his lifetime was well-known in most European musical circles.

Although Mikiel Anġ Vella lacked the cosmopolitan flair of Abos, all the same he represents one of the more important figures in Maltese music of the early 18th century. Like Abos, Vella was born in 1715 in Bormla where he died in 1792. Apart from his artistic activity, Vella is also remembered as being the first person to take a deep interest in starting a school of music in Malta on the same lines as those of the Conservatories in Italy. Among his students, we find some names that had a great say on the course of Maltese music later on in the century – Azopardi, Isouard, Burlò and Magrin. M.A. Vella is also historically important for his pioneering work in the field of the secular cantata. With the opening of the Manoel Theatre in 1732 this type of composition came to full bloom and was very popular with the knights and other concert goers, especially during the *"Calendimaggio"*. Before Vella, these cantatas were invariably the work of Italian composers (Giuseppe and Melchiorre Sammartini). Vella was the first Maltese to infiltrate this area of musical activity with works like *Astra e Pallade*, (1740), *La Virtù Trionphante*, (1741), *La Giustizia di Nettuno e la Religione*

Gerosolimitana, (1746) and *Gli Applausi della Fama*, (1758).

According to F.G. Fetis (1784-1871) Vella, for some time, was active in Paris (c. 1750). Whether he was there studying or working is not very clear. What we know for sure is that during his stay Vella published two trios and six quartets and his impact in Parisian circles was such that Charon and Fayolle in their *Dictionaire Historique des Musiciennes* deemed him important enough to be included, while Fetis in his *Biographie Universelle des Musiciennes et Bibliographie Generale de la Musique* published in 1881 described M.A. Vella as being a contrapuntist of the top order.

The most important composers active in Malta round the middle of the 18th century are undoubtedly Benigno Zerafa and Francesco Azopardi. Benigno Zerafa was born in Rabat on the 25th August 1726, the fifth of eight children. At the very early age of 11, Benigno already formed part of the *"Cappella Musicale"* at the Cathedral after having been recommended by the Church Deputies for Music as being suitably qualified. He was accepted as a *"soprano"* under the directorship of Pietro Gristi. Fr John Azzopardi in his short biography of Benigno Zerafa writes:

"Benigno's service at the Cathedral was brief, for at the age of twelve, and following the premature death of the Chapel Master, Don Pietro Gristi, on the 4th of March 1738, he departed for Naples to be trained in the same institute *(Conservatorio dei Poveri di Gesu Cristo)*, where his master at the Cathedral had received his musical education."

A document of 1738, preserved in the *Archivio Storico Diocesano* of Naples records: *"A 8 detto (July 1738) entrato Benigno Zerafa, Maltese, posto da Sua Eminenza per alunno"*. (On the 8th of July 1738 the name of Benigno Zerafa, Maltese, was registered on the recommendation of His Eminence).

In Naples, Zerafa studied with, amongst other professors, his compatriot Girolamo Abos and after a six year course returned to Malta. Abos thought highly of young

Zerafa and before the latter left Naples to return to Malta he wrote him a very good recommendation extolling the young Zerafa's abilities as a composer.

It was to be expected, then, that when Zerafa applied for the post of *"maestro di cappella"* at the Cathedral in Mdina an office which had been vacant ever since the premature death of Pietro Gristi (1738), his application was very favourably and enthusiastically received by the Church authorities, so that on the 22nd of August 1744 Bishop Alpheran

"issued a decree appointing Benigno Zerafa, aged 18, 'Maestro di Cappella' of his Cathedral, with the obligation to conduct music, teach Canto Fermo and Canto Figurato, holding at least two rehearsals every week".
(Fr John Azzopardi *ibid.*).

Although time would eventually prove Francesco Azopardi to be a more prolific composer, yet in certain musical aspects Zerafa's art was far more progressive. It shows a close familiarity with musical tendencies in pre-classical Europe and in this *"stile galante"*, I find Zerafa to be more advanced than Azopardi, who was rather conservative in this respect. These characteristics of Zerafa are very evident in his orchestration, very often of a florid nature and with intricate musical figuration. His frequent use of the triplet rhythmic division, also makes him stand out among his contemporaries and immediate successors. Likewise, the formal structure of some of his arias. I have yet to meet an 18th century Maltese composition as truly *"rococco"* in style as Zerafa's *"Nisi Dominus"* of 1764 originally scored *"a voce sola con violini, stromenti di fiato e mandolino obbligato"* with, of course, continuo. Notice also the unusual but interesting use of the mandolino as an obbligato instrument.

Fortunately, the majority of Zerafa's compositions, (which include quite a number of psalms, masses, antiphons, motets etc.), are still extant because through a notorial act of the 7th February 1787, he bequeathed all his works to the Cathedral.

Francesco Azopardi (1748-1809) by nature was of a more cosmopolitan inclination than his older contemporary Benigno Zerafa. Azopardi had begun his musical studies with M.A. Vella. But like Zerafa, he soon found his way to Naples to study at the Conservatorio of "San Onofrio". His teacher here was none other than the famous Nicolo Piccini (1728-1800) who during the late 1770's features so notoriously as C.W. Gluck's (1714-1787) rival in the Parisian "*Guerre des Buffons*". After finishing his studies in Naples Azopardi stayed on for about another four years working very successfully along, and sometimes in competition with, famous composers like Tommaso Traetta (1727-1779) and Piccini himself.

This artistic success by a Maltese composer in such a famous city could not but attract the attention of interested parties in Malta, not least the Cathedral authorities in Mdina. As early as 1772, the Chapter had already hinted to Azopardi that he would be very favourably considered as their next "*maestro di cappella*" if he had so desired. However, another two years had to pass before Azopardi could finally be persuaded to return to his homeland to be given his appointment in Mdina in 1774.

To commemorate this occasion (and also, no doubt, to introduce himself with a bang to the Maltese music loving authorities and general public) he composed what is perhaps one of his major works, namely the Mass in G major for two separate four-part choirs, soloists and orchestra. This great mass was performed with huge success in 1775.

Azopardi's vast opus includes many important and prestigious works like for example the two masses of 1776 and 1798, both structured on the style of the "*Messa in Sol*" already mentioned. Besides, we find scores of psalms, antiphons, hymns and the like. One of his reputedly greatest creations, the oratorio "*La Passione di Cristo*" is unfortunately untraceable

and what we know about it comes to us from contemporary reviews and mentions. The text of this oratorio was written by none other than the famous Metastasio.

It is a curious fact, however, that though most of his sacred compositions are extant and readily available in several local musical archives (mostly in Mdina), his secular works are very hard to come by. Suffice it to mention that although the archives in Mdina are so rich as regards Azopardi's church music, there are only three secular works of his on their catalogue, namely, three sinfonie (overtures), two of which are "*con oboe obbligato*".

No less important were Azopardi's other activities, both as a theoretician and as a teacher. His musical treatise *Il Musico Prattico* dedicated to Vincenzo Vergoda y Ribera, was a great success when it was first published in Italy and later on in France, where it was translated and put on the market in 1786 by the Belgian Framery. Eventually, *Il Musico Prattico* found its way even to the exalted aulae of the conservatoire in Paris after it was approved by Andre Gretry. Gretry opined that "*l'opera era l'unica nella quale eccellenti esempii, e scritti bene in musica, sono congiunti alla teoria ordinaria degli accordi*". (The only work where excellent, well-written musical examples are quoted against theoretical statements and harmonic rules). Even the great Cherubini, whose influence shadowed even such a colossus like Beethoven, thought very highly of Azopardi. This, to the point where in his treatise on counterpoint, he saw fit to include excerpts from *Il Musico Prattico* as exemplary elucidations.

In 1774 Azopardi published another didactic book, the manuscript of which is preserved in the Archives in Mdina, "*Origine della Regola della Musica nella Storia del suo Progresso, Decadenza e Rinnovazione*". Here Azopardi challenges the theories expounded by a certain Antonio Eximio in his book *Sull'Origine della Musica* published in Rome, which because of its destructive philosophy had been described by the Italians as *"un bizarro romanzo di musica"* (a bizarre tale of music).

Like Azopardi, both Salvatore Magrin (1770-1848) and Giuseppe Burlò (1772-1856) started their musical studies with M.A. Vella in his school at Bormla (Cospicua). Magrin and Burlò did not measure up to the stature of their two immediate forerunners – Zerafa and Azopardi. Yet, they have endowed and enriched our national musical patrimony with quite a few worthy musical compositions, mostly of a sacred nature.

Salvatore Magrin, after his initial studies with Azopardi went to Naples to finish his training and when he returned to Malta he was immediately appointed *"maestro di cappella"* at Bormla. Apparently, for some reason, Giuseppe Burlò failed to emulate the contemporary custom of proceeding to Palermo or Naples to round up his musical studies. These were limited to courses in Malta, especially with Azopardi, as already indicated. However, rather than the composer, a work of his seems to have eventually found its way there! P.P. Castagna in his *Malta bil-Gżejjer Tagħha* maintains that Burlò's treatise *Memoria sul Contrapunto* was used for didactic purposes at the Conservatorio in Naples.

One of the giants of Maltese musical history is undoubtedly Nicolò Isouard. His exact date of birth has been the subject of controversy for some time. Until a few years ago, the year 1775 was held to be Isouard's date of birth (Castagna, Rolandi, Trecanni, Larouse and the Oxford Companion to Music). Dominic Cutajar's recent research seems to have settled the issue and pins the date to the 17th of May 1773.

Isouard was the composer who towards the end of the 18th century made Malta known to all European musical circles, especially since he preferred to be referred to as Nicolò de Malthe. This despite the fact that like the Italian Giovanni Battista

Lulli (Jean Baptiste Lully 1632-1687) before him he practically lost his national identity and became totally imbued with the manner and style of his adoptive Paris. This loss however, was more on a social rather than artistic level.

Isouard had begun his studies in Malta and it was only to be expected that he would be sent to Naples to finish his schooling. Here, at a very tender age, he began to make a name for himself, especially with the production of his first opera *L'Avviso ai Maritati* (1794, in Florence) which proved to be an immense success. Shortly afterwards De Rohan called him back to Malta to occupy the post of *"maestro di cappella"* at St John's Cathedral in Valletta.

Isouard was a great Francophile and when the French were forced to end their two-year occupation of the Island 1798-1800, he decided to leave Malta and settle in Paris, never to return to his homeland again.

From the middle of the 17th century to the end of the 18th, European music was largely dominated by the Italian style in such a way that this type of music served as a *"lingua franca"* all over the continent. Where this style did not completely absorb local musical customs as had happened in London, St Petersburg and obviously Malta, it co-existed with the local style, but in a state of great rivalry (France and Germany). In France, the rivalry between the two factors was great indeed.

The *"Guerre des Buffons"* had started in the time of Jean Jacques Rousseau (1712-1728) and reached its climax round about the year 1780 when Christoph Willibald Gluck (1714-1787) was "imported" from Germany to champion the French cause (*Tragedie Lyrique*). The rivals were not to be outdone and we find Nicolo Piccini (1728-1800) being asked from Naples to take up the cudgle on behalf of the pro-Italian faction (*Opera Comique*). This was the scene in Paris some twenty years before Isouard's arrival and the latter, bred as he was in the

Nicolò Isouard (1773-1818)

Antonio Nani (1842-1929)

Paolino Vassallo (1856-1913)

'Dulcis Amor Jesu' by Luigi Mataron (c.1650), Archives of Cathedral Museum, Mdina.

Neapolitan school and tradition, could only end up in the camp of Piccini, namely in the world of the *Opera Comique.*

Isouard started to compose several operas in this style which made him an instant success with the Parisian public. He soon became a household name in Paris where he was simply and rather affectionately known as Nicolò or Nicolò de Malthe.

Moreover, works of his like *Jeannot et Colin, Joconde* and *Cendrillon* soon broke the confines of French opera houses and spread the name of Nicolò all over Europe. There is not one single library or archive where I have been (Italy, Austria, Czechoslovakia, Norway) which does not list a substantial number of works by Isouard in its catalogue.

In France, especially, his was a huge success indeed. Some detractors, however, like to point out that this popularity was won for reasons which were circumstantial rather than artistic – Cherubini had by this time become very, very old; Mehul seemed to have lost interest in composition and practically stopped his activities; Kreutzer was grossly and deeply involved only in Grand Opera; Breton had almost disappeared from the scene, while Boieldieu emigrated to Russia to work in the court at St Petersburg.

For some time, therefore, Isouard had been working in Paris almost without any competition. This ended only in 1811 when Boieldieu returned from Russia. Francois Adrien Boieldieu (1775-1834) picked up again a career in Paris which he had launched eleven years earlier (1800) with the production of his highly successful opera *The Caliph of Baghdad.* For his return, Boieldieu presented *La Dame Blanche* which again proved to be highly popular. After this success, Boieldieu's popularity began to mushroom to sweeping proportions, very often to the detriment of Nicolò Isouard's. In fact, Nicolò's biggest disappointment came at the hands of his rival Boieldieu. The latter was in fact chosen as director of the Academie in Paris, a post which Isouard had greatly

aspired to and had wanted so very badly. This incident had a telling effect on his work and health and Isouard died a year later, in 1818.

With the beginning of the 19th Century, we find in Malta three families who were to contribute greatly to the musical life of the island, both in the way of composition and performance.

The Nani family is perhaps the one with the longest roots. In fact, we know that as early as the time of Grandmaster De Rohan, a certain Angelo Nani (1751-1844) came to Malta to be employed as violinist with the Order. Angelo Nani originally hailed from Venice but seems to have found life in Malta very congenial because he settled here for good. He was a top-notch violinist and soon made a name for himself and his music. The next generation Nani was his son Emanuele (1768-1860), who not only followed his father's profession as a violinist, but was also very active as a musical director. His conducting career took him all over Europe (Palermo, Venice, Naples, London and Paris). It is probable that during the two years of the French occupation, Emanuele was not on the island. But he did return when the French left, because it was Emanuele who conducted the concert given in honour of Sir Alexander Ball at the Manoel Theatre. For this occasion, he performed one of his compositions – *Torno Febo dal Gange Festoso*, a cantata.

Dr Paolo Nani (1814-1904) was Emanuele's son. He was sent to Naples to further his musical studies and amongst his teachers we find Zingarelli and the famous Donizetti. Paolo Nani was perhaps the most prolific of the Nani line of composers with many worthy compositions to his credit. Paolo's son, Antonio Nani (1842-1929) after his initial studies in Malta, also went to Naples where he was coached in harmony and counterpoint by the Neapolitan Barbati and De Gioiosa. Back in Malta, Antonio established himself as one of the most successful and popular "*maestri di cappella*" in which capacity he provided the music for some of Malta's major parishes. Because of his job, he had to compose several antiphons for the titular feasts, compositions which are still played today with much relish, one may add, both on the part of the performers and the listeners. The Nani family line continued with another Paolo (1906-1986), Antonio's son. Paolo studied in Rome, and in Malta he will be remembered mostly for his conducting, not only as *"maestro di cappella"*, but also for introducing "new" works from the symphonic and concerto repertoire to the general public.

The origins of the Bugeja dynasty of musicians may be traced back to the end of the 18th century. Since then and for a long time afterwards, the Bugeja family together with that of the Nani's dominated the musical scene in Malta. A member of either one of these families could be found to occupy the post of *"maestro di cappella"* in practically every church in Malta. Typical of the Maltese mentality, we soon find rival groups of supporters forming round the two families and enthusiasm on the part of these "clans" was at times known to get slightly out of hand.

Pietro Paolo Bugeja (1772-1828) was the first in the long line of composers which spanned almost two centuries. V. Caruana dei Conti Gatto in his *Malta Artistica Illustrata* says that Pietro Paolo probably began his studies with Francesco Azopardi. Like so many others before him the young Bugeja left Malta to continued studying in Naples when he was 19.

His first encounter with the music public of this city was when he composed a Solemn Mass in honour of San Ivo. This success led to his being appointed *"maestro di cappella"* at the Church of San Ivo in Naples, a place he occupied for about four years.

While he was in Naples, Pietro Paolo got to know his compatriot Nicolo Isouard, whom he greatly admired. After the success that Isouard had with his *L'Avviso ai Maritati*, he seems to have

become interested in composing an operatic work, a project which however never came to fruition.

After six years in Naples, Bugeja returned to Malta in 1797 and soon became very active in several *"cappellas"*. His fame as a composer grew wider especially when he also started to involve himself in conducting. In fact, during the season 1806/1807, Bugeja held the post of musical director at the "Teatro Reale", the name by which the Manoel Theatre was called at the time. We find him occupying this post again during the 1812/1813 and 1815/1816 seasons. It is interesting to mention here that Angelo Nani, the first generation of the Nani dynasty, served as Bugeja's first violinist for most of these times.

Meanwhile, when Francesco Azopardi died in 1809, Pietro Paolo was appointed *"maestro di cappella"* at St John's. His sacred opus includes four *Messe da Requiem*, a *Messa di Gloria*, twenty shorter masses, about thirty psalms, various hymns, antiphons and responses. There are also nine syphonies.

Another secular work of his, the musical allegory *Il Primo Omaggio* (text by Cesare Vassallo) was composed and performed at the Teatro Reale for the welcome ceremonies for the new governor of Malta Sir Francis Hastings in 1824. His sacred oratorio *Gioas, Re di Giuda* (text by Pietro Anastasio) is also worthy of mention.

On the whole, Bugeja's worthiest contribution was his work in sacred music. His secular works, especially his symphonies, are rather simplistic in conception, form and orchestration.

Pietro Paolo had several children, two of whom Vincenzo and Filippo were to carry on the family standard. Vincenzo Bugeja was born in Valletta in 1805 and died in 1860. At the early age of 23, he found himself being asked to replace his father as *"maestro di cappella"* at St John's following the latter's death in 1828, a post he seems to have reluctantly accepted.

In fact, the year after he left for Naples. At the *"Conservatorio San Pietro di*

Maiella'', Vincenzo studied under Furno and Zingarelli, and his fellow students included the famous Mercadante and Bellini. Mifsud Bonnici writes that when Zingarelli was asked by King Vittorio Emanuele II to nominate two of his best students in order that they could be commissioned to compose a theatrical work he put forward the names of Vincenzo Bellini and Vincenzo Bugeja. The opera *Lodoviska* is said to have been Bugeja's effort which he finished in 1831. Its Maltese premiere took place a year later at the Teatro Reale on the 15th March 1832.

On his return to Malta he took over the post of musical director to the numerous churches where his father Pietro Paolo had established himself. Vincenzo was especially popular in the parish church of Floriana where his antiphon *O Melitae Digna Prolis* in honour of St Publius is still played to the present day. His work also includes solemn masses, funeral masses, motets, antiphons and six symphonies.

As already mentioned, Filippo (1808-1891) was Vincenzo's younger brother. Unlike his brother and his fater before him, Filippo did not go abroad to study. His only musical training was received from his father. Although he seems to have left his mark locally as a pianist, organist and music director, Filippo is perhaps the least important of the Bugeja line of musicians. His life is also rather obscure and few facts about his activities are known with certainty. Unlike the other Bugeja's who left a very rich patrimony for posterity, Filippo's works were either lost or else he was not a very assiduous composer. Granted that he probably wrote more than there is evidence for, yet his extant works are only a handful.

The onus of carrying on the musical torch of the Bugeja family fell on Riccardo, Filippo's nephew. Ricardo Bugeja was the eldest son of Vincenzo. He was born in 1844 and died in 1926 at the venerable age of 82. In 1862 Riccardo

followed his father's footsteps to the conservatorio San Pietro di Maiella in Naples. One of his teachers was the famous Mercadante with whom Riccardo seems to have forged a strong bond of friendship. Mifsud Bonnici in his *Mużiċisti, Kompożituri Maltin u Għawdxin* says that when Mercadante went totally blind Riccardo on various occasions served as his *amanuensis*. The author singles out Mercadante's symphony *Il Rammento del Bardo* also saying that it was dedicated to Riccardo. Like his father Vincenzo, Riccardo was quite a prolific composer. His symphonic overture *Cordelia* written in 1880 remains one of his more popular pieces to this day.

The coming into force of the "moto proprio" decreed by Pope Pius X in 1903 came as a blow to most composers versed and saturated as they were in the traditions of Neapolitan operatic-imbued sacred music. The moto proprio sought to abolish from regular church services excesses of operatic style singing and writing which by the end of the 19th century had permeated every nook and corner of church music-making. It aimed at reinstating as much as possible a simpler accessible style, opting for the simpler forms of the mystic tradition of the Gregorian chant, whenever possible, for the liturgical functions.

Riccardo was one of those composers who had to adapt themselves to the new laws of composition for sacred music, but unlike most of his colleagues he seems to have adapted himself without much difficulty to the recently imposed parameters.

With Riccardo's son Vincent (1910-1967) we come to the end of the Bugeja dynasty. Vincent started his musical studies with several Maltese teachers but when he decided that it was time for him to go and specialize abroad, unlike his father, grandfather and great-grandfather before him, he went to Rome not to Naples. He was 17 by that time and he successfully sat for an entrance examination at the *Istituto di Musica Sacra* where he studied with Refice, amongst others. He returned in 1934 and soon took up the post of musical director in several churches in true respect for a long standing family tradition.

The departures of the Italian opera company in 1939 just before the war broke out, provided the young Vincenzo with the opportunity to break into new ground. He formed the Malta Amateur Theatrical Company (notice the changing Maltese mentality reflected in the choice of an English rather than an Italian title, something which a few years before would have been taken for granted) to help fill the void created by the departure of the Italian singers and musicians. As musical director he performed many (admittedly Italian) operas but always with a totally Maltese cast.

The other family, minor in regards to the Nanis and the Bugeja's both as regards the number of creative members and span of activity, was that of the Vella's. It was started by Dr Giuseppe Vella who was born in Valletta in 1827, by which time both the Nani and Bugeja families had been active for more than 50 years. In Malta Giuseppe Vella had been the pupil of Don Giuseppe Scicluna before proceeding to Genova to specialize.

He was appointed "*maestro di cappella*" to the Cathedral and Co-Cathedral in 1861 after the death of Vincenzo Bugeja. He was also professor of music in the Jesuit College. Giuseppe Vella was quite a popular composer and his works seem to have had an immediate appeal on his listeners. During his time, he was mostly known and lauded for his *Requiem Mass*. He died in 1912. All three of his sons, namely Alberto (1866-1931), Luigi (1868-1950) and Paolo (1873-1948) were also composers, mostly of music of a lighter vein. Several of their pieces were published. However, their stamp on local music is very lightly marked and their importance is more historical than artistic.

Having drawn a historical line down the path of Malta's three best known musical dynasties right through the 19th century

and well in the 20th century, one can retrace one's steps back to the early 1800 to pick up the thread with regards to other composers contemporary to the Nani's, the Bugeja's and the Vella's.

With Alessandro Curmi (born in Valletta 1801) we come across a composer whose stature in our national musical heritage is not as yet given its due recognition. A cosmopolitan man by nature, Curmi worked in the main cities of Europe performing his works and operas. P.P. Castagna lists amongst others his *Gustavo d'Orxa* produced in Rome, the *Elodia d'Herstall* produced in Naples, *Il Proscritto di Messina* and *La Rivoluzione* both produced in Paris. Mention is also made of three operas which Curmi presented in London namely *La Rosiere, La Lolodich* and *La Reine de Fate*. These operas, with a French text, are very much in the style of the opera comique, a fact which would put him in line with his compatriot and predecessor Nicolò Isouard. Alessandro Curmi died in Naples in 1857.

An equally unresearched and as yet obscure figure is that of Francesco Schira (probably a foreign corruption of the local name Sciriha). Grove's Dictionary of Music quotes his date of birth as being 1809 in Malta, and that of his death, 1883, in London. Schira was a composer and conductor of a truly international fame.

When only nine years old he was already studying at the Conservatorio in Milan, and he received his first artistic commission at the young age of 17. This was an opera by the name *Elena e Malvino* performed on the 17th of November 1832 at the Teatro alla Scala. The immense success of this production earned Schira an immediate invitation to the Teatro Santo Carlos in Lisbon. In this city, Francesco sojourned for eight long years as the theatre's artistic director, conductor of the orchestra and also resident composer. He shared all these with the post of professor of harmony and counterpoint at the Lisbon Conservatoire. In 1842, Schira left Lisbon for Paris. His stay here was short-lived because he soon had to leave for London after signing a contract as Musical Director for the Princess Theatre. A short time later he also had under his wings the artistic direction of the Drury Lane Theatre. Schira's expected appointment with Covent Garden arrived in 1848 with his opera *Kenilworth* based on Sir Walter Scott's story.

Other minor figures active during the first half of the 19th century were Emanuele Muscat (1790-1837) who studied in Naples; Emanuele Galea (1790-1850) reputedly active even in Russia where he is said to have written a hymn purposely for the Czar in 1842; Cesare Vassallo (1801-1880) also a doctor of laws and librarian; Angelo Galea (1806-1890), who served as bandmaster with several regimental English bands; and Don Giuseppe Scicluna (1809-1878).

From among this group of minor composers, Giuseppe Spiteri Fremond rises head and shoulders above all the others. Spiteri Fremond (1804-1878) was an Augustinian monk who gave his services in various monasteries belonging to his order in Rome, Genova, France the United Kingdom, Egypt and Palestine. His fame was such that the Musical Society of Bologna found him worthy to be nominated a member (1873) on the strength of the international recognition which his compositions had earned him.

During the span of seventy years starting from the middle of the 19th century, Mons. Giuseppe Farrugia was perhaps Gozo's most famous man of the arts. He was born on the 2nd of June 1852 and died on the 18th of March 1925 after a fruitful life spent in artistic ventures and scholarly pursuits. Farrugia, a canon at the Gozo Cathedral, was indeed a man of many talents. He was a first class preacher and Latinist, poet, author, architect and designer. He was also a very good musician, whose works, in their conception and treatment, were often ahead of what was being written contemporaneously in Malta.

The troubled times of the unification of Italy resulted in a number of Jesuit priests settling in Gozo, and in a thrice, the Seminary in Victoria became a hub of diverse talents and excellent scholarship. One of these settlers, a certain Padre Enrico Scio, became Farrugia's teacher of music at the Seminary, and this would seem to explain how a student whose studies never over-stepped the narrow confines of Gozo, could at the same time write in a contemporary style, as fresh and modern as that of any of his colleagues from Malta. Farrugia wrote various masses, psalms, antiphons, hymns and a few secular works. He is best known for the music which is played during the feast of St George in Victoria.

The most prominent personality after the 1850's was undoubtedly Paolino Vassallo (1856-1913). He was only 19 years old when he went to Paris to study at the Conservatoire and, as teachers, had none other than Charles Gounod, Jules Massenet and Camille Saint-Saens. Vassallo made a name for himself in this city with the composition of diverse cantatas and symphonic pieces. He was also musical director of the then famous *Lamourex Orchestra*.

It is said that Vassallo was even awarded the highly prestigious *Grand Prix de Rome*, a scholarship he could not accept because of his nationality.

In the course of the history of music in Malta, Vassallo represents the first composer who truly severed the close ties which Maltese music had always had with Italian forms and structures. In fact, his secular output is replete with compositions using formal structures which are basically extraneous to Italian idiom, like symphonies, symphonic poems and concert overtures. The harmonic language that Vassallo uses is also quite advanced.

In Malta, Vassallo established a school of music in his hometown Cospicua, and here, Carlo Diacono, Duminku Anastasi and Josie Mallia Pulverenti got their first training.

Paolino Vassallo's historical importance

is three pronged, namely, the influence he had on traditional Italian operatic practices in Malta, the reformed sacred style of the *Moto Proprio* of which he was a great promulgator, and thirdly modern harmonic and formal conceptions which he "imported" from the French School. It is interesting to note that the three students of his just mentioned, Diacono, Anastasi and Mallia Pulverenti each respectively represent these three aspects.

From the point of view of Maltese music, the third branch of influence just mentioned is the most important, because for the first time we can witness a radical break from three centuries of continuous Italian influence. During the middle of the 18th century, Paris was the centre of new artistic ideals which had been given birth and nurtured by such iconoclasts like Monet, Manet, Renoir, Degas and Cezanne. These artists had rebelled against the rules of Romantic art and started the so-called Impressionist Movement. These ideals reflected themselves in the music of Claude Debussy (1862-1918) and later in that of Maurice Ravel (1875-1937). Paolino Vassallo who lived and worked for a whole decade in Paris starting from 1875 till 1885 must surely have been in some way influenced by these artistic convulsions. Any man of his sensibility could not be immune to them.

The "French connection" of Maltese music could make an interesting study on its own. We have seen how musicians from Malta and their art had followed closely Italian (mostly Neapolitan) ideals. Yet, if one delves as far back as the middle of the 17th century one can find a secondary, far less delineated, yet almost uninterrupted line of influence originating from Paris. This had started with Luigi Mataron and Enrico Magi and then on to Mikiel Anġ Vella, Francesco Azopardi, Nicolò Isouard, Alessandro Curmi (or the Francocized form Curmy as he himself mostly signed his name), Francesco Schira and last Paolino Vassallo.

A contemporary of Paolino Vassallo

worthy of mention is undoubtedly Emanuele Bartoli (1852-1933). For a long time he served as a bandmaster in the army and because of this position he has left a great number of original pieces for band and very good arrangements of operas, symphonies and other orchestral works also for this medium. However, he was no less active in the orchestral field. His opera *Simonetta* unfortunately never had an airing, but smaller works of his, especially religious pieces, were widely played. His compositions are notable for their rich harmonic basis, something which Bartoli often integrates with his melodic progressions in such a way as to make the two an essential part of each other.

Vassallo's students, Carlo Diacono (1876-1942), Fr Duminku Anastasi (1886-1938) and Jose Mallia Pulverenti (1896-1964) are the three mainstays of the music of the early decades of the 20th century. Their chief contribution and inclinations as far as Maltese music is concerned has already been hinted at. Of the three, Diacono was perhaps the one to follow most closely the traditional Italian school. Anastasi's art is, in a way, more refined and detached, with elements of a mystic nature surfacing through, especially in his "*a cappella*" works. Both Diacono and Anastasi make liberal use of modal tonalities in their works. Mallia Pulverenti, on the other hand, is the composer with the more "advanced" ideas and idioms. His two symphonic poems *Impressione Sinfonica* and *Espressionismo* attest clearly to this.

Yet, when everything is said, no doubt remains that the influence of Italian music, opera especially, had rooted itself deeply right through to the present time. The building of the Royal Opera House in 1866 was exactly the fruition of this widespread activity and its unquestioned popularity with the Maltese masses. Ulderico Rolandi makes some very interesting and elucidatory comments about opera in Malta in the mid-1850's. He writes that:

"successful appearances on the Maltese operatic stage was considered as an indispensable step in the career of any fledgling artiste"

(he was obviously referring to Italian artistes) and continues saying that:

"the Maltese public were always very enamoured of the lyrical theatre. They showed respect and good manners by refraining from cross talking and making noises with the programmes during the performances, and not coming late"

(apparently ills affecting Italian contemporary theatres).

The above shows the respect that the Italians themselves had for operatic presentation in Malta and how highly they thought of the Maltese stage as a centre for opera production. Moreover, if one looks at the list of operas that were presented during the first operatic season at the Royal Opera House (and most successive ones for that matter) it is not difficult to imagine why.

The first Commission for the Royal Opera House appointed by the government consisted of Lieutenant Colonel John Reel, Mr Henry C. Frendo and Baron Ugo Testaferrata Abela and for the very first season (1866) they programmed the following 16 operas: *I Puritani (Bellini), Gemma di Vergy (Donizzetti), L'Ebrea (Appollone), Mirope (Pacini), Jone (Petrella), Ernani (Verdi), Barbiere di Siviglia (Rossini), Crispino e la Comare (Ricci), Lucrezia Borgia (Donizzetti), Roberto il Diavolo (Meyerbeer* – notice straightaway and significantly, the Italianized version of the French original *Robert Le Diable), Elisir D'Amor (Donizzetti), Rigoletto (Verdi), Poliuto (Donizzetti), Il Trovatore (Verdi)* and *La Traviata (Verdi)*.

The average number of operas presented for each season was fifteen, two of which had to be new to Malta. In all, during a particular season, more than 120 performances were presented, and considering the size of these islands, operatic life then could be considered very rich indeed.

The main bulk of the operas presented were Italian with a sprinkling of French

ones, though always in their Italian version. The following French operas (with the dates of their Maltese premiere) cropped up regularly on the "cartellone" of the Royal Opera House – *Faust* (1868) by Gounod, *Fra Diavolo* (1872) and *La Muta dei Portici* (1866) by Auber, *Roberto il Diavolo* (1866), *Gli Ugonotti* (1868), *L'Africana* (1870), *Il Profeta* (1872) and *Dinorah* (1873) by Meyerbeer, *L'Ebrea* (1876) by Halevy and *Carmen* (1880) by Bizet.

German opera was practically non-existent with the exception of *Martha* (1862) by Flotow and *Don Giovanni* (1847) by Mozart. The first Wagnerian operatic drama, *Lohengrin* arrived during the season 1895-1896.

Reference has already been made to the Nani, Bugeja and the Vella families, some of whose members were extremely active as "*maestri di cappella*" during the first half of the 20th century. However there were quite a few other musicians worthy of mention, active not only in churches but also in the theatre and the very popular local bands – composers like Carlo Farrugia (1881-1961) who studied with Giuseppe Vella; Gaetano Grech (1855-1933) author of a book on the rules of harmony in Maltese; Mario Cirillo (1891-1955) who studied in Naples and Joseph Abdilla (1886-1944) a student of Paolino Vassallo and a well-known contrapuntist.

Another student of Paolino Vassallo was Giuseppe Caruana (1880-1931). Caruana wrote a lot of sacred music but is nowadays chiefly remembered for his hymns. Caruana had a natural flair for writing these simple, attractive semi-religious tunes which over the years seem to have lost nothing of their original freshness and impact. They have a beauty of line rarely met with in Maltese music. I always think of Giuseppe Caruana as the "Schubert" of Maltese music.

Giuseppe Camilleri (1903-1976) and Joseph Abela Scolaro (1910-1979) were both active in the world of the theatre. Camilleri, especially, was for a long time musical director of a local amateur operatic company with whom he produced several operas. Both Camilleri and Abela Scolaro were also very well-known conductors of popular bands and have written some of the best pieces in the "local" repertoire for this medium.

As regards the contemporary scene, four composers stand out clearly both for their vast and varied output and their recognition on an international level — Carmelo Pace (born 1906), Charles Camilleri (born 1931), Pawlu Grech (born 1938), and Joseph Vella (born 1942) who is also very active as a conductor.

Carmelo Pace (1906-1993) has been a shining light to most of his contemporaries. Whether one finds empathy with his music, or faults some of his styles and approaches, his figure none the less looms prominently as that of the "grand old man" of Maltese Music during the greater part of the 20th century. He wrote prolifically in the field of opera, oratorio, chamber music and orchestral works, a substantial number of which have received performances abroad. Pace was the first composer to take an active interest in Maltese folk music. In fact his orchestral Fantasia *Maltesina* was first played in 1931. He also left his mark in the field of teaching, an activity which he assiduously followed right up to his death.

Bibliography

ANON., *Cenni Storici sulla Vita del Maestro di Cappella V. Bugeja*, A. Aquilina, Malta, 1861.

ANON., *Cenni Biografici di Giuseppe Spiteri Fremond*, Tipografia Gutenberg, Malta, 1878.

AZZOPARDI, Fr. J., *Vetera Novaque Concentos et Carmina*, Mid Med Bank, 1985.

    La Cappella Musicale della Cattedrale di Malta e i suoi rapporti con la Sicilia, Daniele Ficola, Palermo, 1985.

    L'Archivio Musicale della Cattedrale di Mdina a Malta: Il Repertorio Siciliano, J. Bonet, Malta, 1986.

    Nicolò Isouard de Malte, PEG, Malta, 1991.

AZZOPARDI, SANSONE, *Baroque & Rennaisance Music in the Mdina Cathedral Archives*, (due to be published).

BADGER, G.P., *Description of Malta and Gozo*, P. Cumbo, Malta, 1851.

BORG, M.A., *Lyric Opera in Malta – Season 1838-39 its Side Issues*, National Press, Malta, 1939.

CARUANA DEI CONTI GATTO, V., *Malta Artistica Illustrata*, Casa di San Giuseppe, Malta, 1910.

CASTAGNA, P.P., *L-Istorja ta' Malta bil-Gżejjer Tagħha*, C. Busuttil, Malta, 1888.

DEGABRIELE, M., CAFFARI, G., *Carmelo Pace – A Maltese Composer*, PEG, Malta, 1991.

EYNAUD, J., *Il Teatro Italiano a Malta 1630-1830*, Lux Press, Malta, 1979.

FARRUGIA, Mons. L., *Maestro Dr Paolo Nani*, Giuseppe Abela, Malta, 1904.

FAURE, G., *Storia ta' Malta u Għawdex*, Andolfo/Magro, Malta, 1916.

HEIGHS, AZZOPARDI, J., *A Concert of Maltese Baroque Music by Benigno Zerafa* (programme booklet), Valletta, 1987.

KROESLER-ILG, B., STUMME, H., *Maltesische Volkslieder*, Berlin, 1909.

LAFERLA, A.V. *Ġrajjiet Malta u n-Nies Tagħha*, Evans Bros, London.

MICELI, A.G., *L-Istorja ta' l-Opera f'Malta* (unpublished).

MIFSUD BONNICI, R., *Mużiċisti Kompożituri Maltin – Maestri di Cappella tal-Katidral*, ABC Fine Arts Printers, Malta, 1950.

    Mużiċisti Kompożituri Maltin u Għawdxin, Giov. Muscat, Malta, 1951.

    Ġrajja tal-Mużika f'Malta u Għawdex, Giov. Muscat, Malta, 1954.

    Dizzjunarju Bibljografiku Nazzjonali, Dipartiment ta' l-Informazzjoni, Malta, 1960.

    Ġrajja ta' Baned f'Malta u Għawdex, Giov. Muscat, 1957.

MUSCAT AZZOPARDI, Ivo, *Bijografija tal-Mużiċist Nicolò Isouard*, Department of Information, Malta, 1958.

    Francesco Azopardi Kittieb tal-Mużika, Casa di San Giuseppe, 1949.

PALMER, Christopher, *The Music of Charles Camilleri*, London, 1975.

PARTRIDGE, J.F., JEAL, F., *Galpin Society Journal*, U.K., 1977.

PELLEGRINI, Maria Vincenzo, *The Making of a Maltese Tenor – Paul Axiaq*, PEG Ltd, Malta, 1989.

PULLICINO, Can. Dr. Paolo, *Notizia Biografica di Francesco Azopardi*, Zefirino

ROLAND, U., *Musica e Musicisti a Malta*, R. Grixti, Livorno, 1932.

SAMUT TAGLIAFERRO, A., *The Royal Opera House: An Historical Sketch*, Progress Press, Malta, 1966.

VELLA, J., *Tfal Maltin Inkantaw*, Government Printing Press, 1987.

WAHL, Eduard, *Nicolò Isouard – His Life and Achievement in the Field of Comic Opera*, Munich, 1908.

WETTINGER, G., FSADNI, M., *L-Għanja ta' Pietru Caxaro*, Printwell, Malta, 1983.

Dissertations

ATTARD, Carmen, *Five Generations of Nani Musicians*, University of Malta, 1986.

ATTARD, Stephen, *Mons. Giuseppe Farrugia*, University of Malta, 1989.

BUTTIGIEG, Maryann, *Giuseppe Vella – His Life and Musical Works*, University of Malta, 1982.

CHIRCOP, Natascha, *Scores Attributed to Giuseppe Balzano*, University of Malta, 1991.

FRENDO, Maria, *Francesco Azopardi – Mass in G. – A Critical Edition*, University of Malta, 1987.

HABER, C.J., *Il-Mużika f'Malta*, University of Malta, 1964.

MICALLEF, Rose Marie, *The Bugeja Musicians*, University of Malta, 1990.

SACCO, J., *Malta – Its Music and Some of Its famous Composers*, St Michael's Training College, 1972.

VELLA, Mary, *Maltese Folk Music and Music Education*, Malta College of Education, 1978.

ZAMMIT, L., *Is-Sehem ta' wħud mis-Surmastrijiet Maltin fil-Mużika Sagra u Profana f'Malta*, University of Malta, 1979.

Folklore

Ġużè Cassar Pullicino

Malta and Gozo possess a rich legacy of folklore. They stand half-way on the land ridge that once joined Sicily to Africa, and their geographical position has influenced their history and traditions.

Besides reflecting the usages and ways of thought of the present, Maltese folklore preserves the soul of the past, embodying the mode of life and the beliefs and practices of preceding centuries. This national heritage of lore and tradition is the product of simple, psychological reactions to the historical environments and to the various culture contacts which our people have experienced in the past. At different times and by various routes, many people have come to these islands and dominated them for varying periods. Each ruling group – Punic, Roman, Arab, Norman, Swabian, Angevin, Aragonese, Castilian, the Knights of St John of Jerusalem and, lastly, the English – brought its own lore, language and way of life in its wake. Most of these left their imprint on local tradition and, in their turn, underwent changes in the process of adaptation to the conditions of the country and subsequent adjustment to the traditional pattern of Maltese life and thought. The result has been an extremely variegated form of folk-culture constituting a distinctive element of Malta's national identity.

Even a short stay in Malta will enable visitors – especially those from a Northern climate – to notice certain features of the local scene. They are struck by the compactness of the buildings, the absence of chimneys and slanting roofs, the prevalence of balconies. They will note an eye – the protective eye of Osiris – painted on the bows of Malta's

characteristic *dgħajsas* and fishing boats. They may see the farmer using a primitive plough (M. *moħriet*), which is now fast going out of use, and the circular threshing floor (M. *qiegħa*) of hard trampled earth. They cannot fail to notice the rubble walls separating the fields, and the wayside shrines, niches and stone crosses. They will hear the cries of the hawkers at town or village festivals, and at the open-air markets held at Valletta and other localities. Besides, there are numerous items of local craft produce to choose from, including silver and gold filigree work, probably introduced into Malta via Sicily during the 17th century, and hand-made lace, which achieved a high degree of perfection in the 18th century and then, after a period of decline, was revived by Lady Hamilton Chichester and others in the 19th century. These and other aspects of the Malta scene, however, will not enable them to look into the heart of things or to understand the working of the Maltese mind in its various manifestations. It takes a much longer period to get into touch with the inner life of the people and discover the varied structure of their folklore as it has evolved in the course of centuries.

Birth and Infancy

Maltese tradition has preserved the memory of several rites of passage characteristic of a pre-industrial community. From the cradle to the grave a series of time-honoured customs marked the main events of human life. Many pious beliefs and practices were associated with the birth of a child. When the delivery was difficult, the mother borrowed a withered plant known as *Il-Warda tal-Passjoni* (The Passion Flower) which was put into some water. Popular belief claimed that the mother was delivered of her child as soon as the branches of the dried plant opened out. The help and protection of certain saints – St Lukarda, St Blaise, St Raymond, St Spiridion of Corfu, St Calogero and St Victor – were especially invoked during childbirth. Delivery often took place in a small room known as *l-alkova*, 'the alcove', which served as a labour or delivery room.

The birth of a girl was not as welcome as that of a boy. It was considered advisable to have the baby baptized as soon as possible, one reason being that if, unfortunately, the child died before it was baptized it would go to limbo. When the christening took place within twenty four hours it was believed that a soul was freed from Purgatory. So long as the baby remained unbaptized it was not considered to be a Christian, but a Turk. In some localities, the unbaptized child was laid in the cot facing left. After the christening, however, the midwife could put the baby either on his back or facing right.

Up to the 16th century the Gallican rite of baptism by immersion was practised in some parishes. In 1575 Mgr Pietro Duzina, the Apostolic Visitor, prohibited the practice on account of its unhygienic effects. Traditionally, the first children are named after their grandparents, the deceased ones taking precedence over those still alive. A child born with a caul (M. *bil-borqom*) is believed to grow up exceptionally strong and invulnerable. Old fishermen will tell you that if you keep a piece of caul on you the sea will have no power over you, the reason being that the caul in reality forms part of another human being.

From the Child Health Clinics two interesting folk-beliefs were communicated to the present writer in 1945. At Mosta and Tarxien it was held that the mother of a newly-born baby has to eat a hen's neck and head on the day following childbirth;

if she failed to do so the child would take more than three months to start keeping his head erect. The other belief was that the placenta or afterbirth (M. *is-sekonda* or *seħbitha*) must be left in the rain till it is washed away, or be buried in the soil and water poured on it; if this is not done the baby will suffer from skin eruptions.

Weaning generally took place when the child was twelve months of age, hence the saying: *It-tnax fattâm*, i.e. at the twelfth month one must wean the baby. To wean their young, mothers smeared their nipples with the juice of the aloe plant (M. *sabbara*) which tastes bitter.

To ward off the harmful effects of the evil eye, children are made to wear amulets in the form of a horn, a cowrie shell (M. *baħbuħa*), or a holy medal hung round the child's neck. Some blessed olive leaves and, up to a few years ago, a piece of candle used in church in Holy Week known as *xemgħa tat-tniebri*, 'candle of the Tenebrae', were also considered effective. On Easter Saturday, at Qormi, children who took an unduly long time to walk were made to stand up and to try and walk at the *Gloria*.

The child's hiccup was formerly cured by the mother with the utterance of the following lines, which were reputed to have the effect of transferring the child's hiccup to someone else:

> *Solluzzu buzzu,*
> *Mur għand min jobgħodni;*
> *'K m'għandix min jobgħodni*
> *Erġ'ejja għandi.*
>
> O nasty hiccup,
> Go to someone who hates me;
> And if there's none who hates me
> Return to me.

A similar Sicilian formula given by Giuseppe Pitrè runs as follows:

> *Suggiuzzu, sugguzzieddu,*
> *Ramuzza ri funtana,*
> *Vattinni ni to mamma,*
> *Va' viri s'idda t'ama.*
> *Si t'ama, statti dda.*
> *S'un t'ama, veni cca.*
>
> Hiccup, little hiccup,
> Little branch of the fountain,

Go to your mother,
See if she loves you.
If she loves you, stay with her,
If she does not love you, come here.

When the child loses his first tooth, he is urged not to leave it lying about but to bury it in a flower pot. It is believed that, as a new plant emerged from the flowerpot, so a new tooth emerges from the child's gum to replace the buried one.

These beliefs and practices are closely related to similar concepts and customs reported from North African and other Arabic-speaking countries (Morocco, Algeria, Palestine) as well as in Sicily and among some other Mediterranean people.

On the child's first anniversary a special ceremony, known as *quċċija*, is held. This is a special party to which relatives and friends are invited, and when the company is assembled, if the child is a boy, they give him articles such as corn and comfits, jewels, money, an inkstand, Rosary beads, a sword, etc., and if a girl, needles, silk, ribbon, and similar articles. The child's choice is thought to determine the profession or character he will develop when he or she grows up. If the boy chooses corn, it is a sign of generosity; if he prefers the inkstand, he is destined for trade or the Bar; if he seizes the sword, it is believed that he will become a soldier, and so on. This divination ceremony seems to be gaining favour once more among a wide circle of Maltese society.

Lullaby – Children's Rhymes

A traditional lullaby or cradle song survived up to some years ago. It runs into some sixteen stanzas making up an exquisite piece of popular composition, rich in imagery and poetic feeling, opening with the following lines:

Orqod, orqod, ibni, orqod
Fil-benniena tal-ħarir ...Laam!
Dik ommok il-Madonna
Missierek Ġesù Bambin ...Laam!

Sleep, sleep, little child
In the cradle made of silk ...Sleep!

The Holy Virgin is thy Mother,
The child Jesus is thy Father ...Go to sleep!

The Christian inspiration and wording of this lullaby links it up with similar compositions in nearby Sicily, but the word *Laam* or *Naam*, from Arabic *nam* 'to sleep', betrays also an earlier Semitic influence.

Nursery rhymes introduce the child to the first wonders of life. Children experience their first journey on their parents' knees as they are rocked to and fro to the accompaniment of a special rhyme beginning with the lines:

Banni bannozzi,
Ġej it-tata ġej ...

Clap, clap your hand
For Daddy's coming ...

which closely resemble those of the corresponding Sicilian rhyme

Manu manuzzi ...
Veni lu tata ...

as well as the English exhortation

Clap hands! Clap hands!
Till Daddy comes home ...

Very few children's rhymes reach up to the standard of the lullaby mentioned above. A few, however, are quite serious in tone and content. One well-known stanza, in particular, reflects the people's preoccupation with the lack of sufficient rain in Malta:

Agħmel, xita, agħmel,
Ħalli jinbet il-ħaxix;
Il-ħaxix intuh lill-mogħża
U l-mogħża ttina l-ħalib;
Għandi nagħġa mmur nirgħaha
Bis-suf tagħha nagħmel qmis.

Rain, rain, rain,
That the grass may grow;
We shall give the grass to the goat
And the goat will give us milk;
I'll take out my sheep to graze
And I'll make me a shirt of her wool.

Incidentally, this presents a sharp contrast to the English nursery rhyme in which English children drive off rain far away to Spain:

Rain, rain, go to Spain,
Never show your face again.

In a few rhymes one can trace a definite link with a probable Semitic stream of thought. Thus, the opening lines of a rhyme heard at Birkirkara during the last war, i.e.

> Tat-tila tula!
> X'kilt illejla?
> – Hobż u għejna!
> Minn fuq?
> – Terż ilma ...

> Thou of the long dress!
> What have you eaten tonight?
> – Bread and a small cheese.
> And after that?
> – A measure of water ...

have a direct relationship with the following *rengaine populaire* from Lebanon given by M. Feghali in his *Syntaxe des Parlers Arabes actuels du Liban* (Paris, 1928, p.467):

> Wáin ként el-bârha
> 'énd 'éhté sâḷḥa
> 'aš tá 'mtak
> Ġébnè mâlḥa

> Where were you yesterday?
> At my sister Salha's house.
> What did she give you to eat?
> Salted cheese.

Children's Games

One can still find a diversity of traditional games among children of school age. It is a pity that Maltese games of the playground type do not figure in the organised play activities of the pupils. These are boys' games and girls' games, and in many instances counting out and other rhymes add to the zest of the games. Quarrels between children at play are made up by crossing the little fingers of their right hands while they say:

> Paċi kulaċi,
> Il-Madonna fuq rasi;
> Kristu jaħbini
> U l-Madonna ssibni;
> Kristu fuq l-altar
> Qed ibierek it-tfal żgħar.

> Peace between us,
> The Holy Mother over my head;
> Christ hides me away
> And the Holy Mother finds me;
> Christ on the altar
> Blesses the little children.

Some games show signs of native freshness and vitality, while others reflect outside influences, mainly Sicilian, and, in more recent ones, English. The very names by which some games are known, such as *faraboj* (It. *fare a boia*), *it-tiġieġa l-għamja*, 'the blind hen', recalling the Italian game *fare a mosca cieca* and the English *blind man's buff*, immediately suggest the probable origin of the games. In the case of the game known as *ċiknatur* a French origin has been suggested, from *chacun a (son) tour*, 'every one in his turn'. Furthermore, under direct British influence other games have been assimilated and given a Maltese garb. Such are the games known as *Master*, explained by J. Aquilina in his *Maltese-English Dictionary* (Vol.2, 1990, p.790) as "a game consisting in throwing a heavy flattish stone at a small standing stone with coins placed on it or under it", *gardinaw* (Eng. guarding out?), the English game 'hopscotch', a popular pavement game in both towns and villages of Malta and Gozo under the name of *passju*, and the words *kikks*, uttered in a game of marbles when one marble hits another, and *ġakk* (pl. *ġakkijiet*) [Eng. jack], a marble used in a children's game. In addition, the use of such words as *gastell*, 'castle' (Sic. *casteddu*) in games involving the use of glass beads or nuts, or of *brilli*, 'skittles' (It. *birilli*), no less than certain game-rhymes with foreign sounding words such as *siamo sette* and *in giro in giro ngella* suggest earlier or long-standing contacts and links with Sicily and Italy.

First Communion and Confirmation

In a predominantly Catholic country such as Malta, First Communion and Confirmation constitute important rites of passage, providing occasions of great joy both to the children receiving these Sacraments and to their parents. A special dress is worn for the occasion. After the church ceremony, the children go to the local premises of the MUSEUM, a lay religious organization which prepares children for these Sacraments, where they are given breakfast, a bag of sweets and a small present. For Confirmation they receive, instead, an ice cream and sweets. A larger party, attended by relatives and friends, awaits the children when they get home. Holy pictures with the child's name printed on the back are distributed on both occasions. The child is usually taken to a photographer and the photograph is then framed and put in a prominent place and prized ever after as a happy remembrance of childhood. Nowadays a video cameraman is often hired to shoot the salient parts of the church ceremony and of the party.

Marriage Customs

Ancient marriage rituals have suffered rapid and successive changes since the first decades of the present century, with the result that modern marriage customs in Malta largely conform to the rites and practices of other European countries. However, the 18th century historians G.A. Ciantar and Agius De Soldanis, followed by various 19th century writers, have left us a clear picture of the older ritual. We read, for example, that a marriageable daughter was hardly consulted at all in the choice of her husband. A young man's first indication that he could pay court to a daughter of the house was a pot of sweet basil placed on a stone bracket on the outer wall of the house where the girl lived. He usually employed an old woman as an intermediary (M. *ħuttaba*) to arrange the match. When his suit has been accepted, the contract signed and the dowry stipulated, the young man sent his beloved a present of a fish with a gold ring in its mouth. Then followed the betrothal feast (M. *il-kelma* or *ir-rabta*) when the bride was first introduced to her future husband in the presence of parents and friends, and he would offer her an engagement ring, on

which were engraved two hands joined in token of fidelity, while she, for her part, reciprocated with a handkerchief edged with lace.

On the day of the wedding, musicians and singers celebrated in verse the virtues of the happy couple, and handfuls of grain, nuts and wheat were showered on them on their return from the church for the nuptial feast. The guests usually stayed for the wedding banquet, to which they often contributed in kind – capons, wine, etc. The bride ate in a separate apartment, but after the repast she would come and sit near her husband, and drink out of the same cup. There was also dancing with castanets after the Spanish fashion. In the intervals the guests threw presents into the lap of the bride, who sat at the top end of the room. Eight days after the wedding, and not before, the bride would leave her father's house (M. *il-ħarġa*) and be received with due pomp and ceremony by her husband in their new home.

Courtship and marriage rituals have changed considerably, especially since the inter-War years (1920-1940). Under direct British influence the bestman and the bridesmaid have made their appearance and worked their way down to all classes of the population. And with the new customs came fresh beliefs and taboos. Should the bridegroom see the bride's dress before the wedding day, bad luck is sure to follow. To avoid the effects of the evil eye, the last stitch in the bride's dress must be made by the dressmaker shortly before the bride puts it on. Some people also believe that the bride should not make her own dress as this may bring her bad luck.

The transition to today's usages has taken place in stages over a fairly long period. Up to within living memory, according to the head dress worn by the bride, people could tell that she was married (i) *bil-għonnella*, with the old-fashioned faldetta – now gone out of use – in which case she wore a whole corded silk or black costume, (ii) *bil-kappell*, with the hat, usually wearing a faun or silver-grey dress, or (iii) *bil-mant*, with a white veil, dress and train. Since World War II the veil has come into general use.

If either the bride or the groom happened to be in mourning, the bride usually wore a hat instead of a veil. Among the upper classes, if the bride is a widow, she puts on a lilac, pink or cream gown. When the bride wore the *għonnella*, or a hat, the groom put on a simple, black or Navy blue suit. Otherwise he wears a frac or cutaway.

The wedding reception may be of two kinds: (a) *bit-trattament*, with waiters carrying various rounds (M. *passati*) of drinks, sweets and other delicacies to the guests, who are seated round the walls of a hall or a yard, or (b) *bir-ripò* (Fr. *repas*), in which case the guests gather round the table, sometimes extravagantly laid out with all imaginable kinds of sweets, savouries, drinks etc., and help themselves.

The bride, assisted by the groom, cuts the wedding cake, which has now come into general use, and then makes her way among the guests, offering pieces of cake to the males, while the groom looks after the females. A smaller cake is given as a present to each of the witnesses. At country weddings there was no wedding cake. The newly married couple received two heart-shaped tarts (*tal-marmorata*) which they passed on as a present to the witnesses. Instead of grain and nuts, rice is showered nowadays on the newly-weds before they leave for the honeymoon.

Jeremy Boissevain, a well known anthropologist, has noted other details of present-day marriage ritual in his Paper "Changing Betrothal and Marriage Ceremonies in Malta", read at *The Life Cycle — SIEF's Third Congress*, held between April 8-13, 1987 in Zurich, Switzerland. The couple spend a period of 'talking' to each other, without the parents' knowledge, before they become formally engaged and have their rings blessed by a priest. At the engagement party they receive as presents many useful items for household and kitchen. The

majority of the guests present in church for the wedding ceremony are relatives or friends of the couple. Those invited by the groom sit on the right hand side. In addition to, or instead of bridesmaids, the bride may have one or more flower girls.

The groom, bestman, the father of the bride and groom and the ushers all wear tails. The groom carries a top hat and gloves during much of the ceremony and the reception. In the church the hired photographer or, nowadays, video cameraman and his assistant are busy shooting the most important scenes for the wedding film.

The same writer observes that in most cases the reception takes place at the local club or other hired premises. After changing into their going away clothes the couple are carried shoulder high by relatives and friends and are encouraged to catch hold of each other and kiss three times. Finally they drive off, generally in the groom's car, which his friends have covered with wet flour or foamy shaving cream, etc. The guests then leave after congratulating the bride's parents and thanking them for inviting them. Upper class couples generally spend their honeymoon abroad.

Death and Funeral Customs

The death and funeral customs of the ancient Maltese presented various features that look rather strange to our modern way of thought. When a man died, hired women mourners known as *newwieħa*, dressed in long mourning cloaks, entered the house, singing the praises of the deceased in low, surrowful voices. They would cut vine branches and run through all the rooms, overturning the flower-pots on the window-sills and smashing some of the ornamental furniture. They then went into the room where the corpse lay, surrounded by female relatives dressed in black and heavily veiled. The *newwieħa* wept, beat their breasts, and cut off locks of their own hair, which they placed in the coffin. Boiled corn was distributed on that day to all the relatives, and they cut off the hair of their horses' tails. For three days they would light no fire in the kitchen, but relatives and friends or neighbours sent meals in to the family. The women remained indoors for forty days; the men went out, unshaven, on the eighth day. The mourning period lasted one or two years, according to the degree of consanguinity.

Although the general practice of these rituals was not resumed after the plague of 1676, some of them survived, in transmuted form, up to the present century especially in Gozo and in some villages in Malta. Mirrors and looking glasses in the room where the body was lying were covered, and some families even removed, or turned round both furniture and pictures hanging on the walls. Door knockers were also removed, or draped with black crepe; housedoors were kept closed for several days, while neighbours half shut their own out of respect for the bereaved family. Window blinds were pulled down for some months or else linen sheets replaced window curtains. A dish of salt was usually placed on the belly of the dead body in the belief that the salt in the dish prevented the corpse from swelling through early decomposition. This custom, first noted by A. Cremona in 1922, is shared with other ethnographically unconnected people, for it was not only practised by the Arabs of Algeria but also survived in a corresponding usage in Cumberland rural districts up to the present century.

For more than a century now mourning customs have tended to become simpler and less complex. The Maltese word for mourning is *vistu*, whence *vistuż*, 'in mourning', obviously derived from Sicilian *visitu* with its twofold meaning, i.e. *purtari lu visitu*, 'to put on mourning', and *tiniri visitu*, 'to receive complimentary visits of sympathy''. This latter custom has now practically gone out of use in Malta.

Wearing of a full mourning dress on the death of parents, formerly observed for two years, has now been reduced to some few days, or weeks. Business premises are sometimes closed, and a notice affixed to the door with English and, formerly, Italian wording: *Family mourning – Lutto di famiglia*. In rural areas some people still keep away from festas, theatres, dances and merrymaking. For many years the coffin was carried in a horse-drawn carriage. Class distinctions were reflected in the kind of funeral chosen by the family of the deceased – *tal-prima*, 'first class', with richly decorated carriage drawn by four horses sporting a black feather on their head; *tas-sekonda*, 'second class', providing only a carriage and pair, and *tal-povri*, for the poorer classes, having just the bare essentials. White coffins, indicating purity or chastity, were used for unmarried women. Black carriages were invariably used, but babies were laid in a white coffin and carried in a white carriage. As from April, 1970 the motor hearse replaced all other funeral conveyances.

Wreath laying on the graves is generally practised, but some people object to these floral tributes at the funeral and they try to discourage the custom by including, in the obituary notice published in the Press, the words: "No flowers by requests, but donations to (a charity) will be appreciated". Sympathy cards are sent by friends to the family of the deceased, who acknowledge the condolences by sending them printed epitaphs often carrying a photograph of the deceased.

Costume

Dress and costume are another important feature of ancient folk-life in Malta. Early travellers' accounts contain many allusions to peculiarities of Maltese dress, a common feature being that, until well into the latter half of the 18th century, the women of Malta went about veiled, like Oriental women. In 1776, Maltese ladies, who were always attended by a black slave, dressed exactly like her mistress but in inferior quality material, plotted to discard the old-fashioned, Sicilian-style dress and to adopt French fashions. The *faldetta*, or *għonnella*, which was considered the national head-dress up to the period between the Wars, has now gone out of use. In his book *Malta: An Account and an Appreciation* (Harrap, 1949, p.26), Sir Harry Luke described it as

"a voluminous hood of rich silk — black everywhere save in the villages of Żabbar and Żejtun, where it is blue and is called *xurqana* — stiffened inside the top edge by a piece of cardboard about a yard long, one end of which rests on the head, while the other end has to be held. Originally, it was really, like the Turkish *charshaf*, a skirt or petticoat (which is what the word *għonnella* means) thrown up over the head. Later it was curtailed, for which reason it is sometimes called *nofs għonnella*, a half skirt; but it is still cut to show the placket-hole — in point of fact, half the placket-hole — of the garment from which it has sprung".

Cookery

Turning to Maltese cookery, we find that the vocabulary of local food presents the pattern of Semitic words for primitive kinds of food and Romance loan-words for the more refined cooked foods: exx. *ħobż*, 'bread' (Ar. *khubz*); *ftira*, 'any disc-like bakery product that is flat and round' (Ar. *fatira*); *ġobon*, 'cheese' (Ar. *gubn*); *sfinġa*, 'battered fish portions fried in oil' (Ar. *'asfanġa*); *maqrut*, 'date-filled pastry fried in oil' (Ar. *maqrūt*); *kawlata*, 'a kind of vegetable soup with pork' (It. *cavolata*); *imqarrun*, 'macaroni' (It. *maccheroni*); *torta*, 'pie' (It. *torta*); *qubbajt*, 'nougat' (Sic. *cubbaitu*); *irkotta*, 'a milk substance resembling cottage cheese' (Sic. and It. *ricotta*); *pudina*, 'pudding' (Eng. *pudding*) and *minestra*, 'vegetable soup' (It. *minestra*). The ever-popular *pastizz*, known locally in English as "cheesecake", derives from Italian *pasticcio*.

The late Vincent Bugeja stressed the eclectic character of the dishes laid on Maltese tables. Writing on "Maltese Style

of Cooking" in the *Times of Malta* of March 22, 1955, he said

"During my long residence in France I discovered that the majority of our dishes are the specialities of one French province or another, and in my travels through Spain, Italy, Austria and Southern Germany I was always struck by the similarity between the fare of country inns and our own culinary productions sometimes considered as specifically Maltese".

The historical explanation he suggested is that these savoury dishes from so many different countries of Western Europe came to us

"from the kitchens of the Knights' auberges, the Grand Master's palaces and the country residences of the dignitaries of the Order. The Knights, noblemen brought up on large country estates, naturally preferred their regional cooking to what Malta had to offer in this respect. So it seems quite likely that they brought over their own cooks, especially for the auberges where they were bound by their rule to dine in hall three or four times a week,... These cooks had Maltese aids, and these in turn passed on the recipes of the best regional dishes of the Continent to Maltese families...".

One may add that, according to the *Notizia della Sacra Infermeria* published in Rome in 1713, the hospital diets prescribed to the Infirmary patients contained various items — soups, meat and poultry, vegetables and sweet dishes — that survive to this day in many a humble household in the villages of Malta and Gozo. And after the Knights left Malta in 1798, as a result of trade and travel links with Sicily and Italy, of contacts with Italian political refugees during and after the *Risorgimento*, and of direct British influence, fresh elements have been added, including the English Christmas turkey, cakes and puddings, to make up the rich variety of Maltese cooking that we have today.

The 'Festa'

The Maltese *festa* is an occasion of great rejoicing, enlivened by illuminations, feastings, fireworks, water regattas and other open air entertainments. No other aspect of Maltese life is as full of warm external appeal as the *festa*, which is a flourishing institution that has evolved gradually in the course of the last four centuries.

In every town and village of Malta and Gozo special celebrations are held each year in honour of the patron saint. With the exception of a few localities, these festivities nowadays take place between May and September, the so-called "*festa-season*". As a result of this arrangement the *festa* is generally celebrated on a different date from that assigned to the Saint in the Church's liturgical calendar.

Its organization is the result of the people's efforts, voluntary work and contributions. Feverish preparations for the *festa* are fanned by the rivalries of the *każini* or band-clubs of which there are two in most towns and villages. The local bands play on two or more days during the week preceding the feast, while visiting bands play on the eve and on the feast day proper. They march through the main streets and finally take their place on a stand built in the middle of the square, surrounded by a crowd anxious to hear the musical excerpts selected for the occasion.

There is an unmistakable festive air about the place on *festa*-day. The bells ring merrily. Walking through the streets, hung with flags, banners, paper decorations and baskets of flowers one notices that the facades of the houses have been neatly whitewashed recently for the occasion, and that the doors and windows as well as the balconies are freshly decorated.

In a few localities which were particularly affected by the Great Sieges of 1565 and 1940-45 one can see wooden pillars, topped by life-sized statues, arms and other trophies recalling the two sieges. However, the majority of statues which surmount the wooden pillars lining the streets in most places in Malta are those of angels painted in attractive colours, holding electric brackets and emblems of the saint whose *festa* is being celebrated. Other statues portray saints, popes, bishops, Doctors of the Church, etc. who were in some way connected with the saint. Others depict the next of kin of saints, or statuary groups representing some episode in the saint's life.

Here and there, at improvised counters or from fast-food vehicles, nougat (M. *qubbajt*) and other dainties are sold. On the eve of the feast a great display of fireworks starts at about 11 p.m., to the admiration of thousands of spectators who pack the square and the overlooking terraces and balconies or, in certain places, watch the spectacle from the sea in boats.

On the day of the feast the whole family and one or more guests of honour assemble at noon to partake of the specially rich fare prepared for the occasion. And people put on a new dress, or a new pair of shoes, for the feast!

The great event of the *festa* is the procession with the Patron Saint's statue through the streets of the town or village. There is a good deal of noise and glare, but the rejoicing reaches its peak when the statue is about to re-enter the church. This is called the *briju*. There are deafening shouts of *evviva*, 'long live'; the bands play, while the firing of crackers, rockets and petards mix with the peal of the church bells and the cries of the vendors of nougat, ice-cream and cheesecakes.

Since the last war the *festa* celebrations in many localities have been expanded so as to include a noon band-march and parade during which youths and others demonstrate wildly. It has also become customary for families and friends from the same neighbourhood to go to the seaside on the morrow of the feast. This outing is often an elaborate form of picnic (M. *xalata*) with decorated cars and buses, and enlivened with the playing of guitars or accordions, lots of fun, loud singing, dancing and plenty to drink.

Carnival

In addition to the *festa* there are calendar customs whose recurrence ensures a break in the routine of daily life during the year. Carnival is undoubtedly the most colourful of all public entertainments in Malta – an officially sponsored period of carefree merrymaking. Historically it can be traced back to the early 1400's. Encouraged in various ways by the Grand Masters of the Order of St John of Jerusalem (1530-1798) Carnival declined in the 19th century but its revival in 1926 made it possible for the folk entertainment to survive the period of British Rule (1800-1964) as a strong living tradition.

The outdoor festivities in Valletta are organised by the National Festivities Committee appointed each year by the Ministry of Youth and Culture, and over the years Carnival has become a major tourist attraction. Prizes are awarded for the best artistic dances, costumes, floats and grotesque masks. Between 1972 and 1987 Carnival was held in May, but in 1988 it was restored to its traditional period, and celebrations now take place during the five days immediately preceding Lent. Some innovations have also been introduced in recent years, including the shifting of merrymaking on the last Carnival day (Tuesday) from Valletta to Floriana. Carnival festivities in Gozo, first organized in 1952, follow the main lines of the Malta Carnival.

During the Merry Monarch's reign Valletta presents a unique spectacle. Grotesque masks and triumphal cars follow the majestic float of King Carnival in a regular train through the main streets of the capital. The balconies and roofs of the houses are full to overcrowding, while the streets below are thronged with people from all over Malta eagerly watching the Carnival defile. The boisterous enthusiasm of the young men and women manning the floats infect with carefree mirth the spectators lining the route or occupying vantage points. Small groups of men dressed as females, and vice-versa, or clad in other carnivalesque attire, indulge in fun and frolic among the bystanders.

Beneath the surface of the present spectacle older motifs linger on, folk elements that helped to maintain and spread the tentacles of the Carnival tradition in the past. A few have been retained, or are being revived, though their significance has been lost. Up to some years ago this folk festival was ushered in by the *Parata* dance on the morning of Carnival Saturday. This is an ancient Maltese sword-dance commemorating the Maltese victory over the Turks in the Great Siege of 1565. The dance was once concluded by raising a little girl, known as the 'Bride', splendidly arrayed and girt with a small dagger – as a sign of the Christian victory. Under the Knights the *Parata* had a special significance because the rule was "No *Parata*, no Carnival". As soon as the Grand Master granted permission to hold Carnival and signified his approval to the Maltese waiting in the Palace Square through a Knight of the Grand Cross, various companies of dancers ranged through the City and performed their mock fight to the accompaniment of strolling music. Every effort should be made to restore the *Parata* to its pristine importance as it is one of the few surviving links in the chain of *Moresca* dances that were once popular throughout most countries of Southern and Central Europe.

Another entertainment known as *Kukkanja* (Cockaigne) was introduced by Grand Master Zondadari in 1721 but did not outlive the Order. A crowd assembled on the Palace Square on Carnival Monday and at a given signal attacked the sausages, hams and live animals tied to the long beams fixed against the guard house and covered over with branches of trees in leaf. The provisions became the property of those who, having seized them, were able to carry them off in safety through the crowd. Revivals of this folk-entertainment took place in 1960-1962 and, more successfully, in 1992 and 1993.

Traces of an ancient folk-drama known as *Qarċilla*, together with the burning of King Carnival on the last day of the festivities, survived up to some years ago. Although these and other folk elements belong to the past now, the Carnival spirit lives on unabated.

Holy Week

Holy Week traditions in the Maltese Islands present features of strong vitality and of ever-expanding popular ritual. Apart from the offices of the church, the people visit the *sepulkri* or altars of repose found in practically every church, going from one church to another on what is known as the Round of the Seven Churches. V. Busuttil in *Holiday Customs in Malta* (6th ed., 1922, p.30) describes this custom as "a very striking scene" and adds:

"Hundreds, from every rank and class of the people, generally in couples or in groups, are seen most devoutly performing the visit of the churches, reciting prayers all the time as they move from one church to another".

In many localities, following the example of the Oratory of the Dominican (Blackfriars) priory in Valletta and of the Pius X Oratory in Cospicua, a replica of the Last Supper scene is put up for public viewing. In some localities a Passion Play is staged, with actors drawn mostly from the village community or from among the membership of the club or other organisation concerned. As a folk production, the one at Għarb, in Gozo, which featured regularly for some years (1940-48) deserves special mention.

However, the Good Friday processions with life-sized images representing the main events of the Passion and Death of Our Lord form the characteristic feature of Holy Week celebrations in Malta and Gozo. There is an air of accentuated suffering and martyrdom about these statuary groups recalling similar scenes in Southern Italy, Sicily and Spain. Their effectiveness is heightened by the grim realism of the gory wounds and ghastly pallor of the suffering Christ no less than by the daggers in the bleeding heart of the *Mater Dolorosa*. As specimens of Maltese popular art, these statues represent the highest form achieved in the *papier mâché* technique which is believed to have been introduced to Malta by a Sicilian lay brother whose name has not come down to us.

This tradition has evolved over a long period. By the end of the 16th century the lay confraternity of St Joseph attached to the Friary of Franciscan Minors in Rabat was the first to organize such a procession in Malta, followed by its counterpart attached to the Valletta friary in 1645. During the 18th century the custom spread to eight other localities, i.e. Vittoriosa (c.1700), Senglea (c.1719), Żebbuġ (c.1742), Żejtun (c.1742), Cospicua (c.1700), Naxxar (c.1750), Qormi (c.1764), and Luqa (c.1795). In the 19th century similar progress was recorded in four parishes, i.e. Għaxaq (c.1820), Rabat, in Gozo (c.1830), Mosta (1866) and Ħal Għargħur (1866). During the present century this development continued both in Gozo — Nadur (1913), Xagħra (1914), Żebbuġ (1918) and at the Gozo Cathedral (1968) — and at Paola, in Malta, between 1944-1976. A set of statues commissioned for Xewkija, in Gozo, between 1922 and 1924, has never been taken out in procession.

These "mystery groups" were successfully grafted on to an already existing, deep-routed local tradition, for the Passion drama had, since the Middle Ages, exercised the mind of our folk and found expression in the form of a considerable repertoire of folk-prayers built on rich imagery and unsophisticated language, which reflect the people's reaction to the events of the Passion Drama. Nowadays these folk-prayers are all but forgotten, but they link with similar compositions and traditions from Sicily, Central Italy and Spain.

Christmas

The modern Christmas scene in Malta includes brightly-lit shop windows, a variety of toys and sweets, artificial

Christmas trees and carol singing mingled with a profuse exchange of greetings. Honey ring-cakes (M. *qagħaq tal-għasel*) are displayed everywhere as a local Christmas speciality. One can see artistic, often mechanised cribs in various localities and, since 1964, street decorations and illuminations in Valletta and other centres have been introduced. More characteristic, and of local growth, is the procession, held for the first time in 1921, staged in most towns and villages, in which children take part, carrying an image of the Baby Jesus and singing sweet carols in Maltese. A talk on the Nativity is then recited by a boy — a custom mentioned in the local Press as a novelty in 1883.

The Christmas tradition in Malta centres round the *presepju*, or crib. Every year the M.U.S.E.U.M. Christian Doctrine Society distributes some 20,000 small cribs to children who attend their religious doctrine classes. Exhibitions of cribs are held annually in Valletta and other localities, while the National Festivities Committee organizes crib competitions every year. Since the early Sixties a Live Crib at Lija has provided a unique attraction, with children dressed as shepherds, and with live donkeys, lambs, hens, ducks, pigeons etc.

After the Second World War the use of artificial Christmas trees spread to the homes of the Maltese, together with Father Christmas, as an added decoration for the festive season. Previously their use was generally restricted to families of British Service personnel and to some Maltese hospitals. The custom had been slowly gaining ground since at least 1887, when it is recorded that Prince George, later King George V, attended a Christmas Tree gathering held at the Governor's Palace of San Anton. The presence of convalescing British and Allied troops in Malta, not to mention the many German prisoners of war during the First World War, also helped to boost the custom.

The Christmas festival in the past was characterised by the music of bagpipes. Folk memory in Gozo records that for the midnight service on Christmas Eve bagpipers played in the principal churches, striking a genuinely pastoral note, while during the *novena* preceding Christmas they performed in the streets. There were also rustic games in which players used nuts and other seasonal produce, while age-old proverbs relating to the Christmas period in the agricultural year have withstood the test of centuries.

Some country people still indulge in a curious form of weather-forecasting. From St Lucy's Day (Dec. 13) till Christmas Eve they regard the sky with attention, note the way of the wind and other signs known only to themselves. In this way they believe they can establish a reliable forecast for the coming year, the weather on December 13 ruling the proximate months of January, and so on until December 24, which is believed to rule the weather of December twelve months later. The signs observed on these twelve days are called *l-irwiegel*, 'the rules'. Analogous beliefs and usages are found in Sicily and various other countries.

Finally, a surviving custom associated with the Christmas crib links up with certain pre-Christian rites known among scholars as "Gardens of Adonis". Each year, with the approach of Christmas, and generally on December 8, Maltese children sow wheat, barley, vetch and canary seed in plates, which they keep in the dark and water every two or three days. The plants soon shoot up, and the plates containing them are then placed near the Child Jesus in churches and in the cribs set up in the homes. Similar practices, observed also in Sicily, in Calabria and in Sardinia on different occasions, have been described as a continuation, under a different name, of the worship of Adonis, who was a deity of vegetation and especially of the corn.

Other Customs

These customs include the blessing of animals, which takes place on the Sunday nearest to the 17th January (feast of St

Antony Abbot) at the door of St Augustine's church at Rabat. Here the animals, mostly quadrupeds, are blessed by an Augustinian friar and they partake of some barley, which is placed in a tray for them. In the time of the Knights the first animals that came up for the blessing were the horses drawing the Grand Master's stately carriage. Nowadays a blessing ceremony also takes place at Xagħra, in Gozo. At Mosta the blessing is held a week later, on the parvis of the old church of St Antony, built in 1608, while at Naxxar it takes place in front of the oratory on one of the Sundays preceding the feast. Since 1987 the blessing of animals at Lija has been held near the old parish church in Saviour Street. In recent years the custom has also spread to other localities but not necessarily linked to the cult of St Antony.

Easter is associated with a special kind of pastry, known as *figolla*, which has been described as "a flat baked dough, cut in the shape of a woman, a Turk, an eagle, a horse, a star, or a basket, with one or more eggs, having the shell stained red or some other colour, embedded in its centre..." On Easter Sunday, processions with the statue of the Risen Christ are held in several parishes. From Vittoriosa and Cospicua, which have a deep-rooted Easter tradition influenced by the Greek Rhodiotes who followed the Order to Malta from Rhodes in 1530, the practice of carrying the statue at a run at certain specified spots of the traditional route has spread to various localities in recent years.

On the first Wednesday after Easter, people flock to the fishing village of Marsaxlokk to picnic there after witnessing at Żejtun a procession which, according to tradition, was instituted centuries ago in fulfilment of a vow for the deliverance of Malta. Up to some years ago bonfires were lighted on St John's Eve (June 23), while Ascension Day (M. *Lapsi*) sees the opening of the swimming season. The folk-festival of *L-Imnarja* on June 29 is marked by folk-singing at Buskett on the eve of the feast, an Agricultural Show organized by the Agrarian Society since 1854, and by traditional horseraces in which the animals are ridden bare-backed. On the feast of St Martin (first Sunday after November 12) children receive a bag full of autumn produce – figs, nuts, chestnuts and oranges. Space does not allow more than a passing mention here of other periodical ceremonies such as those on 8th September or on Candlemas Day, of popular iconography, including *ex-votos* found in various churches and rural chapels, or of *Blason Populaire*, (collective nicknames).

Primitive Beliefs and Practices

Various primitive seasonal customs and beliefs still survive in folk-memory. According to an old tradition, the oldest woman (M. *l-għaġuża*) living in the parish was thrown from the church steeple on the mid-Lent Thursday. This corresponds to the notions behind the beliefs in *La Vecchia di Quaresima* and the practice of *sega-Vecchia* in Sicily and Italy. Up to a few years ago, the figure of a child stuffed with straw (M. *trajbu*) was cast into the flames of the bonfires lit on the eve of the Feast of St John. On St John's Day (June 24) village girls used to melt some lead and then pour it into a vessel filled with water. According to the shape assumed by the lead when it cooled down and solidified, it was foretold whether the girl would be happy in her choice of a husband.

In addition to these customs, which are linked with various midsummer and divination practices in other countries, there are some survivals of fertility rites. A heap of manure is often left standing in Maltese fields until it is carried away by the first rains. To this is given the symbolic name of *l-għarus*, 'the bridegroom'. Peasants sometimes leave a ring, the symbol of marriage, on the branch of a pear-tree in the belief that the tree will become more fruitful. Farmers were used to hang two puppets, representing a

Turkish man and woman, on their vines to ensure an abundant yield.

Fear of the moon and its influence on human beings lies behind various folk-beliefs and practices. It is firmly believed that one should never curse the moon; rather, one should propitiate it, for otherwise it may cause a great deal of unhappiness. Various tasks connected with animals and husbandry are regulated by the phases of the moon. The March and August moons are particularly recommended as a time to place eggs under brooding hens. Olives should be picked with the new moon or during its first phase — and only when the North wind is blowing. The best time for planting palm-trees is when the moon is waxing. Unmarried girls were advised to comb their hair in the light of the moon, and in order to find a rich husband they were to hold a coin in their hand while they looked at the moon. There are various sayings connected with the moon's mysterious power.

The Evil Eye

The cause of evils such as misfortunes, accidents, illness or death is often attributed to the agency of a mischief-maker known as *l-għajn*, 'the evil eye'. In 1923 A. Cremona wrote at some length about "Some Myths and Beliefs in Maltese Folklore" (*Melita*, Vol.III, pp.111-120). He considers the Maltese custom of fumigating with olive leaves which have been blessed on Palm Sunday as "a typical christianized counterpart" of an old heathen charm. The exorcism is commonly carried out

"to free the house from the evil of a haunting spirit or from an illness afflicting a patient. It is also done after the recovery of the patient from a serious illness. Prayers are in the meantime also offered...".

The same writer explained that

"the Maltese word *seher*, meaning witchcraft, sorcery, answers to the Arabic *seher*, meaning also witchcraft, sorcery, seduction, while the term *għajn*, 'eye' and the derivative verb *għajjen*, 'to bewitch' are correspondingly the Arabic forms *għajn* and *għajjen*, having respectively the same meaning".

As for the Maltese word *magħmul*, also meaning witchcraft and charm, this is

"a synonym of the primitive *seher* and appears to be a mere version of the Italo-Sicilian word *fattura* and of not such an old type as the former designation".

Ancient Maltese myths are still designated by a Semitic terminology, examples being *ħâres*, 'a ghostly guardian of the house or of any property', *għafrid*, 'evil spirit', *għul*, 'wild beast', *waħx*, 'ogre, monster', *Iblis*, 'Satan'. Recalling that the Arabic imprecatory expression *Hamsa f'għajnek*, 'five fingers in your eye' is also known by the Maltese, i.e. *Għajnek f'għajnek*, 'your eye in your eye', Cremona concludes that

"it is evident that... all the Maltese expressions indicating an elementary knowledge of the belief must have been chiefly derived from or highly influenced by a Semitic tradition".

Riddles (*Haġa Moħġaġa*)

The art of riddling, at one time indulged in by adults of all classes and looked upon as an accomplishment of royalty in biblical times, has nowadays survived mostly among children. A 'true' riddle is a composition in which some creature or object is described in an intentionally obscure manner, the solution fitting all the characteristics of the description in the question, and usually resolving a paradox. The following examples come to mind straightaway:

Haġa moħġaġa:
Aktar ma tiekol minnha
Aktar tikber.

(Tarxien)

Me riddle, me riddle,:
The more you eat (take) from it
The bigger it gets.
(Solution: a hole in the ground)

Hawn haġa:
Dejjem timxi rasha 'l isfel.

(Birżebbuġa)

A riddle:
Always walks on its head.
(Solution: A nail in your boot)

194

Ħaġa moħġaġa:
Ħamra ħamra – nar m'hijiex
Ħadra ħadra – ħaxix m'hijiex
Tarmi l-ilma – għajn m'hijiex.

(Tarxien)

Me riddle, me riddle:
Though red as fire it is not fire,
Green as grass but it is not grass,
Gives out water but it is not a spring.

(Solution: Water Melon)

The descriptions which the rhyming riddles give of their solutions are usually phrased highly imaginatively in terms of something else. Thus, a bed is seen as a person who gets tired at night and rests all day; the sky is a basket full of pears (roses) which, when turned upside down, will not fall; the clouds look like a bed sheet with patches but without any threads; the sea is thought of as an old grumbler who makes love, or as a garden without trees or leaves or flowers, whose fruit tastes exquisitely good; an onion is likened to a pretty white-faced girl wearing a pink dress who will make you cry if you ill-treat her; a cabbage is conceived as made up of numerous carpets set on top of each other, each more beautiful than the one before it. Such images are perhaps the fittest introduction to poetry that a child can have.

Many notions underlying Maltese riddles are similar to those adopted by riddlers both inside and outside Europe. In this respect one has to underline the historical importance of Sicilian and Arabic influences in the formation of Maltese riddling. Certain correspondences, verbal or other, appear to be so close as to call for particular mention. Thus, the notion "Mother begets and kills Daughter (Son)" appears in the following Maltese riddle:

Ħaġa moħġaġa:
Imwieled minn ommu,
Jitrabba bix-xemx,
Jekk imiss m'ommu jerġa' jmut.

Me riddle, me riddle:
Born of Mother,
Reared by the sun,
If he touches his mother again he dies.

(Solution: Salt)

Archer Taylor (*English riddles from oral tradition*, University of California Press, 1951, pp.394, 790) explains that

"the Levantine – Modern Greek, Arabic and Syriac versions exemplify best the ideas of begetting and killing, and are probably derived from a common source... These parallels are: Modern Greek: 'Water begets me and I feed in the sun; yet if I see my mother, I die'; Arabic: 'Son of water and it dies on touching water'; Syriac: 'It lives when taken out of water, it dies when put into water'."

The Maltese riddle for "Doors" runs as follows:

Ħaġa moħġaġa:
Bil-lejl ibusu 'l xulxin,
Bi nhar miġġeldin.

Riddle me riddle:
They kiss one another at night,
They separate (lit. quarrel) during the day.

With this one may compare the corresponding Sicilian versions: (a) *Lu juorno si talianu, La sira si vasanu.* "By day they look at one another, by night they kiss one another", and (b) *Lu juornu su' spartuti, La sira 'nzimmulati,* "By day they are separated, at night they come together". The Tunisian version given by J. Quemeneur (*Enigmes Tunisiennes*, Institut des Belles Lettres Arabes, Tunis, 1944) is close enough: *'ala zweyz akhwa / fel lîl it'anquou / fen-nhâr itfârqou.* "Two brothers / By night they embrace / By day they separate". Unlike proverbs, local riddles do not set out to teach or to lay down rules of conduct; their intention nowadays is only to amuse.

Proverbs

A rich legacy of proverbial lore has been handed down orally, and age-old sayings are used frequently in everyday conversation, in which they are quoted with the persuasive force of established tradition and with the authority of an unwritten law. A few examples in English translation are given here to illustrate this branch of Maltese folklore: 1. The older you grow, the more you learn; 2. Don't pollute the spring from which you may want to drink; 3. One man dies of drunkenness, and another dies for want of a drop; 4. A sleeping man catches no fish; 5. If a man spits towards the sky, it will come down in his own face; 6. See whose daughter she is, and you will know what she is; 7. For the sake of rings and earrings today she has eaten nothing; 8. He who is born round will not die square; 9. A new bride whatever she touches smells sweet; 10. What the eye doesn't see, the heart doesn't grieve over; 11. He who eats the meat must also gnaw the bone; 12. Not everyone who beats his breast is a saint.

In 1972 the University of Malta published Professor J. Aquilina's *A Comparative Dictionary of Maltese Proverbs* containing more than 4,630 proverbs collected from oral and written sources. In the Introduction he pointed out that some Arabic proverbs are still current in the spoken language "in spite of the nearly 1,000-year-old discontinuation of direct contact with the Arabic world". Five years before he had already referred to the similarity between some Maltese and Arabic proverbs.

In his paper, written in 1967, entitled "Comparative Maltese and Arabic Proverbs" (in *Maltese Linguistic Surveys*, University of Malta, 1976, p.142), he wrote:

"Of the whole collection of proverbs, comparatively very few are of Arabic origin, but the total list of correspondences in all the work is fairly impressive. Some of these proverbs are mixed in the sense that they may be Arabic and European at the same time, sometimes literally and sometimes approximately. Here arises the question as to the criteria that must be adopted to establish which is the original version. Comparatively only a small number of Maltese proverbs corresponds to Arabic ones because since 1090, when the Normans conquered Malta, the social context of our country moved in the direction of Sicily..."

Further on in his paper Aquilina explained that

"many Maltese proverbs, though couched in a completely Arabic vocabulary, are the translation of Italian, and generally Sicilian proverbs, many of which can be compared with those collected by the famous Sicilian paremiologist Giuseppe Pitrè (1841-1916)". His final conclusion is that "when all is said there is no doubt that the greater paremiological heritage reached Malta via Sicily".

Oral Poetry

Oral poetry survives as a living tradition in Malta. It is still one of the main sources of popular folk-entertainment. The Maltese word designating orally performed poetry is *għana*, or song, which covers a wide range of poems in sung form with musical accompaniment by guitarists. These folk compositions are of three types:

1) extemporised (M. *spirtu pront*) short (four-line) stanzas normally sung by individuals, or by a group of two or more singers as a song-duel which can take various forms — for example (a) hitting back, stanza for stanza, with guitar interludes, or (b) an impromptu reply by the second man within the same quatrain immediately after the two lines presented by the first singer — this is called *għanja maqsuma*, or 'broken or shared song';

2) long elaborate narratives in verse, generally known as *fatt* (It. *fatto*, 'deed, event'), either on well-known local heroes as well as on sensational or tragic events (ballad type), or on recent humorous topics, and

3) songs in high register (M. *għanja fil-għoli*), also known as *la bormliża*, i.e. Bormla style — Bormla being one of the three historic cities facing Valletta across the Grand Harbour — short haiku-like poems normally sung by two persons and requiring a full voice capable of sustaining long phrases. This style of singing has now practically died out.

The characteristic form of Maltese folk quatrains is the four-line stanza, rhyming *a b c b*, each line consisting mostly of eight, sometimes seven syllables. The argument used, whether serious or humorous, is followed closely by the audience; clarity of expression in the performance is expected, no less than correct rhyming and maintenance of subject. Assonance rather than rhyme is sometimes employed. In this respect Maltese quatrains have no connection with the songs of Sicily, consisting mainly of eight hendecasyllabic lines. Giuseppe Pitrè,

Folk musical instruments — the Rabbâba, Tambourine and Żaqq (Bagpipes) — which have now gone out of use.

A traditional dance during the Independence festivities in 1964.

197

the well-known Sicilian folklorist, admitted this and asserted that 'the lyric of the Maltese people ... recalls faintly that of Sardinia, and has nothing in common with the *canzuna* of Sicily'. However, the four-line single stanza is not unknown in Sicily, and sometimes occurs in Greek and Spanish popular poetry, while the same form and rhyme-scheme are employed by the boatmen of Rabat and Salè in Morocco.

In 1953 a Folksong Competition organised by the present writer was held on the occasion of the popular *Imnarja* folk-festival. It continued to be held over the following years and it is now recognised that it had a lasting, salutary effect. Quoting from Ranier Fsadni's perceptive article "The Modernity of Maltese *Għana*" (*Sunday Times*, August 30, 1992):

... It (i.e. *għana* singing) became more elaborate ... This formal elaboration was a consequence of the first Maltese Folklore festival, held in 1953, which not only inspired the new rules (and conventions governing the composition of the extemporized quatrains) but also changed the way the *għannej* regarded himself... 1953 is the decisive date, for it set off a process which changed the way *għana* was perceived by the middle classes and how the *għannejja* came to see themselves and the role they played ... They were now the subject of some attention from intellectuals, asked to sing at festivals and hotels, and even sent abroad to represent Malta on cross-cultural exchanges. *Għana* as en entity became mythologised, the soul of tradition which had to be preserved..."

A new generation of folksingers and guitarrists has indeed modernised the folk-art and raised the standard of *għana* performances. Many singers, or their supporters, possess their own tape-recorders and exchange tapes containing recordings of their extemporised songs with emigrated friends in America, Canada or Australia. Occasionally, local singers tour towns and cities in Australia or Canada at the invitation of Maltese migrant communities. Tourism and modern mass media, such as cassettes, radio and TV also contribute to keep the tradition alive.

Folk-Dance

From folk-singing to folk-dancing it is but one short step. Two traditional folk-dances have survived. One of them, known as *Il-Parata*, has already been mentioned. The dancers, making up two concentric circles, represent the besieging Turks and the defenders (Maltese and Knights). The dance has three main movements. The leader, dressed up as Grand Master, directs the dance by means of a whistle. *Il-Parata* was concluded with a final movement whereby the Turks knelt down as a sign of defeat, the Maltese (or Knights) placing their swords over the heads of the Turks. The 'Bride' was then carried round on a platform while she threw kisses all around.

Il-Maltija is considered to be Malta's national dance. It is danced either in peasant costume, known as *Ta' Żepp u Grezz*, these being characteristic peasant names, or, for formal occasions such as a royal visit, celebrations of national importance, or charity balls at the President's Palace, in 18th century costume, the ladies wearing brocade dresses, with full skirts and bodices with battlements, and the gentlemen wearing black velvet tights, long coats of the same period, lace fichus and white satin waistcoats. All the dancers – a leading couple and sixteen other couples – wear white wigs. As the various movements are called, couples do not move until the leader calls *Imxu* (Forward). At the conclusion of the dance each couple in turn approaches the dais to honour the President.

The *Maltija* was most probably introduced to Malta as a Court dance in the later years of the 18th century. When the Knights left it was taken up by the 'folk' where it lingered on until it was revived by Maltese officers of the Royal Malta Fencibles Regiment at the Fancy Dress Ball given at the Palace by Lady Stuart, the Governor's wife, on February 18, 1844.

Folk-Tales

A rich heritage of folk-tales and legends has come down from the past. Unfortunately, the popular art of story-telling has very much degenerated but enough texts have been collected in the present century, especially by the Jesuit Fr E. Magri, to establish the variety of types and motifs of the local folk-narrative material. Most impressive are the tales of magic in which, as in the household tales of the Brothers Grimm, we meet supernatural adversaries and helpers, enchanted princes and talking animals. Open-eyed dragons, guarding fair maidens or golden apples, are fast asleep, while lions with closed eyes are fully awake. We shudder at seven-headed dragons and admire the Maltese Samson, whose strength lies not in his hair but in his tail – a belief still common in these islands where the general opinion is that a baby born with a hairy growth at the lower end of the spine will grow to be a very strong man. There are interesting parallels with the Hercules cycle of Greek stories in the tales of the Wise Woman's Son (M. *Bin il-Għarfa*) and also specimens of the tales of King Solomon, so widespread in Mediterranean countries. One of these attributes to the boy Solomon, assisted by his much wiser sister, the use of the first boat formed of the upturned skeleton of a horse.

Numerous jokes and anecdotes (M. *praspar*) are also told. Among the numskull stories stand out the humorous adventures of 'Ġaħan', a lovable character who does things topsy-turvy but invariably manages to come out all the better for his experience. His amusing adventures are still related to children: how he lost a chicken pea and earned a fortune, how he poured boiling water on his sister, how he sat on a grimy pot because his mother told him not to sit where other usually sit, so as to keep his suit clean, and, finally, how he pulled the door off its hinges and dragged it all the way to the church looking for his mother, whose instructions to shut (lit. to pull) the door behind him he had obeyed so literally. 'Ġaħan' is a Mediterranean folk-hero, called *Si-Ġoħa* or *Ġoħa* by the Arabs, *Gha* in North Africa, *Ġuħa* by the

Persians, *Ġohħa* in Palestine, *Giucca* in Tuscany, and *Giufa* in Sicily.

Legends

The legendary material falls under three main headings: (a) historical, (b) religious, and (c) treasure stories. Historical legends are by far the most numerous as well as the most important. They present the popular version of history, that is, history not as it actually was but as the ordinary people would like it to be, retaining only the kernel of historical fact. Legends are often attached to particular place-names and other features of the landscape and sometimes they are only an attempt to explain the origin of a particular place-name (folk-etymology) which cannot otherwise be accounted for.

A crop of such legends preserves the memory of St Paul's Shipwreck, connected with such place-names as *San Pawl il-Baħar* (St Paul's Bay), *San Pawl Milqi* (St Paul's Welcome), and *Għajn Rażul* (The Apostle's Fountain). Another cycle of legends centre on the figure of Count Roger the Norman, who freed Malta from the rule of the Arabs. The period of Turkish ascendancy and of Moslem corsair activity – the days of the notorious Rajjes Dragut – has contributed a good number of legends, especially in Gozo, while the rule of the Knights of St John (1530-1798), together with the Inquisition, also figure in Maltese folk-memory. The hurly-burly days of the French Revolution (1798-1800) are still remembered in legend and folk-song while the period of British Rule (1800-1964) has produced mainly stories of ghostly apparitions haunting old houses and fortified buildings such as Verdala Castle and Fort St Angelo.

There are legends which centre on a religious personage, and stories told against a religious background with saints, church sites, street crosses, niches and statues as their subject-matter. In some of these one notes a popular attempt to attribute the present site of a church to supernatural intervention prevailing over human decisions, examples being the site of the parish church at Qormi, that of the chapel of Our Lady of Loreto in the limits of Gudja, in Malta and, in Gozo, the site of the Cathedral Church and of Nadur parish church.

In yet another type of legends we learn of treasure troves discovered through the help of the family spirit (*Il-Ħares*). Such legends are generally connected with old houses dating from the days of the Knights, houses in which a hidden treasure is associated with a murdered Knight who lived in the house. The disclosure of the treasure may be subject to conditions that make it practically impossible to unearth it. Thus, 20 *skudi* lie buried under the principal gate of Imdina, destined to be taken by that couple who after a long period of married life find nothing to complain of. Needless to say, no one has ever taken the money, and the legend has given rise to the following humorous expression when referring to an unhappy couple: *Ma jmorrux għall-għoxrin skud!* (They won't go for the 20 *skudi*!)

By and large, the majority of Maltese folktales and legends follow the main stream of the European folk-tale but the subject calls for further analysis on a comparative basis.

Conclusion

We have covered much of the ground making up the field of Maltese Folklore and we have shown that Malta's folkloristic heritage is definitely rooted in a Mediterranean context. Its main constituent elements are (i) Semitic, i.e. Arabic and (ii) European. The latter element pervades practically all aspects of present-day folk-life, being of more recent origin and moulded over the past six centuries or so by contact mostly with Sicily, Italy and Spain, and with a lesser English strain introduced under British rule.

The European element is also much easier to identify, for the formative contacts with Arab culture during the 9th-13th centuries were then interrupted and under the Knights (1530-1798) exchanges could only take place in some measure through the local slave population, through piracy or trade. Emigration to North Africa in the 19th century re-opened possible routes for cultural transmission at the folk level. Otherwise, all outward traces of the preceding Arab heritage – this of course does not apply to the language – were practically obliterated by the superimposition of richer and more varied layers of European cultural elements. The influence of the Catholic Church has also been a vital factor linking Malta to Europe.

Over the past 50 years or so the present writer has studied the Maltese folklore material within the context of similar traditions recorded in countries on both sides of the Mediterranean. His general conclusion is that the affinities of Maltese folklore, already clearly established with Sicily, Italy and Spain, can also be traced in the Arabic-speaking countries of the Maghreb and the Middle East. The examples included in this chapter show that the identification of other surviving Semitic elements is important for a better appreciation of the unique synthesis with the European cultures that has occurred in these islands.

Bibliography

ATTARD, A.F., *Logħob folkloristiku ta' Għawdex*, Union Press, Valletta, 1969.
Mill-Folklor ta' Għawdex – ġabra ta' taqbil u għana folkloristiku, Għawdex, 1986.
Mill-Ħajja ta' l-Imgħoddi – Tagħrif folkloristiku minn Għawdex, Għawdex, 1991.

BERNARDY, A.A., "Forme e colori della tradizione maltese" (IV Congresso Nazionale delle Arti e Tradizioni Popolari, Venezia, 8-12 Settembre 1940). Estratto dalla rivista *Lares* (N. 4-5, agosto-ottobre 1940).

BEZZINA, J., *Forty Legends from Gozo – stories of bygone times*, Bugelli, Valletta, 1991.

BOISSEVAIN, J.F., *Saints and Fireworks: Religion and Politics in Rural Malta*, The Athlone Press, University of London, 1965.
Ħal Farruġ: A Village in Malta, Holt, Rinehart and Winston, New York, 1969.

BONELLI, L., "Saggi del folklore dell'isola di Malta", con prefazione di G. Pitrè, *Giornale di Sicilia*, Palermo, 1895.

CASSAR, P., "Medical Folklore", in *Medical History of Malta*, Wellcome Historical Medical Library, London, 1964, pp.421-436.
"Pregnancy and Birth in Maltese Tradition", in *The Chestpiece – Journal of the Malta Medical Students Association*, April, 1976, pp.25-29.

CASSAR PULLICINO, J., *Introduction to Maltese Folklore*, Allied Malta Newspapers Ltd., Malta, 1947.
"Usi e costumi della Settimana Santa a Malta", in *Phoenix – Rivista Trimestrale di Scienze, Lettere ed Arti*, Bari, Anno II, Nos.1-2, 1956, pp.1-24.
"Nursery Vocabulary of the Maltese Archipelago", in *Orbis – Bulletin International de Documentation Linguistique*, Centre International de Dialectologie Générale, Louvain, Tome VI, No.1, 1957, pp.192-198.
Ħaġa Moħġaġa u Taħbil il-Moħħ Ieħor, Parts I-IV, Central Office of Information, Malta, 1957-1959.
Il-Folklor Malti, Malta University Press, 1960; 2nd ed. enlarged, 1975.
"Song and Dance in Malta and Gozo", in *Journal of the English Folk Dance and Song Society*, London, 1961, pp.63-71.
Il-Bennejja tal-Folklor Malti, University of Malta, 1964.
Stejjer ta' Niesna, Department of Information, Malta, 1967.
(Ed), *Maltese Folklore Review*, Nos. 1-4, Giov. Muscat Printers, Valletta, 1962-1973.
Studies in Maltese Folklore, University of Malta, 1976; 2nd ed. rev. and enl., Malta University Press, 1992.
Studi di tradizioni popolari maltesi, University of Malta, 1989.
"Documentary Material relating to 'L-Imnarja' ", in *Littérature Orale Arabo-Berbère*, Association pour l'Étude des Civilisations et des Littératures de l'Afrique Septentrionale, Paris, Bulletin No.14, 1983, pp.1-98.
"Revival and Decline of 'Il-Maltija': 1844-1875", in CLEWS, H.A., (Ed): *The Year Book*, De La Salle Brothers Publications, Sliema, Malta, 1984, pp.359-364.
"Some Parallels between Maltese and Arabic Folklore", in *Acta Ethnographica*, Hungarian Academy of Sciences, Ethnographical Institute, Budapest, Vol.34 (1-4), 1986-1988, pp.143-175.

CASSAR PULLICINO, J., and GALLEY, M., *Femmes de Malte dans les chants traditionnels*, Centre National de Recherche Scientifique, Paris, 1981.
"Oral Poetry in the Maltese Islands: Imagery relating to Love", in NEWALL, V., (Ed.), *International Folklore Review – Folklore Studies from Overseas*, New Abbey Publications, London, Vol.7, 1990, pp.97-101.

CIANTAR, G., "Appendice in cui si da una breve notizia d'alcune antiche usanze dei Maltesi, e della indole e dei costumi loro in generale", in ABELA, G.F., *Malta Illustrata, ovvero Descrizione di Malta* ... corretta, accresciuta e continovata dal Conte Giovannantonio CIANTAR, Stamperia del Palazzo, Malta, Libro Primo e Secondo, 1772, pp.770-813.

CORSO, R., "Malta e le sue feste", in *Maltese Folklore Review*, Vol.1, No.1, 1962, pp.3-7.

CREMONA, A., "Race, Language and Myth", in *Melita – an English and Italian Monthly Periodical*, Valletta, Vol.1, September 1921, pp.394-405.

"Maltese Funeral Customs", *op. cit.*, Vol.II, June 1922, pp.249-259.

"Weather and Husbandry Lore in the Isles of Malta", in *Archivum Melitense*, Società Storico-Scientifica Maltese, Valletta, Vol.VI, No.1, 1922, pp.1-41.

Is the Maid of Mosta a Myth? Reprinted from *The Journal of the Malta University Literary Society*, No.10, March 1934.

Folklor u Lsien Malti. Reprinted from *Leħen il-Malti*, Nos.158-160 and 161-162, Għaqda tal-Malti (Università), Valletta, 1944.

"Folklore Maltese – Lingua, Credenze e Costumi", in *Folklore*, No.1-2, R. Pironti e Figli, Napoli, 1954.

"Le relazioni etnografiche del folklore narrativo e leggendario delle isole di Malta", in *Maltese Folklore Review*, Vol.1, Nos.1-3, 1962-1966, Giov. Muscat & Co. Ltd Printers, Valletta, 1966.

DE GUIGNARD, F.E., Comte de Saint Priest, *Malte, par un voyageur françois*, Malte, 1791.

FARINI, A., *Fiabe, leggende e tradizioni maltesi*, 3 vols., Tipografia Casa di San Giuseppe, Ħamrun, 1934-1936.

GALANTI, B.M., *La Danza della Spada in Italia*, R. Università di Roma e R. Museo di Etnografia Italiana, Roma, 1946.

GALEA, L., and MURRAY, M.A., *Maltese Folk Tales*, Empire Press, Malta, 1932.

GALLEY, M., "A Mediterranean Hero", in *Journal of Maltese Studies*, University of Malta, No.7, 1971, pp.64-70.

ILG, B., *Maltesische Märchen und Schwänke*, 2 vols., G. Schönfeld's Verlagsbuchhandlung, Leipzig, 1906.

ILG, B., and STUMME, H., *Maltesische Volkslieder im Urtext mit Deutscher Übersetzung*, J.C. Hinrichs'sche Buchhandlung, Leipzig, 1909.

KOESSLER-ILG, B., and CASSAR PULLICINO, J., "200 Maltese Folksongs", collected in 1909-1912 and edited, with translation and introduction by J. Cassar Pullicino, in *Maltese Folklore Review*, No.1, 1962, pp.1-39.

LANFRANCO, G., *Duwa u Semm fil-Ħxejjex Maltin*, Klabb Kotba Maltin, Valletta, 1975.

LEGEY, F., *Folklore of Morocco*, translated by Lucy Holtz, George Allen & Unwin Ltd, London, 1935.

MAGRI, E., *Ħrejjef Missirijietna*, "Kotba tal-Mogħdija taż-Żmien", Nos 15, 18, 29, 38-39, A.M. Galea, Valletta, 1902-1904.

X'Jgħid il-Malti fuq id-Dinja ta' Taħt u fuq ir-Rjieħ, "Kotba tal-Mogħdija taż-Żmien", No.44, A.M. Galea, Valletta, 1905.

X'Jgħid il-Malti jew l-Għerf bla Miktub tal-Maltin, Stamperija tas-Salesjani, Malta, 1925.

"Précis de Mythologie Maltaise", *Actes du XIV Congrés International des Orientalistes*, Alger, 1905 – Deuxieme Section, Paris, 1907, pp.23-55. Reproduced in *Maltese Folklore Review*, Vol.1, No.2, 1963, pp.102-109.

MIFSUD-CHIRCOP, G., *A Type-Index of the Maltese Folktale within the Mediterranean Tradition Area*, Unpublished M.A. Thesis, University of Malta, 1978.

MIFSUD-CHIRCOP, M., *Motif-Index of the Maltese Folktale*, Unpublished M.A. Thesis, University of Malta, 1981.

MUSCAT-AZZOPARDI, I., " 'Il-Maltija' – Maltese National Dance", Malta Carnival Committee, *Malta Carnival Programme 1957*, pp.19-28.

NASELLI C., "Manto Siciliano e 'Faldetta' Maltese", in *Bollettino Storico Catanese*, Anno V, 1940. Reproduced in *Maltese Folklore Review*, Vol.1., No.3, 1966, pp.217-225.

PISANI, Ġ., *Għawdex joħlom fil-leġġendi*, Gozo Press, Għawdex, 1980.

PITRÈ, G., *Indovinelli, dubbi, scioglilingua del popolo siciliano*, Carlo Clausen, Torino-Palermo, 1897.

Medicina popolare siciliana, Edizione Nazionale XIX – G. Barbera, Firenze, 1940.

PRINS, A.H.J., *In Peril on the Sea – Marine Votive Paintings in the Maltese Islands*, Said International Ltd., Valletta, 1989.

SCHIAVONE, M. (ed.), *Il-Purċissjonijiet tal-Ġimgħa l-Kbira f'Malta u Għawdex* bi preżentazzjoni ta' Alexander Bonnici OFM Conv. Pubblikazzjonijiet Indipendenza, Pietà, 1992.

Il-Knejjes Parrokkjali ta' Malta u l-Festi tagħhom, Vol. I u II, bi preżentazzjoni ta' Alexander Bonnici OFM Conv., Pubblikazzjonijiet Indipendenza, Pietà, 1993.

STUMME, H., *Maltesische Studien. Eine Sammlung prosaischer und poetischer Texte in maltesische Sprache nebst Erläuterungen*, J.C. Hinrichs, Leipzig, 1904.

WETTINGER, G., "The Arabs in Malta", in *Mid-Med Bank Limited: Report and Accounts 1984*, pp.23-37.

ZAMMIT MAEMPEL, G., "The Evil Eye and Protective Cattle Horns in Malta", in *Folklore*, The Folklore Society, London, Vol.79, 1968, pp.1-16.

Law

Hugh W. Harding

The geographical position of Malta — in the centre of the Mediterranean — with its excellent harbour has given it an importance which is out of proportion to its size. As a result it has through the centuries been the coveted possession of many major powers and indeed its fate has been inevitably interwoven with the fate of the principal Mediterranean power of the time. Most of these powers — especially since the Middle Ages — have left in some way or other a mark on the evolution of the Maltese legal system. Indeed it can be said that the present legal system has been the result of a slow and gradual evolution throughout the centuries and that several factors have contributed to this evolution as each and every successive domination left its imprint on the Maltese legal system.

It would appear from modern methods of dating, such as radio-carbon and dendrochronology, that man first settled in Malta about the year 5000 B.C. There is no evidence at all about the legal system followed during Malta's prehistory. The presence of so many prehistoric temples in such a small island as Malta postulates the existence of a comparatively large population as is also evidenced by the fact that the bones of some 7000 individuals were found buried in just one place — the Hypogeum. An eminent historian observes that the collective tombs and ancestor cult suggest that the inhabitants produced no powerful chiefs or kings but lived rather in extended family or clan groupings and if there was any powerful class among them it was probably the priests. Their economy was based on farming and the temples and tombs furnish abundant evidence of stockbreeding. The evidence available also seems to show that the Maltese Islands

were connected by a web of trade relations that were more than sporadic with most of the neighbouring lands of the Western Mediterranean, some of which lay at considerable distance. All these activities must have been governed by some legal system, but what this system was we do not know and we are not likely to know.

Malta's prehistory came to an end with the coming of the Phoenicians which is generally said to have taken place at some time in the 9th century B.C. The Phoenicians were mainly concerned with commerce and became, commercially at least, a world power. However, they never attained political unity as well and the cities which they founded remained politically independent of each other, each looking after its own immediate interests and having territory around it which formed its kingdom. There was never a Phoenician confederacy, still less a Phoenician nation. Malta must have been one of these Phoenician colonies but the Phoenician tombs and other remains which have been found do not cast any light at all on the system of Government which was in point of fact followed and the legal system which governed Malta.

The exact period when the Carthaginians supplanted the Phoenicians in Malta is not known. However historians agree that by the time of Ashur-Bani-Pal king of Assyria between 668 and 626 B.C., the authority of Phoenicia was no longer recognised in any of the colonies which had been formerly hers. Carthage herself as well was not imperial in the strict sense of the word and its cities enjoyed a certain amount of independence, though they trusted to Carthage to defend them when attacked. After the end of the Magonid domination, an oligarchy took the place of hereditary royalty and the constitutional power in Carthage rested in the hands of two Magistrates (called kings or *suffetes*), a senate and a general assembly. A Maltese inscription mentions a constitution in Malta consisting of *suffetes*, senate and people, such as Carthage had. What laws, if any, were enacted by this body we do not know.

Carthage lost Malta at the close of the second Punic War (218 B.C.) when following the victory of the Roman fleet over the Carthaginians at Marsala (then known as Lilybaeum) the Consul Titus Sempronius Longus sailed to Malta and there accepted the surrender of Hamilcar with some two thousand men. This was the beginning of a long period of Roman rule marked by the diffusion of Roman culture as evidenced by several architectural remains and inscriptions. It does not appear however that the political change which took place at the end of the Second Punic War was accompanied immediately by a cultural and legal change. At this time Malta had begun to coin its own money. This Maltese coinage struck during the last two centuries B.C., it has been held, is a perfect reflection of the double culture of the island during this period: the fundamental Punic or Carthaginian one resulting from the basic ethnic character of the population which was Punic and the Roman one introduced by the conquerors in 218 B.C. The Roman culture ultimately prevailed during the first and second century A.D., with the romanisation of Malta.

This development in the cultural field appears to have been accompanied by a parallel development in the legal field. Sicily had become a Roman province in 218 B.C., and Malta became part of this province. The subjects of the province (including therefore the people living in Malta) were considered by the Romans as aliens (*peregrini*) and to them, as was observed by the distinguished historian James Bryce:

"Roman law was primarily inapplicable not only because it was novel and unfamiliar, so strange to their habits, that it would have been unjust as well as practically inconvenient to have applied it to them but also because the Romans, like the other civilised communities of antiquity, had been so much accustomed to consider private legal rights as necessarily connected with membership of a city community that it would have seemed to be unnatural to apply the private law of one city community to the citizens of another."

This legal position gradually changed in the course of time. The main reasons given for this change by historians is that there was no pre-existing body of law deeply rooted and strong enough to offer resistance to the spread of Roman law and it was also unlikely that the Maltese, who had upheld the policy of the Romans and who had given themselves up to Rome without war, would have preferred the obsolescent laws of Carthage to those of the Romans.

According to A.P. Vella when peace returned to the Mediterranean after the Punic Wars, the Maltese archipelago became a *"civitas sine foedere libera"*, which meant that the Islands enjoyed an internal autonomy until it pleased the Romans, subject only to the payment of a tax to the Roman *quaestor*. Moreover Cicero's *"In Verrem"* brings out the historical fact that about the year 70 B.C. the Maltese enjoyed the quality of *socii* which must have entailed a certain degree of participation in the rights of Roman citizenship. However the Acts of the Apostles, a document of the period describing St Paul's shipwreck off Malta in A.D. 60 and his three month sojourn in the island, shows how gradual this process of change must have been because the author therein refers to the inhabitants as *barbari*: a word which denotes that the Maltese were then considered to be neither Roman nor Greek. But the gradual process of romanisation inevitably carried on and Malta became a *municipium* at the beginning of the second century A.D. This meant that the Maltese became Roman citizens (*cives*), their leaders being called decurions. It appears that all Roman *municipia* could enact laws of their own so that Malta potentially could have had laws of its own, though none are known to exist. Roman law however must have completely prevailed during this period of Malta's history.

With the break-up of the Roman empire in the fifth century A.D., as a consequence of the invasions of the Vandals and the Goths the Maltese Islands came under the Byzantines, the Empire of the East which had its seat in Constantinople. This Byzantine rule lasted for some three hundred years until the seizure of the islands by the Arabs in 820 A.D. This period is a very nebulous one especially in so far as the law and its administration are concerned. We can however cull some idea of the government of the island from Justinian's *"De Praetore Siciliae"*, where mention is made of the praetor or civil governor of Sicily and its islands (*insulis adiacentibus* or *et alias insulas*), including therefore also Malta and Gozo, as well as of the duties of the *dux* who was concerned with the military defence.

The Arab domination, which followed and which cut off Malta from its Byzantine-Roman-Christian culture, is even more nebulous. It is a historical fact that many Arabs settled in Malta and these would have been governed by their own customs and laws based on the Koran. What happened in the case of the conquered Maltese one can only conjecture. As they were cut off from Byzantium, the Roman-Byzantine laws could only have been handed down by way of tradition from father to son and eventually became tantamount to customs of general observance.

The importance of customary law seems to have increased during the Norman and Suabian periods which followed the Arab occupation. Historians agree that Count Roger the Norman landed in Malta in 1090, freed the Christian slaves and exacted a yearly tribute from the Arab Emir or governor of the island. But according to modern historians who rely on accounts written at the time by Malaterra and Telesino, Count Roger the Norman did not impose his direct rule on the inhabitants and it was only in 1127 under his son King Roger II of Sicily that Norman rule properly started and Malta once again became a part of the European system, uniting its destiny with that of Sicily for over four hundred years up to the coming of the Order of St John in 1530. At that time there were living in Malta, besides the Maltese inhabitants, a strong Arab community as well as Greeks or Byzantines and Jews. Because of the paucity of their number which made it difficult for them to impose themselves on the subject races, the Norman rulers allowed the different communities to continue to be governed by their own laws and customs — the Normans themselves being governed by the *Coutoumier de Normandie* which was a collection of Norman customs. There was therefore no Norman Code and the Normans limited themselves to enacting special laws called *Assizes* dealing mainly with the repression of crime and with the feudal system which they introduced. In fact, in the preamble to the *Assizes* of Ariano of 1140 Roger II decreed as follows:

"The laws newly promulgated by our authority are binding on everyone, but without prejudice to the habits, customs and laws of the peoples subject to our authority, each in its own sphere .... unless any one of these laws or customs should be manifestly opposed to our decrees".

This system of personality of the law, where the origin and status of a man indicated the system of law by which all his legal acts were to be regulated, was gradually supplanted by the system of territoriality when the distinct races, originally living side by side, started to amalgamate with the passing of time. When this system of territoriality became gradually established, general laws were enacted applicable to all persons living within the realm.

These laws, with one notable exception to be referred to later, were completely permeated by the old Roman law. This predominance of Roman Law in the Sicilian legal system (whereof Malta then formed part) is explained in many ways. At that time Roman Law had returned to its splendid heritage on the Continent through the halls of the Bologna School. The religious reorganisation carried out by the Normans contributed to its re-introduction since it placed the people, who still enjoyed a substratum of Roman culture and traditions, in touch with ecclesiastics who were well versed in that law and indeed followed its rules in many parts of the Canon Law then applicable to Malta. Another factor contributing to this predominance was the desire of the Sicilian monarchs to justify in some way their absolute and supreme power. Such Roman Law maxims as *"princeps legibus solutus"* and *"quod principi placuit legis habet vigorem"* contained in the Digest must have been most welcome to the absolute Sicilian rulers, particularly to the Swabian Frederick II crowned Holy Roman Emperor in 1220 by Pope Honorius III in St Peter's Basilica, King of Sicily and Jerusalem, he was referred to by his contemporaries as *stupor mundi et immutator mirabilis* because of his extraordinary character and versatility. Frederick, with the help of his erudite Chancellor Pier della Vigna, enacted in 1231 the *Liber Augustalis* also known as the *Constitutiones Regni Siciliae* based almost entirely on Roman Law.

Moreover, Frederick expressly ordered his judges to decide according to the Sicilian Constitutions and, in default thereof, according to established customs and the common laws, that is to say the Lombard Law and the Roman Law, as the circumstances of the litigants required. Since Malta never came under Lombard domination and there were no people of Lombard origin in Malta, this meant that in the silence of the Sicilian constitutions and recognised customs, the judges were, in Malta, to decide according to Roman Law — the *jus commune*. Thus Roman Law became a supplementary law to be

applied by the judges. It may be added that this *jus commune* was not the pure Roman Law of Justinian's *Corpus Juris* since many cross-threads of diverse textures had been woven into the web of the system.

An important document of the year 1240 published by Winkelmann shows that at the time Frederick's constitutions were enacted, Malta had its own customs and constitutions which were different from those obtaining in Sicily. In fact, in that document, Frederick II, addressing himself to the Abate Giliberti in answer to the *Capitoli* which the people of Malta had sent to him, ordered that as a general rule the Imperial Constitutions and the customs of the Kingdom of Sicily were to be observed in Malta. However if the customs and constitutions of the Maltese were to the greater advantage of the King, then the Maltese were to be governed by them: *"Quod si mores et constitutiones eorum redundant ad maius comodum curie nostre, eos permittat, secundum soliti sunt mores."* What these constitutions (applicable solely to Malta) referred to in the document were, the present writer has been unable to establish but, in his *Storia della Legislazione Civile e Criminale di Sicilia*, Lamantia expresses the opinion that the reference to these constitutions must have been to the laws enacted by the Norman kings for Malta.

However as regards customs, the position is different. Although there was no law-making body proper in Malta during this period of its history, yet there existed a body called the *Commune* or the *Consiglio Popolare* wherefrom were chosen the Capitano della Verga (Captain of the Rod), four jurats and other officials who constituted the *Consiglio Particolare* or *Università*. This body did not possess legislative powers but had the right to send to the King for his approval "Capitoli" containing requests regarding the particular requirements and needs of Malta. The Capitoli, when approved by the King, acquired the force of law. They contained *inter alia* requests for the approval or amendment of customs special to Malta and the King's decision thereon. An examination of these Capitoli shows that there existed in Malta customs sanctioned by the King and thus having the force of law which regulated juridical relationships in the silence of the laws enacted by the King.

It has been stated above that generally speaking the laws enacted after the coming of the Normans were completely permeated by Roman Law with one notable exception. This exception consisted in the laws governing the introduction of feudalism whose direct and principal source was the system of beneficiary grants which grew up under the Frank kings and emperors. When the bands of the Germanic warriors settled in the Roman provinces, some portions of the conquered territory, called allodial land, were left in the hands of the provincials. The greater part, however, were occupied by the invaders and large demesnes were held for the King. Out of the royal demesne the sovereign granted lands to his favoured followers under the title of fiefs. These fiefs, which gradually became hereditary, were subject to certain conditions such as military service, respect for the person and honour of the grantor and pecuniary contributions in certain emergencies. In consideration of these conditions corresponding duties of protection devolved on the grantor so that the relations between lord and vassal were those of a mutual contract of support and fidelity. The vassal frequently had vassals of his own to whom he carved out portions of his own fief and the subgrantee became his vassal.

The first feudal concessions of which we have record occurred under Tancred, the last of the Norman Kings, who granted Malta in fief to his admiral Margheritone of Brindisi to reward him for his services in the naval battles against the fleets of Pisa and Genoa in 1191. This was the beginning of the numerous feudal concessions of Malta made by the Sicilian Kings which were interrupted only during those periods when Malta, following the representations made by its *Commune*, became by Royal Charter part of the royal demesne. In fact Malta became part of the royal demesne by Royal Charter in 1240 during the reign of Frederick II, in 1350 during the reign of Ludovico and again in 1397 during the reign of Martin I and finally in 1428 under Alfonso V. During these periods several fiefs regarding particular tracts of land were granted by the sovereign, such as the fief of Dar il-Bniet granted to the Noble Francesco Gatto by King Ludovico of Sicily in 1351 and the fief of Gariexem granted to Henrico de Osa in 1372 during the reign of King Frederick III. The grant of these fiefs gave rise to a local aristocracy. When a tract of land was granted by a sovereign to one of his followers, it was called a *"feudum nobile"* and conferred nobility on the person to whom it was granted. These nobles were called barons. By Act XXIX of 1975 titles of nobility are no longer recognized.

The fact that feudalism had been introduced in Sicily by the Normans and that Malta formed part for a considerable time of the Kingdom of Sicily, leads to the obvious conclusion that it is to the Sicilian system that we have to look for guidance when studying the effects of feudalism in Malta. This rule was recognized on 9 June 1882 by the Maltese Civil Court in the case "Nobile Augusto Testaferrata Abela vs. Nobile Dottor Pietro Paolo Testaferrata Abela Moroni."

Feudalism affected the system of land tenure. Property could be either feudal or allodial. Under the first category came all property held in fief, under the second all property which could be freely disposed of. It also affected the law of succession. Although the law based on the Roman model remained unchanged in so far as allodial property was concerned, yet, as regards feudal property the mode of succession was that established by the conditions of the investiture. This was held by the Court of Appeal in "Sceberras Trigona Testaferrata Falzon Dorell vs Sceberras D'Amico" on 3 August 1885 and in "Formosa Montalto vs Attard Montalto" on 15 November 1885.

The legal system established by the Normans and the Swabians did not change under the subsequent very short Angevin domination which was marked by continuous wars. Neither did it change under the Aragonese and Castillian dominations which followed. The laws enacted during these dominations provided for new matters but did not revoke the previous legislation. Indeed these laws maintained expressly in force the Constitutions enacted by the Emperor Frederick with certain modifications required by the changes which had taken place in society with the passing of time. Neither did they do away with the privileges and customs of the Maltese. Indeed these dominations are marked by frequent *Capitoli* where these privileges and customs were duly recognized by the sovereign. The most important of these were the *Capitoli* of 1428 often referred to as the Maltese *Magna Charta* whereby the islands, following the payment by the Maltese of 30,000 gold florins to the feudal overlord Monroy, were irrevocably united to the royal demesne in the same way as Messina, Palermo and Catania. Alfonso V also granted to the Maltese the right to resist with the force of arms (*manu forti*) any future attempt to grant the Islands in fief. The local Courts were given unlimited jurisdiction and the inhabitants were allowed the privilege of being judged by their own Courts only. These *Capitoli* also confirmed the privileges which had been recognised by the predecessors of Alfonso V and were themselves followed by other *Capitoli* which granted and recognised further privileges and customs.

With the coming of the Order in 1530 Malta ceased to be a political appendage of Sicily and laws were enacted locally by the Order. The laws enacted in Sicily after the grant made by Charles V could not, and did not, have any legislative authority in Malta. However the legal position with regard to Sicilian Law enacted before the grant was different. The grant was not made forcibly to a sovereign who had conquered the island but was a concession made "*ex munificentia et pietate*" of Charles V, as was stated by Pope Clement VII in his bull of the 7th May 1530 confirming the said concession. By that grant Charles V, in agreement with the Pope, made Malta a bulwark against the incursions of the Saracens, giving therein a stable and permanent refuge to a military and religious Order, whose mission was that of fighting the enemies of Christendom, after it had been expelled from its ancient seat in Rhodes. Neither was such a grant given effect to before an agreement was entered into in the records of Notary Giacomo Saliva on the 21st June 1530 between the Deputies of the Maltese people and the Commissioners representing the Order, subsequently confirmed by Grand Master Villiers de L'Isle Adam on the 16th July 1530 prior to his taking possession of Malta. In that agreement the privileges, laws and customs of the Maltese were expressly preserved and confirmed: *omnia et quaecumque privilegia, indulta Regia, leges municipales, usus, consuetudines, praeminentias, prerogativas et honores indistincti scriptos et non scriptos.* The Grand Master himself, when taking possession, swore on the cross that he would observe the said privileges, laws and customs. The Order, therefore, came in possession of the Maltese Islands by virtue of a compact expressly stipulated and signed as well as confirmed on oath by the party stipulating. Moreover, the Grandmaster who, by the said concession, took the place of Charles V, could not have brought with him other laws to be substituted for the pre-existing ones since he was only the head of a religious body without a State. It was not the case of a sovereign of a people having its own laws who had come as a conqueror and who could therefore have imposed on the Maltese, had they been conquered, the laws of his people instead of the laws which the Maltese had.

It followed that until the pre-existing Sicilian laws were revoked or amended by the Grandmaster they continued to be in force even after the grant of Malta to the Order. As a consequence, the legal doctrines enunciated by Sicilian authors continued to be followed and the Latin and Italo-Sicilian legal terminology continued to be used in Court proceedings and in public documents. It also followed that Maltese customs continued to be observed though in the course of time these were considerably whittled down either because they were superseded by express legislation or because they were incorporated in such legislation. Amongst these institutes of customary origin one may mention the institute of conjugal partnership (*società coniugale*) and that of pre-emption (*irkupru*) which were incorporated in the Code de Rohan of 1784.

Particular mention is to be made in this respect of the mercantile law of Malta. Up to 1697 Malta continued to be governed as regards mercantile matters by the *Consolato del Mare* of Messina. With the passing of time the laws of Messina were found to be insufficient to meet the increasing needs of the country and hence Grandmaster Perellos promulgated the *Consolato di Mare di Malta*. This notwithstanding, it was expressly laid down therein that in cases not provided for by Maltese Law, the commercial usages of Messina were to be observed. When later the mercantile law was again amended and included in the *Costituzioni di Manoel* promulgated in 1723 it was expressly laid down that controversies not provided for in Maltese Law were to be decided according to the *Consolato del Mare* of Barcelona and that of Messina. As a consequence the teachings of the commentators of the *Consolato del Mare* of Barcelona, such as Targa and Casaregis, started to exercise a considerable influence

on the development of this branch of law besides the teachings of the commentators of the *Consolato del Mare* of Messina.

When the Order came to Malta, Sicilian Law also continued to be the substratum of Maltese procedural law, though with the passing of time several laws were enacted by the Grandmasters. This applies especially with regard to the Code de Rohan, enacted in 1784, which contains several rules of civil, commercial and criminal procedure. This Code was also greatly influenced by the legal reforms carried out by Vittorio Amadeo II of Savoy in 1729 and by Carlo III of Bourbon and by Ferdinand his successor, though, of course, the main influence in Maltese Law (and this applies to most legislation – except mercantile legislation – enacted during the Order's rule) remained that of Roman Law particularly in the field of the law of property, the law of obligations and the law of succession. As was pointed out by the Royal Commission of 1812:

"The Code de Rohan, so differently viewed and represented by different writers, is founded on the Roman Law and partakes of all the merits and demerits of its great original. With the exception of some modifications and additions rendered necessary by local circumstances, we may consider it as a compilation of the same law by which the greater part of the Continent of Europe continues to be governed."

Roman Law also continued under the Order to perform the important function of a supplementary law or a *jus commune* to which recourse was to be made in cases not provided for by Maltese Law. This *jus commune*, it must be again stressed, was not the pure Roman Law of Justinian but Roman Law as modified by the comments and treatises of influential writers as well as by judgments delivered by various Continental courts, particularly those of the Rota Romana.

During the Order's rule the authority of Canon Law increased considerably because the Order, although a militant body, was also at the same time a religious one whose supreme head was the Pope. During this period the old Canon Law was modified by the decrees of the Council of Trent. These decrees were formally accepted by Fra Martino Royas, the accredited ambassador of the Order, which ratified his action when reported by him, on his return, to the Council of the Order. It may also be added in this connection that King Philip of Spain (who under the deed of donation of 1530 was the suzerain lord of Malta) by Proclamation of the 17th July 1564 had ordered all his subjects to conform to the decrees of the Council of Trent.

The Order's rule came to an end on the 12th June 1798 with the cession of Malta to France. This event, however, did not bring about the abolition of the existing laws. The deed of donation of 1530, whereby Charles V had granted Malta to the Order as a noble fief, had contained a very important clause of reversion which was intended to ensure that Malta either belonged to the Order (to whom it suited Charles V to belong) or to no one else but him and his successors. In fact this clause stipulated that if the Order were to succeed in reconquering the Island of Rhodes and ' for this reason or for any other cause were to depart from Malta and establish its home elsewhere, it would not be lawful for the Order to transfer the possession of Malta to any person under whatsoever title without the express sanction of its feudal lord. If the Order alienated Malta without any such sanction or licence, then it was to revert to Charles V and his successors in full sovereignty. The cession made to Napoleon therefore had no legal effect because when the Order left Malta, it immediately reverted to the King of Naples as successor of Charles V and indeed the rights of this sovereign had been expressly reserved in the "Convention" of the 12th June 1798 by his representative the Bali of Torino. The French, therefore, could only enact administrative measures to maintain public order and could not, without the consent of the legitimate sovereign, enact legislative acts which were not necessary for this purpose. Moreover, the French had only a *de facto* possession which was

neither peaceful for a sufficient period nor recognised by other nations. Indeed the Maltese rose against the French within less than three months – on the 2nd September 1798 – and besieged the French garrison behind the walls of Valletta and Cottonera, raising the Sicilian flag in the other parts of the country. During this period of hostilities the former laws of Malta were applied as if no change had been effected by the French and, after the French Capitulation of the 4th September 1800, they were applied in Valletta without any act expressly revoking the laws enacted by the French as if these laws never existed. All these reasonings are to be found in "De Piro vs Grech Delicata" decided by the Court of Appeal on 7 January 1885.

Therefore, generally speaking, the laws in force at the beginning of British rule remained those contained in the Code de Rohan. If a case occurred on which the Code was silent, then recourse was to be made to the *jus commune* of Malta which, as already stated, consisted in the Roman Law as modified by the comments of influential writers and by judgments of the Continental Courts. This Code remained in force until the major legal reforms carried out in the second part of the nineteenth century. However, even before these extensive reforms, a number of important and lasting reforms were also introduced. Amongst them one may mention the laws rendering the judges independent and the laws setting up the different Courts promulgated by Governor Sir Thomas Maitland in 1814, the laws introducing *viva voce* proceedings and other salutary rules of the English law of evidence, the laws introducing appeals to the Privy Council which remained in force throughout British rule, the laws abolishing sanctuary and subjecting all classes of H.M.'s subjects in temporal matters to the jurisdiction of H.M.'s lay tribunals, the law introducing the system of trial by jury in criminal cases which succeeded beyond all expectations and which, with some modifications, has remained in force up to the present day, and the law abolishing censorship and providing against the abuses of the freedom of publishing printed matter.

This was a period where the legislative power appertained up to 1835 exclusively to the Governor and after the 1st May 1835 to the Governor advised by a Council consisting of four official members and three unofficial members, the latter consisting of two Maltese selected from among the chief landed proprietors and merchants, and of a British-born principal merchant of the Island. It was only in 1849 that a new constitution was granted where provision was made for elective representation. In fact the Council set up by this Constitution was to consist of the Governor (with an original and a casting vote) and eight elected unofficial members and nine official members, four of whom had to be English. This Council was given the power to make laws provided that such laws were not repugnant to the law of England, to the statutes of the United Kingdom, to any Order-in-Council extending to Malta, to the Letters Patent themselves constituting the Council and to the accompanying Royal Instructions. The power was reserved to the Crown to legislate generally for Malta by Order-in-Council. The power of disallowance was also reserved to the Crown and the power of veto was reserved to the Governor.

However, although, as stated above, the major legal reforms were carried out in the second half of the nineteenth century, the first steps in this direction were taken as far back as 1831 when a Commission was set up — consisting of the Chief Justice Sir John Stoddart, Mr John Kirkpatrick, a member of the Supreme Council of the Ionian Islands, Mr Baron Field, Chief Judge of Gibraltar, and Maltese Judges Bonnici and Bonavita — with the express purpose of proceeding to draw up successively five codes of law: a Criminal Code, a Civil Code, a Commercial Code, a Code of Civil Procedure and a Code of Criminal Procedure. Attorney General Langslow was later included in the Commission. The history relating to the enactment of these Codes was destined to be a long one and, indeed, in the case of the Criminal Code and Code of Criminal Procedure, a highly eventful one and many years had to pass before Malta got its Codes.

In fact, the Commission, which started its work on the Criminal Code, found itself confronted by two major fundamental problems. The first problem was whether the authoritative text of the Codes was to be the English language or the Italian language. After considerable correspondence where the members of the Commission advanced their separate views, the British Government decided to accept the view of the Maltese judges, which had been upheld by Kirkpatrick and also shared by Lieutenant Governor Ponsonby, and ordered that the Italian language was to be the text of the Codes, care being taken that they were to be accompanied by a clear literal translation into English.

The other major problem concerned the basis of the Codes. Diametrically opposite views were expressed by Chief Justice Stoddart and Attorney General Langslow on the one hand and by Judges Bonnici and Bonavita on the other. The British Government, after considering the detailed submissions made by the Commissioners, arrived at the conclusion, in view of the discordant opinions and the past proceedings of the Commission, that there was no reasonable hope that any useful result could be expected from a continuation of the labours of the Commission and it therefore ordered its dissolution. Government at the same time requested the Maltese Commissioners, Judges Bonnici and Bonavita, to continue to prepare a Project of the Criminal Code and a sketch of the Code of Criminal Procedure. When these were completed, Government decided to have them published granting at the same time a period for observations on the proposed reforms. In point of fact the Criminal Code and the Code of Criminal Procedure were published on the 31st July 1836. At that time political agitation in Malta was at its height and the British Government had decided to send a Royal Commission to Malta consisting of two Royal Commissioners — John Austin and George Cornwall Lewis — who recommended *inter alia* the suspension of the coming into effect of the Criminal Code and a careful and skilful revision thereof. This revision was carried out by Sir Ignazio Bonavita (who had become President of the Court of Appeal) and Judges Falzon and Chapelle. But again Government hesitated as it considered the Code to be a transcript of the Neapolitan Code with some alterations in order to adapt it for trial by jury. In fact, the Code was eventually revised by a Scottish lawyer — Sir Andrew Jameson. However the Code had to pass through many further vicissitudes before it became law, particularly because of the Title containing the provisions dealing with offences against the religious sentiment, which distinguished between the Catholic Church and other religions. As the British Government found these provisions objectionable, it enacted the Code by an Order-in-Council dated 30th January 1854 omitting from the Order the provisions considered objectionable and leaving to the Maltese legislature full power to amend its provisions from time to time: a power made use of by the Maltese Parliament in 1933 when by Act XXVIII it introduced a number of provisions under the title "Crimes against the Religious Sentiment". The Code, it may be added, also expressly discarded Roman Law in its very first section, the object being that of ensuring certainty in the Criminal law.

The Criminal Code, as so enacted, is with certain minor amendments, still in force today and consists of two books — the first book dealing with the substantive part of criminal law and the second book dealing with laws of criminal procedure. The first book is based mainly on the plan and spirit of the Neapolitan Code, which, in its turn, was based on the French Penal Code. The second book was founded almost entirely on the existing procedure introduced mainly by the Governor Sir Thomas Maitland, with some modifications which were necessary to adapt it to the system of trial by jury (which was also maintained and, indeed, has been maintained up to the present day). The Code has proved that it is possible to apply successfully the substantive criminal laws of the Continental system in a court where the procedure followed was that belonging to a different system i.e., the English system.

The other Codes did not have such a chequered history. Following the dissolution of the 1831 Commission for the reasons mentioned above, another Commission was set up in 1834 consisting solely of Maltese judges and lawyers with instructions to proceed to draw up three Codes of law — a Civil Code, a Commercial Code, and a Code of Civil Procedure. The Italian language was to be the authoritative text of all the Codes — as it remained up to the 1936 Constitution — and the three Codes were to be, as far as circumstances permitted, founded upon and comfortable to the principles and rules of the most approved Codes of foreign countries, provision being nevertheless made for all those cases and exigencies in which local reasons required the preservation of any law or custom prevailing in Malta. In drawing up the Codes the Commissioners were not required to invent original Codes but were to frame them upon the principles, spirit, system and rules which pervaded the French Code and other Codes based on it.

In point of fact, as regards the Commercial Code, the Commission adopted as its model the French Code of Commerce of 1808 which had been adopted by most Continental states and to which we owe the principle of the freedom of trade, the duty of traders to keep books and the prohibition to brokers from

The pre-war Law Courts at the Auberge D'Auvergne.

trading in their own name. The Project of the Commission was published on the 3rd December 1853. With the exception of the second book thereof the Project was approved and formed the subject matter of several Ordinances passed in 1857 and 1858. The second book which contained the merchant shipping laws was not acceptable to the British Government as it was felt that its provisions were contrary to those of the British Merchant Shipping Act of 1854. Therefore, merchant shipping continued to be regulated by this Act, and later by the British Merchant Shipping Act of 1894. Today we have our own Merchant Shipping Act (Cap. 234, Rev.Ed. 1984) which was enacted by Act XI of 1973 and is based mainly on United Kingdom legislation and on international conventions. In 1927 the Commercial laws were considerably amended by Act XXX based on the Italian Project of a Code of Commerce (itself based on the German Commercial Code) prepared by Professor Vivante. All these laws were later embodied in the Commercial Code (Cap.17 Rev.Ed. 1942). It must be added that by an express provision therein the usages of trade have remained one of the important sources of our commercial laws.

As regards the Code of Civil Procedure, a Project (the work of a new Commission set up in 1848) was published in 1850. This Project was intended to bring some order to Maltese procedural law which at that time was based on Sicilian Procedural Law, on Roman Law, on previous judgements and on a large number of ordinances enacted from time to time to deal with specific matters. This Project was also revised (and praised) by Sir Andrew Jameson and finally became law on the 1st August 1855 and, except for a number of amendments, still constitutes our procedural law.

However no Civil Code as such was ever drawn up during this period and in fact we owe our present Civil Code to the genius of Sir Adrian Dingli who, during his long tenure of office as Crown Advocate,

drafted several Ordinances which were approved by the Council of Government and subsequently embodied in Ordinances VII of 1868 and I of 1873. These Ordinances, dealing respectively with the law of things and the law of persons, together with other subsequent ones, were later consolidated by the Statute Law Revision Commission 1942 and became our Civil Code which, with some amendments, is still in force today. These two Ordinances were mainly based on the Code Napoleon which, in its turn, in many parts had reproduced with modifications the principles of Roman Law long established in Malta. These Ordinances were, in certain respects, more progressive than the Code Napoleon because they incorporated provisions containing solutions to the controversies which arose after the promulgation of the Code Napoleon. In drafting these Ordinances Dingli also consulted the provisions of other leading Continental Codes and the treatises of textwriters of repute, and did not lose sight of the ancient laws and customs obtaining in Malta as well as the basic principles of Roman Law. He also referred to the Code of Louisiana, itself based on the Code Napoleon.

After the promulgation of the Codes several new laws were enacted (especially after 1921 when Malta enjoyed self-government) dealing mainly with commercial, maritime, fiscal and administrative matters. These were at first mainly inspired by English law but since the attainment of independence in 1964 the Maltese legislator is, more and more, relying on other foreign legislations as well as international conventions. Amongst these conventions one cannot but mention the European Convention for the Protection of Human Rights and Fundamental Freedoms which, with some reservations, became a part of Maltese domestic law by Act XIV of 1987 and which, together with Chapter IV of the Constitution, protects fundamental rights in Malta.

The Malta Constitution has been since 1974 a republican constitution and its head of state is a President. Besides protecting fundamental rights, it has maintained the traditional threefold division of the powers of the state — the executive, the legislative and the judicial powers — introduced in Malta by Governor Sir Thomas Maitland as far back as 1814. The Constitution provides *inter alia* for the composition, the powers, the procedure and the summoning, prorogation and dissolution of Parliament. It lays down provisions dealing with the executive authority, particularly with regard to the Cabinet, the appointment and tenure of office of Ministers, the powers and functions of the President of Malta and of the Prime Minister, the appointment of the Leader of the Opposition as well as the office of Attorney General. The Constitution moreover recognises and protects the independence of the judiciary and the power of the Courts to declare a law invalid.

It may therefore be concluded from this necessarily brief survey that the present legal system reflects Malta's chequered history. During the long period before 1530 when Malta was under a foreign ruler and when, as far as is known, there was no law-making body proper in Malta, the laws of the successive foreign rulers applied to Malta, though due recognition was also given to local customs. During this period — particularly during the latter part thereof — Malta became part of the European system and was governed by the legal principles recognised and developed by the Continental system of law which itself was inspired by Roman Law. During the subsequent period running from 1530 up to the early part of this century, although laws were enacted in Malta, still these depended on the decision of the foreign ruler, though Maltese legal talent started contributing in great measure — especially during British rule — towards Malta's legal development. This contribution necessarily greatly increased when Malta was granted self-government in 1921 and again in 1947 and became exclusively Maltese with the grant of independence in 1964. Malta's connection with the Continental system of law acquired before 1530 was never severed although attempts were made to do so in the early years of British rule. It still exists today though with the passing of time other factors have contributed to Malta's legal development, mainly English legislation and more recently other foreign legislations and international conventions. The Maltese legislator very wisely studies these recent legal developments and introduces them after adapting them to the circumstances of Malta.

Bibliography

BRES, O., *Malta Antica Illustrata*, Rome, 1816.

COLEIRO, E., "Maltese Coins of the Roman Period", *Numismatic Chronicle*, Seventh Series, Vol. XI, 1971.

DEBONO, P., *Storia della Legislazione in Malta*, Tipografia del Malta, Valletta, Malta, 1897.

EVANS, John B., *Malta*, Thames & Hudson, London, 1963.

FRENDO, H., *Party Politics in a Fortress Colony: The Maltese Experience*, Midsea Books Ltd, Malta, 1979.

GANADO, J.M., Maltese Law, *The Journal of Comparative Legislation and International Law*, November, 1947.

HARDEN, D., *The Phoenicians*, Thames & Hudson, London, 1962.

HARDING, H.W., *Maltese Legal History Under British Rule 1801-1836*, Progress Press Co. Ltd, Malta, 1968.

LAMANTIA, V., *Storia della Legislazione Civile e Criminale di Sicilia*, Clamis e Roberti, Palermo, 1858.

MIFSUD, A., *Origine della Sovranità Inglese in Malta*, Tipografia del Malta, Valletta, Malta, 1907.

MIFSUD BONNICI, C., *Del Comune Maltese*, Empire Press, Valletta, Malta, n.d.

MONTALTO, J., *The Nobles of Malta*, Midsea Books Ltd, Malta, 1979.

TRUMP, D.H., *Malta: An Archaeological Guide*, Faber & Faber Limited, London, 1972.

VELLA, A.P., *Storja ta' Malta*, Klabb Kotba Maltin, Malta, 1974.

WINKELMANN, E., *Acta imperii inedita saeculi XIII et XIV*, Two Volumes, Innsbruck, 1880-1885.

ZAMMIT, T., *Malta: The Islands and Their History*, Malta Herald Office, Valletta, Malta, 1926.

Medicine

Paul Cassar

The story of disease and healing in the Maltese Islands begins with the earliest inhabitants of Malta and Gozo about 3600 to 2500 B.C.

The most ancient remains of medico-cultural interest have been found in the Stone Age temples of Mnajdra, Ħaġar Qim and Tarxien. The sick resorted to these shrines to implore the deity to restore them to health. By way of thanksgiving for recovery from their illness they were in the habit of depositing in these temples small "ex-votos" of pottery in the shape of the diseased parts of their body: there are examples of a swollen face and foot, and a torso with a prominent abdomen.

That these temples were associated with the healing art is also shown by the figure of the serpent which, since very early times, has symbolised the practice of medicine in the ancient Near East, Egypt and Greece. Pottery objects showing two intertwined coils come from Mnajdra while in the temple of Ġgantija in the neighbouring island of Gozo the figure of a serpent-like creature is carved on a large block of stone.

The underground temple at Ħal Saflieni – known as the Hypogeum and also belonging to the Stone Age period – has furnished us with two statuettes each representing a sleeping woman on a sort of couch. These statuettes are reminiscent of the rite of incubation by which the patient was put to sleep by the priest to have the line of treatment to be followed inspired by the god while the patient was in the hypnotic state.

With the advent of the Phoenicians to Malta about 800 B.C. the god Exmun was honoured as the protector of the sick.

During the Roman period, which begins with the capture of the Maltese Islands from the Carthaginians in 218 B.C., we come across more tangible evidence of the medical art among us such as feeding bottles of baked clay for babies and invalids; a large stone slab used for plugging the entrance of a Roman burial chamber in a catacomb at Rabat (Malta) bearing carvings of surgical instruments including a vaginal speculum, forceps and cupping vessel; the provision of a supply of running water for domestic purposes; the presence of heating arrangements in Roman houses; and the existence of toilet sets made of stone with a notch on their front edges at the public baths at Għajn Tuffieħa – a design anticipating the modern U-shaped lavatory seat.

The most outstanding medical event of Roman rule was the shipwreck on the Island of Malta in 60 A.D. of St Paul and his companions among whom was the physician Luke. This evangelist is the first medical man known to have come to Malta. His Acts constitute the earliest written document known to us dealing with the presence of disease and its treatment in Malta.

Practically no records relative to the years that followed the fall of the Roman Empire have survived in our islands except two – both of which are of a funereal character. One is a tombstone in Greek testifying to the presence of a Christian physician, named Domesticus, who was buried in the vicinity of Mdina which was then the capital city and citadel of Malta. The inscription is difficult to date but it is likely that it belongs to the period from the third to the fifth century A.D.

The other record consists of a series of stone slabs from a cemetery in Gozo bearing the armorial crests of church dignitaries and noblemen who were taking part in the crusade of 1270 against Tunis and who are believed to have died of plague in Gozo on their way to the North African coast.

Plague has been one of the scourges of seafarers in the Mediterranean since the early Middle Ages; hence the establishment by maritime communities of quarantine measures which were already in existence in Malta by 1458. Among the penalties laid down against breaches of the quarantine laws was the burning of merchandise and also of the homes of offenders to ensure the elimination of the fomites of the disease as then understood.

Not far from Mdina was the hospital of *Santo Spirito* which according to legend was founded by St Francis of Assisi on his way to Africa in 1220. Although this tradition remains unsupported by documentary sources, there is evidence that the hospital was already in existence in 1372 when it was under the direction of a Franciscan Friar of the Order of the Minor Conventuals who came to Malta in that year. In 1575 it was described as consisting of a small church containing only four beds in each of which two patients were placed in accordance with the usage of the time.

Besides the sick, this hospital also received foundlings: for this purpose it had a contrivance called *rota* which was a cot revolving on a vertical axis that communicated with the outside of the hospital by means of a small window through which the unwanted baby was deposited inside the cot.

The hospital building was enlarged in subsequent years and its bed complement increased considerably. It continued to function uninterruptedly as a hospital until 1967 when it was closed down by the government for reasons of economy. Until then it could boast of a continuous history of over six hundred years and claim to be one of the oldest surviving hospitals in Europe.

A new phase in the medical and cultural history of Malta begins with the granting of our islands as a fief to the Knights Hospitallers of the Order of St John of Jerusalem in 1530 by the Emperor Charles the Fifth but our association with this band of autocratic rulers opens rather sadly. In the midst of these political changes we come across the earliest Maltese physician on record. He is Giuseppe Callus who was born in the early years of the sixteenth century. He was already in practice in 1530 and had served in a medical capacity in the naval service of the Order of St John on board of the *Sant'Anna* and later as a District Medical Officer at Mdina.

On taking possession of Malta, the Order of St John had solemnly declared to respect the political and other liberties of the Maltese but Grand Master Jean de la Vallette soon forgot this promise and took the imposition of taxes into his own hands. A group of discontented citizens decided to appeal secretly to Philip II, King of Spain, but their petition fell into the hands of the Grand Master instead of reaching the King. Dr Giuseppe Callus is said to have been the author of the document meant for the King. He was arrested and condemned to death, his execution taking place at Rabat in 1561.

The Order of St John had its origin in Jerusalem about the mid-eleventh century with the aim of nursing those pilgrims that fell ill during their journeys to the Holy Sepulchre. Hence their name of Hospitallers. In later years they developed into a military and naval power as they had to defend themselves and their patients from the attacks of the harassing Moslems.

On coming to Malta one of their first acts was to found a hospital at Birgu, the maritime city where they had initially settled. This hospital was later transferred to Valletta in 1574. It was known as the Holy Infirmary and there the knights, and at times even the Grand Master, served the sick in person in silver plate. This hospital was exclusively reserved for men, the sick being classified into medical and surgical cases and housed in separate wards according to the nature of their illness.

The Holy Infirmary had its own pharmacy. An early mention of this pharmacy (*apotheca*), with sleeping accommodation for the apothecary (*aromatarius*), occurs in 1587. Drugs and medicaments were imported from Sicily (Palermo, Messina), Italy (Naples, Venice, Leghorn, Florence), France (Marseilles) and Spain (Madrid, Cadiz), the purchases being made by the Order's agents (*ricevitori*) in these places.

Among the pharmaceutical manuals consulted by the apothecary in the compounding of medicaments were the Italian versions of M. Macquer's *Elements de Chymie Theorique* (Paris, 1753) and the *Elements de Chymie Pratique* (Paris, 1756).

Laboratory equipment, such as glass retorts, flasks and alembics were imported from the places already mentioned. No specimens of these utensils have survived apart from a large bronze mortar with the coat-of-arms of Grand Master Ramon Perellos moulded on it. The date 1710 is near its base.

The pharmacy of the Holy Infirmary was renowned for the beauty and variety of its maiolica drug jars and pots, some of which were decorated with the armorial bearings of the Grand Masters Alofius Wignacourt (1601-22) and Ramon Perellos y Roccaful (1697-1720). Most of this ware is of the Caltagirone type.

Near the Holy Infirmary at Valletta was another hospital reserved for women, while a district medical and nursing domiciliary service was set up in the towns for the benefit of sick women who could not be admitted into hospital.

At the Holy Infirmary, Grand Master Nicolas Cotoner founded the School of Anatomy and Surgery in 1676. From this origin has evolved our present Medical School which was later incorporated with the University of Malta when this institution was established by Grand Master Emanuel Pinto de Fonceca in 1769.

At the School of Anatomy and Surgery the greatest importance was attached to the performance of human dissection and of post-mortem examinations for teaching purposes so much so that to provide the necessary material it was decreed in 1739 that the corpses of knights and of laymen dying in the Infirmary were to be made over to the teacher of anatomy.

One of the famous Maltese surgeons who worked and taught at the School of Anatomy and Surgery was Michel'Angelo Grima (1731-1798). He was a contemporary of the renowned English surgeon John Hunter and like the latter received some of his surgical experience on the battle field during the Seven Years War of 1756-63, though the two surgeons were on opposite sides. Grima recorded some of his war cases in his book on traumatic surgery (*Della medicina traumatica*, Florence, 1773). He promoted the spiral suture of the intestine after resection of this organ and experimented successfully on the removal of the spleen in dogs. He also published the results of his work on the *contre-coup* phenomenon of head injuries and on popliteal aneurysm, the latter being published in London in 1773.

Grima was also one of the members of a commission appointed by the Grand Master to investigate the claims of mesmerism as advocated by Franz Anton Mesmer (1734-1815), an Austrian physician, in October 1783. It is significant that this commission reported adversely on this method of therapy several months before the French Royal Commission of King Louis XVI issued its condemnation of mesmerism.

Another prominent Maltese surgeon, whose name is still alive on the continent of Europe, was Joseph Barth (1745-1818). He was born at Valletta and began his studies at the Holy Infirmary but later went to Vienna where he studied eye diseases and became the oculist of the Empress Maria Theresa. In the Austrian capital he occupied the Chair of Ophthalmology at the University of Vienna – this Chair being purposely founded for him in 1773 by the Empress in recognition of his professional services to her son, later Joseph II. Barth died in Vienna in 1818.

At the Holy Infirmary of Valletta there was a School of Pharmacy apart from the School of Anatomy and Surgery already considered. It is not known when the School of Pharmacy was founded but it is likely that it was set up in 1676 in conjunction with the School of Anatomy and Surgery. In 1690 a botanical garden of medicinal herbs was planted in the ditch of Fort St Elmo – very close to the Holy Infirmary – for the practical instruction of the pharmacy students. By the following century the Pharmacy School had made considerable progress and in 1729 rules and regulations were laid down concerning the curriculum that had to be followed to qualify as a pharmacist.

One of the aims of the School of Anatomy and Surgery was the training of surgeons for service afloat on board the galleys of the Order of St John that often engaged Moslem ships in mortal combat. Some of these galleys had a crew of some three hundred men including knights, sailors, soldiers and slaves to man the oars. To look after the health of this mass of men there was a physician, a surgeon and a number of barber-surgeons, the latter being entrusted with such duties as blood letting, application of dry cupping and teeth extractions.

The fear of bubonic plague – a disease then rampant in the ports of the Mediterranean and the Middle East – had induced the Order of St John to device sanitary means to guard against the introduction of pestilence into the Maltese Islands by contaminated ships. Those suspected of carrying the plague were kept for a period of observation and isolation in Marsamxett or Quarantine Harbour before the crew and merchandise were allowed ashore. Severe punishments – including the death penalty – were laid down for transgressors of the quarantine laws. Soldiers guarding ships in quarantine had orders to shoot any sailor who tried to leave his ship as well as any inhabitant who attempted to communicate with ships detained in quarantine. These measures may, today, seem to be unduly harsh but it must be remembered that in those times there was no medical means of combating plague so that once this disease had gained a foothold on the island it caused not only an extensive mortality but also a wholesale disorganization of the social and economic state of the country as happened, for example, during the epidemics of 1592 and 1675-76.

During the first two months of the outbreak of 1592 some five hundred persons lost their lives but the worst feature of the epidemic was the famine that followed in its wake as Sicily and other Mediterranean ports were so terrified of catching the pestilence from Malta that they refused to trade with the island. Thus the Maltese found themselves cut off from all sources of food supplies so much so that the Grand Master was compelled to order his galleys to leave harbour and seize foreign ships laden with corn and bring them to Maltese ports.

The epidemic dragged on for a whole year killing three thousand persons out of a population of twenty-seven thousand.

The pestilence of 1675-76 was even more distressing. It began in Valletta and soon spread to other areas. The mortality at Tarxien and Birgu was so great that there were not enough men to bury the dead. The outbreak lasted nine months with a loss of eight thousand to eleven thousand souls among whom were twenty-six physicians and surgeons.

From these two epidemics originated in our island the devotion to the saints protectors against the plague Saint Roque and Saint Sebastian. Chapels and altars were dedicated to them by the survivors who also erected statutes, by way of thanksgiving, on the fronts of houses and at street corners of towns and villages, many of which are still extant.

Following the expulsion of the Order of St John from Malta and the occupation of the Maltese Islands by Napoleon Bonaparte in 1798, the Holy Infirmary of Valletta was taken over by the French for their sick troops.

The civilian patients were transferred from the Holy Infirmary to the nearby monastery and Church of St Mary Magdalen. As the monastery was not large enough to accommodate all the sick, the church was adapted as a ward for surgical cases and its choir as a pharmacy.

When the French evacuated Malta in 1800 this Civil Hospital, as it was called, remained in use for many years as the erstwhile Holy Infirmary passed into the hands of the British military authorities for their own soldiers, and continued to function as a Garrison or Station Hospital until 1920 when a new military hospital was built at Mtarfa.

The Civil Hospital at Valletta showed itself to be ill-adapted for the adequate care of the sick and in 1850 was replaced by the Central Hospital set up at Floriana.

The Quarantine System devised by the Order of St John was retained and strictly applied under British rule as it not only safeguarded the public health of the Maltese Islands but also provided a protective barrier for European ports on the Mediterranean coastline. In fact large quantities of goods thought to be liable to harbour the "contagion" of plague were landed at the Lazzaretto on Manoel Island to undergo a period of quarantine before they were shipped to the ports of Livorno, Marseilles and Algiers to reach European and North African markets.

The aetiology of plague – the chain of causation and transmission formed by a germ, a rat and a flea – was still unknown. The accepted epidemiological concept of the time still blamed personal contact and "contaminated" clothing and paper as the means of catching plague. In practice this way of thinking meant the isolation of travellers and crews at the Lazzaretto.

The Lazzaretto was a complex of buildings that had its origin in 1643 on Manoel Island away from inhabited areas. Here the traveller was kept under observation for any manifestation of plague under the custody of Health Guards.

Merchandise was "purified" by being unpacked and exposed to the air for "ventilation" – a time-consuming process that sometimes took as many as eighty days to perform.

Heavily infected ships were burned with all their rigging and fittings. The seamen on board were shaved of all their hair and plunged repeatedly into the sea before being admitted to the Lazzaretto.

An essential function of the quarantine set-up was the "smoking" or "fumigation" of letters from abroad as it was believed that paper could carry the "contagion" of plague. The process was carried out by an *ad hoc* employee known as the *profumatore* (literally the "perfumer").

Before being "smoked", the letters were not touched by hand but were held by means of a pair of pincers and incised by a scalpel or chisel in two places to ensure that the fumes of the "perfume" penetrated inside them. They were then placed over a grille inside a cabinet over a stove and exposed to the fumes of burning straw and aromatic herbs for half an hour.

Paper, as a carrier of plague, was so much feared that during the epidemic of 1813 it was avoided completely for the purpose of correspondence and drawing up a will, so much so that such documents were written on wood – a material that was not considered to be susceptible to convey the plague.

Intellectual and cultural developments in Malta have for centuries reflected the evolution of ideas and events in Europe.

It was inevitable, therefore, that Maltese medicine should share the same direction of progress in its growth and ultimate pattern.

Italian influence was a major formative force in moulding medical thought and practice in Malta. This was due not only to our geographical proximity to Sicily and southern Italy but also to our political links with these countries since the Norman Count, Roger of Hauteville, occupied Malta in 1090 following his conquest of Sicily.

One of these Sicilian links is associated with the earliest known hospital to be established in Malta in the fourteenth century; when set up at Rabat under the name of St Francis Hospital (later changed to *Santo Spirito* Hospital) this was placed under the Rectorship of a Minor Conventual Friar from Palermo, Fra Nicolò Papalla (1347).

In the following century the Jews formed an important element of the Maltese community, then based at Mdina, with very close contacts with the Jews of Sicily. In Malta, Jews appear to have monopolised the exercise of medicine and surgery after obtaining their licence to practice at Palermo and Randazzo.

With the granting of the Maltese Islands the Order of St John in 1530, Italian and Sicilian physicians, surgeons and pharmacists were employed in the medical services of the Order. In times of a sanitary crisis, medical "experts" were purposely engaged from Sicily. Thus during the plague of 1592-93 Dr Pietro Parisi was sent from Trapani to Malta by the Viceroy of Sicily to endeavour to check the progress of the malady. Another "expert", this time from Messina, Dr Domenico Bottone, was brought over to treat Grand Master Raymon Perellos who was suffering from a "rheumatic fever". Bottone later published an account of the Grand Master's illness in 1712.

The early Chief Government Medical Officers or *protomedici*, who occupied the highest post in the medical hierarchy of the island, were Italians. Whenever doubts arose regarding the application of rules of conduct in medical practice they were to be decided in accordance with the regulations issued by the Sicilian *protomedico*.

For many years before the foundation of the Malta University in 1769, Maltese youths who wished to follow a medical career proceeded to study and graduate in the universities of Salerno, Florence and Bologna; others went to Rome and Palermo to train in pharmacy.

Dissection of the cadaver, as part of the teaching of anatomy, was introduced in 1723 by the Italian Grand Master Marcantonio Zondadari who sponsored the young Maltese surgeon, Gabriele Henin, to study anatomy and surgery at the Hospital of Santa Maria Nuova in Florence. In 1750 another surgeon, Michel'Angelo Grima, trained at the same hospital where, during a stay of eight years, he carried out animal experiments on the removal of the spleen and on intestinal suture.

Italian was the language of literary and scientific culture among professional people in eighteenth century Malta. At the university, lectures were delivered in Italian and the graduation ceremony at the end of the various courses was based on that of the University of Bologna.

When surgeon M.A. Grima, who was lecturer in anatomy and surgery at the Holy Infirmary, published his treatise on traumatic surgery and a textbook on anatomy for his students he wrote them in Italian. Even as late as the nineteenth century the medium of communication of the first medical journals to be published in Malta, such as *L'Ape Melitense* (1838), *Il Barth* (1871) and *La Rivista Medica* (1890) was Italian.

Italian medical influence began to decline at the beginning of the twentieth century owing to the increasing British impact that reached its peak with the outbreak of World War II (1939-45). Italian, as a cultural medium, was replaced by the English language and by the British pattern of medical thought and practice with the consequent break of the past medico-cultural links between Malta and Italy.

France, like Italy, played a beneficial role in medical developments in Malta especially during the seventeenth and eighteenth centuries. The most distinctive French imprints that left their mark on our medico-cultural past were: – (a) the presence in the island of French physicians and surgeons; (b) the education and training of Maltese medical men in France; (c) seeking medical advice and obtaining hospital supplies; (d) the diffusion of French medical literature among Maltese practitioners and (e) the persistence of medical links in the nineteenth and twentieth centuries.

It is of interest to note that when the Order of St John came to Malta in 1530, it was a French Grand Master – Fra Philip Villiers de L'Isle Adam – who laid the foundation stone of their first hospital to be erected in the island i.e. the Holy Infirmary at Birgu. It was also during the rule of another French Grand Master – Fra Jean Levesque de La Cassiere – that the building of a new Holy Infirmary was commenced at Valletta in 1574.

The highest official in the hierarchy of the Order that presided over the administration of the Holy Infirmary was the Head of the French Langue who bore the title of Grand Hospitaller. Under him was the Infirmarian, who was also a French knight, and who was responsible for the day-to-day running of the Infirmary.

It has been observed that during the seventeenth and eighteenth centuries Malta became politically, though not legally, a French dependence in the sense that more than half the knights in the island were French and that a substantial amount of the Order's revenues were derived from its possession in France. The weight of this French influence became even more manifest in the social and cultural life of Malta following the accession to the Grand Mastership of Fra Emmanuel de Rohan in 1775.

In the medical field this French bias exerted a decidedly profound impact when the Order sought and obtained the professional services of a nucleus of French physicians and surgeons for the care of the sick in Malta particularly in times of some medical emergency as happened during the bubonic plague of 1675-76 when a French physician from Marseilles was engaged by the Order to treat the plague-stricken.

Concurrently with the policy of employing French practitioners, the Order endeavoured to form its own Maltese medical and surgical personnel by training Maltese youths in France. The physicians-to-be proceeded to Montpellier and the budding surgeons to Paris. They received financial assistance from the Order and were placed under the protection of some highly placed person to ensure that the trainee was attached to the best teachers available. In the case of surgeons emphasis was laid on such specific surgical procedures as the removal of stones from the urinary bladder and operations for cataract.

The following physicians and surgeons were trained in France: – (a) Joseph Cossaeus, probably the Latin rendering of Cassia or Cossai or Casha (1636); (b) Giorgio Imbert who wrote a Latin treatise on melancholia published in Montpellier in 1723. He served at the Holy Infirmary of Valletta and the Order's navy and eventually became *protomedico* or Chief Government Medical Officer; (c) Gaetano Azzopardi (1734); (d) Gaetano Delicata (c.1734); (e) Giuseppe Demarco (1742), the author of several publications in Latin; (f) Giorgio Locano (1749) who was appointed Professor of Medicine at our university (1771) and (g) Salvatore Bernard (1724-1806) who graduated at the University of Aix-en-Provence (1749).

Among the surgeons mention may be made of (a) Giuseppe Grillet (c.1709); (b) Antonio Grillet (1704); (c) Giuseppe Farrugia (1754); (d) Michel'Angelo Grima (1758) who after spending three years in Paris joined the French army as surgeon during the Seven Years War (1756-63). As a result of his war experiences he published a book on the surgery of wounds in 1773. In teaching this subject he followed the methods of his French contemporary Antoine Louis, the Physician-in-Chief of France.

Apart from the training of Maltese doctors and surgeons in France, French medical thought and practice reached Malta through a stream of medical literature in the form of books and the printed proceedings of the *Academie de Chirurgie* of Paris and by means of publications in the libraries set up by two French knights – Joseph De Saint Jay and the Bailly de Tencin – who donated their books to the Public Library in 1714 and 1756 thus rendering this literature available for perusal to members of the profession.

Thanks to this French influence, Malta could boast of a fair-sized group of Maltese professional men who were highly competent to impart medical knowledge to their students and to provide treatment on the French model and, therefore, of the highest European standards to the sick.

Relations between Malta and France became strained following the French Revolution which despoiled the Order of its estates in France with consequent loss of revenues. Five years later *General en Chef* Napoleon Bonaparte captured Malta from the Knights of St John. The French eventually departed from the island in 1800 when Malta passed under British rule with the consequence that the current of medical thought and influence veered mainly towards Edinburgh and London. In spite of this turning point, however, a number of Maltese practitioners continued to seek in France the opportunities to advance their academic medical status and enrich their therapeutic experience.

The French lead was reflected especially in the management of the mentally sick. Thus when Dr Thomas Chetcuti (1797-1863) was appointed Director of the Mental Asylum in 1838, he made it a point to visit institutions not only in Italy and

Great Britain but also in France. He returned to Malta imbued with the spirit of the humanitarian reforms of Philippe Pinel (1754-1826) carried out at the Bicetre Asylum. Like Pinel, Chetcuti liberated disturbed mental patients from the chains with which they were restrained. In diagnosing mental illness he adopted the classification of the French psychiatrist Jean Etienne Dominique Esquirol (1772-1840) and, in accordance with the tenets of two other French pioneers in the mental field – E.J. Georget (1795-1828) and William Ferrus (1784-1861) – who stressed the importance of the concept of occupational therapy as an integral element in the management of psychiatric illness.

The French imprint of nineteenth century advances in the areas of general medicine, surgery and neurology was spread in Malta by Dr Gavino Gulia (1835-1889) by means of his medical journal *Il Barth* (1871-77) especially in connection with the investigations of Louis Pasteur (1822-95) in the new field of bacteriology.

One of the last outstanding links with French medicine was forged by Dr. (later Sir) Themistocles Zammit (1864-1935) – the discoverer of the germ of brucellosis in the blood of the goat in 1905 – who in 1891 went to Paris to widen his knowledge of laboratory procedures. There he met Louis Pasteur whom Zammit ardently admired till the end of his life.

At the time of the centenary celebrations of the birth of Pasteur by our university on the 22nd January 1923, Sir Temi Zammit was the Rector of that institution. When, on the 17th October of the same year the *Camera Medica*, representing the Maltese medical profession, presented a bronze bust of the French scientist to the University this gift was very appropriately received by Sir T. Zammit. That bust is displayed at the Medical School as a reminder of Malta's past medical bond with France.

The dawn of the nineteenth century stands out as a turning point in Maltese history – politically and culturally. On the 5th September 1800 the Maltese Islands came under the protection of King George III and in 1814 passed in full sovereignty to His Britannic Majesty. Thanks to these events Maltese medicine came in close touch with British medical thought and experience. This contact occurred mainly through the physicians and surgeons attached to the British Navy and Army stationed in the island.

The earliest instance concerned the prevention of smallpox which was prevalent in Malta in the late eighteenth century. Protective vaccination against this illness had been discovered in England by the general practitioner Edward Jenner in 1798 and the British Government took steps in 1800 to promote vaccination among its naval and military forces overseas including Malta.

Dr Joseph Marshall and Dr John Walker were sent as vaccinators to the British Fleet in the Mediterranean. Dr Walker eventually went to Egypt but Dr Marshall remained in Malta to introduce vaccination among Maltese practitioners. The first doctors to be initiated in its use were Dr Lorenzo Cassar, the personal physician of Sir Alexander Ball (the British Royal Commissioner) and Dr Aloysio Caruana, the Chief Government Medical Officer. Because of the indifference of the people to avail themselves of this preventive measure, vaccination was made compulsory in 1855.

Malta derived other benefits from the presence in our island of several British doctors who took interest, and recorded their observations, in the medical and natural history of Malta. Among these was Dr F.F. Sankey who put Malta on the map of medicine in two ways – by directing the attention of British physicians in the island's assets as a winter resort for invalids from Britain and by publishing in Malta in 1846 what appears to be one of the earliest – if not the earliest – First Aid books to be printed. In this short work he enunciated three maxima forming a

sound guide line for the medical profession world wide and which are still valid today i.e. (a) One must not expect to find in an individual patient all the signs and symptoms of disease as set down in books; (b) when prescribing medicines one must be prepared to be disappointed with their effects; and (c) drugs may be looked upon as poisons which do not always arrest disease and which may cause other complaints in addition to the ones they are given to cure.

Another British physician who left his legacy to Maltese patients was Dr John Davy (1790-1868) who spent seven years in Malta on the army medical staff and who was the moving spirit behind the creation of the first public dispensary at the Auberge d'Italie in Valletta for the out-patient treatment of the needy poor. This is how the present Government polyclinics – until a few years ago known as *il-berga* – originated. Davy has also left his imprint as the practitioner who treated two distinguished visitors to Malta i.e. Sir Walter Scott (1831) and the Rev. (later Cardinal) John Henry Newman (1838).

An initial attempt to form a non-private medical library in Malta goes back to 1687 when Dr Fra Giuseppe Zammit, the first Director and Lecturer at the School of Anatomy and Surgery at the Holy Infirmary, donated his personal collection of medical books to the Infirmary for the use of its professional staff. With the passage of time these books ceased to be of practical value as they became outdated.

The next effort to found a medical library occurred in 1824 when a British benefactor – the Hon John Hookham Frere (1769-1846) – who had settled in Malta in 1821 – was appointed Chairman of the University Council. In 1833-4 he donated thirty-three works on medicine, surgery and allied subjects to the university for the use of medical students. The title-page of each volume carries his *dedit* and autograph.

These books were written by the established medical authorities of the time who dominated the contemporary and therapeutic fields and who represented the leading minds of continental universities and of the medical schools of Edinburgh and of Glasgow and the London teaching hospitals of St Bartholomew and of St George.

This collection, now of historical interest, is on show at the Medical School as the John Hookham Frere Memorial Medical Library set up in 1985 to remind students of the origins of the medical library of today.

Two early advantageous developments that resulted from the British connection were the re-establishment of the University, that had been abolished by the French in 1798 on the 6th November 1800; and the appointment of Dr Cleardo Naudi (1780-1837) to the Chair of Experimental Chemistry and Natural History (1805).

In April 1812, Dr Naudi was sent to London by the government to acquaint himself with the running of the schools of medicine and of the hospitals of that city. During his twentyone months stay there he followed lectures in medicine, surgery and chemistry at St Thomas's and at Guy's Hospitals and attended courses in midwifery, dentistry and eye diseases. He returned to Malta enriched with a representative range of British medicine which formed the basis of his lectures to students.

By the early decades of the nineteenth century Maltese young men went to the United Kingdom to pursue their medical studies. The first to qualify there were Dr Vincent Dionysius Portelli (1834) and Dr Salvatore Luigi Pisani (1853). The latter volunteered, with other Maltese doctors, to serve in a medical capacity with the British Army during the Crimean War and had the honour of working with Miss Florence Nightingale who spoke very highly of his surgical skill.

This, however, was not a one-way current; indeed there was a time — between 1826 and 1886 — when no fewer than twelve British physicians obtained a doctorate from the Malta Medical School. Most of them were serving in the British Navy but others belonged to British families residing in Malta.

In April 1813 plague again invaded the island disrupting commerce, agriculture and social life. As no one knew what caused the disease and how the illness passed from one individual to another no really efficacious preventive measures could be taken against the malady which spread over the island in spite of the quarantine precautions enforced by the health authorities.

The plague-stricken were isolated at the Lazzaretto but owing to the great incidence of cases this establishment could no longer cope with the great number of patients brought to it. To provide the necessary accommodation, wooden huts were built to shelter the sick in the ditches outside Porta Reale and Portes des Bombes. The Bishop of Malta, Francesco Saverio Caruana, used to visit the patients in these places and administer the sacraments.

So many attendants on the sick and other public employees died that ultimately the government had to press convicts into the service to clear houses of corpses, to drive the dead cart and to bury the dead. But the convicts, too, were wiped out by the disease. They were replaced by fifty prisoners brought from Sicily but these also were mowed down.

The epidemic came to an end in September 1814 after carrying off four thousand six hundred persons out of a population of one hundred thousand.

Twenty-four years later a new enemy reared its head. This was the dreaded cholera. Of the eight cholera epidemics that visited Malta over a period of seventy-four years i.e. from 1837 to 1911 that of 1865 claims our attention. It was then held that cholera was transmitted from one place to another by means of infected air. Dr Antonio Ghio, the Chief Government Medical Officer of the time, thought otherwise. He felt convinced, from his observations, that the disease was not spread by the atmosphere but by a microbe that passed from one person to another. To appreciate the great significance of Dr Ghio's idea one must recall that the concept that certain diseases were due to microbes was still quite new to medical science. In fact the cholera germ was discovered twenty years later by the German researcher Robert Koch when Dr Ghio was still living and thus had the satisfaction of knowing that the new science of bacteriology had proved him right.

Although the nineteenth century was often darkened by the tragedy of epidemic illness, it was also a period of achievement and developments in Malta's medical services.

In 1832 the British Navy established a hospital for its seamen on the site of an old villa, that had belonged to the Knight of St John Giovanni Bichi, on the headland between Kalkara Creek and Rinella Bay in the Grand Harbour. This hospital, which was known as Bichi Hospital until its closure in 1970, played a very conspicuous role in Malta's medical history as it was the scene of the first surgical operation to be carried out under ether anaesthesia in Malta. This occurred in March 1847 barely three months after the administration of the first anaesthetic to be given in a London Hospital. The anaesthetist at Bichi Hospital was the naval surgeon Dr (later Sir) Thomas Spencer Wells. Dr Wells showed the apparatus — and how to use it — to his Maltese colleagues and even demonstrated the effects of ether inhalation on two Maltese doctors who volunteered to submit to the experiment which was attended with success. Dr Thomas Spencer Wells eventually left the navy and settled in London where he gained a world-wide renown as a surgeon.

Up to one hundred years ago many of the Maltese midwives and hospital attendants were illiterate and uncouth folk with no background of organised training in midwifery and nursing. The Comptroller of Charitable Institutions, Sir Ferdinand V. Inglott, who was responsible for the administration of our hospital services, had been insisting with government to tackle this problem. He had even entered into a correspondence on the subject with Florence Nightingale who had organised the nursing service in the Crimea during the war of 1854-56 and who was afterwards responsible for the foundation of nursing education and training in England.

A course for the training of midwives was eventually begun in 1869 by Professor Salvatore Luigi Pisani who published a book in Maltese for the use of his student-midwives.

Instruction of hospital nurses was pioneered in 1882 by Dr Teodoro Bonnici when he was a Resident Junior surgeon at the Central Hospital at Floriana.

From these small beginnings has gradually evolved the St Luke' School for Nurses (1938) now forming part of the Institute for Health Care attached to the University of Malta.

Substantial progress was registered in the area of public health with the enactment of appropriate legislation for the provision of a wholesome water supply, the laying down of a drainage system, the prevention of the introduction and spread of communicable diseases and the abolition of burials inside churches.

The highlight of the nineteenth century was the discovery in the human spleen of the causative germ of Brucellosis, then known as Malta or Mediterranean or Undulant Fever, by the British Army surgeon (later Sir) David Bruce with the help of the Maltese laboratory worker Dr Giuseppe Caruana Scicluna (1853-1921). Bruce published his results in 1887 from the Station Hospital of Valletta, the former Holy Infirmary of the Knights of St John.

The source of the germ — then called *Micrococcus melitensis vel Brucii* — and how it invaded the human body was unknown and, therefore, no preventive measures against the illness could be devised. The number of cases per year among the Maltese was 3.2 per thousand of the population. The British army and navy were equally interested in controlling the disease as, through its prolonged course and high invaliding rate, this fever was seriously undermining the strength of the twenty-five thousand soldiers and sailors of the Mediterranean garrison.

The British military authorities finally took action as the incidence of the fever reached alarming figures among the garrison. The Royal Society, at the request of the Admiralty, War Office and the Colonial Office undertook its investigation and sent out a joint commission to Malta for that purpose representing the army, navy and the Malta Civil government. The commission, of which David Bruce and Themistocles Zammit formed part, set to work at the Public Health Laboratory at Valletta in 1904. Many bacteriological experiments on animals were carried out but in spite of all their labours the source of the microbe continued to elude them.

The investigation had started to become tedious and unrewarding when the discovery was made that the goat was the reservoir of the micrococcus. The actual discovery of the microbe in the blood of the goat was made by Themistocles Zammit on the 25th June 1905.

Armed with the new knowledge that the microbe passed from the blood of the infected goat to the animal's milk, practical steps were taken to prevent the infection from reaching human beings by boiling the milk before its consumption. These steps finally culminated in 1938 in the introduction of the pasteurization of goat's milk which covers the whole of the Maltese Islands and which has resulted in the almost complete eradication of Brucellosis amongst us.

Maltese doctors gave their services during the two World Wars, joined the ranks of the British Colonial Medical Service and of the medical branches of the Army, Navy and Air Force. An appreciable number have made the British Isles their home being engaged in general practice or occupying consultant and academic posts in various specialities. Others are in Africa, Canada, Australia and in the United States of America.

The World Health Organisation has availed itself of Maltese physicians in connection with public health projects such as the control of trachoma and tuberculosis in various parts of the globe.

Bibliography

BRUCE, D., Note on the Discovery of a Micro-organism in Malta Fever, *The Practitioner*, 1887, Vol. 39, p.163.

CASSAR, P., Dr Thomas Chetcuti, *Scientia* (Malta), 1949, Vol.XV, pp.110-124.

Medical History of Malta, London, Wellcome Medical Library, 1965.

The Use of Wood as Writing Material during the Plague of Malta of 1813, *Medical History* (London), Vol.X, July 1966, pp.275-280.

Slitting of Letters for Disinfection in the Eighteenth Century in Malta, *British Medical Journal*, 14th January 1967, p.105.

Overseas Medical Graduates and Students at the University of Malta in the Nineteenth Century, *Melita Historica*, 1981, Vol.VIII, pp.93-100.

Rapporti medico-culturali tra Malta e l'Italia nel passato, *Rivista di storia della medicina* (Roma), Anno XXI, 1977, pp.1-22.

The John Hookham Frere Memorial Medical Library and the Origins of the Malta Medical School Library, Malta, The University Press, 1985.

French Influence on Medical Developments in Malta, Malta, Ministry of Education, 1987.

Malta's Role in Maritime Health under the Auspices of the Order of St John in the Eighteenth Century, Lombard Bank Publications, Malta, 1989, pp.1-25.

DAVY, J., Notes and Observations in the Ionian Islands and Malta, London, 1842, Vol.1 and 2.

DEMARCO, G., Dissertatio de Cocholata ejusque usu et abuso in medicina, Malta, 1760.

GRIMA, M.A., Instituzioni d'anatomia, Venice, 1781.

Della medicina traumatica, Firenze, 1773.

HOWARD, J., An Account of the Principal Lazarettos of Europe, London, 1779.

HENNEN, J., Sketches of the Medical Topography of the Mediterranean, London, 1830.

HARDMAN, W., A History of Malta, London, 1909.

HENIN, G., Observatio chirurgo-anathomica, Messina, 1749.

IL BARTH, 1871-77.

IMBERT, G., *An aegrotantes imaginarii sola diversitate idearum sanandi sint*, Monspelli, 1723.

INGLOTT, F.V., Brief Historical Account of the Treatment of the Insane in Malta, Malta, 1867.

Notizia della Sacra Infermeria, Rome, 1725.

PARISI, P., Avvertimenti sopra la peste, Palermo, 1593.

Aggiunta agli avvertimenti sopra la peste, Palermo, 1603.

PISANI, S.L., Report on the Cholera Epidemic in the year 1887, Malta, 1888.

Reports of the Commission for the Investigation of Mediterranean Fever, Part III, London, 1905, p.83.

SCHEMBRI, G.B., *The Midwife's Guide Book*, Malta, 1896.

Storia della Società Medica d'Incoraggiamento di Malta, Malta, Vol.I, 1845.

ZAMMIT, T., Undulant Fever in the Goat in Malta, *The Annals of Tropical Medicine and Parasitology*, 1922, Vol.16, p.1.

The Medical School of Malta, *Proceedings of the Royal Society of Medicine*, 1920, Vol.XII, pp.133-142.

The Economy

Lino Briguglio

I. Introduction

The Maltese economy is one of the smallest in the world. In 1991, the Maltese GNP was approximately US$25,000 million and the Maltese population was just under 360,000, occupying a land area of around 320 square kilometres.

In terms of GNP per capita, however, Malta is not on the low side by international comparisons. Although usually classified as a developing country, its average 1991 per capita GNP, amounted to approximately US$7,000, which is higher than most third world countries. The World Bank, in its 1991 *World Development Report* classified the Maltese economy as an upper middle income one.

As is well known, GNP per capita has a number of shortcomings as an indicator of development, and sometimes other indicators are utilised for making development comparisons across nations. One such indicator is the percentage contributed by the manufacturing sector to GDP (see Table 1). In Malta this amounts to just under 30%, which compares well with the manufacturing percentage pertaining to developed countries.

Some social and educational indicators suggest that Malta is more akin to industrial market economies than to third world countries. Literacy rates, school enrolment rates, average life expectancy, the number of hospital beds and the number of physicians per head of population are very similar to the rates found in Western European countries (Briguglio 1988).

This paper gives a very brief overview of the structure and performance of the Maltese economy during the period 1960-1991. Following this introduction, a brief account of Malta's development planning, and its results, is given. Sections three and four give some details on cyclical and structural changes over time. The fifth section discusses changes in expenditure patterns, while section six deals with changes pertaining to the Maltese balance of payments. Section seven describes the most important weaknesses faced by the Maltese economy today, and section eight concludes the paper.

II. Maltese Development Planning

The most important change that has occurred in the Maltese economy during the past 30 years relates to the expansion of the manufacturing sector and the phasing out of the British forces bases in Malta.

Up to the fifties, the Maltese economy relied heavily on British military expenditure (up to 1964 Malta was a British colony). Exports of merchandize was minimal, and very little regard was given to international competitiveness. Every year, the Maltese government drew up a budget, asking for funds from Britain to balance its administrative accounts and to create employment in British military establishments in Malta.

During the second half of the fifties, it became manifestly obvious that changes in the British defence policies were going to result in massive rundowns of employment with the British services in Malta, and the

Malta's Central Bank in Valletta, with the suburb of Floriana and part of the Grand Harbour in the background

need was felt to implement a coordinated development plan to diversify Malta's economy (see Balogh and Seers, 1955, Stolper, 1964 and British Government, 1957, 1963).

Between 1959 and 1986, six development plans were launched (see Maltese Government, 1967, 1972, and Development Plans). Although during this time Malta had governments of different ideologies, the basic objective of successive plans was essentially the same, namely that of making Malta a viable economic unit, which by its own efforts would provide jobs for those who sought them.

To achieve this aim, steps were taken to increase the share of manufacturing, tourism and agriculture in the domestic product. Since Malta's internal market is very small, industrial expansion had to be sustained through increased reliance on the export market, and therefore the importance of competitiveness for attaining economic objectives was always stressed. All plans and strategies were based on the need for adapting attitudes and methods of production to the changing structure of the Maltese economy.

The major differences between the planning and strategic approaches under different governments were related to the role of the state in directly productive activities. The Nationalist governments (1962-71) believed that state organs should only take a supportive role in such activities, leaving the private sector to take business initiatives according to market forces. The Labour governments (1971-87) on the other hand, tended to base their economic policy on the tenet that the state should participate directly, especially where the private sector failed to take the initiative.

Since 1987, the year the Nationalist party (conservative with liberal economic orientation) was elected in government, no plan was published as such, but the market oriented strategy of the government was clearly expressed. Malta is at present seeking to join the European Community,

and reliance on international competitiveness has been emphasised more than ever due to the fact that as full EC member, Malta would eventually have to remove all import barriers on goods, services, capital and labour coming from and going to the other members of the community.

The development process in Malta was beset by a series of difficulties, which were not all of Malta's own making. These included the successive and sometimes unexpected decreases in the British defence expenditures during the sixties, the international energy crisis and unprecedented inflationary pressures during the seventies, and the international recession during the early eighties.

A satisfactory measure of success has however been achieved, and this is evidenced by the expansion of the manufacturing and the services sectors and the phasing out of dependence on British military service, the growth in the number of the gainfully occupied persons and the rise in real per capita national income.

III. Cyclical Changes

During the period under consideration, the Maltese economy experienced a cyclical pattern of change.

The economy grew at a very slow rate during the first half of the sixties. During this sub-period, emigration and unemployment reached very high rates. The trend was however reversed during the second half of the sixties, a sub-period characterised by very fast growth rates in GDP and employment.

The economy slowed down again during the first half of the seventies. Although between 1970 and 1974 GDP tended to grow, the number of persons employed did not grow significantly, and had employment not been created in government labour corps, the number of persons employed would have actually decreased. Again, this sub-period of unsatisfactory economic performance was followed by fast growth rates in output and employment in the second half of the seventies.

Between 1982 and 1985 the Maltese economy performed at its worst. The rate of growth of GDP was a very slow one. Employment decreased at a very rapid rate – the fastest decline when all sub-periods are considered. Unemployment, on the other hand, increased and reached very high rates. Had the labour force not decreased, the official unemployment figures would have been much higher.

The economy picked up again after 1985, and GDP in real terms grew at a rate of about 6% per annum between 1986 and 1991. Between 1988 and 1991 unemployed averaged around 4%.

The fluctuations in the Maltese economy are reflected in the ups and downs of GDP and the rate of unemployment shown in Figures 1 and 2. Figure 1 gives the pattern of change of GDP compared to a 33 year trend and Figure 2 shows the ups and downs of unemployment and emigration. The figures show graphically that the economy performed at its best, in terms of rates of growth of GDP during the second half of each decade. The most rapid increase in GDP occurred between 1975 and 1979 and the lowest rates of unemployment occurred during the second half of the seventies and the second half of the eighties.

Probably the most important factors which accounted for the satisfactory performance of the Maltese economy during the second half of the sixties and of the seventies were the so-called construction boom during the sixties, and the rapid increase in tourism during the seventies. These two types of expenditures have relatively low import contents (see Briguglio, 1992 and Tarling and Rhodes, 1989 for the multiplier effects of tourism) and therefore also have relatively high multiplier effects on domestic value added and employment.

The rapid rate of economic growth during the second half of the eighties and early nineties could be attributable to process of liberalisation introduced by the Nationalist government since 1987. There is considerable debate in Malta as to whether or not economic liberalisation is beneficial to the Maltese economy, but it appears that it has so far given good results in terms of growth of GDP and employment.

IV. Structural Changes

The patterns of change just described have been accompanied by changes in the composition of GDP. Table 2 presents data on the contribution of major sectors during the period under consideration.

It can be seen from this table that the fastest growing sector was manufacturing, which accounted for just under 17% in the early sixties and increased to about 33% during the late seventies. There was a decline in the percentage share of this sector during the eighties.

The manufacturing sector itself also changed structurally during the past thirty years. The textile and clothing sub-sector has tended to increase its share up to the seventies and to decline again during the eighties. The machinery sub-sector expanded its relative shares between 1960 and 1990. On the other hand, the transport equipment sub-sector (mainly representing shiprepair and shipbuilding) has experienced a decline in its share of the manufacturing sector.

An important sector during the sixties was the British military base. The data in Table 2 shows that this sector reduced its share of GDP from an average of 15% in the early sixties to zero during the eighties. As already explained, this was in line with the development strategy adopted in the Maltese development plans.

The changes in the shares of other economic sectors were not as dramatic as those pertaining to manufacturing and the British bases. During the thirty year period, construction and quarrying

Table 1   The composition of the Maltese gross domestic product, 1990

	Lm million	%
Agriculture and fishing	23.6	3.1
Construction and quarrying	24.9	3.3
Manufacturing	197.3	25.8
Market services	285.6	37.4
Domestic property income	55.2	7.2
Public sector[a]	177.1	23.2
Total	763.7	100.0

[a] The public sector as defined here excludes limited liability companies with government majority shareholding.
Source: *Economic Survey*, 1992. (The average rate of exchange of the Maltese lira against the US dollar was Lm1 = $3.15.

Table 2   Sectoral net output as a percentage of GDP at factor cost (averages for six sub-periods)

	1960-64	1965-69	1970-74	1975-79	1980-84	1985-90
Manufacturing	16.6	20.8	24.3	32.7	30.5	27.9
Construction and quarrying	4.4	4.4	4.2	2.9	5.0	4.1
Market services	33.7	33.3	30.4	30.9	34.3	34.4
Agriculture and fishing	7.3	7.2	7.2	5.3	4.2	4.1
Public sector[a]	17.9	19.8	21.8	19.8	18.7	21.8
British forces	15.1	9.5	6.3	2.3	–	–
Property income	5.0	5.0	5.8	6.1	7.4	7.8
Total	100.0	100.0	100.0	100.0	100.0	100.0

[a] This covers public administration and public enterprise, but excludes companies with government majority shareholding.
Source: *National Accounts of the Maltese Islands*.

contributed an average of 4.2%, market services an average of 32.7% and the public sector an average of 19.5% of GDP. The share of agriculture and fishing averaged 6.1% but tended to decrease during the period under consideration.

Table 3 shows the changing pattern of the distribution of employment in different sectors. In general, with the notable exception of the public sector, the changes in employment shares reflected the changes in the shares of GDP. For example, the increasing share of the manufacturing output has increased employment in manufacturing from just over 18% of the gainfully occupied in the first half of the sixties to about 30% in the eighties.

The changing structure of the Maltese gainful employment is shown graphically in Figure 3, where the sectoral distribution in the early sixties is compared with that of the second half of the eighties. The growing share of the manufacturing sector and the disappearance of the British military sector in the eighties are clearly shown in the pie-charts.

As stated earlier, there was also a structural change within the manufacturing sector itself. Table 4 gives a breakdown of the percentage share of employment in some manufacturing sub-sectors. It can be seen that the textile and clothing sub-sector has increased its share of the manufacturing sector from 13% in the first half of the sixties to 30% during the second half of the seventies, and by the end of the eighties its share went down again to 25%. The machinery industries expanded their relative shares between 1960 and 1990. On the other hand, the transport equipment industry has decreased its share of the manufacturing sector from 39% in the first half of the sixties to 22% in the second half of the eighties.

Another interesting tendency, shown in Table 3, is that female employment as a percentage of total employment increased from just over 18% in the first half of the sixties to about 26% in the second half of the seventies. The percentage has decreased slightly during the eighties. In recent years, the percentage of female employment has again started to increase reaching 26% in 1992.

Female employment tended to increase at a faster rate than male employment between 1960 and 1980. The bulk of the increases in female employment occurred in the manufacturing sector, mostly in the clothing, textile, and electrical machinery industries.

V.   Changes in Total Final Expenditure

Total final expenditure is composed of consumption, investment, exports and government current expenditure. These represent all the possible expenditures on goods and services sold by domestic firms. These expenditures have an import content and a domestic value-added content. The latter is called the gross domestic product.

Aggregate expenditures in Malta have also tended to follow a cyclical pattern of change (see Figure 4). In general, these tended to increase rapidly during the second half of the sixties, of the seventies, and of the eighties and to increase slowly or even decline during the other sub-periods.

The type of expenditure that fluctuated most was that related to investment. Exports of goods and services also tended to fluctuate widely around the thirty year trend, with rapid growth rates during the second half of the sixties, seventies and eighties. Exports have tended to decrease during the early sixties and the first half of the eighties.

Imports, measured in real terms, tended to grow at a slower rate than total final expenditure during the seventies and the eighties. This means that the real import content of total final expenditure tended to decrease and the real domestic value added content tended to increase during these two decades. This tendency, shown in Figure 4, has been brought about by the policy of

Table 3 Sectoral employment as a percentage of total employment (averages for six sub-periods)

	1960-64	1965-69	1970-74	1975-79	1980-84	1985-90
Manufacturing	18.2	21.3	27.0	31.3	31.8	29.0
Construction and quarrying	8.6	10.7	8.0	4.2	5.8	5.5
Market services	28.4	29.8	30.4	30.8	32.7	33.3
Agriculture and fishing[a]	8.9	7.3	6.3	6.4	5.2	3.0
Public sector[b]	19.6	20.6	22.9	25.2	24.6	29.3
British forces	16.2	10.3	5.3	2.1	–	–
Total	100.0	100.0	100.0	100.0	100.0	100.0
Male	81.1	79.6	76.0	74.0	75.0	75.0
Female	18.2	20.4	24.0	26.0	25.0	25.0

[a] This covers public administration and public enterprise, but not companies with government majority shareholding.
[b] Agricultural employment statistics have been revised in the 1985-89 sub-period and are not therefore strictly comparable with previous sub-periods.
Source: Annual Abstract of Statistics.

Table 4 The composition of employment in the manufacturing sector (average percentage shares for six sub-periods)

	1960-64	1965-69	1970-74	1975-79	1980-84	1985-90
FBT	20.3	16.9	13.3	11.1	11.3	12.1
TC	13.1	18.0	22.0	29.9	28.6	25.3
MME	5.6	6.9	11.3	11.3	11.6	14.1
TE	39.2	32.9	24.2	19.9	20.8	21.5
OTHER	21.9	25.3	29.3	27.7	27.7	27.0
TOTAL	100.0	100.0	100.0	100.0	100.0	100.0

Legend: FBT: Food, Beverages and Tobacco
TC: Textiles and Wearing Apparel
MME: Metals, Machinery and Electrical Machinery
TE: Transport Equipment (mostly ship repair/building)

Note: Figures are approximate.

Source: *Annual Abstract of Statistics.*

import substitution and import controls which have been resorted to with increased intensity since the seventies and up to 1987. The tendency was reversed somewhat after 1987, when a trade liberalisation policy was ushered in.

Measured at current prices, however, the Imports/Total Final Expenditure ratio did not exhibit a marked tendency to decrease or increase, fluctuating around 50%.

VI. The Maltese Balance of Payments

The balance of payments gives a picture of a country's transactions with the rest of the world. It is usually divided into three parts, namely the Current Account, the Capital Account and Official Financing Account.

Table 5 gives a summary of the main entries in the balance of payments during the 1960-1990 period. The data is presented as five-yearly annual averages, with the exception of the last sub-period which is a six-year average.

Briefly, Malta has always experienced a relatively large deficit in its merchandise trade, as shown in the table, and a positive but smaller surplus in its services trade. Thus the balance between exports and imports of goods and services taken together (the resource balance) was negative during all sub-periods.

There has been major changes in the composition of Maltese exports of goods and services between 1960 and 1990, as shown in Table 6. It can be seen that during the sixties, the bulk of exports were associated with "other services" an item which mainly represented British military expenditure in Malta. During the seventies, this type of exported service declined in importance, whereas exports associated with tourism and with clothing and textiles increased their percentage share.

During the eighties, dependence on British military expenditure was phased out. The percentage share of exports

associated with tourism continued to grow, whereas exports of clothing and textiles experienced a decline. There was a marked increase in the share of exports associate with electrical machinery, mainly attributable to one company which produced electronic components.

Another important change associated with trade relates to its direction. Table 7 shows the direction of merchandise trade between 1960 and 1990. The table shows that the UK was Malta's main trading partner during the sixties with Italy taking second place. During the seventies, Germany emerged as Malta's most important export market, with the UK and Italy remaining Malta's most important sources of imports. Germany retained its dominant position as Malta's most important client during the eighties, with Italy taking second place and the U.K. third. Italy was also the most important source of imports during the same period.

The deficits which Malta experienced on trade in goods and services tended to be partially offset by investment income from abroad, the net inflows from which are shown in Table 5.

Another source of foreign exchange on Current Account are transfers which consist of remittances and pensions to households and foreign exchange grants to the Maltese government. Considering all these inflows and outflows of foreign exchange, the overall balance on Current Account was generally a surplus, with the exception of the last sub-period, as shown in Table 5. A closer look at the balance of payments statistics would indicate that, in many years, the Current Account surpluses would not have been possible without official transfers (grants).

With the exception of the first and the last sub-period, the Capital Account has tended to be in surplus, indicating that, on average, capital inflows from abroad offset capital outflows to foreign countries. The capital account includes borrowing from abroad by the government. Of interest in this regard is that Malta's external debt as

Table 5 Statistics pertaining to the Maltese balance of payments (annual averages for six sub-periods, Lm million)

	1960-64	1965-69	1970-74	1975-79	1980-84	1985-90
Trade:						
Merchandise trade	-22.9	-27.1	-42.9	-61.4	-116.5	-144.0
Services trade	16.6	13.3	15.9	37.8	62.2	76.2
Merchandise & services	-6.3	-13.8	-27.0	-23.6	-54.3	-68.8
Net investment income	3.7	5.2	8.6	17.1	41.4	36.1
Transfers	4.2	11.2	24.6	30.6	28.8	33.8
Current account balance	1.6	2.6	6.1	24.1	16.0	1.2
Capital account balance[a]	-1.9	3.7	5.8	11.0	17.7	-15.1

[a] Includes net errors and omissions.
Source: *National Accounts of the Maltese Islands*.

Table 6 The composition of exports of goods and services (average percentage shares for six sub-periods)

	1960-64	1965-69	1970-74	1975-79	1980-84	1985-90
Merchandise:						
Primary Products	3.5	3.8	1.3	1.0	0.7	0.6
Food, Beverage, Tobacco	1.0	2.0	2.8	3.4	2.6	1.3
Clothing/Textiles	3.4	10.7	19.3	25.1	21.2	12.0
Electrical machinery	–	–	1.3	1.6	2.6	18.0
Ship repair/building	3.5	7.0	5.1	3.2	3.0	2.9
Other manufacturers	1.5	2.5	7.9	15.8	18.8	15.8
Re-exports	9.0	7.9	8.3	6.6	5.4	4.2
Services:						
Tourist expenditure	4.4	14.4	20.1	22.6	24.0	26.9
Transportation	11.6	15.6	16.1	12.1	14.6	12.7
Other services	62.1	36.1	17.8	8.6	7.1	5.6
Total	100.0	100.0	100.0	100.0	100.0	100.0

Note: Figures are approximate due to the fact that the classification of exports has been changed during the period under consideration.
Source: *Trade Statistics*.

a proportion of GNP is rather low by international standards. It should be noted also that the outflows of foreign exchange on Capital Account do not include those by the monetary authorities.

If we add the net surpluses (or deficits) of foreign exchange in the Current Account to the net surplus (or deficits) in the Capital Account we obtain the total net surplus (or deficit) in the balance of payments above "the line". This residual is computed after taking into account all foreign exchange transactions, with the exception of Official Financing.

During any one year, this residual broadly approximates the net additions (or reductions) of foreign exchange holdings of the monetary authorities. These official external reserves have tended to grow rapidly during the seventies and early eighties, as a result of the surpluses shown in Table 5.

As at 1990, the Maltese monetary authorities still held large amount of reserves invested abroad, in spite of the recent deficits in the balance of payments. The amount of Maltese official external reserves is very high by international standard, when measured in terms of monthly imports. It is much higher than the amount requested by law to serve as backing for the domestic currency.

VII. Major Problems of the Maltese Economy

Although the Maltese economy has grown at a relatively fast rate since 1960, it faced, and still faces, a number of weaknesses. These will be briefly discussed in this section. (More detailed analyses of problems facing the Maltese economy are given in Briguglio, 1988; Delia, 1988 and Scicluna, 1992).

Small Size

An obvious feature of the Maltese economy is its very small size in terms of its total GNP, land area and population.

Smallness does not necessarily render a country underdeveloped, since there are small countries, such as Luxemburg, Iceland and Cyprus that have done rather well in terms of economic development. However there are a number of drawbacks associated with small size.

Malta's small land area, coupled with its small domestic market, renders it difficult to reap the benefits of large scale production in domestically oriented industries. This tends to push up unit costs and inhibits the use of modern technology. For this reason, a large proportion of Malta's output has to be exported, giving rise to a very high degree of dependence on conditions in the rest of the world. Small size also reduces the possibilities for diversification in the economy.

Imports

Like other small countries, Malta depends to a large extent on imports, due to the lack of natural resources and limited variety of domestic production.

Malta's dependence on imports has, during the seventies and the first half of the eighties, prompted the government to embark on a policy of strict import controls. This policy brought about a marked reduction in the import content of total final expenditure, but it had in many instances encouraged inefficient production and markedly reduced consumer choice.

There is an ongoing debate in Malta as to whether or not it is to Malta's benefit to abolish import controls. Since 1987, the government has adopted a more liberal trade policy, giving rise to more efficient forms of production and a wider variety of consumer products, but at the same time this aggravated Malta's balance of trade problems, as shown in Table 5. It has also resulted in a loss of jobs in domestically oriented industries which lost protection.

Unfortunately, a sizeable proportion of the manufacturing sector still depends on import controls for survival. A considerable amount of employment would

242

disappear if import controls are totally dismantled. This question is of utmost importance at present because Malta is aspiring to join the European Community as full member and this would necessitate the eventual complete liberalization of imports from the Community.

However, it appears that a more liberalized economic environment has, on balance, generated enough employment to absorb the loss of jobs in domestically oriented industries which were not able to withstand competition.

Exports

To finance a large import bill, Malta has to export a large proportion of its output. Moreover, given that its domestic market is very small and that certain types of production are only feasible on a relatively large scale, it follows that Malta has to rely on exports. About 45% of Malta's total final expenditure consists of exports, which is a very high percentage by international standards.

An area of concern is that Malta's range of exports is too narrow, with a very high percentage consisting of clothing and electronic components. In this regard, the advantages of specialization arising from concentration on a few products has to be weighed against the disadvantages of having too many eggs in one basket.

A related problem is that a very large percentage of exported services are connected with tourism. Tourism has had an important beneficial effect on the Maltese economy, in terms of foreign exchange earnings and employment. However, past experience has shown that excessive reliance on this type of service presents a danger in that the tourist industry tends to be volatile.

As regards exports in general, the major recurrent problem is the need to maintain competitiveness vis-a-vis foreign countries. This touches upon the question of exchange rate policy (see Scicluna, 1984; Briguglio, 1989 and Delia, 1991). The

Maltese Monetary Authorities have during the first half of the eighties adopted a policy of tying the Maltese lira to relatively strong foreign currencies. This policy has had beneficial as well as adverse effects on Malta's economy. It has helped to contain the disadvantages associated with imported inflation. But at the same time, it has adversely affected export competitiveness.

The international value of the Maltese lira is now based on a trade weighted basket of exchange rates, with the objective of attaining exchange rate stability with respect to the currencies of Malta's trade partners.

Terms of Trade

Another problem, which Malta used to face during the seventies, and which has emerged again during the late eighties (and will probably persist during the coming years) is a deterioration in the terms of trade. This means that the prices of Maltese imports rise faster than the prices of Maltese exports, so that every year the country has to export more to pay for the same quantity of imports.

A look at the Maltese balance of payments statistics would indicate that between 1970 and 1983 Malta has had a consistent deficit in its resource balance (see Table 5). This deficit would have been turned into a surplus in most years had the prices of imports not risen faster than the prices of exports, everything else remaining constant.

One possible reason for the deteriorating terms of trade is that Malta tends to export goods and services in competition with developing countries, and the prices of exports are therefore influenced to a high degree by this tendency. On the other hand, a large proportion of Malta's imports originate from developed countries, and the prices of imports therefore reflect this reality (see Briguglio, 1993).

The Manufacturing Sector

The Maltese manufacturing sector faces

Table 7   The direction of trade (average percentage shares for six sub-periods)

	1960-64	1965-69	1970-74	1975-79	1980-84	1985-90
Exports:						
UK	32.4	32.3	33.1	19.9	17.8	12.1
Italy	12.3	9.4	9.1	4.5	8.4	21.8
Germany	0.7	3.3	10.1	29.9	30.5	26.2
Belgium	0.9	2.2	7.1	4.5	5.2	2.2
Libya	9.5	6.7	4.5	9.3	6.1	6.0
USA	0.9	5.9	3.3	1.5	3.3	6.7
Others	43.3	40.2	32.8	30.3	28.7	25.0
Total	100.0	100.0	100.0	100.0	100.0	100.0
Imports:						
UK	39.5	41.0	30.9	24.5	18.4	16.8
Italy	10.1	14.8	17.1	19.4	27.4	26.0
Germany	4.2	3.8	7.0	11.9	15.3	15.2
France	5.1	3.5	4.5	5.1	3.6	5.2
N'Lands	5.3	4.0	4.9	4.2	3.2	3.0
USA	2.0	3.1	5.4	7.5	7.6	6.1
Others	33.8	29.8	30.2	27.4	24.4	27.8
Total	100.0	100.0	100.0	100.0	100.0	100.0

Source: *Annual Abstract of Statistics.*

two distinct problems. The first is that many firms in the export oriented sub-sector, so far, enjoy a competitive edge in terms of wage rates, but still depend to a large extent on relatively old technology. The wage advantage is continually being eroded by new competitors from the developing world. In all probability, competing on the bases of cheap labour will no longer be an option for Maltese exporters within a few years, given that wage rates in Malta are rising much faster than those in many of its competitor countries. The alternatives include competing on the basis of technological advance, or specialising in up-market products and in "niche" markets. The objective would be to avoid dependence on low wage rates for attaining competitiveness.

The second problem is that the domestically oriented sub-sector is still heavily protected, despite the process of liberalisation that was ushered in after 1987. This situation cannot continue to exist if Malta joins the EC (see Coopers and Lybrind, 1991). It can be anticipated that the gradual liberalization of imports, in preparation for Malta's EC membership, would result in the closing down of a number of firms, which in 1991 employed around 7% of the Maltese gainfully employed population.

Although the two problems just described are distinct, they have a common solution, namely the attainment of competitiveness, through the upgrading of the manufacturing capital stock to allow for technologically advanced production processes and the seeking of "niche" markets, which can be serviced without resort to large scale production.

Monetary Aspects

On the monetary side, the Maltese economy is characterised by (a) a very high proportion of currency in circulation to GNP, (b) a very high propensity to invest funds abroad and (c) an excessively regulated market (see Galdes, 1990 and Azzopardi, 1991).

In Malta, currency in circulation, in relation to the formal GNP is extremely high, amounting to around 50%. This is probably due to the tendency to settle certain transactions in cash to evade taxation. The high Currency/GNP ratio suggests that the underground economy is relatively large in Malta. The most important factors giving rise to this tendency are (i) tax rates in Malta rise very progressively, even though the maximum rate is 35% and (ii) the rate of interest on fixed deposits, which is related to the opportunity cost of holding currency, is relatively low, and regulated directly by the monetary authorities.

In Malta the personal sector, as well as the banking sector, tend to have a very high propensity to invest funds abroad. in spite of very rigid exchange controls. One reason for this would be that interest rates in Malta are relatively low. This propensity will most probably increase if foreign exchange control is relaxed. It is ironical that while Malta craves for investment, the Maltese people and their financial institutions look elsewhere to invest their money.

It appears also that Maltese financial institutions and Maltese households tend to consider investment in Malta as too risky compared to the cushy deposits in foreign banks, which carries with it a low risk and a relatively high interest yield. In this regard, the basic problem in Malta would not seem to be lack of funds, but the utilization of funds for Malta's own economic development. Fortunately, recent institutional developments, in particular the establishment of the Stock Exchange, appear to be having a positive effect in channelling funds for investment in Malta.

The Labour Market

There are also a number of problems directly associated with the labour market. The major problem in this respect appears to be that of skill mismatches, causing a considerable amount of frictional unemployment. One solution is of course training and retraining schemes to develop and upgrade skills in line with the development needs of the Maltese economy.

Another problem is that a large proportion of the gainfully occupied (around 30% in government departments and corporations and around 40% in companies with government majority shareholding are included) are employed in the public sector. This sector tends to be characterised by low labour productivity in the lower grades, and a shortage of efficient and motivated personnel in the higher grades. The relatively large size of this sector in the Maltese economy is probably giving rise to inefficient use of resources, and creating an artificial labour shortage in the private sector. Many economic analysts are of the opinion that the Maltese public sector needs trimming down.

Integrating with Europe

The Maltese economy is to a very large extent tied to the European Community. The bulk of its merchandise and services exports are directed towards the EC. The EC is also the major supplier of Malta's imports.

The association agreement with the EC in the early seventies, had as one of its aims the eventual establishment of a Customs Union between Malta and the EC, which involved the gradual removal of Maltese import controls and the opening up of Malta's market to European products. This objective was however abandoned by the Labour government. As a result, during the seventies and up to 1987, Malta remained a very heavily protected economy, with a non-tariff access to the European markets for most of its merchandise exports, while at the same time retaining the option of imposing import controls on goods originating from Europe.

As stated, a process of gradual liberalisation began in 1987, following a change in government. In July 1990, the Nationalist government lodged an application for Malta to join the European Community.

At present there are two major problems associated with this application. The first is that the process of adjustment involves a number of changes which are not easy to implement (Redmond, 1993). The major problems are those associated with Malta's small size, its regulated financial sector, and the proliferation of restrictive practices working against competition.

The second problem is that it is not certain that the Maltese economy would be better off if Malta joins the EC. The arguments for and against joining the EC have been aired in a number of publications in Malta (see for example EC Directorate, 1990; Pomfret, 1989; Frendo and Bonnici, 1990; and Malta Labour Party, 1990). The most important issue in this regard relates to the trade-off between protection and efficiency.

Those in favour of EC membership stress the need for competition and efficiency, and those against emphasise the inability of small enterprises to survive with the dismantling of import controls.

However, as indicated in many other parts of this paper, recent developments in Malta have shown that under a more liberalized structure, growth in the non-protected sectors of the economy – particularly services – has more than made up for the losses in the protected

sector, the end result being historically high rates of employment, low rates of unemployment and relatively high growth rates in GDP, during the past five years.

While it may be true that the existance of inefficient enterprises may be prolonged via protectionism, it is also true that the well-being of the economy cannot be fostered in a protective set-up. On a macroeconomic level, there is overwhelming evidence to suggest that countries which have embarked on a policy of protection, tend to end up using their resources inefficiently, and therefore have a much lower standard of living than other countries who utilise their resources efficiently to meet international competitiveness. This is especially so for small countries that have to rely on exports for survival.

VIII.   Conclusion

This paper has given a brief overview of the patterns of change in the Maltese economy during the past thirty years and described some weaknesses inherent in the economy at present.

During the period under consideration, incomes have arisen substantially in real terms, and the Maltese population has enjoyed marked improvements in the standard of living. The economy has been restructured from one depending on expenditures related to British defence needs to one based on marketed exports of goods and services. It is now being again restructured to meet the challenge that will emerge from full EC membership.

The weaknesses in the Maltese economy described in this paper are formidable, but not insurmountable. Perhaps the most difficult ones to overcome are those associated with the dismantling of import and exchange controls. Suitable policies are called for to improve import and export competitiveness and to reverse the tendency of looking abroad for a good return on investment.

Statistical Appendix

Employment and Population in Malta
December 1992

	Total	Males	Females
Labour Force	135,157	101,470	35,687
Employment	131,609	96,892	34,627
Unemployment	5,548	4,488	1,060
Population	362,900	179,400	183,500

Number of persons employed by sector

	Number	Percentage
Private direct production	*37,952*	*28.8%*
of which:		
Agriculture and fishing	3,210	2.4%
Quarrying and construction	5,436	4.1%
Manufacturing	29,306	22.3%
Private market services	*37,485*	*28.5%*
of which:		
Wholesale and retail	13,814	10.5%
Insurance and real estate	1,454	1.1%
Transport and communications	5,780	4.4%
Hotel and catering	7,683	5.8%
Others	8,754	6.7%
Public sector	*51,276*	*39.0%*
of which:		
Government departments	30,452	23.1%
Armed forces and airport	1,691	1.3%
Public corporations	9,325	7.1%
Govt/MDC controlled companies[a]	9,808	7.5%
Temporary employment[b]	4,896	3.7%
Total Employment	131,609	100%

Source: *Economic Trends*.

[a] Employment in government controlled companies includes direct production employment (3,217 persons) and market service employment (6,591 persons). In some official publications, such employment is listed with the private sector.

[b] Temporary employment includes apprentices and trainees, pupil and student workers.

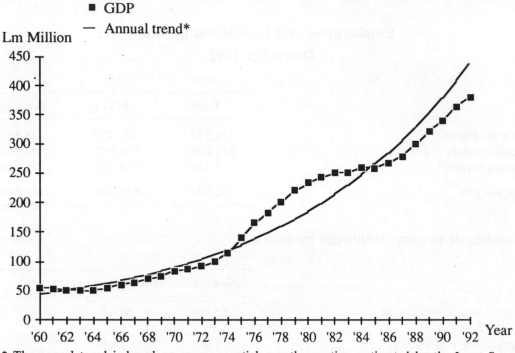

Figure 1. The Gross Domestic Product at 1973 Prices compared to a 33 Year Trend.

* The annual trend is based on an exponential growth equation, estimated by the Least Squares Method.

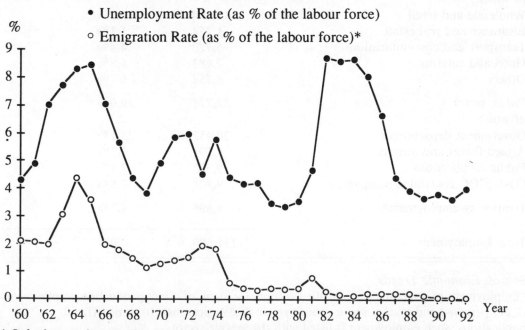

Figure 2. The Rate of Unemployment and of Emigration.

* Only those emigrants who were members of the labour force (i.e. were employed or registering for employment) before they emigrated are considered here.

248

Figure 3. Sectoral Composition of Gainful Employment

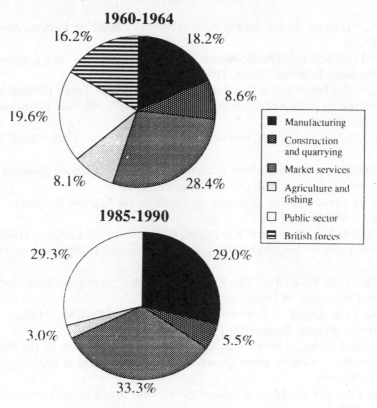

Figure 4. The Import Content and the GDP Content of Total Final Expenditure.

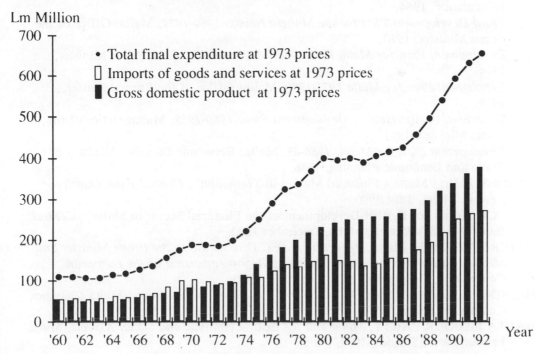

References

AZZOPARDI, P., "Interest Rate Liberalisation in Malta", *Bank of Valletta Review*, Autumn 1991.

BALOGH, T., and SEERS, D., *The Economic Problems of Malta – An Interim Report*, Malta, Government Printing Office, 1955.

BRIGUGLIO, L., "The Impact of a Devaluation on the Maltese Trade Balance with Special Reference to Price and Income Reversal Effects", *Applied Economics*, 1989, Vol. 21, pp.325-338.

The Maltese Economy – A Macroeconomic Analysis, Malta, 1988, David Moore Publishing.

"Tourism Multipliers in the Maltese Economy" in *Perspectives on Tourism Policy*, P. Johnson and B. Thomas (Eds), U.K., Mansell, 1992.

"The Terms of Trade and the Direction of Trade in the Maltese Economy", *World Development*, 1993, Vol. 21, No.2.

BRITISH GOVERNMENT, *Defence White Paper*, Command 124, London: HMSO, 1957.

The Next Five Years – Statement on Defence, Command 1639, London: HMSO, 1963.

COOPERS & LYBRAND EUROPE, *The Effect of EC Membership on Industry in Malta*, Malta Federation of Industry, 1991.

DELIA, E.P., *The Task Ahead – Dimensions, Ideologies and Policies*, Malta Confederation of Private Enterprise, 1988.

"Malta's Trade Account. Labour Cost and the Rate of Exchange of the Maltese Lira: An Overview", *Central Bank Quarterly Review*, September 1992.

DEVELOPMENT PLANS

Development Plan for the Maltese Islands 1959-1964, Malta: Department of Information, 1959.

Development Plan for the Maltese Islands 1964-1969, Malta: Department of Information, 1964.

Third Development Plan for the Maltese Islands 1969-1974, Malta: Office of the Prime Minister, 1970.

Development Plan for Malta 1973-1980, Malta: Office of the Prime Minister, 1974.

Supplement Plan for Malta 1973-1980, Malta: Office of the Prime Minister, 1977.

Guidelines for Progress – *Development Plant 1980-1985*, Malta: Office of the Prime Minister, 1981.

Development Plan for Malta, 1986-88, Malta: Economic Division, Ministry of Trade and Economic Planning, 1986.

GALDES, A.P., "Malta's Financial Market in Transition", *Central Bank Quarterly Review*, Malta, June 1990.

"Conditions for Further Development of the Financial Sector in Malta", *Central Bank Quarterly Review*, Malta, December 1990.

EC DIRECTORATE, Malta, *Report by the EC Directorate to the Prime Minister and Minister of Foreign Affairs regarding Malta's membership of the European Community*, Department of Information, 1990.

FRENDO, M. and BONNICI, J., *Malta in the European Community*, Malta Chamber of Commerce, Malta, 1989.

MALTA LABOUR PARTY, *Malta and the EEC: Economic and Social Aspects*, Malta Labour Party, Senglea, 1990.

MALTESE GOVERNMENT, *Joint Mission for Malta Report*, Malta, Department of
    Information, 1967.
    *Agreement between the Government of Malta and the Government of the United
    Kingdom*, Malta, Department of Information, 1972.
METWALLY, M.M., *Structure and Performance of the Maltese Economy*, Aquilina,
    Malta, 1977.
POMFRET, R., *The European Community: Three Issues*, European Documentation
    Centre and the Chamber of Commerce, Malta, 1989.
ROBENS REPORT (See Maltese Government, 1967).
REDMOND, J., "The European Community and the Mediterranean Applicants: Malta,
    Cyprus and Turkey", *Bank of Valletta Review*, No.7, Spring 1993.
SCHUSTER REPORT (See British Government, 1950).
SCICLUNA, E.S., *Export Competitiveness and the Maltese Lira*, Malta Federation of
    Industry, 1984.
    The Outlook for the Maltese Economy in 1992 and Beyond: A Sober Assessment,
    Malta Federation of Industry, 1992.
STOLPER, W.F., HELLBERG, R.E.R. and CALLENDER, S.O., *Economic Adaptation
    and Development in Malta*, United Nations Commission for Technical Assistance,
    Department of Economic and Social Affairs, 1964.
TARLING, R.J. and RHODES, J., *A Study of the Economic Impact of Tourism on the
    Economy of Malta*, Malta, P.A. Cambridge Consultants for the Ministry of
    Tourism, 1989.

Additional Literature on the Maltese Economy

The most important sources of statistical data are the *National Accounts of the
Maltese Islands*, and *Annual Abstract of Statistics*, both published by the Central Office
of Statistics, Malta. The Economic Planning Division of the Office of the Prime Minister
also publishes a quarterly *Economic Survey*.

A number of journals on topical issues are published in Malta. Two publications of
this type are *The Central Bank Quarterly Review* and *Bank of Valletta Review*. The
former is a good source of monetary data and contains articles on monetary issues and
the latter contains articles on a wide variety of topics related to the Maltese Economy.

Some Maltese business and professional bodies also publish material with
information about the Maltese Economy on a macroeconomic level. Two publications of
this nature are the *Industry Trends Survey*, published by the Malta Federation of
Industry and *The Commercial Courrier* published by the Malta Chamber of Commerce.

Emigration

Lawrence E. Attard

On June 9, 1798, Napoleon Bonaparte appeared on Malta's horizon, ostensibly to ask for water for his fleet, and eventually received from Grand Master Ferdinand von Hompesch the capitulation of the island. Napoleon brought to an end an era that had endured for 268 years. In spite of the ease with which the French took Malta from the Knights of Saint John, their presence on the island lasted only two years and they spent much of that time behind the massive fortifications till General Vaubois capitulated to the British and to the Maltese on September 5, 1800.

The defeat of the French heralded the beginning of Malta's incorporation within the British Empire. On May 30, 1814, Europe's leaders met at Paris to formally sign a treaty. The Treaty of Paris aimed at bringing peace to a continent shattered by long years of wars. According to article seven of the Treaty, Malta was to pass formally under the sovereignty of the British monarch.

When Napoleon left Malta he took with him some 2,000 Maltese who had enlisted with the French and formed the so-called *Légion Maltaise*. Many of these recruits were to perish because of Napoleon's · misadventures in Egypt, but R. Vadalà considers these men as the first arrivals of what was later to become one of the most populous Maltese colonies in North Africa.

Marc Donato believes that Maltese emigrants started leaving their islands as a consequence of 1798. He refers to the presence of Maltese immigrants in Algeria before 1830, the year when the French took over that country. Donato mentions a certain Eugène Fénech who was in Malta at the time of Napoleon's invasion. Fénech went to Paris to study medicine and his degree helped him in no small way to make his name known in Malta. In later years Eugène and his brother Antoine left for Algeria. Eugène practised as a doctor in Bone while Antoine became mayor of the same town and a representative of France in Philippeville.

The Imperial Bond

The transition from a self-contained island ruled for many years by the paternalistic Knights of St John to a colonial status within the vast British Empire was bound to produce radical changes in the life of the Maltese. It is for this reason that 1798 is considered as a milestone in Maltese history. That year marked the end of a Medieval system and paved the way for Great Britain to obtain a valuable base in the middle of the Mediterranean. The end of the rule of the Knights and the hurried departure of the French caused Malta to abandon centuries-old ties with Europe. What was previously an intensely Catholic state ruled by a Religious Order whose roots were Latin and aristocratic, became now a small colony and a strategic naval base. Great Britain, Anglo-Saxon, Protestant, and very distant, became the Mother Country of the Maltese.

The French interlude and the subsequent British connection put Malta's Mediterranean role in a secondary position of importance. Henceforth Malta's place was in the Empire and Imperial representatives in Malta made it clear that to their way of thinking Malta was a fortress with excellent harbours from which London intended to keep watch on what was going on in the Mediterranean. That Malta was home to the Maltese was secondary to Imperial considerations. The men of Malta were employed to keep the military and naval facilities in good shape ready to defend the primacy of the British fleet in the Mediterranean. Those not involved in the maintenance of the Fortress were advised to seek employment overseas. Emigration was the only feasible solution for those unemployed who had no place within the defence system of the island.

The first years of British rule were relatively prosperous. Maltese harbours were busy owing to the international situation. In 1812 a Commission of Inquiry had noted that the Maltese had done well for themselves from 1800 till the end of the Napoleonic wars in 1815. The presence of the British fleet in the Mediterranean had helped to reduce the piratical activity of the Barbary corsairs and Maltese entrepreneurs began to approach the shores of North Africa as traders when previously most Maltese had entered those areas as slaves captured by pirates. Agile speronaras owned by the Maltese were plying the narrow waters between Sicily, Malta and the neighbouring Arab lands. Maltese traders soon established contacts with the Arabs and with other Europeans in Algeria, Tunisia, Tripolitania and Egypt. The emigrant followed the trader and small colonies of Maltese came into being along the southern shores of the Mediterranean.

Algeria and Tunisia

Maltese haphazard emigration to the western regions of North Africa proceeded rapidly after 1830 when the French under King Louis Philippe conquered Algeria thus opening that part of the Ottoman Empire to thousands of French and other European colons. Among the Europeans the Maltese were at one time the fourth largest group after the French, the Spaniards and the Italians.

Algeria was for many years the most important country for emigrants from Malta. Indeed, by the 1850's more than half of those who had emigrated opted for that country. Miège, the French Consul in Malta, encouraged this movement because the French had difficulty in finding enough settlers from France itself and he considered the Maltese as safe foreigners because they had no political ambitions. Another prominent Frenchman who wished to see more Maltese emigrate to French North Africa was Cardinal Charles Lavigerie, who was in Malta in 1882. He spoke of the Maltese workers in Algeria as hard working people loyal to France and to the Catholic Church.

By 1847 the number of Maltese living in Algeria was estimated to be slightly over 4,000. In 1903 there were probably some 15,000 persons in Algeria who claimed Maltese ancestry, most of them living in Algiers, Philippeville and Bone. In a village near Bone called Allelik, a Gozitan immigrant family had a son on Christmas Day 1891. They named him Laurent. When he grew up Laurent Ropa became a well-known novelist whose works reflected the life of Maltese immigrants in Algeria.

On the east side of Algeria lay the territory now known as Tunisia which eventually was also drawn into the French sphere of influence. Since the shores of Tunisia are so close to Malta, settlements in that country began to take shape in various localities such as Tunis, Susa, Monastir, Mehdia and on the island of Jerba. By 1842 the Maltese population in Tunisia rose to 3,000 and in less than twenty years that number increased to 7,000. Paul Cambon, an influential French politician, urged the government in Paris to encourage more Maltese to settle in Tunisia because the Italians there were very numerous and Italy itself had schemes to take over the territory. Cambon referred to the Maltese in Tunisia as the "Anglo-Maltese Element" and he felt that the Maltese in North Africa owed their allegiance to France. In 1882 Cambon was administering Tunisia for France and he wrote to the French consul in Malta to encourage more migrants from Malta to settle in Tunisia.

Close to Tunisia lay the two provinces of Cyrenaica and Tripolitania. For centuries they languished under inefficient Turkish rule, but in 1911 the Italians occupied them and created a zone which they called Libia Italiana. As was the case with Algeria and Tunisia, Maltese traders had long-established links with the ports of Tripoli and Benghazi. They carried goods which Saharan traders had brought to the coast. There had been schemes for Maltese colonisation of Cyrenaica but the Italian occupation brought them to nothing. Unlike the French, the Italians did not like the presence of the Maltese because they feared British influence. They also had enough migrants of their own from the Mezzogiorno to meet their needs in Africa. It is probable that the number of Maltese in Tripolitania and Cyrenaica never rose to more than 3,000.

The Maltese in Egypt

When the Treaty of Paris had been signed there were about 1,000 Maltese in Egypt. These included the survivors of those who had enlisted in Napoleon's Légion Maltaise. By 1882 Egypt was under the effective rule of the British who were to expand their sphere of influence over the Dark Continent from Cairo to the Cape. Politicians like Benjamin Disraeli had grasped the strategic value of Egypt and the Sudan especially when work on the digging of the Canal was finalised in 1869. By that time the Maltese population in Egypt had risen to 7,000. This number kept on increasing until just before the Second World War there were about 20,000 people of Maltese origin, mostly in Alexandria, Cairo, Suez, Rosetta and Port Said.

In the later years of the last century the Maltese in Egypt issued publications like "Melita" and "Eġittu". In 1909 George J.

Vella edited a weekly newspaper under the name of "Li Standard tal-Maltin"; it ceased publication in 1912 but was resumed in 1919 and survived till 1924. Toni Said founded an association for the preservation and diffusion of the Maltese langauge. He tried to achieve this by publishing a literary review called "Il-Qari Malti", which appeared at intervals and survived till 1946.

There were other Maltese publications in Egypt supported by various societies. As the Maltese communities prospered, the children of the original immigrants received a sound education and many of them became accomplished linguists fluent in Maltese, English, French and Arabic. This flair for languages opened for them the doors of different careers. Maltese were to be found in consular offices and European companies operating in the Canal Zone found the polyglot Maltese very useful.

By 1926 Egypt had practically achieved independence from Great Britain though British forces were still stationed there. The Maltese, like other aliens living in that land, felt secure as long as there were British soldiers guaranteeing their lives and property. This dependence on external forces made many immigrants nervous and there were some who soon after the end of the Second World War started packing their belongings to seek a new home somewhere else, even if Egypt was the only country in the world that they knew. When the fateful year 1956 arrived the Maltese joined the mass departure of foreigners and sought refuge in Great Britain and in Australia where they began to rebuild their lives again.

Corfù, Constantinople and Smyrna

The Ionian islands became a British protectorate in 1815. The British encouraged Maltese immigration into the islands because they needed workers and also to strengthen their position in an area which felt distinctly Greek. Sir Thomas

Maitland wanted migrants from Malta because he knew that they would be loyal supporters of the British connection.

In 1901 there were 1,000 people in Corfù who claimed Maltese ancestry. In Cephalonia the Maltese were just over 200. In 1864 the islands were returned to Greece and Maltese interest in the Ionian islands waned. Some of the Maltese decided to re-emigrate; this time their destination was Great Britain. They went to Cardiff where their descendants are still living. But the original Maltese colony in Corfù did not vanish. Two villages still bear names with a Maltese connotation: Maltezika (Malta) and Cozzella (Gozo). In the latter the Franciscan Sisters of Malta opened a convent and a school in 1907.

Constantinople and Smyrna also attracted a number of Maltese migrants. During the middle years of the nineteenth century the Sublime Porte had opened the capital to European traders because the Sultan needed Western cash and expertise. The Maltese were attracted by the prospects of work and trade in the Empire. In Constantinople they congregated in the district of Galata where they frequented the church of St Peter. R. Vadalà mentions two prominent Maltese who made a name for themselves in Constantinople: Dr Lewis Mizzi and Dr Parnis. The former was a well-known lawyer who also edited a newspaper, "The Levant Herald", while the latter was a legal adviser to the Sultan. Vadalà suggests that at the beginning of this century there were about 3,000 Maltese in Constantinople.

The sea-port of Smyrna (Izmir) on the Aegean coast of Anatolia was the other important town where some Maltese lived. There were about 2,000 Maltese living in Smyrna at the turn of the century, but tension between the Turks and the Europeans kept on rising until 1922 when the Young Turks turned on the Christians who fled in their thousands. By 1932 the Turkish leader, Kemal Ataturk, had practically expelled all aliens. Some of the Maltese, none of whom had been born in Malta, found refuge in the island of their forefathers.

Gibraltar and Marseilles

At the westernmost extremity of the Mediterranean lies the Rock of Gibraltar which became British in 1713. The presence of the navy attracted many foreigners, including Maltese, who found work at the dockyard and in the running of small businesses. By 1885 there were about 1,000 Maltese living in Gibraltar but in later years few Maltese went there. However, unlike the history of Maltese settlements in Moslem lands, the Maltese colony never became extinct and the descendants of the first immigrants from Malta are still to be found living in Gibraltar.

Still in the western basin of the Mediterranean lies the great French sea-port of Marseilles. Some Maltese who had emigrated to the Maghreb eventually settled in there while others left directly from Malta to Marseilles in the hope of finding work in the busiest port of the Mediterranean. By the end of the nineteenth century more than 600 Maltese were earning their living in Marseilles as stevedores, artisans and general labourers. From 1919 to 1929, 4,172 Maltese were recruited to work on building sites in the regions which had been devastated by the war. Many of these went back to Malta once their contracts had expired, but some did stay in Marseilles. According to Angelo Camilleri, a priest from Gozo working with the Maltese in Marseilles, in 1929 there were about 3,000 Maltese in Marseilles. It was in that year that he acquired a chapel for his community. Today Marseilles must hold a considerable number of people with Maltese ancestry because many of the Maltese who were living in Algeria and Tunisia sought refuge there after they were compelled to leave North Africa.

South America

Emigration from Malta was for many years haphazard and without any serious planning; nor were those who wished to emigrate prepared for life in a foreign country. There was no one willing to help financially those who had the will to emigrate but had no cash to realise their wish. When in 1912 a special offer appeared in the Maltese press of a free trip to Brazil, interest was naturally aroused. Some Brazilian landlords had contacted a local agent to recruit workers for their coffee plantations. The offer was tempting: free transport from Marseilles to Santos with work and accommodation guaranteed.

The first batch left for Brazil on March 28, 1912. Another group left on April 18. In all 179 migrants, including women and children, left on what was naively described as "the founding of our little Malta beyond the ocean". The first arrivals were accommodated on the fazenda of San Josè de Fortaleza while the others were put on the fazenda of Santa Eulalia.

The Brazilian landlords were not impressed by the newcomers. None had any training for the work they were expected to do and they had no interpreter with them. The Maltese soon found out that food and wages were conditional on the amount of work they were able to do in one day. They also complained about the local food. As had happened before, they soon broke their contract and drifted towards the cities, destitute and very lonely. By August 1913 the Brazilian venture had ended in dismal failure.

In general the Maltese failed to grasp the potential of South America where millions of Europeans were emigrating. As has happened so often in Malta emigration became a political issue and the pro-British party was against interest in the vast regions of Latin America because these were places beyond the pale of the British Empire. The failure of the Brazilian project thwarted any real attempt at establishing a permanent foothold in that part of the world. In 1924 Senator A. Cassar Torreggiani went to Paris to contact government officials from Argentina. The senator's report was presented to the Maltese Government on July of that year. According to that report Argentina welcomed agricultural workers who would be housed at the expense of the state. Politicians like Enrico Mizzi and Ignazio Panzavecchia supported emigration to Argentina even though Mizzi complicated the matter by saying that Italian was a useful language to learn because it was so similar to the Spanish language spoken in Argentina. Nothing was done to direct the flow of Maltese emigration to Latin America.

Emigration to the USA

Europe after 1918 was a continent of confusion. Millions of displaced Europeans felt they had had enough of the quarrelsome nations in the Old Continent, and opted for a new life in the New World. In the first four months of 1920, 3,461 Maltese had applied for their passports stating that their final destination was the U.S.A. However by 1921 the American authorities checked the unrestricted entry of aliens by enforcing a Provisional Immigration Measure on May 19, 1921. This was also known as the First Quota Law and it limited the number of immigrants to 3% of the total of foreign-born persons as they were in 1910. Maltese immigrants prior to 1910 were few in number. Malta was placed with a group of small countries such as Andorra and Monaco. These were to share between them the grand total of eighty-six immigrants each year.

Before the First Quota Law interfered with the Maltese migratory movement to the U.S.A., a few thousand Maltese had settled in New York, Detroit and San Francisco. Detroit had the largest Maltese community not only in the U.S. but in the whole of North America. By the middle

1920's the Maltese in Michigan numbered 5,000. They were mostly men working in the automobile industry. Eventually they organised themselves into various associations and published some newspapers such as *Il Malti-American* and *L'Ecu Malti*.

Although the Maltese in New York were not as numerous as those in Detroit, yet their presence in that city preceded that in Detroit. In 1830 a certain Carmelo Caruana had a business in New York where he was known as "The Merchant Prince". Jean Piper, writing in the "Brooklyn Daily Eagles" of August 16, 1925, said that in that year there were 2,000 Maltese living in New York, spread out in Manhattan, Brooklyn and the Bronx.

A report published by the Malta Emigration Committee in 1900 stated that the Maltese in California numbered then about 200. A year later Charles Mattei claimed that he had helped 500 emigrants to settle in North America, most of whom had settled in San Francisco. In 1915 the Maltese in San Francisco had acquired a hall in the Bay View District which was converted in 1922 into a chapel and was given the title of St Paul of the Shipwreck Maltese Church.

By the late 1920's the Maltese living in the areas of San Bruno and Butcherstown had increased to about 5,000. A certain Francis Grech opened on February 1, 1930, the Maltese Club of San Francisco and in less than five years the Club had 750 members. However the crash of the Stock Market in 1929, coupled with severe restrictions on immigration, severely hampered the growth of the Maltese communities in the U.S. The rate of returnees was high. Within the ten-year period, April 1921 – March 1931, there were 2,891 departures from Malta to the U.S.A. Of these 2,188 came back, most of them beaten by the Depression.

When the dust of war began to settle down after 1945 an enormous movement of displaced people began taking place on a pattern not unlike that of 1918. In Malta the situation was rendered more difficult by the intention of the British Government to run down the facilities of the Services with significant redundancies looming on a dark horizon. Again, emigration was thought to be the easiest way out of the two major problems facing the island: over-population and unemployment. Up to 1947 Malta was under direct colonial rule from Whitehall and the will to develop the island industrially was not there yet. Between 1947 and 1948 a little more than a thousand Maltese left their homes for a new life and security in employment. These migrants, among the first to travel directly by ship from Malta to the U.S.A., settled in the traditional receiving cities such as Detroit, San Francisco and New York where they were likely to be helped by friends and relatives.

In February 1950 the American Consulate in Malta was again reopened. According to the Emigration Report of the time the Consul was issuing visas at the rate of 200 a month. Between 1950 and 1952 3,146 emigrants left for destinations in the U.S.A., but again restrictive legislation was enacted in 1952 which established a nominal annual quota of 100 entrants for all colonial territories of the British Commonwealth. This enactment was the U.S. Immigration and Nationality Law, commonly known as the McCarran-Walter Act.

On the first of December 1965 an amendment was made which abolished the National Origins Quota System, but the effects of the amendment did take a long time to be felt. The annual intake of emigrants from Malta from 1954 onwards never reached the 300 mark.

The Call of Canada

North of the American border lay the vast open spaces of British North America. During the nineteenth century very few Maltese had ventured that far, though a successful businessman from Malta, Louis Shickluna had settled in St Catherine's, Ontario, in 1836. Shikluna had his own shipbuilding yard and was a very well-known person when he died in 1880.

In 1910 the Malta Emigration Committee stated that British Columbia was a region capable of absorbing many of Malta's unskilled labourers. There had been a few isolated cases of immigrants from Malta who had settled in British Columbia. Others were to be found in Toronto and Winnipeg. The major obstacle to emigration to Canada at the time was the expense involved. Among those who managed to make it, many were illiterate, unable to speak English and unprepared for life in that part of the world. The class of emigrants needed in Canada were farmers with capital. The unemployed labourers in Malta were labourers with no capital.

Between January 1909 and May 1912 82 prospective emigrants had applied for passports to go to Canada. Later on such applications were on the increase, and between January and July 1913, a total of 471 had actually left for Canada. A gentleman on the Emigration Committee, Dr Charles Mattei, made an extensive tour of Canada in 1912 to prepare the way for more emigrants. According to Mattei the Maltese could be easily employed in the canneries, in market-gardening, in the building industry and in the construction of railways.

In 1911 a few young men from Malta had found jobs in Winnipeg. Their success encouraged others to follow. A relevant comment on Winnipeg came from "The Malta Herald" of May 23, 1912:

"The rapid growth of Winnipeg during the last three years is almost unimaginable. From every country in the world the tide of emigration is steadily pouring to that place. Many are those here in Malta who are anxious to go there, but owing to the lack of money necessary to defray the voyage expenses, they cannot realise their wish."

After the end of the First World War the migratory movement from Malta to Canada began gaining momentum. Between 1918 and 1920 the number of Maltese emigrants was 611. However in 1919 the Canadian authorities imposed the Literacy Test and a year later foreigners entering the country were expected to have sufficient cash to help them settle in their place of destination. No immigrant was to enter Canada unless he had travelled directly from his own country. Since at the time there was hardly any direct shipping between Malta and Canada, this condition effectively barred many from reaching Canada.

In 1922 it was decided that no immigrant of any Asian race was to be allowed into Canada unless he carried on him the sum of 250 dollars. Eventually even the Maltese were required to have such money on them. A Canadian official told Henry Casolani, the Superintendent of Emigration in Malta, that he thought that the Maltese were physically unfit for life in a cold country like Canada and therefore their entry was not to be encouraged. In 1923 Ottawa issued a Privy Council Order which indicated the categories of British subjects allowed entry. That order specifically excluded the Maltese. In his report on emigration for 1930, Casolani complained that the Maltese alone seemed to fall victims to Canada's exclusion order: "All British, thousands of Italians and other European nationals are welcome. The Maltese alone are excluded."

Casolani called Canada a *"terra clausa"*. He found Canadian indifference to the Maltese hard to understand, especially as the numbers of Maltese living in Canada in the 1920's were insignificant. Between April 1921 and March 1931, 631 Maltese had entered Canada. Of these 335 decided to come back to Malta, leaving a balance of 296 for ten years, or less than thirty Maltese migrants for every year in the period under consideration.

In 1939 the Maltese in Canada could not have been more than a thousand. They were mainly in Toronto in the area known as the Junction. There they had their own Church which had been acquired through the initiative of their own priest, Alphonse Cauchi. He had also given his support to the creation of the Maltese-Canadian Society of Toronto which was to become a permanent feature in the life of the Maltese in that city.

On March 1, 1948, Malta's newly-elected Prime Minister Paul Boffa declared in Parliament that Canada had accepted 500 construction workers from Malta. These workers left on May 3 and on June 16, on the two ships "Marine Perch" and "Vulcania". By the end of March of that same year the Report on Emigration for 1948 showed that nearly 3,000 had registered to emigrate to Canada and by the end of April that figure had increased to 15,000.

In 1951 the number of assisted emigrants who actually arrived in Canada was 1,607. Statistics show that this was the highest figure ever achieved in the migratory movement from Malta to Canada though in 1964-1965 a total of 2294 Maltese went to live in Canada.

Up to 1957 the selection procedure of emigrants wishing to go to Canada was largely based on the sponsorship system. After that year the policy of Open Placement was introduced. A Canadian selection team used to interview applicants in Malta even if these had no one to sponsor them. If approved they were sent to receiving camps and jobs were provided. Three years later married men were allowed, for the first time, to proceed to Canada accompanied by their families. Those who chose to go on their own were usually joined by their dependants in less than a year. In 1962 there were only 371 emigrants going to Canada but 133 of them had been allowed to go because they had been approved under the Open Placement Scheme and they were able to take their families with them.

1962 saw the introduction of new immigration regulations. The Canadians finally decided to abandon all restrictions emanating from reasons based on race or other considerations while accepting applicants solely on grounds of education, health, conduct and skill. Hence emigrants wishing to enter Canada no longer needed a sponsor nor had they to be accepted under the Open Placement Scheme. This meant that more Maltese were able to emigrate to Canada. In the period 1963-1965 there was an upsurge of 3,199 emigrants. Interest in Canada continued and by 1974 about 17,000 Maltese had made their new home there since the end of the Second World War. This made Canada the third most popular receiving country for Maltese emigrants after Australia and the United Kingdom.

What made emigration to Canada successful was the decision to base the migratory policy on the family unit. A man accompanied by his wife and children was bound to make a greater effort to succeed in a new land, a policy which brought stability to the Maltese ethnic group.

Maltese in the United Kingdom

During the heyday of post-war mass emigration from Malta, Great Britain was the second most important receiving country. Emigration to the United Kingdom did not have as long a history as emigration to the U.S.A., Canada, Australia or North Africa. At the beginning of the twentieth century very few Maltese thought of settling in the United Kingdom, even if a tiny nucleus of Maltese immigrants had been forming in London in and around the Commercial Road. A Maltese priest from Valletta, Innocent Apap, was working in London in 1907 and from his correspondence we know that in 1912 he organised a gathering for his fellow countrymen and he gave them lectures in their own language during Lent of that year.

The First World War had brought the Maltese and the British that little bit closer and in Malta a number of mixed marriages had taken place. After the Armistice many Maltese brides accompanied their husbands when they went back home, giving rise to an interesting Anglo-Maltese community in places with sea-going tradition such as London, Southampton and Portsmouth. The Anglo-Maltese element kept on increasing till well after the Second World War.

Between 1919 and 1929 there were 3,354 Maltese officially listed as having emigrated to the United Kingdom, though 1,445 of these are known to have come back in later years. Even those listed as having stayed in Great Britain did not actually stay in the country but moved on to the U.S.A., Canada, Australia and to other parts of the Empire. The report on emigration for 1918-1920 states:

"It may seem strange that in the present unsettled state of the labour market in England, 225 Maltese emigrants should have gone to the United Kingdom between Armistice Day and March 31, 1920. On a small scale a certain number of Maltese have always filtered to the Mother Country. They are attracted by friends, or go to join relatives who are there, and they belong as a rule, either to the Dockyard or Domestic classes".

Emigration from Malta to the United Kingdom intensified after 1946. By 1974 more than 30,000 had left Malta for Great Britain. This intake is second only to that of Australia. That figure includes those emigrants who had been processed by the Emigration Department in Malta. Those who had emigrated on their own initiative or arrived in the United Kingdom not directly from Malta (as many Maltese from North Africa did), are not included in that figure.

For many years no formal arrangements were made to regulate the flow of emigrants from Malta to Great Britain. An applicant was allowed to go if he was considered suitable for settlement overseas and had a good conduct. He only paid one fourth of the passage money and was given a passport free of charge. Those who did not apply for financial assistance were free to go without too much formality.

On November 1, 1961 the government at Westminster introduced the Immigration and Deportation Bill which took effect on July 1, 1962. This was an effective measure to control the entry of Commonwealth citizens. The Emigration Report for 1962 noted that "Paradoxically the new British legislation would appear to have had an opposite effect on Maltese migration in as much as the number of emigrants admitted during the year was the largest for some years." The number referred to was that of 1,129 immigrants. That ascending trend continued for a few years. Only in 1967 did the total intake fall under the one thousand mark. From that year onwards Maltese emigration to the United Kingdom kept falling until by the end of the seventies it became insignificant.

Pioneers in Australia

In strict geographical terms the very distant land of Australia should have been the last place to attract Maltese migrants. Attract it did, in thousands. In 1991 it was estimated that there were 57,778 people in Australia whose births had been registered in Malta. According to the Melbourne-based newspaper "Il-Maltija" of October 1, 1991, there were in Australia about 119,504 people of Maltese ethnic origin.

It is probable that some Maltese reached the shores of the "*terra incognita australis*" soon after the Treaty of Paris (1814) when the Maltese Islands joined the same British Empire of which Australia was a major possession. Of course these unknown arrivals by no means point to the beginning of Maltese emigration to that part of the world.

Although before 1900 Maltese interest in Australia was mild and sporadic there were those who felt that Queensland was the part of Australia capable of absorbing Malta's surplus population. Alexander Balbi and two brothers, Joseph and Charles Busuttil, had done well in Queensland where the sugar industry was expanding and workers were in such a demand that in spite of the Australian determination to keep Asians out some of the landlords were recruiting workers from the Solomon Islands.

The first governor of Queensland, Sir George Bowen, knew the Maltese and he preferred to have them on the sugar plantations rather than the Kanakas. It is for this reason that he wrote to Malta suggesting that Maltese workers should be sent on contract to his State. According to C. Price, some Maltese were interested but there was general ignorance in Malta at the time about Australia. The problem of how to finance transport to Queensland was also difficult and Bowen's suggestion eventually came to nothing.

It is not correct to state that the Maltese had ignored the possibility of establishing some contact with Australia. Some twenty years after Bowen's suggestion a Maltese businessman, Francesco Decesare, was invited to go to Australia to inquire about the possibility of sending Maltese workers there. Again it was the landlords of Queensland who showed the greatest interest because opposition to the presence of the Kanakas was growing and the landlords needed the Maltese to fill the place of the Kanakas.

The mission of Decesare resulted in the sending of the first organised group of Maltese emigrants we know of to date. About seventy men left Malta for Australia in October 1883 on board the ship S.S. Nuddea. They had a priest with them, Ambrose Cassar. They travelled as steerage passengers and disembarked at Brisbane some six weeks later. From Brisbane they were taken to Townsville and were given work on a five-year contract. Fr Cassar wrote to Malta to complain that the Maltese were not receiving the same wages as other European workers. Some complained about the hot weather and others were downright homesick. By the end of 1884 most of them had broken their contract and drifted towards Sydney. But Fr Cassar himself stayed in Australia for the rest of his forty-five years. He worked among immigrants of different nationalities as he was conversant with various languages. He also encouraged some of his own relatives to emigrate to Australia and their descendants are now living in and around the city of Mackay.

Emigration to Australia before 1939

Australians were acutely aware of the important decision they had to make regarding the future of their country: populate or perish. In 1912 Percy Hunter, Director of Immigration for New South Wales, stated that it was Australia's goal to swell its population to twenty million. Another Australian who was also the president of the Immigration League, Richard Arthur, wrote in 1912 to some politicians in Malta suggesting that the Maltese had better forget all about other countries such as Brazil and Canada and think of Australia as the land of their future. The suggestion had its supporters in Malta as the comment of "The Daily Malta Chronicle" of September 28, 1912 rightly shows:

"Whom could Australia admit after Englishmen, with greater advantage to herself than emigrants from Malta? We have the same flag as Englishmen and Australians. Our skin is about as fair, except for the tanning done by a semi-tropical sun. We are as proud of our place in the Empire as they are of theirs. Our physique is all that could be desired by the most fastidious selectors of immigrants. Our moral values are above dispute."

Dr Richard Arthur had first-hand knowledge of the Maltese as he had been on a visit to Malta. He claimed that Australia should admit the Maltese especially in the more remote regions where they could withstand the climate better than Englishmen. Such writing sounded like sweet music to those who championed Malta's British connection. By emigrating to Australia Malta would be helping to keep that large island under the British Crown and would also strengthen its own ties with Great Britain. The teaching of the English language would receive a great boost and the supremacy of Italian would be done away with.

One politician who agreed with the pro-British platform was Sir Gerald Strickland. Although born in Malta in 1861 he had a British father and had connections with Australia where he had been governor of various States. On becoming Prime Minister of Malta in 1927, besides strengthening Malta's ties with the Empire and reducing cultural ties with Latin Europe to a minimum, Strickland also sought to establish a Maltese colony in Australia. On February 22, 1928 he informed Malta's Legislative Assembly that his Australian friend, Sir James D. Connolly had written to him to let him know that the Australian Government was

..."strongly disposed to encourage Maltese emigration to the Berkeley tableland, a portion of Australia with a climate very similar to that of Malta, with an assured rainfall and a very fertile soil."

Some Australians were willing to accept Maltese immigrants with one important proviso: they were to stay in the outback and avoid at any cost the cities. Thus when Richard Arthur wrote about allowing the Maltese into Australia he had in mind the vast and empty regions of North Queensland and the Northern Territory. He was certainly not referring to cities like Sydney and Melbourne. There was strong opposition from the trade unions against foreigners competing for city jobs. A letter, written in 1912 by a Maltese living in Melbourne, illustrates this point:

"No Australian or Englishman will work with the Maltese. We are beginning to feel ashamed of ourselves on this account. In Sydney the Maltese are utterly cold-shouldered. A few days ago I read that the unions decided against Maltese membership."

It was only four years after this letter that the Maltese were subjected to a nation-wide series of humiliations. Some 214 emigrants, hailing mostly from Gozo, had departed for Australia on board the French steamer "Gange". The world was at war and many young Australians had lost their lives in Europe. As the "Gange" approached the port of Fremantle, the Australian Prime Minister, W. Hughes, was conducting a vigorous campaign in

favour of conscription. His opponents raised the alarm about the Maltese who were about to enter the country when the Prime Minister was intending to send young Australians to the fronts. The ship was not allowed to enter any Australian port but was told to proceed to Noumea in the French island of New Caledonia. The Maltese were kept there for three months. Even when they returned to Sydney their trial was not over yet. They were transferred to an old ship away from public view until employment was found for them.

The "Gange" affair was discussed at the sitting of the Council of Government in Valletta on January 13, 1917. During that meeting a certain E. Bonavia complained that

"there has been for some time past a good deal of unrest in Australia in the matter of importation of labour and a strong public feeling has all along existed against any newcomers who could, with or without reason, be regarded with suspicion as people who were willing to work long hours for low wages. They are not looked upon with any friendly eye by the Labour unions."

By 1919 Australia had stopped the entry of Maltese except for wives and dependent children of Maltese nationals who were already permanently living in the country. Those few who were admitted were urged not to walk in groups or speak Maltese aloud. They were strongly advised to avoid the cities.

Between April 1, 1920, and March 31, 1921, there were 278 Maltese who expressed their intention to emigrate to Australia. Even before President Harding of the U.S.A. had passed the First Quota Law in 1921, Australia was already receiving the highest intake of emigrants from the Maltese Islands.

In May 1922, Malta's chief spokesman on emigration, Henry Casolani, was in London on an official visit to contact representatives of Canada, U.S.A. and Australia. Casolani met Percy Hunter and urged a more liberal attitude from the Australians towards the Maltese. Casolani noted:

"I am glad to be in a position to state positively that Mr Hunter's views are very favourable to our migrants."

John McWhae, the Agent General for the State of Victoria, was not convinced. He was a staunch supporter of the White Australia Policy and for him White meant British and British meant what it said: a person born in Great Britain of pure British parentage. To McWhae the Maltese were aliens and he told Casolani that he intended to keep all aliens away from Australia to make sure that his country remained Anglo-Saxon.

In 1925 McWhae was back in Australia more determined than ever in his opposition to foreign immigration. At the same time there was a recrudescence of anti-Maltese articles in the Melbourne press. In 1924, Adelaide witnessed some ugly disturbances and when the police intervened it was revealed that among those arrested were some immigrants from Malta. In Sydney and in Perth people were warned about the imminent take over of Australia by hungry undesirables from Southern Europe. Organisations speaking on behalf of returned soldiers insisted that any available jobs should go to those who had fought for king and country.

As far as the Maltese were concerned there was no imminent danger from their part of taking over "the Lucky Country". In 1922 there were less than 2,000 Maltese in Australia. (Malta Government Gazzette, Vol. XIV, no.36). At that time the entry of Maltese into Australia was regulated by the quota system which allowed 260 immigrants each year. In later years the quota was abolished and by 1927 the Maltese population in Australia was near the 3,000 mark. In that same year Casolani published his book "*L-Emigrazzjoni tal-Maltin*" where he still complained about the prejudices against the Maltese which were rampant in some sections of the press in Australia. The author urged the Maltese not to be discouraged by such prejudices. In a later book published in 1930 under the title "Awake Malta" Casolani insisted on

the need of preparing those who intended to emigrate and that those who were selected should settle in the country not in the crowded cities.

Casolani also insisted on three basic points in order to make Maltese emigration successful: First, educate prospective emigrants. Second, appoint an official representative to speak and act on behalf of the Maltese living in a foreign country. Third, encourage priests to settle permanently in areas inhabited by the Maltese.

It did take some years before these suggestions were taken up by the Maltese authorities. The choice of Captain Henry Curmi in 1929 was a good one. Curmi was in Australia in that year and his arrival coincided with the Depression. He therefore warned the Maltese authorities against sending too many emigrants while the situation remained as it was. In 1930 no new passports were issued for would-be migrants unless they had close relatives in Australia who would be willing to help them out during the initial months of their arrival.

Although Captain Curmi had to give up his work soon after his arrival in Australia because of failing health he was back as Malta's commissioner on June 8, 1936. At that time there were about 4,000 Maltese, mostly in Queensland, but there were other communities in various States of Australia. In 1937 Curmi was in New South Wales and he found out that the Maltese in that State actually outnumbered those in Queensland. Curmi was of the opinion that New South Wales and Victoria were to become the major focal points of Maltese immigration into Australia. During his visits to the two States, Curmi noted that the Maltese did not stick to one particular type of work. Many worked in factories, hotels, shops, and on the wharves. Others owned small businesses such as general stores, groceries, cafes and fish shops.

In the western suburbs of Sydney and Melbourne Curmi noticed how successful Maltese market-gardeners were. He thought that some Maltese, particularly the Gozitans, had holdings which in 1937 were worth £10,000 or more. He wrote:

"It is a pleasure to mention that I have seen a poultry farm and a dairy farm each owned and kept by a Maltese and both of which are models of their kind. The success of the Maltese as market-gardeners is proverbial and landowners have written to me to obtain settlers from Malta because they knew that the Maltese have proved to be a success in their avocation."

A great achievement for Captain Curmi was when in March 1938 the Australians finally decided to accord British status to the migrants from Malta. It was a belated decision but a very welcome one at that time. Casolani had worked hard for a British status and Curmi reaped the results. A British status for the Maltese meant that henceforth applicants from Malta were considered on a par with applicants from the United Kingdom. There were no objections to their being approved for entry into Australia except that they had to abide by the general rules concerning health and general adaptability. By 1938 the negative effects generated by the Depression were nearly over and as the economy improved, Australia began recruiting more workers. The Government of Malta was offering financial assistance by paying half the passage of those families who had been nominated by sponsors already living in Australia.

Post-War Migration

In 1947 the Maltese were again granted self-government and the ensuing elections returned the Labour Party to power. The new government faced the old and double problem of an expanding population due to numerous marriages contracted as soon as hostilities were over and the lack of employment because of the redundancies made by the British forces. Peace brought the same old problems to an island that knew much of its prosperity to fighting in the Mediterranean region. This was the prediction Christopher Marlowe's *Jew of* *Malta* had in mind when he said that nothing was more welcome to Malta than wars. It came as no surprise to anybody when Paul Boffa's administration declared emigration as "the safety-valve" of the nation.

One of the first moves of the new government was to create a Department of Emigration with a minister and director responsible for it. A Standing Committee was formed to advise the minister on how to encourage the Maltese to emigrate. This Standing Committee was described by John Axisa, the director of emigration, in these words: "It is today a powerful element in the formation of Government policy with regard to emigration." In just over a year after taking power the Labour Government needed all the advice it could get because on its books it had more than 25,000 Maltese who had registered in order to emigrate.

In September 1948, a Ministerial Mission left for Canada, U.S.A. and Australia. The minister responsible for emigration, J.J. Cole and his director, J. Axisa, obtained from the Australian Government an agreement on passage assistance which was to take effect as from January 1, 1949. The Australians also agreed to nominate a large number of workers for important State projects. This made the emigration of those with no one willing to sponsor them possible. There was also an agreement on the inception of a Child Migrant Scheme which had been in operation with the United Kingdom for many years and which was to be extended to Malta with the cooperation of Church authorities in Malta and in Australia.

By 1953 a Maltese migrant going to Australia was paying the nominal fare of £10. There was also an allowance of £20/£30 to the dependants of migrants when the heads of families were emigrating ahead of their wives and children. These financial concessions had removed the great barrier which had hindered the development of emigration to distant lands on a significant scale. Direct shipping from

from Malta to Australian ports also facilitated the transport of thousands of migrants. This was even more improved when emigrants started leaving Malta by air. Besides such obvious advantages emigration to Australia received a considerable boost when the Archbishop of Malta, Michael Gonzi, went on a pastoral visit to see the Maltese in Australia in 1953. The effect of this visit is clearly seen in the emigration figures for 1954 when 11,447 assisted emigrants left Malta, with 8,470 preferring to settle in Australia. This was the highest figure ever achieved in the history of emigration.

Yet only two years after that exodus the trend of emigrations to Australia went on a downward direction. In 1957 the number of those who left for Australia with an assisted passage was only 1,286. This trend lasted for three years, when during the 1960's emigration to Australia was again on the increase. It was at this time when some people began to have second thoughts on how wise it was to accept emigration as an inevitable fact of life.

Plans began to be considered for the economic development of the island, though a political solution had to be found so that the Maltese would free themselves of the humiliation of being a colony. The great British Empire was now only a weak shadow of what it was before 1939. The British wanted to retain their bases but did not feel bound to provide the same amount of jobs they formerly generated. If Malta were to take the road to economic development, emigration had to be controlled and the Maltese people were to have the full reins of their own country in their own hands.

This way of thinking began to attract a lot of people. Not only fewer people wanted to emigrate but some of those who had gone began returning home. The emigration figure of 1,286 for 1957 has to be examined against the number of returnees for the same year which was 1,097. Unfortunately words were not matched by facts. Many of the returnees

had to reluctantly admit that the Maltese situation was still in a state of flux and they went back. For much of the sixties there was a lot of political turmoil coupled with widespread industrial unrest. All this made life unpredictable. The very year of Malta's independence, 1964, saw the exit of 8,788 of its citizens. Again it was Australia that received about 59% of Maltese wishing to settle abroad.

In 1960 the Single Young Women Migrants Scheme (SYWMS) was launched to help ladies in the age-group between eighteen and thirty-five years to emigrate. Mass emigration had produced an unpleasant side effect. Malta, and to a larger extent Gozo, became a country where young women did not find enough male partners. In 1960 there were more than 9,000 girls of marriageable age than there were young men. In some villages in Gozo the young male population had vanished. The Governments of Malta and Australia enlisted the support of Church authorities to redress this imbalance, especially when on the Australian side the problem was the reverse. The Church in Malta, through its Emigrants' Commission which had been active since 1950, helped to run this scheme in conjunction with the Female Catholic Immigration Committee of Australia.

In 1962 Church and State collaborated in working the Child Migration Scheme which has been already referred to. Children from local institutions and others with no particular bright prospects for their future, were sent to institutions in Australia where they received a good education and were trained for particular jobs. More than 250 boys and girls were eventually sent to Western Australia, their ages raging from six to sixteen. Their progress was monitored by welfare officers till they reached the age of twenty-one. This scheme did provide an opportunity for a completely new start for some. However the Scheme had its critics too. They argued it was not right to send children to another country at an age when they did not fully realise what was being decided for them.

Eventually the scheme was allowed to die out.

In 1962 the quota for Maltese emigrants to Australia was increased from 2,000 to 3,000 a year. Half of this quota was made up of persons sponsored by close relatives who were permanently resident in Australia. These were financially helped under the Passage Assistance Agreement which had come into force in 1949 and which had been periodically renewed. The other half consisted of those who qualified for help from the Maltese side.

According to a census held in Australia in June 1966 there were in the country 55,104 persons who had been born in Malta. Maltese interest in Australia continued till 1974 when a total of 2,595 assisted emigrants left for various destinations in Australia. After that year there was a decline, punctuated by two exceptions in 1980 and 1981. The low figures for emigration contrasted with the high numbers of returnees. It can be said that as from 1975 emigration to Australia and to other traditional receiving countries ceased to be a relevant factor in the life of the Maltese.

Significant to the changes of the times was the Maltese Government's decision in May 1991 to "reconstruct" the Department of Labour and Emigration. The very term "emigration" was dropped and a new body came into being known as Secretariat for Maltese Living Abroad. There was also to be a Commission under a similar title which was supposed to suggest policies concerning people of Maltese origin living in other lands and to present them to the Government for approval.

The Maltese living abroad are a statistical fact which should not be ignored. Between 1946 and 1974 more than 137,000 emigrated. The number of those who returned should be taken into consideration but it is also a fact that most of those who left did so with the intention of settling permanently in their country of adoption.

Although the situation of our migrants world-wide differs considerably from one country to another, it is possible to arrive at some conclusions. To begin with the oldest category: the Maltese of North Africa. Most of their descendants are spread out in many countries. There are significant groupings in the U.K., France and Australia. Those in Australia have established contacts with the other Maltese, though they are careful to preserve their individuality and can be marked out by their flare for business and pursuit of higher learning. A number of people in the professions in Australia who carry Maltese names are in fact Maltese from Egypt.

In the United Kingdom and in France there are associations made up of people who had to leave their homes and possessions in North Africa. In England most of the immigrants are from Egypt whereas in France they were originally refugees from Algeria and Tunisia. The British and the French governments offered them shelter and these people are now proud of their British and French citizenship. In Great Britain there is an Association of Maltese Communities of Egypt, originally founded in Alexandria in 1854 and transferred to London in 1956. It is still very active and publishes its own newsletter. In Paris there is the Association France-Malte, which among other activities, organises tours to Malta for members eager to discover their own roots.

More recent emigrants settled in Australia, Canada, Great Britain and the U.S.A. Those who went to the United Kingdom and to the U.S.A. are not as vibrant in their identity as the others. Although more than 30,000 Maltese left for Great Britain between 1946 and 1974, the rate of returnees was very high so much so that it is probable that the present population of Maltese in Great Britain is about half that total. As Russel King noted, "the whole idea of Maltese emigration is more in the nature of an adventure, a relatively short-term work contract, than permanent migration." Since a number of those who did actually remain were single men they married non-Maltese women and in such mixed marriages the children were unlikely to be brought up as Maltese. In some cases there was a cultivated attitude to ignore one's past so as to become thoroughly assimilated. Then there are those who because of the ease with which one can travel between Malta and Great Britain spend some time in one place and some time in another.

The case of the Maltese in the U.S.A. is roughly similar to that of their brethren in the United Kingdom. Not only are they relatively few but they are also scattered in different cities which are miles and miles apart. For many years foreign immigrants in America were under intense pressure to conform with the majority. There was an evident dislike of the unlike. The Americanisation Committees insisted on conformity in habits and in language to such an extent that many were encouraged to change their names. The situation did change after the Second World War and the Americans slowly adopted the Canadian policy of respecting ethnic culture; hence the idea of multiculturalism.

The Maltese in Detroit, New York and San Francisco had their own clubs, some of which still function to this day. Some of the earliest Maltese newspapers away from Malta were published in Detroit. The Maltese in the U.S.A. were also very generous in supporting the Malta Relief Fund to help the besieged population of Malta during the war. However, the total intake of Maltese immigrants after the war was not impressive, perhaps just over 9,000. As in the United Kingdom, the number of unmarried men who emigrated to the U.S.A. was considerable. This brought about a situation with similarities already noted with the situation prevailing in Great Britain.

The Maltese presence in Canada and in Australia is identifiable with permanence.

During the peak years of Maltese emigration the two countries received more than 97,000 men, women and children. Agreements between the two receiving countries on one hand and the Maltese authorities on the other, ensured that the migratory movement was based on preserving the unity of the family. A number of priests not only accompanied the emigrants but also settled in places where the Maltese were present in good numbers. Priests also acted as welfare-officers and interpreters.

Both Canada and Australia have accepted the principle that they are multicultural. The immigrant can be integrated without being assimilated. Multiculturalism allows an ethnic group to take pride in its own language, culture and religion without being considered as a despised minority. There are newspapers published by the Maltese in Canada and in Australia. These are either bilingual or in Maltese. The editor is sometimes elevated to the status of a spokesman of the community. Prof. H. Frendo says on the ethnic press in Australia: "People would phone to enquire about anything and everything, occasionally reducing the editor and his staff to journalists – turned – counsellors."

Some libraries have sections of Maltese books. There are ethnic radio and television programmes with the radio broadcasts in Maltese perhaps being one of the most popular means of communication. Religion also helps to preserve a national identity because, as H. Frendo asserts, "most central to this unmistakable feature of Malteseness is the festa of the patron saint of the town or village of origin, in which the brass band plays an active part."

Will the Maltese language survive in an alien environment? Emigrants born in Malta with Maltese as their native language will undoubtedly speak Maltese till the very end. Children born to Maltese couples stand a fair chance of retaining the language. Maltese however tend to enter into mixed marriages and the children of such unions, especially when the mother is not Maltese, will not be able to speak the language of their father.

It is also unfortunate to note that the Maltese are poorly represented in the professional classes, and although some have gone to university and entered State parliaments, their impact on cultural circles in the receiving countries, including Canada and Australia is negligible; it is certainly not commensurate with their numbers.

Bibliography

ATTARD, L.E., *Early Maltese Emigration (1900-1914)*, Gulf Publishing Ltd., Malta, 1983.
The Great Exodus (1918-1939), P.E.G. Ltd., Malta, 1989.
"Maltese Ethnic Identity in Australia", *I.C.M.C. News* No.2, Geneva, 1979.

CASOLANI, H., *Reports and Correspondence on Mission to London*, 1922.
Awake Malta, 1930.
L-Emigrazzjoni tal-Maltin, 1927.

CAUCHI, M.N., *Maltese Migrants in Australia*, M.C.C., Victoria, 1990.

CORDER, F.J., "Maltese links with Australia" in *The Victorian Historical Magazine*, Vol.XXVI, No.4, June, 1933.

DENCH, G., *Maltese in London*, Routledge & Kegan Paul, London & Boston, 1975.

DONATO, M., L'Émigration de Maltais en Algérie au XIXème Siècle, *Africa Nostra*, Montpelleir, 1985.

FERGUSSON, E., *Immigrants in Canada*, University of Toronto, 1974.

FRENDO, H., "Religion and Ethnic Identity in the Maltese Australian Community" in A. Ata (ed): *Religion and Ethnic Identity. An Australian Study*. Spectrum, Melbourne, 1988.
"Australia's Maltese Language Press", Abe Wade Ata and Colin Ryan (eds): *The Ethnic Press in Australia*, Academia Press, Melbourne, 1989.
"Maltese Cultural Identity in Australia" in *The Maltese Herald*, Sydney, 7, 14, 21 July, 1992.

HARTMANN, E.G., *A History of American Immigration*, Rand & McNally and Co., Chicago, 1967.

HARVARD Encyclopaedia of American Ethnic Groups, H.U.P., 1980.

JONES, H.R., "The Regional Origin of Emigrants: Findings from Malta" in *International Migration*, Vol.XI, 1973.

JUPP, J., "Settlement patterns in Melbourne", Jupp J. (ed): *The Australian People*, Angus and Robertson, 1988.

KING, R., "Post-War Migration Pattern and Policies in Malta" in *European Demographic Information Bulletin,* Vol.X, No.3, 1979.

MAGRI-OVEREND, I., "Humble Beginnings – Great Achievements" in *Lil Hutna*, 1976-1978.

MORISON, S.E., *The Oxford History of the American People*, O.U.P., New York, 1965.

PRICE, C., *Malta and the Maltese*, Georgian House, Melbourne, 1954.

SMITH, T.E., "Malta and the Commonwealth Connection" in *Commonwealth Migration: Flows and Policies*, Macmillan, London, 1981.

TENCAJOLI, O.F., *L'Emigrazione Maltese in Australia*, Rome, 1927.

VADALÀ, R., *Les Maltais hors de Malte*, Paris, 1912.

YORK, B., *The Maltese in Australia*, A.E. Press, Melbourne, 1986.
Empire and Race, N.S.W. University Press, 1990.

Notes on Contributors

LAWRENCE E. ATTARD is a Catholic priest and has written extensively on Maltese migration. His works include *Early Maltese Emigration 1900-1914* and *The Great Exodus 1918-1939*.

ANTHONY BONANNO is Full Professor and Head of the Department of Classics and Archaeology at the University of Malta. His works include *Roman Malta* and *The Archaeological Heritage of the Maltese Islands*.

ALEXANDER BORG is a dialectologist and ethnolinguist with a special interest in Semitic studies. He has worked mainly in Israel from where he has co-edited the *Mediterranean Language Review*. Works include *Cypriot Arabic* (1985).

LINO BRIGUGLIO, Associate Professor in Economics, is Director of the Islands and Small States Institute at the Foundation for International Studies and of the University Gozo Centre. Works include *The Maltese Economy* (1988).

PAUL CASSAR, a medical doctor, has lectured in medicine and law and written extensively in the areas of medical and social history. Works include *Medical History of Malta* (1965) and *La Sacra Infermeria* (2nd ed. 1994).

ĠUŻÈ CASSAR PULLICINO is a folklorist and has published numerous works on Maltese language and history. His books include *Il-Folklor Malti, Papers in Maltese Folklore, Il-Bennejja tal-Folklor Malti*.

ANTONIO ESPINOSA RODRIGUEZ is Curator of Fine Arts in the Malta Museums Department and directs the Maritime Museum in Vittoriosa. His works include *Paintings at the National Museum of Fine Arts in Malta* (1990).

HENRY FRENDO is Professor of History at the University of Malta and since 1970 has had several books published on Maltese history and politics. A former newspaper editor and UN diplomat, he chairs the European Cultural Foundation's Malta committee.

OLIVER FRIGGIERI is Full Professor of Literature and Head of the Department of Maltese at the University of Malta. His numerous books and studies have been published in Malta and in various countries.

271

HUGH W. HARDING is a retired Chief Justice, a Fellow of the Royal Historical Society and Fellow of the Society of Antiquaries of London. His works include *History of Roman Law in Malta* and *Maltese Legal History under British Rule 1801-1836*.

LEONARD MAHONEY (1928-1993), an architect and civil engineer, served with Malta's Public Works Department for thirty years, retiring as Chief Engineer. Works include *A History of Maltese Architecture* (1988) and a voluminous sequel to it due to be published posthumously.

PATRICK SCHEMBRI is Full Professor in the Department of Biology at the University of Malta. His research interests are marine benthic ecology, faunistics of the Maltese Islands. He has authored several papers in scientific journals.

JOSEPH VELLA is Associated Professor of Music at the University of Malta. He is the composer of numerous works, including oratorios and cantatas and was the first to edit and perform old Maltese music.